CAREER
OPPORTUNITIES
in

THE RETAIL AND WHOLESALE INDUSTRY

SECOND EDITION

CAREER OPPORTUNITIES in

THE RETAIL AND WHOLESALE INDUSTRY

SECOND EDITION

SHELLY FIELD

Foreword by JOHN R. SOHIGIAN,
Senior Vice President, Marketing, Orange County Choppers

Ferguson
An imprint of Infobase Publishing

Career Opportunities in the Retail and Wholesale Industry, Second Edition

Ferguson
An imprint of Facts On File, Inc.
132 West 31st Street
New York NY 10001

Library of Congress Cataloging-in-Publication Data

Field, Shelly.
  Career opportunities in the retail and wholesale indstry / Shelly Field ; foreword by John R. Sohigian. — 2nd ed.
    p. cm.
  Includes bibliographical references and index.
  ISBN-13: 978-0-8160-7779-3 (hardcover : alk. paper)
  ISBN-10: 0-8160-7779-7 (hardcover : alk. paper) 1. Retail trade—Vocational guidance. I. Title.

  HF5429.F434 2009
  381.023'73—dc22   2008053240

Ferguson books are available at special discounts when purchased in bulk quantities for businesses, associations, institutions, or sales promotions. Please call our Special Sales Department in New York at (212) 967-8800 or (800) 322-8755.

You can find Ferguson on the World Wide Web at http://www.fergpubco.com

Series design by Kerry Casey
Cover design by Takeshi Takahashi

Printed in the United States of America

VB Hermitage 10 9 8 7 6 5 4 3 2 1

This book is printed on acid-free paper and contains 30 percent postconsumer recycled content.

This book is dedicated to my parents, Ed and Selma Field, who were always there to cheer me on through every step and every milestone. Thank you for believing in my dreams and helping me along the way.

———————————————

CONTENTS

E-COMMERCE, MAIL ORDER, AND DIRECT RESPONSE SHOPPING

TELEVISION SHOPPING CHANNELS

WHOLESALE

APPENDIXES

HOW TO USE THIS BOOK

Since the first edition of this book was published in 2001, the retail and wholesale industries have expanded more than anyone ever could have imagined. While some major stores have merged, department stores, chains, and specialty stores continue to be abundant. And although a number of well-known retailers have closed their doors, others have emerged to fill the void. Developers continue to build new malls and shopping centers to replace older, less appealing centers. There are superstores and mini-marts to shop in as well as large supermarkets, warehouse clubs, small groceries and more. Shopping as an activity continues to be a national pastime, drawing people to stores and malls.

All you need to do is turn on your TV late at night to see infomercials filling the airwaves into the early morning hours. Televised shopping channels have become an accepted option for both buyers and sellers. Some of the most prominent designers now create exclusive lines specifically for television shopping channels, because they have seen the opportunity to sell millions of dollars of merchandise in a very short time period. Manufacturers of electronics, computers, housewares, toys, gourmet foods, and more also see the opportunity to sell thousands of pieces of merchandise in a few short minutes of on-air time.

Catalogs still sell every conceivable item and most now have an online shopping presence as well. Online shopping has exploded. There is virtually no major retailer that does not offer an online alternative for their customers. Companies can send out an e-mail blast to thousands of people touting a special sale at a moment's notice. EBay and similar sites are more popular than ever both with buyers and sellers. Because of the Internet, individuals and large companies can open online stores for customers from almost anyplace in the world. Many online stores are stand-alone entities that built their success with great customer service and creative marketing.

The retail and wholesale industry offers a wide array of career options. No matter what your interest or your experience level, opportunities exist. Retail and wholesale jobs are located almost everywhere. There are full-time and part-time jobs. Openings are available for those who choose retailing and wholesaling as their main career choice, for young people still in high school, and for retirees seeking to augment a fixed income or start another exciting career. There are also a wide array of opportunities for those seeking to start their own retail business.

This book was designed to help you prepare for interesting, exciting, fun, and rewarding careers in the retail and wholesale industry. One of the best things about a career in retail is you can generally always find employment. Another is that dedicated, hardworking employees can quickly move up the career ladder—often even if they don't have higher education.

Thousands are currently working in the retail and wholesale industries. Many more are eager to enter but have no concept of what career opportunities are available, where to find them, or what training and qualifications are required.

Career Opportunities in the Retail and Wholesale Industry is the single most comprehensive source for learning about job opportunities in this growing field. This book was written for everyone who aspires to work in retail and wholesale whether just for the jobs it provides or to create a career. It will give you an edge over other applicants. The jobs discussed in this book include careers not only in selling, but also in the business, administration, marketing, creative, and management areas.

The retail and wholesale industry offers an array of opportunities and requires people with a variety of skills and talents: salespeople, secretaries, bookkeepers, property managers, Webmasters, artists, leasing people, security employees, administrative assistants, special event coordinators, advertising directors, customer service representatives, store managers, buyers, mystery shoppers, executives, car salespeople, copywriters, call center representatives, trade show representatives, television shopping show hosts, directors, producers, stylists, merchandisers, and more. The trick to locating the job you want is developing your skills and using them to enter these exciting and expanding industries. Once you have your foot in the door, you can climb the career ladder to success.

What Is New in the Second Edition

The second edition of *Career Opportunities in the Retail and Wholesale Industry* is full of updated information. All salaries, employment and advancement prospects, training and educational requirements, and unions and associations for each job profile were reviewed and updated when necessary. The information in every appendix has been updated as well, giving you the most up-to-date names, addresses, phone numbers, and Web sites of colleges and universities, trade associations, unions and other organizations, chain stores, department stores, supermarkets and groceries, catalog companies, television shopping channels, and manufacturers and other companies. New books and periodicals complete the bibliography.

A new appendix has also been added to make it easier for you to find more job opportunities with a listing of career and employment Web sites.

While the first edition of *Career Opportunities in the Retail and Wholesale Industry* was very comprehensive in its coverage of careers and key jobs, nine new job profiles have been added to the updated edition of the book. This brings the total number of career opportunities to 90.

Sources of Information

Information for this book was obtained through interviews, questionnaires, and a variety of books, magazines, newsletters, literature, and television and radio programs. Some information was gathered through 14 years of personal experience as a marketing, public relations, and mall management consultant. Other data was obtained from business associates in various areas of the retail and wholesale industry.

Among the people interviewed were men and women in all aspects of retailing and wholesaling. These include individuals working in the business, administration, and management end of the industry as well as frontline employees and support personnel. Also interviewed were human resources directors and staff, training managers, publicists, marketing managers, property managers, salespeople, store managers, leasing directors, district managers, security people, maintenance supervisors, mall management personnel, developers, marketing coordinators, public relations directors, benefit coordinators, store managers, sales associates, television show hosts, producers, directors, secretaries, administrative assistants, and others. Interviews included personnel from large and small malls and shopping centers, outlet centers, manufacturers, specialty stores, discount stores, chains, department stores, car dealerships, groceries and supermarkets, television shopping channels, distributors, online stores, schools, colleges, unions, and trade associations.

Organization of Material

Career Opportunities in the Retail and Wholesale Industry is divided into six general employment sections. These sections are: Malls and Shopping Centers; Department Stores; Stores, Chains, Shops, and Boutiques; E-Commerce, Mail Order, and Direct Response Shopping; Television Shopping Channels; and Wholesale. Within each of these sections are descriptions of individual careers.

There are two parts to each job classification. The first part offers job information in a chart form.

The second part presents information in a narrative text. In addition to the basic career description, you will find additional information on unions and associations as well as tips for entry.

Eleven appendixes are offered to help locate information you might want or need to get started looking for a job in the field. These appendixes include four-year colleges and universities offering degree programs in apparel and accessory marketing; public relations; and advertising; two-year college degree programs in retail management; listings of trade associations and unions and other organizations; a bibliography of books and periodicals related to the retail and wholesale industry; directories of chain stores, department stores, supermarkets, and groceries; catalog companies; television shopping channels; manufacturers and other companies; retail and wholesale career Web sites; and a glossary.

This book will help you take the first step toward preparing for a great career. Job opportunities exist throughout the country and the world and are increasing every day. Opportunities exist in malls, shopping centers, outlets, discount stores, chains, department stores, specialty shops, auto dealerships, television shopping channels, catalogs, manufacturers, wholesalers, online, and more.

No matter which facet of the retail or wholesale job market you choose to enter, you can find a career that is rewarding, exciting, challenging, and fun. The jobs are out there waiting for you. You just have to go after them.

Persevere. I know you will have a great career!

Shelly Field
www.shellyfield.com

ACKNOWLEDGMENTS

I would like to thank every individual, company, union, and association that provided information, assistance, and encouragement for this book.

I acknowledge with appreciation my editor, James Chambers, for his help and encouragement. I would also like to express my sincere gratitude to Sarah Fogarty for her assistance in the completion of this book.

I gratefully acknowledge the assistance of Ed Field for his ongoing support in this and every other of my projects.

Others whose help was invaluable include Ellen Ackerman; Advertising Club of New York; Advertising Council; Advertising Research Foundation; Advertising Women of New York, Inc.; Harrison Allen; Julie Allen; American Association of Advertising Agencies; Allan Banish; Dan Barrett; Lloyd Barriger, Barriger and Barriger; Steve Blackman; Theresa Bull; Earl "Speedo" Carroll; Eileen Casey; Catskill Development; Anthony Cellini, Town of Thompson supervisor; Brandi Cesario; Patricia Claghorn; Dr. Jessica L. Cohen; Lorraine Cohen; Norman Cohen; Jan Cornelius; Crawford Library staff; Margaret Crossley; Meike Cryan; Daniel Dayton; W. Lynne Dayton; Carrie Dean; Charlie Devine, Devine Realty, Inc.; Direct Mail/Marketing Association, Inc.; Direct Marketing Educational Foundation, Inc.; Joseph Doucette, general sales manager, Middletown Honda; Dress Barn; Michelle Edwards; Scott Edwards; Cliff Ehrlich, Catskill Development; Dan England; Ernest Evans; Julie Evans; Sara Feldberg; Field Associates, Ltd.; Deborah K. Field, Esq.; Edwin M. Field; Greg Field; Lillian (Cookie) Field; Mike Field; Robert Field; Selma G. Field; Rob Fier; Finkelstein Memorial Library staff; David Garthe, CEO, Graveyware.com; John Gatto; Sheila Gatto; Gem Communications; Morris Gerber; Alex Goldman; Larry Goldsmith; Sam Goldych; Gail Haberle; Lillian Hendrickson; Hermann Memorial Library staff; David Hernandez, Community College of Southern Nevada; Hank Hershey; Joan Howard; International Brotherhood of Electrical Workers; International Council of Shopping Centers; Isle of Capri Casinos; Jimmy "Handyman" Jones; Linda Joslin; Dave Kleinman; Janice Kleinman; K-LITE Radio; Bruce Kohl, Boston Herald.com; Crystal Lauter; Karen Leever; Liberty Central School; Liberty Public Library staff; Ernie Martinelli; Robert Masters, Esq; Pat Matthews; Richard Mayfield; Judy McCoy; June E. McDonald; Phillip Mestman; Rima Mestman; MGM Grand, Las Vegas, NV; Beverly Michaels, Esq.; Martin Michaels, Esq.; Middletown Honda, Middletown, N.Y.; Monticello Central School High School Library staff; Monticello Central School Middle School Library staff; Jennifer Morganti; David Morris; National Association of Music Merchants; National Association of Recording Merchandisers; National Music Publishers Association; National Retail Federation; Earl Nesmith; Newburgh Free Library; Marvin Newman; New York State Employment Service; Nikkodo, U.S.A., Inc.; Ellis Norman, UNLV; Peter Notarstefano; Heather Dawn O'Keefe; Outlet Bound; Ivy Pass; Ed Pearson, Nokkodo, USA; Herb Perry; Barbara Pezzella; Public Relations Society of America; Doug Puppel; QVC; Harvey Rachlin; Ramapo Catskill Library system; Doug Richards; John Riegler; Diane Ruud, Nevada Society of Certified Public Accountants; Bob Saludares, Community Employment Training Center, Las Vegas, NV; Michael Seiter; Joy Shaffer; Stuart Slakoff, Professional Programs, Inc.;

M. D. Smith; Raun Smith; Smith Employment Agency; John Sohigian, Orange County Choppers; Laura Solomon; Debbie Springfield; Matthew E. Strong; Sullivan County Community College; The Teenagers; United States Department of Labor; Brian Vargas; Brian Anthony Vargas; Sarah Ann Vargas; Pat Varriale; Amy Vasquez; Pat Vasquez; Kaytee Warren; Marc Weiswasser; Carol Williams; John Williams; Ann Williamson; John Wolfe, general manager, WTZA-Television; WSUL Radio, WVOS Radio and WTZA.

My thanks also to the many people, associations, companies, and organizations that provided material for this book that wish to remain anonymous.

FOREWORD

When Shelly Field asked me to write the foreword for this book, I was happy to do so. The retail and wholesale industries have given me the opportunity to have a great career, and I wanted to share some of my thoughts about how this book can do the same for you.

When I was first starting out, I wasn't sure what career path I would take. And while I knew there were a lot of different opportunities, I wasn't sure where I would fit in. I knew that whatever I did, I wanted to make a difference. I wanted every day to have challenges that I could meet. I wanted to see a company succeed because of the work I did.

I knew I had a lot of skills and talents, and I wanted to be able to use them effectively. And I knew I loved the sports and entertainment businesses and wanted to somehow find a way to have them be part of my career.

Through a lot of work and a bit of luck, I have been able to carve out an exciting and fulfilling career in both the retail and wholesale industries. If this is your goal as well, *Career Opportunities in the Retail and Wholesale Industry* is *the* book to help you take the next step in your career. It is important to know that no matter what segment of an industry you choose to work in, there will be an array of careers for you to choose.

As a 25-year veteran of the sports and entertainment businesses, I have been in sales for my entire career. While your career aspirations might be in a different area of either the retail or wholesale industry, I think you'll find this new edition of Shelly's book will help you zero in on exactly what you might want to do and help you find ways to prepare for your career.

In my current position as the senior vice president of Orange County Choppers, I work with a team that is first and foremost sales oriented. Orange County Choppers is the world's premier custom motorcycle manufacturer.

Orange County Choppers is also an entertainment property. The motorcycle shop is featured on *American Chopper,* TLC's popular television series. I would venture to guess that when most people watch *American Chopper,* they often don't even consider that the show is based on a huge retail and wholesale business. As a manufacturer of motorcycles, Orange County Choppers buys parts, manufactures and sells other parts, and of course sells motorcycles. We wholesale to dealers as well as selling directly to the public.

Our buyers search for the best parts at the best prices. Our warehouse manager makes sure that the right parts are stocked in appropriate quantities. Our sales manager makes sure that the right quantity of each model is built to meet dealer and consumer demand. And our sales team keeps up to date on all product attributes as well as industry trends to be knowledgeable for all consumer questions.

At Orange County Choppers, our business touches on just about every retail channel imaginable. It relies on retail to bolster its image and drive the bottom line by selling products with their logos and similar intellectual property. Retailers rely on these properties to drive sales and add excitement and popular culture to their product mixes and in-store promotions.

Orange County Choppers, like many other companies, licenses its logos and images to consumer products companies to manufacture products using those marks. From T-shirts, hats, and other apparel to video games, toys, pet products, and even trucks and auto aftermarket products, licensed products account for billions of dollars in retail sales annually.

Orange County Choppers sells goods directly to consumers through our Web-based e-commerce store, as well as our own retail operation. We sell licensed products as well as products that we source directly. As part of this chain, there are manufacturers' sales representatives, merchandisers, promotion managers, retail buyers, retail salespeople, and more.

We have someone who sources products from different vendors, such as apparel and die-cast motorcycles, etc. We have a buyer who is responsible for all products in our store and on our Web site, a store manager who is responsible for all store employees including scheduling, training, customer service, etc., as well as a senior vice president who oversees all aspects of the consumer products business.

Virtually all of these functions can be found in some form in this book. As you embark on your job search, be aware that there has probably never been a more challenging time for the entire retail industry. It is important to note that following years of unprecedented growth, a global economic crisis has caused consumers to stop spending. However, with that said, no matter what the economy is, people will still have to eat and clothe themselves. They still will want to buy the little extras that make life worth living. What this all means is that no matter what, the retail/wholesale industry is not going to go away.

If you have the desire, opportunities will always exist to have a fulfilling career in wholesale and retail. The industry needs smart, hardworking people who are capable of following and predicting trends, tracking consumer habits, and thinking outside the box. Shelly's book is chock-full of information about the types of jobs that exist, skills necessary to secure those jobs, tips on how to stand out, and, most important, a directory of key organizations to seek employment.

Use this book as a tool to assist in the process of your career growth. Make it your career workbook. Take its cues; look for subtle suggestions and recommendations that can help you in your job search. Compare your interests and skill set with job requirements. Rank the jobs by your interest level and passions. Ask yourself what intangibles you can bring to a job that might set you apart from other applicants.

Step up and stand out, and you can look forward to an exciting and fulfilling career in this industry.

—John R. Sohigian
SVP, Marketing
Orange County Choppers

INTRODUCTION

Imagine what life would be like if, when you needed something, you could not just go to the store and buy it. Imagine what life would be like without supermarkets, discount stores, department stores, specialty shops, online shopping, etc. Luckily, you do not have to. Retail is bigger today than ever before. And while we now take it for granted that when we need groceries, clothing, housewares, electronics, automobiles, or almost anything else, we simply go to a store, go online, or go to one of the other many types of retail outlets available, it was not always like this.

Trade has always existed. It was not the sophisticated form of shopping that we know today, but it was trade just the same. Throughout history, people traded with each other first to get necessities such as food and clothing, and then to obtain the luxuries of the day. Barter may have preceded the exchange of money in trading and still exists to some extent, but today money is the medium of exchange.

Before there were marketplaces, there were peddlers, traveling salespeople, and trading caravans. Then people traveled to marketplaces in towns where small stalls sold specialty items and wares. As time went on, towns established general stores where almost anything could be purchased. In 1879, Aaron Montgomery Ward founded the company known as Montgomery Ward. That same year F. W. Woolworth opened its first five and dime. By 1902, James C. Penney founded his company, JC Penney. In 1961, Target was founded, followed in 1962 by the founding of Wal-Mart by Sam Walton.

Over the years, retail and wholesale have evolved into a multibillion-dollar business. We all reap the benefits and pleasures of this trade and would find it difficult to live if it did not exist. There are department stores, specialty stores, supermarkets, malls, outlets, and shopping centers for people to buy everything they want and need. Catalogs, televised shopping, and online options also are available. Thousands and thousands of people work in the various segments of the retail and wholesale industry. You can be one of them.

As you read the various sections in this book searching to find the perfect job, keep in mind that every job can be a learning experience and a stepping stone to the next level. I have given you the guidelines. You have to do the rest.

Within each section of this book you will find all of the information necessary to acquaint you with most of the important jobs in the industry. A key to the organization of each entry follows:

Alternate Titles

Many jobs in retail and wholesale, as in all industries, are known by alternate titles. The duties of these jobs are the same; only the name is different. Titles vary from company to company.

Career Ladder

The career ladder illustrates a normal job progression. Remember that in many parts of retail and wholesale there are no hard-and-fast rules. Job progression may not necessarily follow a precise order.

Position Description

Every effort has been made to give well-rounded job descriptions. Keep in mind that no two companies are structured exactly the same. Therefore, no two jobs will be exactly alike.

Salary Ranges

Salary ranges for the job titles in this book are as accurate as possible. Earnings for a job will depend on how large and prestigious a company is, where it is located, and the applicant's experience, education, training, and responsibilities.

Employment Prospects

If you choose a job that has an EXCELLENT, GOOD, or FAIR rating, you are lucky. You will have an easier time finding a job. If, however, you would like to work at a job that has a POOR rating, don't despair. The rating only means that it may be difficult to obtain a job, not that finding one is totally impossible.

Advancement Prospects

Try to be as cooperative and helpful as possible in the workplace. Don't attempt to see how little work you can do. Be enthusiastic, energetic, and outgoing. Go that extra step that no one expects. Learn as much as you can. When a job advancement possibility opens up, make sure that you're prepared to take advantage of it.

A variety of options for career advancement are included. However you should be aware there are no hard set rules for climbing the career ladder in the retail and wholesale industry. While work performance is important, advancement in many jobs is based on experience, education, training, employee attitude, customer service, and of course individual career aspirations. Many companies in both retail and wholesale promote from within. The best way to advance your career is to get your foot in the door and then climb the career ladder.

Education and Training

This section presents the *minimum* educational and training requirements for each job area. This does not mean that you should limit yourself. Try to get the best training and education possible. A college degree or background does not guarantee a job, but it might help prepare a person for life in the workplace. Education and training also encompass courses, seminars, programs, on-the-job training, and learning from others. Volunteer work, internships, and even helping out in family businesses can look good on your résumé.

Experience, Skills, and Personality Traits

This section indicates experience requirements as well as specific skills and personality traits necessary for each job. These will differ from job to job. Whatever job you want, being outgoing helps. Networking is essential to success. Contacts are important in all facets of the business. Make as many as you can. These people can often be helpful in advancing your career.

Best Geographical Location

Most jobs in retail can be located throughout the country. Wholesale jobs may be easier to locate in large cities or areas where there is more industry. If you are creative in your job hunting, opportunities may be found most anywhere in the country.

Unions/Associations

This section offers other sources for career information and assistance. Unions and trade associations offer valuable help in obtaining career guidance, support, and personal contacts. They may also offer training, continuing education, scholarships, fellowships, seminars, and other beneficial programs.

Tips for Entry

Use this section to gather ideas on how to get a job and gain entry into the area of the business in which you are interested. When applying for any job always be as professional as possible. Dress neatly and conservatively. Don't wear sneakers. Don't chew gum. Don't smoke. Don't wear heavy perfume or men's cologne. Always have a few copies of your résumé with you. These, too, should look neat and professional. Have them typed and presented well and checked and rechecked for grammar, spelling, and content. If asked to fill in an application, fill in the entire application even if you have a résumé with you. Print your information neatly. When applying for jobs and filling in applications, be prepared. Make sure you know your Social Security number. Ask people *in advance* whether you can use them as references. Make sure you know their full names, addresses, and phone numbers. Try to secure at least three personal references as well as three professional references you can use.

The ability to go online, whether from your home computer or one in a school or public library, puts you at a great advantage. No matter which aspect of the industry piques your interest, you need to be computer literate. It is always a plus. Many retail and wholesale companies today have Web sites that may be helpful in your quest for a perfect job. You can obtain information about companies and their current job opportunities. You can also read up on industry news or even check the classifieds from newspapers in different areas via their online version of the paper.

Use *every* contact you have. Don't get hung up on the idea that you want to get a job by yourself. If you are lucky enough to know someone who can help you obtain a job, take him or her up on it. You'll have to prove yourself at the interview and on the job. Nobody can do that for you. (Remember to send a thank you note to the person who helped you as well as to the interviewer after the interview.)

Once you get your foot in the door, learn as much as you can. As noted previously, doing a little bit more than is expected will be helpful in your career. Be cooperative. Be a team player. Don't burn bridges; it can hurt your career. Ask for help. Network. Find a mentor.

Remember that customer service is very important in every segment of the retail and wholesale industry. Even if you feel a customer is wrong, try to make him or her feel important and valued. The ability to provide excellent customer service will help you excel in your career no matter the area you work in. I can't stress enough how critical it is to be on time for everything. This includes job interviews, phone calls, work, and meetings. People will remember when you're habitually late, and it will work against you in advancing your career. Have faith and confidence in yourself. You *will* make it to the top eventually, but you must persevere. In many instances, the individual who didn't make it in the career they wanted is the one who gave up too soon and didn't wait that extra day.

The retail and wholesale industry has wonderful opportunities for a great career. Have fun reading this book. Use it. It will help you find a career that is rewarding and exciting. When you do get the job of your dreams, do someone else a favor and pass along the benefit of your knowledge. Help them too.

We love to hear success stories about your career and how this book helped you. If you have a story and want to share it, go to www.shellyfield.com. I can't wait to hear from you!

Good luck!

—Shelly Field

MALLS AND SHOPPING CENTERS

PROPERTY MANAGER— SHOPPING CENTER/MALL

Duties: Overseeing one or more shopping center properties; handling the day-to-day management of shopping center properties; acting as owner's agent; negotiating leases and rental agreements

Alternate Title(s): Real Estate Manager

Salary Range: $40,000 to $125,000,000+

Employment Prospects: Fair

Advancement Prospects: Fair

Best Geographical Location(s) for Position: Jobs may be located throughout the country

Prerequisites:

  Education and Training—Educational requirements vary; see text

  Experience—Experience in mall management, real estate management, or related fields necessary

  Special Skills and Personality Traits—Problem solving skills; negotiation skills; communication

skills; ability to deal well with people; administrative skills

  Special Requirements—Voluntary certification for shopping center management

Position Description

The retail Property Manager is responsible for overseeing one or more shopping center properties. The individual acts as the owner's agent representing landlords, owners, and investors of shopping centers and malls. In some situations, the Property Manager also oversees additional income producing properties such as office buildings, residential buildings, and commercial properties.

The responsibilities of Property Managers vary depending on the specific situation and structure of the company with which he or she works. In smaller companies, the Property Manager may have more general duties. In larger companies, the individual may handle more specific responsibilities. The Property Manager at one company may, for example, oversee mall managers at various malls. Another company may not employ on-site managers and the Property Manager must float from center to center making frequent visits to each.

This job involves a great deal of bookkeeping and paperwork. The Property Manager may do this alone or it may be handled by an on-site manager, bookkeeper, and/or secretaries. While tenants are supposed to pay rents and other fees on a timely basis, this doesn't always happen without some prompting. The Property

Manager is expected to make sure all the rents and fees are collected and credited properly. He or she must also pay all bills, mortgages, taxes, insurance premiums, and payrolls and account for all expenditures.

The Property Manager must be adept at tenant relations. It is essential that the individual deal well with people and keep tenants as happy as possible. Tenants need to feel that their problems and concerns are taken seriously. If they feel otherwise, they will not renew their leases.

One of the most important functions of Property Managers is problem solving. A leaky roof, a lack of customers, a negative story about the mall in the media, a snow covered parking lot, a flood in one of the stores, or a new store which is not ready on time can all turn into disasters if not handled quickly and efficiently. A successful Property Manager will know what to do and who to call to resolve every situation.

Property Managers lease empty stores and other vacant space. They may do this alone or with the help of leasing managers, leasing agents, or leasing consultants. As part of the job, they negotiate leases and other rental agreements under the direction of the mall owners, developers, or landlords.

An important responsibility of Property Managers is bidding and negotiating contracts for services. These might include grounds keeping, snow removal, security, janitorial, maintenance, and other services. Managers might also bid on and negotiate for equipment and supplies including cleaning supplies, paper products, landscaping, or office products.

Additional duties of Property Managers might include:

- Overseeing construction
- Dealing with governmental officials, community and public interest groups, and public utilities
- Overseeing consultants
- Hiring and supervising on-site personnel

Salaries

Annual earnings for Property Managers working in shopping centers can range from approximately $40,000 to $125,000 or more. Compensation is determined by the size, prestige, geographic location, and number of properties the Manager oversees as well as the experience, responsibilities, and education of the individual. Property Managers in some situations may receive bonuses or a small percentage of ownership in projects.

Employment Prospects

Employment prospects for Property Managers are fair. Property Managers may find employment throughout the country. Individuals may be employed by malls or work for real estate developers, development companies, or property management companies. It should be noted that relocation may be necessary to take advantage of job openings.

Advancement Prospects

Property Managers can climb the career ladder in a number of ways. More experience, additional training, and certification help individuals obtain better paying jobs. One of the most common methods of career advancement in this field is locating similar positions with larger, more prestigious real estate development companies and property management firms.

Education and Training

Much of the training Property Managers receive is on the job. However, whether the individual works directly for malls, shopping centers, real estate developers, or property management companies, most employers require or prefer applicants with a college degree. Relevant majors might include real estate, business administration, liberal arts, retail management, public administration, finance, or communications.

Professional and trade associations often offer helpful seminars and courses in all aspects of construction, finance, marketing, human resources, and retail management.

Special Requirements

The International Council of Shopping Centers (ICSC) offers a voluntary certification program for shopping center management.

Experience, Skills, and Personality Traits

Experience is essential in order to become a Property Manager. Some individuals begin their careers as on-site mall managers, promotion, marketing, or public relations managers or in some aspect of real estate.

Property Managers should be energetic, detail-oriented and highly motivated. Individuals need to know a great deal about many different areas. To begin with, Property Managers should have a basic understanding and knowledge of maintenance, construction, human resources, tenant relations, community relations, leasing, budgets, advertising, and marketing.

One of the most important skills that a good Property Manager should have is the ability to solve problems while remaining calm. Communication skills, both written and verbal, are essential. The ability to work with and get along with a variety of people on all levels is necessary.

Unions and Associations

Property Managers may be members of a number of trade associations. These include the International Council of Shopping Centers (ICSC), the Building Owners and Managers Institute International (BOMII) and the Institute of Real Estate Management (IREM).

Tips for Entry

1. Many larger property management and real estate development companies have internships and training programs.
2. There are a number of search firms dealing exclusively with jobs in shopping centers and malls.
3. Send your resume and a cover letter to retail property management companies, real estate development companies, and large malls.
4. Positions are often advertised in the classified sections of newspapers. Look under classifications including "Property Management," "Property Manager," or "Retail Real Estate Management."

5. Jobs in this field, might also be located on-line. Begin your search on some of the more popular job search sites such as the Monster board (www.monster.com) and Yahoo! HotJobs (www.hotjobs.com).

6. Positions may also be advertised in trade journals such as *Value Retail News*.

7. Attend seminars and classes to hone skills and make professional contacts.

MALL MANAGER

Duties: Overseeing the day-to-day management of mall or shopping center; negotiating leases and rental agreements; acting as owner's agent

Alternate Title(s): Shopping Center Manager

Salary Range: $30,000 to $100,000+

Employment Prospects: Fair

Advancement Prospects: Good

Best Geographical Location(s) for Position: Jobs may be located throughout the country

Prerequisites:

Education and Training—Educational requirements vary; see text

Experience—Experience in mall management, marketing and/or promotions preferred

Special Skills and Personality Traits—Problem solving skills; negotiation skills; communication

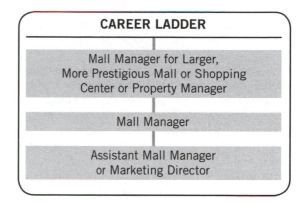

CAREER LADDER

Mall Manager for Larger, More Prestigious Mall or Shopping Center or Property Manager

Mall Manager

Assistant Mall Manager or Marketing Director

skills; public relations skills; ability to deal well with people; administrative skills

Special Requirements—Voluntary certification for shopping center management

---

Position Description

The Mall Manager has a great deal of responsibility. He or she is responsible for overseeing everything that occurs in the mall or shopping center. Some duties may vary depending on the specific structure of the mall, while others are common to all shopping centers.

Mall Managers represent the mall's owner. In this capacity, the individual meets with a variety of people for a wide array of reasons. For example, the Mall Manager might meet with government officials or city or county representatives or attend city or town council meetings to work on changes in zoning, explore grant possibilities, or lobby for tax abatements.

Malls and shopping centers must meet state and local building code requirements. The Mall Manager may meet with state or local building inspectors to learn how to obtain certificates of occupancy for the mall or its individual stores.

Every mall has tenants with problems and concerns that need to be dealt with on a timely basis. Good tenant relations are essential in this job. The Mall Manager is expected to meet with local and corporate tenants, store managers, and owners, and address these concerns. Tenants may, for example, be worried about security issues, increased rents, heavy shoplifting, mall hours, or mall maintenance. Successful Mall Managers

listen to concerns and try to deal with them effectively. It is essential that tenants feel that they are important and are being listened to or they will not be eager to renew their lease. In many centers, Mall Managers also facilitate regular tenant meetings.

The Mall Manager may be in charge of leasing space or may oversee a leasing agent, director, or consultant. He or she may show stores to potential tenants, discuss the pros of the specific mall and negotiate leases. When negotiating, the individual must know the parameters regarding rents and extra charges.

Customers do not enjoy shopping in unkempt, dirty, or poorly maintained malls. One of the most important functions of the Mall Manager is the maintenance of the mall and its property. The most successful malls are clean and well maintained. To do this, Mall Managers must make sure rest rooms are kept clean and working; roofs are not leaking; floors are clean; and carpeting is free of debris, mold, and mildew. In addition the Mall Manager must attend to the outside of the property. This means making sure parking lots are free of potholes, snow and ice are cleaned during the winter months, the building is cared for, and the grounds are neat and clean. The Mall Manager usually oversees a maintenance and janitorial staff who handle these functions.

The Mall Manager works with members of the mall management staff. Depending on the size and structure of the specific property, these might include a promotions director, marketing director, advertising manager, public relations director, construction manager, leasing director, bookkeepers, and secretaries.

There is a great deal of paperwork in this job. The Mall Manager must make sure accurate records are kept of rents received and all expenditures. A bookkeeper may or may not assist with this. The individual is also responsible for keeping records of accidents or incidents involving customers or employees occurring in the mall. He or she might interview customers who slipped and fell in the mall, people who had accidents in the parking lot, or store managers who had shoplifting incidents. It is imperative that every incident be documented for insurance purposes and in case of lawsuits.

A great deal of what the Mall Manager does is solve problems. He or she must constantly try to keep tenants, customers, and the landlord happy.

Additional duties of Mall Managers might include:

- Developing the mall's annual budget
- Attending local community, civic, and not-for-profit meetings on behalf of the mall
- Overseeing construction
- Bidding and negotiating contracts for services, equipment, and supplies
- Hiring and supervising on-site personnel

Salaries
Earnings for Mall Managers can range from approximately $30,000 to $100,000 or more. Earnings are affected by the size, prestige, and geographic location of the mall, as well as the experience, responsibilities, and education of the individual.

Mall Managers in some situations may receive bonuses based on increases of sales, rentals, or the handling of extra projects.

Employment Prospects
Employment prospects for Mall Managers are fair. Individuals may find employment throughout the country. Mall Managers may be employed by malls directly or might work for real estate developers, development companies, or property management companies.

Advancement Prospects
Advancement prospects for Mall Managers are good. As individuals gain experience, they can climb the career ladder by locating similar positions with larger, more prestigious malls or by becoming property managers for larger real estate developers.

Education and Training
Educational requirements vary from mall to mall. While much of the training individuals receive is on the job, most employers prefer their Mall Managers to have a college degree. Others require it. Good majors might include business, real estate, liberal arts, retail management, public administration, finance, communications, public relations, marketing, or related fields.

Professional and trade associations often offer helpful seminars and courses in all aspects of construction, finance, marketing, human resources, and retail management.

Special Requirements
The International Council of Shopping Centers (ICSC) offers a voluntary certification program for shopping center management.

Experience, Skills, and Personality Traits
Mall Managers begin their careers in a variety of ways. Some start out as promotion or marketing directors. Others work in some aspect of real estate, manage stores, or work as assistant mall managers.

The ability to deal with and work well with people is essential for Mall Managers. Individuals need to be good problem solvers, energetic, detail oriented, and highly motivated.

A basic understanding and knowledge of maintenance, construction, security, tenant relations, community relations, leasing, budgets, advertising, and marketing is necessary.

Unions and Associations
Mall Managers do not usually belong to a bargaining union. They may, however, be members of a number of trade associations. These include The International Council of Shopping Centers (ICSC), the Building Owners and Managers Institute International (BOMII) and the Institute of Real Estate Management (IREM).

Tips for Entry
1. There are a number of executive search firms dealing exclusively with jobs in shopping centers and malls.
2. Contact larger property management and real estate development companies to find out what internship and training programs they have available in this area.

3. Consider sending your resume and a cover letter to retail property management companies, real estate development companies, and large malls.

4. Positions are often advertised in the classified sections of newspapers. Look under classifications including "Mall Management," or "Mall Manager," or "Shopping Center Manager."

5. Openings are also advertised in trade journals such as *Value Retail News*.

6. Jobs in this field, may be located on-line. Begin your search on some of the more popular job search sites such as the Monster board (www.monster.com) and Yahoo! HotJobs (www.hotjobs.com).

PUBLIC RELATIONS DIRECTOR— SHOPPING CENTER/MALL

Duties: Develop and implement shopping center and mall public relations and marketing campaigns; handle day-to-day public relations functions; create goodwill between the center and the community; plan and implement special events

Alternate Title(s): Mall P.R. Manager; P.R. Director

Salary Range: $26,000 to $70,000+

Employment Prospects: Fair

Advancement Prospects: Fair

Best Geographical Location(s) for Position: Jobs may be located throughout the country

Prerequisites:

Education and Training—Bachelor's degree in public relations, advertising, business, journalism, marketing, liberal arts, English, communications, or business

Experience—Publicity or public relations experience or training necessary

CAREER LADDER

Shopping Center/Mall Marketing Director or Public Relations Director for Larger, More Prestigious Center

Public Relations Director—Shopping Center/Mall

Assistant Public Relations Director, P.R. Assistant or Publicist

Special Skills and Personality Traits—Creativity; good verbal and written communication skills; knowledge of retail industry

Position Description

All malls and shopping centers have some type of public relations and marketing campaign. The Mall Public Relations Director develops these campaigns. He or she works with the mall marketing or advertising department and the advertising directors of various shops to promote the mall and its image and events. The main goal of the P.R. Director is to get as much positive publicity and exposure for the center as possible.

Depending on the size and structure of the specific center, the Public Relations Director may be referred to as the public relations manager. In certain centers, the Public Relations Director also handles the responsibilities of the marketing director. In others, the P.R. Director works under the direction of the marketing director.

The Public Relations Director is expected to handle the day-to-day public relations functions at the mall. These might include developing and writing a variety of press releases, calendars, newsletters, special interest stories, and feature stories about mall events and special promotions. The P.R. Director must write clearly and concisely in a factual and interesting manner. He or she must develop "hooks" or angles to make stories and releases interesting to the media.

The individual may be responsible for producing both internal and external communications, booklets, pamphlets, posters, or newsletters. He or she may do all the actual writing and layout or work with assistants, publicists, graphic artists, copywriters, or printers, to complete projects.

The P.R. Director may take photographs of special events occurring in the mall or may assign the project to an assistant or professional photographer. Photos may then be used with captions to send to the press or used in other communications.

An important function of the P.R. Director is handling any problems which develop with mall customers, store owners, or managers. He or she might make phone calls to people who have had problems or write letters to try to resolve complaints and situations.

The Public Relations Director keeps in contact with the media to let them know about special events occurring at the mall and must answer calls from the media seeking information.

Often, the P.R. Director is asked to be the spokesperson for the center. He or she must speak on radio and television and to reporters. It is therefore imperative that the individual feels comfortable handling these tasks. It is also essential that the P.R. Director maintains a good business relationship with all media to help ensure that press releases get placed in papers and special events are covered by news people.

The mall P.R. Director is often responsible for developing, planning, and implementing unique special events and promotions that draw people into the mall. These might include contests, weddings in the mall, taste tests, petting zoos, craft shows, antiques shows, classic car shows, or karaoke competitions. In some malls, these tasks may also be handled by an event coordinator.

The individual also is expected to create goodwill between the shopping center and the local community. He or she might, for example, invite local or civic groups such as hospitals, 4-H, schools, Red Cross, American Heart Association, Girl Scouts, or Boy Scouts into the mall to demonstrate activities, pass out literature, or raise money. These groups often hold bake sales, craft sales, or other events to help achieve their goals.

Additional duties of the Shopping Center P.R. Director may include:

- Helping mall stores promote their special events
- Developing media lists
- Attracting bus tours, shopping tours, or other group events
- Designing and developing promotional material

Salaries

Earnings for the Director of Public Relations working in shopping centers or malls can vary greatly depending on a number of variables. These include the size, location, and prestige of the mall as well as the experience and responsibilities of the individual. Annual salaries can range from $26,000 to $70,000 or more. Individuals with experience working in larger, more prestigious malls will earn the highest salaries.

Employment Prospects

Employment prospects are fair for individuals seeking this position. Jobs can be located in malls and shopping centers throughout the country. While smaller centers may have this position, the responsibilities of the P.R. Director may be picked up by the mall manager or marketing director.

There is a fair amount of turnover in this job due to advancement and the general mobility of people in today's job market.

Advancement Prospects

Prospects for career advancement for Public Relations Directors working in malls and shopping centers are fair. Individuals have a number of different options for moving up the career ladder.

One possibility is to move into a similar position in a larger or more prestigious center resulting in increased responsibilities and earnings. Another option is to move into the position of mall marketing director. Some Public Relations Directors move into mall management. Still others advance their careers by striking out on their own and starting P.R. consulting firms.

Education and Training

Most malls and shopping centers either require or prefer the person in this position to hold a minimum of a four-year college degree. Good choices for majors include public relations, advertising, business, journalism, marketing, liberal arts, English, communications, and business.

Courses and seminars in public relations, marketing, publicity, promotion, and the retail industry help give individuals an edge in both obtaining jobs and career advancement.

Experience, Skills, and Personality Traits

Public Relations Directors working in malls and shopping centers should be very creative people who can communicate effectively both verbally and on paper. The ability to deal well with people is essential.

P.R. Directors need to handle many tasks at the same time without getting flustered. Knowledge of publicity, promotion, public relations, and the retail industry will help the Public Relations Director working in this industry excel in his or her job and move up the career ladder.

Unions and Associations

Public Relations Directors working in malls and shopping centers do not usually belong to any union. Individuals may belong to a number of trade associations providing support and guidance. The most prevalent is the Public Relations Society of America (PRSA). This organization provides educational guidance, support, seminars, and important information to members. Mall P.R. Directors may also be members of the International Council of Shopping Centers (ICSC).

Tips for Entry

1. Join the student group of the Public Relations Society of America (PRSA). This association provides many services to help you cultivate your

skills as well offering an opportunity to make valuable contacts.

2. There is quite a bit of turnover in these positions. Consider sending your resume and a cover letter to a number of malls and shopping centers in the area in which you are interested. Ask that your resume be kept on file. Send your letter and resume to the mall owner, developer, or manager. Call each mall's management office to get correct names.

3. You might want to gain some experience in publicity or promotions by volunteering to handle publicity for a local civic or not-for-profit group or a school play or project.

4. Positions are advertised in display ads in newspapers. Look under classifications including "Public Relations," "Promotion," "Malls," "Shopping Center," or "Retail."

5. Larger malls and shopping centers often have internships in the management office. Others may have summer jobs as assistants. Contact malls in your area to check into the possibilities.

6. Take seminars and courses in promotion, public relations, marketing, and publicity.

7. Other seminars in retail management, mall management, and shopping center development will also give you added knowledge in the field as well as helping you make contacts.

8. There are employment agencies dealing specifically with finding employment position in public relations. Check ahead of time to see who pays the fee if you get a job.

9. Check out openings online. Start with traditional job sites like www.monster.com and www.hotjobs.com. Then search for sites specializing in retail career opportunities.

PUBLICIST—SHOPPING CENTER/MALL

CAREER PROFILE

Duties: Publicize mall or shopping center; write press releases and compile press kits; deal with customer service problems

Alternate Title(s): Public Relations Specialist; P.R. Rep; P.R. Representative

Salary Range: $24,000 to $45,000+

Employment Prospects: Fair

Advancement Prospects: Fair

Best Geographical Location(s) for Position: Jobs may be located throughout the country

Prerequisites:

    Education and Training—Bachelor's degree in public relations, advertising, business, journalism, marketing, liberal arts, English, communications, or business

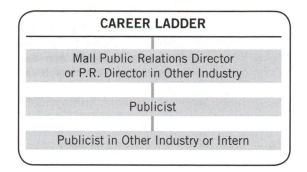

CAREER LADDER

Mall Public Relations Director or P.R. Director in Other Industry

Publicist

Publicist in Other Industry or Intern

Experience—Publicity or public relations experience helpful

Special Skills and Personality Traits—Creativity; good verbal and written communication skills; pleasant personality; knowledge of retail industry

Position Description

The main function of Publicists who work in malls is to publicize the center. Depending on the structure of the mall, individuals may have varied responsibilities. Some malls may employ P.R. directors and one or more Publicists. In these cases, the Publicist will work under the direction of the P.R. director. Other malls might not hire a P.R. director, opting instead to hire only a Publicist. In these cases the individual usually will handle more general duties.

The Publicist is expected to write stock press releases on the center, as well as news releases on special events and promotions the mall is holding. For example, the mall may be having a "Safe Trick or Treat" night for local children or a "Soap Opera Festival" hosting national television personalities. In order to get the most publicity from the event, the Publicist must develop press releases specific to the events and distribute them to the media. The Publicist also takes photographs of special events and promotions or finds someone else to handle the task.

Publicists develop and put together press kits on the shopping center. These might include stock press releases, the history of the center, fact sheets, mall brochures containing a list of stores, photographs, schedules of special events, and other interesting and pertinent information. The Publicist sends these press kits and press releases to the various media, and must compile media lists for the general trade as well as those specific to the retail and shopping center industry.

It is essential that the Publicist have a good working relationship with news editors for print, television, cable, and radio. The individual must also develop a good working relationship with television and radio producers, guest coordinators, and print feature editors, so he or she will be in a better position to have stories placed in print. The Publicist also answers calls from the media seeking information.

Publicists also handle customer relations problems. He or she might make phone calls to people who have had problems at the mall or write letters to resolve complaints and other situations.

If there is no P.R. director, the Publicist will be expected to act as the spokesperson for the center. This may include speaking on radio and television and to reporters.

Additional duties of the Publicist may include:

- Helping mall stores promote their special events
- Developing, planning, and implementing unique special events to draw people into the mall

- Designing and developing promotional material
- Creating goodwill between the shopping center and the local community

Salaries

Annual earnings for Mall Publicists may range from approximately $24,000 to $45,000. Salaries vary greatly depending on a number of factors. These may include the size, location, and prestige of the center as well as the responsibilities and experience of the individual.

Employment Prospects

Employment prospects are fair for individuals seeking this position. Jobs can be located in malls and shopping centers throughout the country. Larger malls may hire a P.R. director and one or more publicists. Smaller centers may hire one or the other.

There is a fair amount of turnover in this job due to advancement and the general mobility of people in today's job market.

Advancement Prospects

Publicists working in malls may advance their careers in a number of ways. After obtaining some experience, some individuals may climb the career ladder by landing jobs as either the assistant P.R. director or a full-fledged P.R. director. Others move into P.R. positions in other industries, some related, some not.

Education and Training

Generally, malls and shopping centers require or prefer the person in this position to hold a four-year college degree. Good choices for majors include public relations, advertising, business, journalism, marketing, liberal arts, English, communications, and business.

Courses and seminars in public relations, marketing, publicity, promotion, and the retail industry help give individuals an edge in both obtaining jobs and career advancement.

Experience, Skills, and Personality Traits

Publicists should enjoy working with people. Individuals should be outgoing, assertive, articulate, and person-able. Publicists need to be creative enough to come up with catchy angles for press releases, media events, and feature stores. An excellent writing style is essential in this job. Verbal communications skills are mandatory.

Unions and Associations

Publicists working in malls and shopping centers do not usually belong to any union. Individuals may belong to a number of trade associations providing support and guidance. The most prevalent is the Public Relations Society of America (PRSA). This organization provides educational guidance, support, seminars, and important information to members. Individuals may also take advantage of activities of the International Council of Shopping Centers (ICSC).

Tips for Entry

1. Join the student group of the Public Relations Society of America (PRSA). This association provides many services to help you hone your skills as well offering an opportunity to make valuable contacts.
2. Send your resume and a cover letter to a number of malls and shopping centers in the area in which you are interested. Ask that your resume be kept on file if there are no current openings.
3. Obtain experience in publicity or promotions by volunteering to handle publicity for a local civic or not-for-profit group or a school play or project.
4. Job openings are often advertised in display ads in newspapers. Look under classifications including "Publicists," "Publicity," "Public Relations," "Promotion," "Malls," "Shopping Center," or "Retail."
5. Larger malls and shopping centers often have internships in the management office. Others may have summer jobs as assistants. Contact malls in your area to check into the possibilities.
6. Take seminars and courses in promotion, public relations, marketing, and publicity.
7. Many shopping centers and malls list job openings on their Web site. Check it out.

MARKETING DIRECTOR— SHOPPING CENTER/MALL

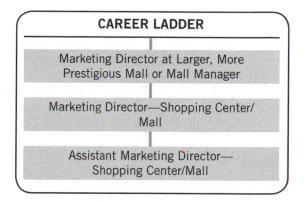

CAREER LADDER

Marketing Director at Larger, More Prestigious Mall or Mall Manager

Marketing Director—Shopping Center/Mall

Assistant Marketing Director— Shopping Center/Mall

Position Description

The Marketing Director of a mall or shopping center is responsible for developing the concepts and campaigns for marketing the center to potential shoppers. The director is expected to determine the most effective techniques and programs for the mall and its tenants, and as part of the job, must plan and coordinate all of the centers marketing goals and objectives.

Shopping centers may utilize a variety of programs and services to attract shoppers. The Marketing Director must select the most viable programs and services for his or her specific center.

For example, does the mall want to market to young families or senior citizens? Does the mall want to attract upscale shoppers or bargain hunters? The Marketing Director will base some of his or her marketing efforts on the answers to questions such as this.

To get this information, the Marketing Director does research by utilizing surveys, questionnaires, focus groups, and comments from shoppers.

Mall Marketing Directors must come up with new and innovative ideas to attract new visitors. These may cover a wide array of promotions, special events, and attractions, and might include exhibits, art shows, craft shows, carnivals, health fairs, and community fairs. Other promotions might run the gamut from cooking and craft demonstrations, antiques shows, career expos, and computer shows to sidewalk sales, wine and cheese tasting, beauty contests, weddings, and bridal shows.

Promotions are designed to bring people in to browse and hopefully buy. Marketing Directors often utilize traditional marketing efforts such as coupon books. Holidays and other annual events might feature Safe Trick or Treating, the Arrival of Santa Claus, the Easter Bunny, or Mother's Day Make-Over Contests. The most successful Mall Marketing Directors are those who devise the most innovative and creative ideas.

Once the ideas are developed, the Marketing Director will work with the public relations and advertising directors to publicize and advertise the promotions. In smaller malls, the Marketing Director may also be responsible for handling the public relations and advertising functions.

Depending on the specific center, the Mall Marketing Director often will work in conjunction with local or corporate tenants on copromotions. For example, the mall may put together a shopping guide showcasing all the tenants, coupon books, or a bus program. Sometimes, the Marketing Director may work with tenants on co-op ads or billboards.

Additional duties of the Mall Marketing Director might include:

- Overseeing the marketing, public relations, and advertising programs
- Supervising the marketing, public relations, and advertising staff
- Developing bus tours, shopping tours, or other group events
- Designing and developing marketing materials
- Conducting marketing research

Salaries

Annual salaries for Marketing Directors of malls and shopping centers can range from approximately $27,000 to $80,000 or more, based on the size, prestige, and geographic location of the specific center as well as the experience and responsibilities of the individual. Generally, those working in larger, more prestigious malls have the highest salaries.

Many malls also have bonus plans for their Marketing Directors, where the individuals receive bonuses for annual or bi-annual increases in sales.

Employment Prospects

Most malls employ Marketing Directors. Employment prospects are fair for this position and getting better every day. Jobs can be located in malls and shopping centers throughout the country. The greatest number of opportunities will be located in areas hosting a large number of malls.

Advancement Prospects

Marketing Directors have a number of options in career advancement. The most common method of climbing the career ladder is locating a similar position with increased responsibilities and earnings in a larger, more prestigious mall.

Another possibility for career advancement is to become a mall manager. Some Marketing Directors move into marketing positions in other industries, while others strike out on their own and start their own marketing firms.

Education and Training

Mall Marketing Directors are usually required to hold a four-year college degree. Good choices for majors include public relations, advertising, business, journalism, marketing, liberal arts, English, communications,

and business. Courses and seminars in marketing, public relations, publicity, promotion, and the retail industry are also helpful.

Experience, Skills, and Personality Traits

Communications skills, both written and verbal, are essential for Marketing Directors. Individuals should be creative, innovative, ambitious, articulate, and highly motivated. Marketing Directors also need to be energetic, with the ability to handle many details and projects at one time without getting flustered.

A knowledge of publicity, promotion, public relations, and advertising as well as research techniques is also necessary.

Unions and Associations

Marketing Directors working in malls and shopping centers do not usually belong to any union. Individuals may belong to a number of trade associations providing support and guidance. These might include International Council of Shopping Centers (ICSC), the American Marketing Association (AMA), the Marketing Research Association (MRA), and the Public Relations Society of America (PRSA).

Tips for Entry

1. Send your resume and a cover letter to a number of malls and shopping centers in the area in which you are interested. Ask that your resume be kept on file. Send your letter and resume to the mall owner, developer, or manager. Call the mall's management office to get correct names.
2. Positions are advertised in display ads in newspapers. Look under classifications including "Marketing," "Marketing Director," "Malls," "Shopping Center," or "Retail."
3. Join trade associations. These will help you in searching for internships, scholarships, and training programs. Jobs may also be advertised in trade journals.
4. Larger malls and shopping centers often have internships in the management office. Others may have summer jobs as assistants. Contact malls in your area to check into the possibilities.
5. Take seminars and courses in marketing, promotion, public relations, publicity, retail management, mall management, and shopping center development. These will give you an edge over other applicants as well as helping you hone your skills and make valuable contacts.
6. Contact recruiters and executive search firms specializing in the shopping center industry.

ASSISTANT MARKETING DIRECTOR—SHOPPING CENTER/MALL

CAREER PROFILE

Duties: Assist the mall's marketing director with plans and campaigns; handle day-to-day marketing functions; assist in the planning and implementation of special events

Alternate Title(s): Assistant Marketing Manager; Assistant Mall Marketing Director

Salary Range: $25,000 to $45,000+

Employment Prospects: Fair

Advancement Prospects: Good

Best Geographical Location(s) for Position: Jobs may be located throughout the country

Prerequisites:

Education and Training—Bachelor's degree in marketing, public relations, advertising, business, journalism, liberal arts, English, communications, or business

Experience—Marketing experience or training necessary

CAREER LADDER

Shopping Center/Mall Marketing Director
Assistant Marketing Director— Shopping Center/Mall
Public Relations, Marketing or Advertising Assistant or Publicist

Special Skills and Personality Traits—Creativity; marketing skills; good graphic sense; good verbal and written communication skills; people skills; knowledge of retail industry

---

Position Description

The Assistant Marketing Director is responsible for helping the mall's marketing director develop concepts and campaigns to market the center to potential shoppers. The individual works with the marketing director coordinating the marketing goals and objectives.

The Assistant Marketing Director may perform research to see what types of programs and services will bring in the most shoppers and where customers are coming from. For example, are all customers local or are they driving distances to reach the center? The individual will work with the marketing director to determine how far customers will travel so they know where to market the mall.

The individual may also help to develop surveys or promotions to identify the most effective media in which to advertise. For example the Assistant Marketing Director might help develop a sweepstakes, where in order to enter, shoppers must write down the newspapers they read, television stations they watch, and radio stations they listen to most frequently. In this manner, the marketing department will know which media is most effective to market the mall. They can then make recommendations to the advertising director.

The Assistant Marketing Director will often brainstorm with the marketing director to come up with unique and innovative ideas and promotions to market the center. Once ideas are finalized, the individual is expected to assist the marketing director in their implementation. Depending on the structure of the center, he or she may work with the public relations and advertising director, promotions coordinator, community relations manager, and mall manager to bring the promotion or program to fruition.

The Assistant Marketing Director is expected to be on hand for special events and promotions when they are taking place. This might mean working on weekends or during the evening.

The most successful Assistant Marketing Directors are detail-oriented. They can keep track of everything that needs to be taken care of for specific promotions. Depending on the project, tables may need to be rented, ads designed, press releases developed, the media notified, and extra security retained.

If the mall does not have a public relations or advertising director, the Assistant Marketing Director may handle many of their functions. He or she may be expected to write press releases, develop ads, handle publicity, and work with the media.

The Assistant Marketing Director will work with the marketing director in dealing with local and corporate tenants on any copromotions. He or she may handle correspondence with the tenants regarding co-op ads, billboards, or promotions. The individual might also set up and attend meetings on behalf of the marketing director.

Additional duties of Assistant Marketing Directors may include:

- Helping mall stores promote their special events
- Assisting in market research
- Tabulating data
- Attracting bus tours, shopping tours, or other group events
- Designing and developing promotional marketing material

Salaries

Earnings for Assistant Marketing Directors can vary greatly depending on a number of variables. These include the size, location, and prestige of the mall as well as the experience and responsibilities of the individual. Annual salaries can range from $25,000 to $45,000 or more.

Many malls also have bonus plans for the marketing director and Assistant Marketing Director, in which individuals receive bonuses for annual or biannual increases in sales.

Employment Prospects

While every mall does not employ an Assistant Marketing Director, there are opportunities in many mid-size and larger malls throughout the country. There is also a fair amount of turnover in this job due to advancement and the general mobility of people in today's job market.

Advancement Prospects

Prospects for career advancement for the Assistant Marketing Director are good. Individuals can find similar positions in larger or more prestigious malls. However, the more common path to climbing the career ladder is for individuals to become a full fledged mall marketing director. This may be in the same mall already employing the individual or might be in a different center completely.

Education and Training

As a rule, individuals seeking this position must hold a four-year college degree. Good choices for majors include marketing, public relations, advertising, business, journalism, liberal arts, English, communications, and business.

Courses and seminars in marketing, public relations, publicity, advertising, promotion, and the retail industry help give individuals an edge in both obtaining jobs and career advancement.

Experience, Skills, and Personality Traits

Assistant Marketing Directors, like individuals working in other aspects of marketing, need excellent verbal and written communications skills. Knowledge of the fundamentals of marketing are necessary in order to be successful in this job.

Assistant Mall Marketing Directors should be creative and innovative with the ability to come up with unique ideas and angles to market the mall.

There are often deadlines which must be met and projects which need to be completed. Individuals need the ability to handle multiple tasks at the same time without getting flustered.

Unions and Associations

Assistant Marketing Directors working in malls and shopping centers may belong to a number of trade associations. These might include the International Council of Shopping Centers (ICSC), the American Marketing Association (AMA), the Marketing Research Association (MRA), and the Public Relations Society of America (PRSA).

These associations provide members with educational opportunities, support, and career guidance.

Tips for Entry

1. Joining trade associations and attending their meetings and conferences will give you an opportunity to make valuable contacts.
2. Send your resume and a cover letter to a number of malls and shopping centers. Ask that your resume be kept on file if there are no current openings.
3. Positions are often advertised in display ads in newspapers. Look under classifications including "Marketing," "Assistant Marketing Director," "Malls," and "Shopping Center."
4. Openings may also be advertised in trade journals such as *Value Retail News*.
5. Larger malls and shopping centers often have internships in the management office. Others

may have summer jobs as assistants. Contact malls in your area to check into the possibilities.

6. Take seminars and courses in marketing, publicity, and public relations to help you hone skills.

7. Other seminars in retail management, mall management, and shopping center development will also give you added knowledge in the field.

ADVERTISING DIRECTOR— SHOPPING CENTER/MALL

Duties: Plan, develop, and implement advertising campaigns for a shopping center or mall

Alternate Title(s): Ad Manager; Advertising Manager; Director of Advertising

Salary Range: $25,000 to $58,000+

Employment Prospects: Fair

Advancement Prospects: Fair

Best Geographical Location(s) for Position: Jobs may be located throughout the country

Prerequisites:

Education and Training—Bachelor's degree in advertising, business, journalism, public relations, marketing, liberal arts, English, communications, or business

Experience—Experience in some facet of advertising necessary

Special Skills and Personality Traits—Creativity; ability to handle details; knowledge of retail industry; knowledge of copywriting, graphics, and layout; ability to meet deadlines

CAREER LADDER

```
┌─────────────────────────────────────┐
│ Shopping Center/Mall Marketing      │
│ Director or Advertising Director    │
│ of Larger, More Prestigious Center  │
└─────────────────────────────────────┘
                 │
┌─────────────────────────────────────┐
│ Shopping Center/Mall                │
│ Advertising Director                │
└─────────────────────────────────────┘
                 │
┌─────────────────────────────────────┐
│ Assistant Advertising Director      │
│ or Advertising Assistant            │
└─────────────────────────────────────┘
```

Position Description

Some communities feature a number of large malls and shopping centers, while others only have one or two small strip centers. In order to attract potential shoppers, malls and shopping centers must advertise.

The Advertising Director working in a shopping center or mall setting is responsible for planning, developing, and implementing advertising campaigns and individual ads for the facility. He or she may work with the center's private shop owners, corporate tenants, store managers, mall owner, and developers.

The Advertising Director is responsible for planning and developing the annual advertising budget for the center. The Advertising Director must develop campaigns for the entire year, including special plans for individual holidays, promotions, special events and sales programs. He or she will call, write, and meet with representatives of various media to get rate sheets, demographics, information sheets, and other useful material. The individual also meets with various representatives of the advertising media to learn more about their publications or broadcast stations.

Customers may come from local areas as well as long distances to shop, so the Mall Advertising Director must decide where his or her advertising dollars would best be spent. Choices might include local or regional newspapers, magazines and other publications, television stations, radio stations, cable stations, billboards, and the Internet.

After the Ad Director has developed the budget, he or she takes it either to the mall marketing director (if there is one), mall management, or the mall owners for review. If the budget is acceptable, the Ad Director then implements it. If it comes in too high, he or she must make adjustments.

In some instances, mall tenants pay an annual advertising fee to a community marketing fund, and these tenants may have more input into the way money is spent on advertising.

Shopping centers and stores often feel that as long as they have people walking and browsing, they will have shoppers. While these people may not make immediate purchases, they may buy at some later date. The Advertising Director works with the marketing, promotional, and public relations departments to come up with ads and campaigns to inform as many people as possible of what the mall offers. The objective for mall Advertising Directors is to attract shoppers and browsers.

Mall Advertising Directors often work with the corporate headquarters of stores and private shops in the mall to put together group or cooperative ads. These are advertisements in which a number of mall stores advertise special sales together at a given time. This might also encompass placing ads advertising all of a mall's stores, shops, and food outlets in publications.

The Advertising Director is responsible for advertising all special events and promotions the mall is hosting. These might include craft, antique and home shows, petting zoos, circuses, celebrity appearances, soap opera festivals, performers, demonstrations, and other events. An Ad Director may develop personally such promotions or may just advertise events developed by the promotion or public relations departments.

The Advertising Director may be required to do actual copywriting, graphics, layout, and production for advertisements or may work with freelance copywriters, graphic artists, and producers. He or she might also sketch out rough ideas for advertisements and have the publication's or broadcast station's advertising department put the final ad together. In some instances, the Advertising Director may also work with advertising agencies which handle some of these functions.

As part of the job, the Advertising Director is expected to decide the best media in which to place ads, specific sections of publications in which to have ads inserted, and when to schedule broadcast commercials. He or she is responsible for making sure all advertisements and commercials have accurate copy and graphics and are mailed or delivered to the correct media before deadline.

Additional duties of the mall Advertising Director may include:

- Developing and putting together shopper's guides
- Tracking tear sheets, clippings, visual cuts, and audio-tapes
- Checking bills for ad placement
- Sending or authorizing payment for ads

Salaries

Salaries for Advertising Directors working in malls and shopping centers range from approximately $25,000 to $58,000 or more annually. Compensation varies according to the size and prestige of the specific mall, its geographic location, size of the advertising budget, and the responsibilities and experience of the individual. Advertising managers also often receive bonuses when there are sales increases in given periods.

Generally, the smaller the mall or the less experience the Advertising Director has, the lower the salary. Larger shopping centers with bigger annual advertising budgets usually offer higher earnings. Malls hosting more prestigious stores and shops may offer salaries on the higher end of the scale.

Employment Prospects

Employment prospects are fair for Advertising Directors in shopping centers. Malls are located throughout the country and more are springing up. Almost every center of any size has someone on staff to fill this advertising function. They may, however, delegate the advertising responsibilities to someone in mall management, public relations or marketing.

Advancement Prospects

Career advancement for Advertising Directors working in malls and shopping centers are fair. Individuals may move up the career ladder in a number of ways.

Some individuals find similar positions in larger or more prestigious centers resulting in increased responsibilities and earnings. Others become mall public relations, marketing, or promotions managers. Some move into mall management positions.

Education and Training

Most malls and shopping centers either require or prefer a four-year college degree. Good choices for majors include advertising, business, journalism, public relations, marketing, liberal arts, English, communications, and business.

Courses and seminars in advertising, copywriting, business, or retail management are also helpful.

Experience, Skills, and Personality Traits

Advertising Directors need to be creative with the ability to communicate both verbally and on paper. Experience working in advertising is usually necessary. This might include knowledge of creating and placing ads, or of copywriting, graphics, and layout.

An understanding of the inner workings of the retail industry is helpful in order to plan successful, effective ads and campaigns. The ability to work on multiple projects at one time and to meet deadlines is essential.

Unions and Associations

Advertising Directors working in malls and shopping centers do not usually belong to any union. Individuals may belong to a number of trade associations providing support and guidance. These may include the American Advertising Federation (AAF) and the Business/Professional Advertising Association (B/PAA).

Tips for Entry

1. There is quite a bit of turnover in these positions. Consider sending your resume and a cover letter to a number of malls and shopping centers in the area in which you are interested. Ask that your resume be kept on file. (Send your letter and resume to the mall owner or developer.)

2. Positions are advertised in display ads in newspapers. Look under classifications including "Advertising," "Promotion," "Malls," "Shopping Center," "Advertising Director," "Advertising Manager," or "Retail."

3. Larger malls and shopping centers often have internships in the management office. Others may have summer jobs as assistants. Contact malls in your area to check into the possibilities.

4. Take seminars and courses in advertising, promotion, public relations, marketing, and publicity.

5. Other seminars in retail management, mall management, and shopping center development will also give you added knowledge in the field as well as helping you make contacts.

6. A good way to gain experience in advertising is to work for a local newspaper, magazine, television, or radio station in the advertising department.

7. Check out openings online. Start with traditional career sites like monster.com and hotjobs.com. Then check out sites that deal specifically with shopping centers, malls, and the retail industries.

ADVERTISING ASSISTANT— SHOPPING CENTER/MALL

CAREER PROFILE

Duties: Assist in the development and implementation of advertising campaigns and individual promotional ads; assist in creating advertisements and commercials

Alternate Title(s): Ad Assistant; Mall Advertising Coordinator; Advertising Trainee

Salary Range: $21,000 to $33,000+

Employment Prospects: Fair

Advancement Prospects: Good

Best Geographical Location(s) for Position: Jobs may be located throughout the country

Prerequisites:

Education and Training—College degree preferred

Experience—Experience in some facet of advertising helpful, but not always necessary

CAREER LADDER

Assistant Advertising Manager

Advertising Assistant—Shopping Center/ Mall

Entry Level, Intern, Secretarial Position, or College Student

Special Skills and Personality Traits—Creativity; detail oriented; knowledge of copywriting, graphics, and layout; good writing skills

Position Description

The Advertising Assistant working in a mall or shopping center is responsible for helping the advertising director. The individual will assist in the development and implementation of the mall's advertising campaign and develop individual ads as well.

Duties of the Advertising Assistant will vary among malls and according to individual experience. The Ad Assistant might be expected to fulfill secretarial duties such as typing letters, updating the returns from mail or ad campaigns, returning phone calls, keeping records of the cost of ad space, checking media prices, etc.

The Ad Assistant may learn how to read and use a book called *Advertising Rate and Data*. This publication lists advertising rates for television, radio, magazines, and newspapers throughout the country. The individual must also become familiar with rate cards which give the prices of ads in various media.

The advertising director might call on the Assistant to write ad copy, create graphics, layout print ads, or develop copy for sales letters, circulars, direct-mail, or other marketing pieces. The individual might be asked to help create storyboards and scripts for broadcast commercials.

The Advertising Assistant may be expected to place ads in publications, purchase space on radio and television and deliver ads and commercials to the media on deadline. He or she will also be responsible for checking

billings, authorizing payments, and keeping accurate records. While the individual may be required to check ad copy for accuracy, he or she will usually be expected to have ads reviewed by the advertising director.

An important function of the Advertising Assistant is helping the Advertising Director plan and develop the annual advertising budget for the center. In this position, the Ad Assistant works with the advertising director and learns how to budget the amount of money to be spent on promotions, the various types of media, and cost-effective places to advertise.

In malls or shopping centers where there is no advertising director, the Advertising Assistant may work with the director of marketing.

Additional duties of the Advertising Assistant working in a mall or shopping center may include:

- Tracking tear sheets, press clippings, visual cuts from broadcasts, and audiotapes
- Overseeing television and radio commercial production and filming
- Conducting research
- Acting as buffer for the advertising director

Salaries

Salaries for Advertising Assistants working in malls and shopping centers range from approximately $21,000 to

$33,000 or more annually. Variables that affect compensation include the size, prestige, and geographic location of the specific mall as well as the responsibilities and experience of the individual.

Employment Prospects

Employment prospects are fair for Advertising Assistants in shopping centers. Individuals may find job opportunities located throughout the country. There is a great deal of turnover in these positions due to promotion and the general mobility of today's population.

Advancement Prospects

Career advancement for Advertising Assistants working in malls and shopping centers are good. Aggressive and enthusiastic individuals may move up the career ladder in a number of ways.

After obtaining experience, some Ad Assistants find similar positions in larger or more prestigious centers resulting in increased responsibilities and earnings. Others become assistant advertising managers or locate other positions in the malls's marketing department.

Education and Training

Educational requirements for this position vary. Some malls and shopping centers may prefer the person in this position to hold a four-year college degree. Others have no educational requirement. For individuals aspiring to advance their career, a college degree is essential. Good choices for majors include advertising, business, journalism, public relations, marketing, liberal arts, English, communications, and business.

Courses and seminars in advertising, copywriting, business, or retail management are also helpful.

Experience, Skills, and Personality Traits

Experience requirements vary from mall to mall. Advertising Assistant is an entry-level position in many malls, but others may prefer candidates with some experience. Internships and training programs are useful.

Advertising Assistants need to be extremely detail-oriented, articulate, personable, and persuasive. Copywriting skills and a knowledge of graphics and layout are helpful. The ability to use computer graphic design programs is necessary.

Unions and Associations

Advertising Assistants working in malls and shopping centers do not usually belong to any union. Individuals may belong to a number of trade associations providing support and guidance. These may include the American Advertising Federation (AAF), the Business/Professional Advertising Association (B/PAA), and the International Council of Shopping Centers (ICSC).

Tips for Entry

1. There is quite a bit of turnover in these positions. Consider sending your résumé and a cover letter to a number of malls and shopping centers in the area in which you are interested. Ask that your resume be kept on file. (Send your letter and resume to the mall owner, developer, or human resources director.)

2. Positions are advertised in display ads in newspapers. Look under classifications including "Advertising," "Advertising Assistant," "Promotion," "Malls," "Shopping Center," "Retail," etc.

3. Attend seminars in all phases of advertising and retail management. These are useful to hone skills and make professional contacts.

4. Larger malls and shopping centers often have internships in the management office. Others may have summer jobs as assistants. Contact malls in your area to check into the possibilities.

5. A good way to gain experience in advertising is to work for a local newspaper, magazine, television, or radio station in the advertising department.

6. Read the trades. These periodicals often advertise job openings and keep you up on current trends in advertising and mall management. If you can't find them in your local library or magazine store, write to the publisher to see if you can get a short-term subscription.

7. Check out shopping center and mall Web sites. Many advertise job openings on their site.

TENANT RELATIONS MANAGER

CAREER PROFILE

Duties: Attending to needs of tenants in shopping center; keeping tenants happy; acting as liaison between mall management and tenants

Alternate Title(s): Tenant Relations Director

Salary Range: $38,000 to $71,000+

Employment Prospects: Poor

Advancement Prospects: Fair

Best Geographical Location(s) for Position: Jobs may be located throughout the country; areas hosting more large malls will provide more opportunities

Prerequisites:

   Education and Training—College degree preferred

   Experience—Experience in retail, mall management, or marketing

   Special Skills and Personality Traits—Problem solving skills; negotiation skills; communication skills; ability to deal well with people; administrative skills

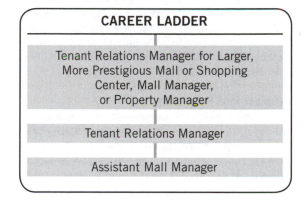

CAREER LADDER

Tenant Relations Manager for Larger, More Prestigious Mall or Shopping Center, Mall Manager, or Property Manager

Tenant Relations Manager

Assistant Mall Manager

Position Description

It is essential to malls and shopping centers to keep tenants happy. The Tenant Relations Manager is responsible for making sure this happens. He or she walks the line trying to satisfy the tenants while competently representing the mall or mall management company.

The Tenant Relations Manager is expected to promote tenant relations, and stay in close contact with tenants. He or she may call, visit, or send correspondence on a regular basis, and may for example, visit stores to see if everything is going well or if they are experiencing any problems. The Tenant Relations Manager may also schedule meetings with local store managers, real estate agents, corporate managers, or store owners.

The Tenant Relations Manager acts as the liaison between the tenants and mall management. When tenants report a problem, the Manager must see how it can be resolved as quickly as possible.

Problems may be easily solved or may be more complex. Tenants may feel the mall is not making repairs which were promised. The Tenant Relations Manager must determine if the repairs were actually promised and if so, why they weren't carried out. A tenant might dispute a charge on his or her CAM (common area maintenance) bill. In this case, the Tenant Relations Manager might speak to the accounting department to straighten it out.

One of the most important functions of the Tenant Relations Manager is making sure that tenants feel that management hears their concerns and cares about them. He or she must establish a good working relationship between the tenant and the mall management.

The individual may deal with various members of the mall management staff including the leasing director, mall manager, marketing, public relations and advertising departments, maintenance department, and management company.

Tenant Relations Managers working for real estate developers or mall management companies may handle the tenant relations of more than one mall.

Additional duties of Tenant Relations Managers might include:

- Discussing tenant problems with mall owners
- Scheduling meetings between mall management and tenants
- Arranging for credits on tenants bills when necessary
- Attending mall meetings
- Handling crises

Salaries

Earnings for Tenant Relations Managers can range from approximately $38,000 to $71,000 or more annually. Variables affecting earnings include the size, prestige, and geographic location of the property and the number of properties for which the individual is responsible. Other variables include the experience, responsibilities, and education of the individual.

Employment Prospects

Employment prospects are poor for Tenant Relations Managers, since not every mall employs a Tenant Relations Manager. Generally, this position can only be found in larger malls or working for a mall management company. In smaller malls the mall manager will be responsible for handling the tenant relations functions.

Advancement Prospects

The most common method of career advancement for Tenant Relations Managers is to find similar positions in larger, more prestigious malls or mall management companies. Depending on career aspirations, some individuals climb the career ladder by becoming mall managers or property managers.

Education and Training

Educational requirements vary from mall to mall. While much of the training individuals receive is on the job, many employers prefer that Tenant Relations Managers have a college degree. Others require it.

Good majors might include business, public administration, marketing, public relations, communications, finance, or related fields.

Professional and trade associations often offer helpful seminars and courses in retail management, mall management, and related subjects.

Experience, Skills, and Personality Traits

Experience requirements vary. Some Tenant Relations Managers start out in marketing, public relations, or community relations. Others may work in mall management.

Tenant Relations Managers need to be diplomatic. The ability to solve problems while remaining calm is essential. The ability to see both sides of a problem also is necessary.

Individuals should be detail oriented and have a basic understanding of everything that goes on in a mall. This includes maintenance, construction, human resources, tenant relations, community relations, leasing, budgets, advertising, and marketing.

Communication skills, both written and verbal are essential. The ability to work with and get along with people is mandatory.

Unions and Associations

Mall or shopping center Tenant Relations Managers may get additional career information by contacting the International Council of Shopping Centers (ICSC) and the Institute of Real Estate Management (IREM).

Tips for Entry

1. Contact larger property management and real estate development companies to find out what internship and training programs they have available in this area.
2. There are a number of executive search firms dealing exclusively with jobs in shopping centers and malls.
3. Send your resume and a cover letter to retail property management companies, real estate development companies, and large malls.
4. Contact the International Council of Shopping Centers (ICSC) to check out what courses they are offering. These will provide valuable training as well as an opportunity to network.
5. Positions may be advertised in the classified sections of newspapers. Look under classifications including "Tenant Relations Manager," or "Mall/Shopping Center Opportunities," or "Retail Opportunities."
6. Openings are also advertised in trade journals.
7. Jobs in this field may be located on-line. Begin your search on some of the more popular job search sites such as the Monster board (www.monster.com) and Yahoo! HotJobs (www.hotjobs.com).

COMMUNITY RELATIONS DIRECTOR— MALL/SHOPPING CENTER

Experience—Experience working with community and not-for-profit groups helpful

Special Skills and Personality Traits—People skills; creativity; good written and verbal communications skills; public speaking ability; organization

Position Description

The Community Relations Director of a mall or shopping center is a great job for anyone who enjoys working with people. The individual coordinates community activities between the mall or shopping center and local agencies, civic groups, schools, community groups, political entities, and governmental agencies. In addition, the Community Relations Director cultivates relationships with these groups.

In smaller areas, the local shopping center is often the gathering place of the community. In larger areas, malls may be utilized for the activities of not-for-profit and civic groups. The Community Relations Director helps coordinate these efforts.

The Community Relations Director plans and designs programs to help the local community and promote the image of the shopping center in a positive manner. While performing these functions, the Director must remain sensitive to the local community and its needs.

The Community Relations Director represents the corporation in beneficial community activities, including the sponsorship of programs such as sporting events, cultural events, and community related programs. For example, the Community Relations Director may arrange to have the shopping center sponsor a Little League team, concert, or local sports team.

The Community Relations Director may develop programs with local community groups such as the United Way or Red Cross to address specific issues, such as a Red Cross program for employees of the mall to volunteer to donate blood.

The Community Relations Director must develop new and innovative community relations programs in which the mall can take leadership. These might include marathons, fairs, art auctions, or parades. These events keep the mall favorably in the public eye and market the mall's name and services to the public. Though sponsored by a single chain of stores rather than a mall, Macy's Thanksgiving Day Parade, which airs on television every year, is an example of this type of event.

The Community Relations Director acts as the mall's representative on not-for-profit organization boards and committees, and is often expected to be an active member of many civic and community groups.

The Community Relations Director should have a good working relationship with the media. In this way, when the mall is sponsoring a local team, helping to raise money for a worthwhile cause, or working on any other community event, the center will reap the benefits of good press coverage.

Additional duties of Community Relations Directors working in malls or shopping centers include:

- Giving speeches on behalf of the mall to local community groups
- Representing the mall at community events
- Appearing on local public service television and radio interview shows to promote the mall's community projects
- Making sure the mall maintains a good public image

Salaries

Earnings for Community Relations Directors working in malls or shopping centers can range from approximately $24,000 to $49,000 or more. Factors affecting earnings include the size, prestige, and geographic location of the mall as well as the responsibilities and experience of the individual. Generally, the larger the mall, the higher the earnings.

Employment Prospects

Employment prospects are poor for individuals seeking this position. Even though there are thousands of malls and shopping centers throughout the country, many do not hire someone specifically for this job. Instead many malls expect someone from the public relations or marketing department to handle the community relations functions.

Advancement Prospects

Advancement prospects are fair in this position. There are a number of different possibilities for climbing the career ladder depending on career aspirations. Some individuals locate similar positions in larger, more prestigious malls. Others move on to similar positions in large corporations. Many land jobs as a mall's director of public relations.

If the individual has developed a good working relationship with a not-for-profit organization that is seeking a director, the individual may be considered for the position.

Education and Training

Most malls and shopping centers require their Community Relations Directors to hold a minimum of a four-year college degree. While majors vary, emphasis should be placed on courses in publicity, public rela-

tions, marketing, advertising, journalism, English, communications, writing, psychology, and sociology.

There are many seminars related to working with not-for-profit groups, community relations, public relations, and publicity that are useful in obtaining a job and excelling in it.

Experience, Skills, and Personality Traits

It is essential in this type of position to enjoy working with people. Individuals should be community minded and have an understanding of non-for-profit civic and community groups.

Community Relations Directors should be outgoing, personable, assertive, and articulate. Good writing, organization, and planning skills are necessary. The ability to speak in front of groups is necessary.

Community Relations Directors working in malls usually have had experience working with not-for-profit or civic groups or as publicity or community relations assistants.

Unions and Associations

Community Relations Directors working in malls and shopping centers may be members of local civic groups, not-for-profit organizations, and service clubs. Individuals may also take advantage of opportunities offered by the Public Relations Society of America (PRSA) or the International Council of Shopping Centers (ICSC).

Tips for Entry

1. Send your resume and a short cover letter to shopping centers and malls in the area in which you are interested in working.
2. Openings may be advertised in the classified section of the newspaper. Look under classifications including "Retail," "Shopping Centers," "Mall," "Community Relations," and "Community Affairs."
3. Jobs may also be advertised on-line at specific shopping center and mall Web sites as well as job sites such as the Monster board (www.monster.com) or Yahoo! HotJobs (www.hotjobs.com) among others.
4. Jobs may also be advertised in trade journals such as *Value Retail News.*
5. Join civic and not-for-profit groups and volunteer to be on committees. This will give you hands-on experience working with these groups.
6. Many large malls offer internships and training programs. Contact them to check out availability.

INFORMATION REPRESENTATIVE— MALL/SHOPPING CENTER

CAREER PROFILE

Duties: Provide information regarding mall, mall stores, and mall services to customers

Alternate Title(s): Information Clerk

Salary Range: $7.50 to $9.00+ per hour

Employment Prospects: Fair

Advancement Prospects: Fair

Best Geographical Location(s) for Position: Jobs may be located throughout the country

Prerequisites:

Education and Training—High school diploma or equivalent preferred

Experience—No experience necessary

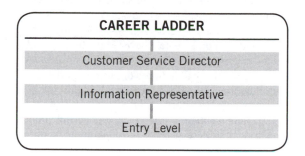

CAREER LADDER

Customer Service Director

Information Representative

Entry Level

Special Skills and Personality Traits—Pleasant personality; outgoing; interpersonal skills; people skills; communications skills

---

Position Description

Many malls and shopping centers host information centers for the convenience of their customers. These centers are usually found in a central location in the mall for the convenience of shoppers and may be a storefront, a counter, or a kiosk.

The Information Representative is the individual who mans the mall's information center. He or she is responsible for answering the questions of mall customers. These might include simple things such as where specific stores are or the location of the closest rest room. The Information Representative may be asked the names of stores in the mall which sell certain merchandise such as children's shoes or electronics.

The Information Representative often will give directions to locations within the mall. In very large malls the individual might use a mall floor plan to help direct shoppers to specific stores as well as verbal instructions. He or she might also give customers directions to places outside the mall such as roads, highways, restaurants, or even other retail establishments.

The Information Representative may answer patron's inquiries about activities, special events, and promotions going on in the mall or mall stores. He or she may, for example, give dates, times, and locations of where a special event is taking place.

The Information Representative will often be asked about mall hours. He or she is expected to know the correct hours that the mall is open daily, as well as holidays. Depending on the specific mall, the Information Representative may also handle the duties of a customer service representative such as wrapping gifts, selling gift certificates, renting baby strollers, or wheelchairs.

This is an ideal job for those who enjoy meeting new people and dealing with and helping others.

Additional duties of the Information Representatives may include:

- Selling gift certificates
- Assisting lost children
- Assisting people who are looking for each other in the mall
- Making announcements in the mall on the public announcement system
- Answering phone inquiries regarding mall questions
- Giving phone numbers of mall stores

Salaries

Information Representatives working in malls or shopping centers may earn between $7.50 and $9.00 or more per hour. Variables affecting earnings include the geographic location, size, and prestige of the shopping center as well as the experience and responsibilities of the individual.

Employment Prospects

Employment prospects are fair for individuals seeking this position. Jobs can be located in malls and shopping centers throughout the country. While every mall does not employ an Information Representative, those who do usually hire more than one.

There is a great deal of turnover in these positions. This may be a result of a number of situations including other career aspirations, advancement, the general mobility of today's society and "Mall Hopping." Many malls and shopping centers have "Mall Hoppers." This means that employees move from store to store and job to job within the mall in hopes of earning more money, better working conditions, increased benefits, or career advancement.

Information Representatives may work full time or part time depending on the specific position.

Advancement Prospects

There are not generally a lot of career advancement possibilities in this area. However, advancement prospects for Information Representatives are dependent to a great extent on the career aspirations of the individual.

Those who are in this position to earn money while in school will probably move to different types of careers as they continue their education. Some individuals may move into administrative assistant positions in the mall management office. Others who are interested in moving up the career ladder in this field might become the mall's customer service manager if the mall has this position.

Education and Training

Most malls prefer their Information Representatives to have a minimum of a high school diploma or the equivalent. The mall provides on-the-job training for this position.

Experience, Skills, and Personality Traits

Generally, this is an entry-level position. Interpersonal and customer relations skills are essential. Communications skills are mandatory.

To be successful at their job, Information Representatives should have a pleasant personality, be outgoing, and enjoy dealing with people.

Unions and Associations

There is no association specific to Information Representatives working in malls or shopping centers. However, individuals may obtain information about this type of career by contacting the International Council of Shopping Centers (ICSC) or mall management offices.

Tips for Entry

1. Jobs may be advertised in the classified sections of newspapers. Look under classifications such as "Information Representative," "Information Clerk," or "Mall/Shopping Center Opportunities."
2. Stop in the mall's management office and ask to fill in an employment application. Ask that your application be kept on file if there are no current openings.
3. Some malls also have a job board posted somewhere in the center. Call the mall management office and ask if they have one.
4. Many local chambers of commerce or community colleges offer hospitality and customer service seminars. These may be helpful in giving you the edge over another applicant.
5. Check out mall and shopping center Web sites. Many list job openings on their site.

CUSTOMER SERVICE REPRESENTATIVE— MALL/SHOPPING CENTER

Duties: Provide special services to mall customers; sell gift certificates; wrap gifts; rent strollers and wheelchairs; give information regarding the mall, mall stores and mall services

Alternate Title(s): Customer Service Clerk

Salary Range: $7.50 to $9.00+ per hour

Employment Prospects: Fair

Advancement Prospects: Fair

Best Geographical Location(s) for Position: Jobs may be located throughout the country

Prerequisites:

Education and Training—High school diploma or equivalent preferred

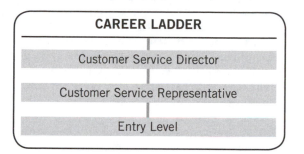

Experience—No experience necessary

Special Skills and Personality Traits—Pleasant personality; outgoing; interpersonal skills; people skills; communications skills

Position Description

Today, there are many places for people to shop. Stand-alone stores, department stores, strip malls, small, mid-sized and large indoor malls, catalogs, television shopping channels, and the Internet are all possibilities. With all these choices, many malls feel that the more services they provide, the easier it will be for people to shop there. As a result, many malls host a variety of special services designed to make shopping easier and more convenient. These services are provided by Customer Service Representatives.

The customer service area of a mall is usually centrally located to make it easy for shoppers to find. The area may be a kiosk, store, or customer service counter in the mall.

The Customer Service Representative's duties vary depending on the specific center, its structure, and the services they provide. In some centers, the Customer Service Representative will also be expected to act as an information representative. This means the individual will be expected to answer mall customers' questions. These might include things like where specific stores are located in the mall, the location of the closest rest rooms, or which stores in the mall sell certain merchandise.

Many malls rent strollers and wheelchairs for customer use in the mall for a small fee or deposit. The Cus-

tomer Service Representative is responsible for helping customers get the stroller or wheelchair, explaining the conditions of use, taking payment, and keeping records of rentals and deposits. He or she must also check in strollers and wheelchairs which are returned.

Certain malls offer gift wrapping services which are offered either gratis or for a small fee. The Customer Service Representative would be responsible for wrapping packages in a neat and attractive manner.

Other malls offer shipping services for the convenience of customers. In these instances, the Customer Service Representative may weigh items, package them for shipping, collect monies, and get the correct shipping information.

The more time a customer spends in a mall, the better the chance he or she will purchase something. With this in mind, many malls feel that customers will be more comfortable shopping without carrying around their other purchases, heavy outerwear, or packages. Therefore, they have areas where customers can store their belongings, outerwear, and purchases while they shop. The Customer Service Representative usually takes the customer's belongings and gives the customer one half of a ticket to use to retrieve their merchandise when they are done shopping. The other half of the ticket is kept with the customer's items.

If a shopper has a problem in the mall, he or she will usually go to the customer service counter or area and speak to a Customer Service Representative. It is the responsibility of the individual to help the customer as much as possible. Problems can vary tremendously in a mall and the Customer Service Representative must be adept at handling an array of situations in a calm and helpful manner.

People lose their wallets, leave their handbags in dressing rooms or rest rooms, and put bags of merchandise down and forget to pick them up again every day in malls. Customers may find large sums of money or jewelry that others have dropped or misplaced or bags of merchandise that someone else has lost.

Some situations are more stressful than others and need more understanding. Children often wander away from parents, customers slip or fall, or accidents occur. The Customer Service Representative must keep everyone calm while following the mall's procedures. Depending on the situation, he or she may be expected to call mall management, security, or even the police when needed.

The Customer Service Representative will answer patron's questions about mall hours and special events and promotions. He or she will give out brochures, coupons, or other materials provided by the mall.

The Customer Service Representative may be responsible for selling mall gift certificates and explaining any conditions and limitations. In some malls, gift certificates may be sold by the mall management office or specific stores in the mall instead.

Additional duties of Customer Service Representatives working in malls may include:

- Assisting lost children
- Assisting people who are looking for each other in the mall
- Making announcements in the mall on the public address system
- Answering phone inquiries regarding mall questions
- Giving phone numbers of mall stores

Salaries

Customer Service Representatives working in malls earn between $7.50 and $9.00 or more per hour. Variables affecting earnings include the geographic location, size, and prestige of the shopping center as well as the experience and responsibilities of the individual.

Employment Prospects

Employment prospects are fair for individuals seeking this position. Jobs can be located in malls and shopping centers throughout the country. While every mall does not employ a Customer Service Representative, those who do usually hire more than one.

There is a great deal of turnover in these positions. This may be a result of a number of situations including other career aspirations, advancement, the general mobility of today's society and a phenomenon called "Mall Hopping."

Many malls and shopping centers have "Mall Hoppers." This means that employees move from store to store and job to job within the mall in hopes of making more money, better working conditions, increased benefits, or career advancement.

Customer Service Representatives may work full time or part time depending on the specific position.

Advancement Prospects

Advancement prospects for Customer Service Representatives working in malls are dependent to a great extent on the career aspirations of the individual. Generally, advancement prospects for Customer Service Representatives working in malls are limited. Individuals may move up to become customer service managers, but these jobs are few and far between. Usually these jobs can only be found at larger malls.

Individuals who want to work in customer service and advance their career may move into customer service positions in other industries. Those who want to stay in a mall environment may move into administrative assistant positions in the mall management office.

Education and Training

Customer Service Representatives working in malls generally are required to have a minimum of a high school diploma or the equivalent. Many malls, however, also hire individuals who are still attending school. The mall provides informal on-the-job training for this position.

A college degree or background is helpful for those aspiring to move up the career ladder in customer service. There are also many seminars, courses, and workshops in the area of customer service which will be useful in honing skills and may give one applicant an edge over another.

Experience, Skills, and Personality Traits

This is usually an entry-level position. Interpersonal and customer relations skills are essential. Individuals should be articulate with good communications skills.

Customer Service Representatives working in malls should be outgoing with a pleasant personality. They should enjoy dealing with the public.

Unions and Associations

There is no association specific to Customer Service Representatives working in malls or shopping centers. However, individuals may obtain information about this type of career by contacting the International Council of Shopping Centers (ICSC) or mall management offices.

Tips for Entry

1. Jobs may be advertised in the classified sections of newspapers. Look under classifications such as "Customer Service Representative," "Customer Service Clerk," "Customer Service," or "Mall/ Shopping Center Opportunities."
2. Visit the mall management office to fill out an employment application. Ask that your application be kept on file if there are no current openings.
3. Some malls also have a job board posted somewhere in the center. Call the mall management office and ask if they have one; if so, check it regularly.
4. Many local chambers of commerce or community colleges offer hospitality and customer service seminars. These may be helpful in giving you the edge over another applicant.
5. Malls often have Web sites where they advertise employment opportunities. Look in the newspaper for ads to find the Web site addresses of the mall you're interested in working in.

ADMINISTRATIVE ASSISTANT— SHOPPING CENTER OR MALL OFFICE

CAREER PROFILE

Duties: Assist mall executives in their functions; screen phone calls for executive; return phone calls; compose correspondence; schedule meetings; coordinate office services

Alternate Title(s): Executive Assistant

Salary Range: $8.50 to $30.00+ per hour

Employment Prospects: Fair

Advancement Prospects: Fair

Best Geographical Location(s) for Position: Jobs may be located throughout the country

Prerequisites:

　Education and Training—High school diploma or equivalent; on-the-job training; additional training may be required

　Experience—Experience requirements vary

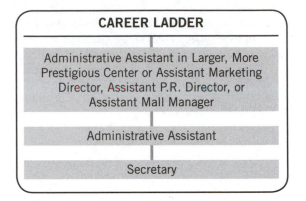

CAREER LADDER

Administrative Assistant in Larger, More Prestigious Center or Assistant Marketing Director, Assistant P.R. Director, or Assistant Mall Manager

Administrative Assistant

Secretary

Special Skills and Personality Traits—Good judgment; communications skills; detail oriented; office skills; computer skills; phone skills; people skills

Position Description

A mall office may have an array of support personnel helping the mall or shopping center run smoothly. Depending on the size and structure of the center, there may be one or more Administrative Assistants helping the mall management staff.

The Administrative Assistant may be assigned to work with the mall manager or one of the other directors, managers, or departments. These might include marketing, advertising, leasing, or tenant relations. In some malls, the Administrative Assistant may work with the entire administrative staff.

The Administrative Assistant has varied duties. His or her main function is to assist the mall management executives. The individual might coordinate the office staff and services. He or she may schedule the work of the office personnel. The Administrative Assistant might assign specific projects to staff on behalf of the mall manager or other department managers. The individual may, for example, assign secretaries to type correspondence or to put together leasing packages.

If the Administrative Assistant is working with a specific department in the management office, he or she might have more specialized duties. Working in this capacity, the individual has the opportunity to obtain experience and learn more about the functions of a department.

The Assistant working in the advertising department, for example, might be asked to call the media to get rate cards or check space availabilities and prices. The individual might be responsible for proofing ads for accuracy and correcting any errors. As the individual gains experience, he or she might even begin to develop simple ads or layouts. Everything, of course, will be done under the director's supervision.

The Administrative Assistant working with the public relations director might have other duties. He or she might be expected to proof press releases, check information for accuracy, or put together press packages. The individual might be asked to schedule meetings with members of the media, help the P.R. director put together a press conference, or coordinate a special event.

In some situations, he or she may act in the capacity of secretary. The individual might screen, take, and return phone calls on behalf of the mall executive. He or she might also prepare, compose, and type correspondence or check correspondence done by secretary.

Administrative Assistants are often called upon to type or handle confidential documents. Individuals might also be expected to handle confidential phone calls or schedule important meetings. It is essential the Administrative Assistant keep information learned in the mall office confidential and be discrete at all times.

In many mall offices, one of the major projects of the year is preparing the annual budget. The Administrative Assistant may help collect information for the budget as well as assist in its preparation.

Other duties of an Administrative Assistant working in a mall office may include:

- Reviewing reports
- Training office staff
- Screening visitors
- Dealing with emergencies

Salaries
Earnings for Administrative Assistants working in shopping centers and malls can range from approximately $8.50 to $30.00 or more per hour. Variables affecting earnings include the geographic location, size, and prestige of the shopping center as well as the experience and responsibilities of the individual.

One of the perks for Administrative Assistants working in malls is that individuals often receive an employee discount from many of the mall stores.

Employment Prospects
Employment prospects are fair for individuals seeking this position. Jobs can be located in malls and shopping centers throughout the country. As noted previously, malls may hire one or more Administrative Assistants.

Advancement Prospects
Administrative Assistants working in mall offices may advance their career in a number of ways. Some find similar positions in larger malls resulting in increased responsibilities and earnings.

Depending on the individual's education and the area he or she has worked in, after obtaining experience the Administrative Assistant might advance to positions such as assistant director of marketing, public relations, advertising, leasing, or even assistant mall manager.

Education and Training
Education and training requirements vary from mall to mall. Generally, most malls prefer their Administrative Assistants to hold a minimum of a high school diploma. Some prefer a college background. This will be especially important for individuals seeking to advance their careers in this field. Depending on the aspirations of the Administrative Assistant, good choices for majors might include retail management, communications, marketing, advertising, public relations, English, liberal arts, or a related field.

Experience, Skills, and Personality Traits
Experience working in an office environment may be required or preferred. However, some malls will hire Administrative Assistants with experience in public relations, marketing, advertising, or leasing instead.

Administrative Assistants need excellent communications skills. Individuals should be dependable, detail oriented, and extremely organized. Interpersonal and customer relations skills are essential. Good judgment is mandatory.

Unions and Associations
Individuals interested in working as Administrative Assistants in mall offices may learn more by contacting the International Council of Shopping Centers (ICSC) or the International Association of Administrative Professionals (IAAP). Those working in specific departments aspiring to move up may belong to more industry specific organizations. For example, those working in the public relations department, might belong to the Public Relations Society of America (PRSA).

Tips for Entry
1. Jobs may be advertised in the classified sections of newspapers. Look under classifications such as "Administrative Assistant," "Mall Office," "Retail Opportunities," or "Executive Assistant."
2. Stop by the mall management office to fill out an application. Ask that your application be kept on file if there are no current openings.
3. You can also send a short cover letter and your resume to the mall management office.
4. Many malls now have Web sites listing their openings. Check out on line the malls in which you are interested in working. If you don't know their web address, you can either call the mall office or see if the address is in advertisements.
5. Some malls have internship programs. Call or write to check the possibilities.

SECRETARY—SHOPPING CENTER OR MALL OFFICE

CAREER PROFILE

Duties: Answering telephones in mall office; returning phone calls; filing; typing; routing mail; greeting people

Alternate Title(s): None

Salary Range: $7.50 to $25.00+ per hour

Employment Prospects: Fair

Advancement Prospects: Fair

Best Geographical Location(s) for Position: Jobs may be located throughout the country

Prerequisites:

Education and Training—High school diploma or equivalent; on-the-job training; additional training may be required

Experience—Secretarial or office experience preferred, but not always required

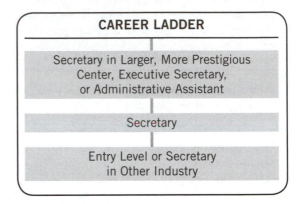

CAREER LADDER

Secretary in Larger, More Prestigious Center, Executive Secretary, or Administrative Assistant

Secretary

Entry Level or Secretary in Other Industry

Special Skills and Personality Traits—Office skills; computer skills; phone skills; typing skills; communication skills; good judgment; people skills

Position Description

Most malls and shopping centers have mall offices. These require the services of an array of support personnel including Secretaries, executive secretaries, administrative assistants, receptionists, and more. Each of these individuals help the mall management office run smoothly.

Depending on the size and structure of the mall, there may be one or more Secretaries employed by the center. The size and structure of each center will also determine the exact functions of each individual.

Secretaries handle a wide variety of clerical duties. They are expected to type a variety of correspondence, envelopes, and reports. Typing may be done on a typewriter, word processor, or computer.

Individuals might additionally use various software programs to accomplish different tasks necessary to the mall on the computer. These might include more common programs such as Microsoft Word or Excel. Many malls also utilize specific mall management software programs to keep track of tenancies, rents, and leases.

The mall Secretary might be asked to take and transcribe dictation or may be required to take shorthand. Depending on the situation, he or she may be expected to assist the mall manager, leasing agent, marketing director, public relations director, or advertising director with their clerical work.

The mall Secretary may photocopy documents such as leases, contracts, letters, or reports. He or she will also be responsible for filing, maintaining files, collating reports, sorting mail, and sending faxes.

An important function of the mall Secretary is greeting in a courteous manner people who visit the mall office. Visitors might include tenants, mall employees, contractors, potential tenants, and customers.

The Secretary must answer the phones and return phone calls in a professional and polite manner. The individual may also be responsible for screening calls and scheduling meetings and appointments.

On occasion, the mall Secretary may deal with emergencies, finding the correct people to handle the problem.

Other duties of the mall Secretary may include:

- Answering letters and other correspondence
- Handling accounts payable and receivable
- Screening visitors
- Answering customer's questions regarding the mall
- Giving directions to stores within the mall

Salaries

Earnings for Secretaries working in shopping centers and malls can range from approximately $7.50 to $25.00

or more per hour. Variables affecting earnings include the geographic location, size, and prestige of the shopping center as well as the experience and responsibilities of the individual.

One of the perks for Secretaries working in malls is that individuals often receive an employee discount from mall stores.

Employment Prospects

Employment prospects are fair for individuals seeking this position. Jobs can be located in malls and shopping centers throughout the country. As noted previously, malls may hire one or more Secretaries.

Advancement Prospects

Secretaries working in mall offices may advance their career in a number of ways. After obtaining experience, some individuals find similar positions in larger, more prestigious malls. Others may climb the career ladder by becoming executive secretaries or administrative assistants.

Education and Training

Education and training requirements vary from mall to mall. Generally, most malls prefer their Secretaries to hold a minimum of a high school diploma or the equivalent. Some prefer some college or secretarial school. Secretarial courses as well as instruction in computers and various software packages are helpful.

Experience, Skills, and Personality Traits

Entry-level positions may be open in some malls. Experience, working in an office environment is usually required or preferred.

Secretaries should have excellent typing skills, with the ability to type accurately between 55 and 65 words per minute. Word processing and computer skills are usually necessary. The ability to take dictation is often required or preferred.

Successful mall Secretaries are pleasant to be around. Interpersonal and customer relations skills are essential. Communications skills are mandatory.

Unions and Associations

Individuals may obtain information about a career in this field by contacting International Association of Administrative Professionals (IAAP). Secretaries working in malls and shopping centers may also want to contact the International Council of Shopping Centers (ICSC) for additional career information.

Tips for Entry

1. There are community colleges, secretarial schools, and vocational and technical schools that offer courses in various aspects of office work, computers, and software. These courses give you the working knowledge which may be useful in giving you the edge over other applicants.
2. Jobs may be advertised in the classified sections of newspapers. Look under classifications such as "Secretary," "Mall Office," "Retail," "Executive Secretary," or "Administrative Assistant," "Office Workers."
3. Stop by the mall management office to see if you can fill out an application. Ask that your application be kept on file if there are no current openings.

BOOKKEEPER—SHOPPING CENTER OR MALL OFFICE

CAREER PROFILE

Duties: Recording accounts receivable and accounts payable

Alternate Title(s): Accounting Clerk, Bookkeeping Clerk

Salary Range: $8.50 to $30.00+ per hour

Employment Prospects: Fair

Advancement Prospects: Fair

Best Geographical Location(s) for Position: Jobs may be located throughout the country

Prerequisites:

    Education and Training—High school diploma or equivalent; on-the-job training; additional training may be required

    Experience—Bookkeeping or accounting experience preferred, but not always required

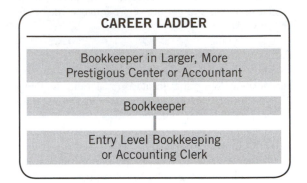

CAREER LADDER

Bookkeeper in Larger, More Prestigious Center or Accountant

Bookkeeper

Entry Level Bookkeeping or Accounting Clerk

Special Skills and Personality Traits—Aptitude for numbers; orderly; detail oriented; office skills; computer skills; communication skills; good judgment

Position Description

A great deal of money is involved in running malls. Rents and other charges are paid to the mall owner in exchange for a location in the center. Other monies are paid out to run the center. The mall Bookkeeper is responsible for accurately recording all money received and spent. This information is invaluable in running the mall. As in all businesses, it will reflect the profit and losses of the mall.

Depending on the size and structure of the mall office, there may be one or more Bookkeepers. In centers where there is only one Bookkeeper, the individual will be responsible for all of the accounting duties. Centers with more than one individual in the department may have more specialized duties.

For example, in some centers the mall Bookkeeper may be solely responsible for accounts receivable or conversely just the accounts payable. In other centers, one Bookkeeper may handle everything. Large malls may also have head Bookkeepers as well as entry-level clerks.

A major function of the mall Bookkeeper is recording tenant rents. In addition to monthly rents, malls charge various other monies to tenants. These might include taxes, CAM (common area maintenance) fees, advertising, or marketing. These various charges must

be billed to tenants on a regular basis. The mall Bookkeeper is responsible for preparing and sending out these bills on a monthly basis.

The individual may also be expected to monitor payments to ensure they are up to date. In some malls, the Bookkeeper may be required to call tenants when bills are not paid by tenants on time.

Running a mall is expensive. There are a wide array of expenses which are paid out. These might include payroll, consultants, advertising, taxes, loans, equipment, and supplies. It is the responsibility of the mall Bookkeeper to handle these account payables. He or she is expected to review invoices and statements for accuracy and completeness, cut checks, have them signed by the correct party, and send them out. Bills must be paid in a timely manner in order to avoid the mall being charged late fees.

Mall Bookkeepers must post the details of each financial transaction. This may be done manually (by hand on paper), with adding machines, or with the help of a computer. Special accounting or bookkeeping software or mall management programs are commonly used.

Malls may have one or more bank accounts. Individuals are responsible for totaling, balancing, and reconciling each account to ensure accuracy.

Many malls have codes for various categories of incomes and expenses. The Bookkeeper must code each invoice properly. This makes it easier to prepare reports detailing transactions and for annual budgeting purposes.

The mall Bookkeeper may be responsible for printing out and reviewing monthly management reports detailing accounts receivable, expenses, or budget comparisons.

Mall Bookkeepers in many centers may also be responsible for handling payroll functions. In these cases individuals may collect time cards, and tabulate hours worked and pay due to each employee.

Other duties of the mall Bookkeeper may include:

- Performing secretarial functions
- Writing letters and other correspondence regarding accounts payable and/or receivable
- Answering tenants questions regarding billings
- Preparing reports for auditors

Salaries

Earnings for Bookkeepers working in shopping centers and malls can range from approximately $8.50 to $30.00 or more per hour. Variables affecting earnings include the geographic location, size, and prestige of the shopping center as well as the experience and responsibilities of the individual.

One of the perks for Bookkeepers working in malls is that individuals often receive employee discounts from mall stores.

Employment Prospects

Employment prospects are fair for individuals seeking this position. Jobs may be located in malls and shopping centers throughout the country. Management companies and developers may also employ Bookkeepers for malls they manage. Depending on the size and structure of the center, there may be one or more Bookkeepers on staff.

Advancement Prospects

Bookkeepers in mall offices may advance their career in a number of ways. After obtaining experience, individuals may take on additional duties or find similar positions in larger, more prestigious malls. Others may climb the career ladder by taking additional training and becoming an accountant.

Education and Training

Education and training requirements vary from mall to mall. Generally, malls require their Bookkeepers to hold a minimum of a high school diploma or the equivalent. Many prefer a college background or some business courses. Classes in bookkeeping, accounting, computers, and accounting software are helpful.

In some properties, the mall will provide in-service training in the use of the software programs or the specific bookkeeping procedures used in the center.

Experience, Skills, and Personality Traits

Bookkeepers should have a strong aptitude for numbers. Individuals need to be careful, orderly, and detail oriented. Mall Bookkeepers should be comfortable using computers and able to use accounting software packages.

Unions and Associations

There is no association specific to Mall Bookkeepers. Individuals working toward becoming an accountant might get additional information from the National Society of Public Accountants (NSPA) or the American Institute of Certified Public Accountants (AICP).

Tips for Entry

1. Courses and workshops in accounting and bookkeeping techniques as well as bookkeeping and accounting software are helpful in making you more marketable.
2. Jobs may be advertised in the classified sections of newspapers. Look under classifications such as "Bookkeeper," "Accounting Clerk," "Bookkeeping Clerk," and "Mall Office Personnel."
3. Stop by the mall management office to see if you can fill out an application. Ask that your application be kept on file if there are no current openings.
4. Look for openings online. Check out sites like hotjobs.com, monster.com and shopping center and mall Web sites.

JANITORIAL SUPERVISOR— SHOPPING CENTER/MALL

Duties: Overseeing center's janitorial staff; keeping mall and property clean and well maintained

Alternate Title(s): Building Custodian Supervisor

Salary Range: $24,000 to $48,000+

Employment Prospects: Fair

Advancement Prospects: Poor

Best Geographical Location(s) for Position: Jobs may be located throughout the country

Prerequisites:

Education and Training—Educational requirements vary

Experience—Supervision experience

Special Skills and Personality Traits—Supervisory skills; ability to deal well with people; knowledge of use of cleaning supplies and equipment

CAREER LADDER

```
┌─────────────────────────────────────┐
│  Janitorial Supervisor for Larger,  │
│       More Prestigious Malls/        │
│      Shopping Centers or             │
│       Maintenance Supervisor         │
└─────────────────────────────────────┘
                 │
┌─────────────────────────────────────┐
│   Janitorial Supervisor—Shopping     │
│           Center/Mall                │
└─────────────────────────────────────┘
                 │
┌─────────────────────────────────────┐
│   Assistant Janitorial Supervisor    │
│            or Janitor                │
└─────────────────────────────────────┘
```

Position Description

It is essential to their success that malls be clean and well maintained. The Janitorial Supervisor is responsible for overseeing the janitors and cleaning people. In some situations, he or she may also function as the maintenance supervisor. In others, the individual must work in conjunction with the maintenance department.

The Janitorial Supervisor coordinates and schedules the other janitors, cleaners, and custodians. Depending on the mall hours, janitors may work various shifts including morning, afternoon, evening, or overnight. The individual may also schedule and oversee independent contractors for special projects such as cleaning windows, skylights, fountains, or carpets.

The Janitorial Supervisor assigns tasks on a daily basis for the mall's janitors to accomplish. Some of these tasks may need to be done on a daily basis, while others may be done on a weekly or monthly basis. For example daily tasks may include emptying ashtrays and trash receptacles, cleaning rest rooms, checking and replenishing rest room paper products, and cleaning and vacuuming floors and food court areas. Weekly tasks might include washing inside mall windows, shampooing carpets, and washing down walls. Monthly tasks might include cleaning vents and major cleaning projects on the property.

Not only must the Janitorial Supervisor assign the tasks, he or she must make sure they are completed correctly. Not every assigned job must be inspected, but the supervisor must see that tasks are executed in a timely manner.

The Janitorial Supervisor also trains new employees. He or she must explain all pertinent procedures, rules, and regulations to employees. The supervisor issues cleaning supplies and equipment to employees and shows them how each is used properly.

Janitorial Supervisors often meet with salespeople from companies selling paper products or cleaning supplies. They may sample cleaning supplies and products for possible use in the mall, and they must inventory cleaning supplies and paper products on a regular basis to be sure supplies and paper products are available when needed. They must also maintain cleaning equipment in good working condition.

Additional duties of Janitorial Supervisors might include:

- Screening, interviewing, and hiring janitors
- Recommending promotions and dismissals
- Preparing reports for budgets and expenses and schedules
- Performing cleaning duties

Salaries

Annual earnings for Janitorial Supervisors working in malls and shopping centers ranges from approximately $24,000 to $48,000 depending on a number of variables. These include the size, prestige, and geographic location of the specific mall or shopping center as well as the experience, responsibilities, and education of the individual.

Employment Prospects

Employment prospects for Janitorial Supervisors are fair. Individuals may find employment in malls throughout the country. As noted previously, in some malls there is a maintenance supervisor who handles the functions of the Janitorial Supervisor. Additionally, some malls contract outside janitorial companies to clean the center.

Advancement Prospects

Advancement is difficult for Janitorial Supervisors. Individuals may find similar positions in larger, more prestigious properties to advance their careers. They might also become Maintenance Supervisors.

Education and Training

Generally, most employers prefer to hire individuals who have completed high school. A great deal of the training Janitorial Supervisors receive is usually on the job. Many malls have in-service training programs to hone skills. Technical schools and trade programs may also offer training.

Experience, Skills, and Personality Traits

Experience handling janitorial work is necessary. Most Janitorial Supervisors were once janitors or custodians. Supervisory skills are essential. A basic understanding and knowledge of the use of cleaning products and equipment as well as maintenance is helpful. The ability to work well with others is also needed.

Unions and Associations

There is no association specific to Shopping Center Janitorial Supervisors. Some Supervisors may take advantage of educational programs of the International Council of Shopping Centers (ICSC).

Tips for Entry

1. Many larger property management and real estate development companies have internships and training programs.
2. Get your foot in the door by stopping in to the mall management office and a filling out an application.
3. Positions are often advertised in the classified sections of newspapers. Look under classifications including "Janitorial Supervisor," "Custodian Supervisor," "Malls," or "Shopping Centers."
4. Openings may also be listed on mall and shopping center Web sites.

MAINTENANCE SUPERVISOR— SHOPPING CENTER/MALL

Duties: Overseeing center's maintenance staff; making sure mall and property are well maintained and in good working order; doing routine preventative maintenance

Alternate Title(s): Maintenance Mechanic Supervisor

Salary Range: $24,000 to $48,000+

Employment Prospects: Fair

Advancement Prospects: Fair

Best Geographical Location(s) for Position: Jobs may be located throughout the country

Prerequisites:

Education and Training—Training requirements vary; see text

Experience—Experience in mall or property maintenance

Special Skills and Personality Traits—Basic knowledge of woodworking, electricity, and plumb-

ing; problem solving skills; time management skills; communication skills; ability to deal well with people

Position Description

The mall's Maintenance Supervisor cares for the physical appearance of the mall. Depending on the size of the mall, he or she may work with and supervise one or more maintenance people. In some malls, the individual also oversees the janitorial staff.

People generally don't enjoy shopping in an unkempt and dirty mall. Every building has things that break, and malls are no exception. The Maintenance Supervisor must constantly look out for things that are not working are in or need of repair or replacement, so that he or she can quickly correct the situation.

Maintenance Supervisor's look for an array of things. These might include stained ceiling tiles, broken paper towel dispensers, nonworking toilets, chipped paint, cracked benches, broken food court chairs, and bulbs that are burned out.

Broken or damaged fixtures of furniture might also be a liability. For example, a big pothole in the parking lot might cause an accident. Cracked blacktop or sidewalks might result in a trip or fall. A leaky roof might allow water to damage tenants' goods and result in insurance claims.

In addition to fixing things, Maintenance Supervisors also do routine preventative work to ensure that things are kept in working order. Individuals may, for example, do routine checks on ballasts, heating and air conditioning vents, and other equipment.

The Maintenance Supervisor is expected to oversee the repair and maintenance of the mall, its property, machinery, and equipment. This might include working on plumbing, electrical, and air conditioning and heating systems. A successful Maintenance Supervisor needs to be a jack-of-all-trades. Generally, the smaller the property, the more the Maintenance Supervisor and his or her staff must know how to do. While the services of outside contractors such as HVAC (heating, ventilation, and air-conditioning) mechanics, certified electricians, and roofers may be utilized, individuals must know the basics. The Supervisor must know how to evaluate a situation and when to call in a professional.

The Maintenance Supervisor and his or her staff are often expected to handle plaster and drywall repairs or putting up walls to cover empty stores. Other responsibilities might include checking and repairing the roof, painting the building, clearing clogged toilets and leaky faucets, and doing work within the building structure to bring it in compliance with local building codes. The Maintenance Supervisor and his or her staff additionally might be expected to repair air conditioning and heating problems. In many malls, each maintenance man or woman has a specialty. In that manner, a Supervisor can then assign the correct person to handle each job.

The Maintenance Supervisor is expected to coordinate and schedule the maintenance staff. He or she assigns tasks on a daily basis to the maintenance staff. The individual may also schedule and oversee the work of independent contractors.

Additional duties of Maintenance Supervisor might include:

- Screening, interviewing, and hiring the maintenance staff
- Recommending promotions and dismissals
- Preparing reports for budgets and expenses and schedules
- Performing maintenance
- Making sure maintenance jobs are performed correctly and on a timely basis

Salaries

Annual earnings for Maintenance Supervisors working in malls and shopping centers can range from approximately $24,000 to $48,000 or more depending on a number of variables. These include the size, prestige, and geographic location of the specific mall or shopping center as well as the experience, responsibilities, and education of the individual.

Employment Prospects

Employment prospects for Maintenance Supervisors are fair. Individuals may find employment in malls throughout the country. The more skilled the individual, the more employable he or she will be.

Advancement Prospects

Maintenance Supervisors may advance their careers by locating similar positions in larger, more prestigious properties. Others climb the career ladder by finding employment with large real estate developers or management companies.

Education and Training

Maintenance Supervisors obtain their training in different ways. Some train informally, learning new skills by watching others. Apprenticeships are an excellent training opportunity in this field. Many individuals also attend trade, technical, or vocational schools to learn various skills.

Experience, Skills, and Personality Traits

Experience working in maintenance is necessary for this job. Most Maintenance Supervisors worked in maintenance prior to their current job. Supervisory skills and the ability to work well with others are needed. An understanding and knowledge of all aspects of maintenance is essential.

Unions and Associations

There is no association specific to Shopping Center Maintenance Supervisors.

Tips for Entry

1. Stop in to the mall management office and fill out an application. Ask that it be kept on file if there are no current openings.
2. Many larger property management and real estate development companies have internships and training programs.
3. Positions are often advertised in the classified sections of newspapers. Look under classifications including "Maintenance Supervisor," "Maintenance," "Malls," or "Shopping Centers."
4. Many malls have Web sites featuring job opportunities. Check advertisements in newspapers or mall brochures for mall Web site addresses.

SECURITY DIRECTOR— SHOPPING CENTER/MALL

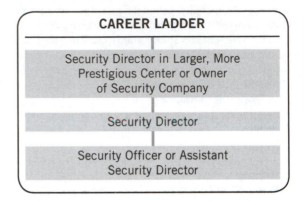

Position Description

Today more than ever, security in malls is of the utmost importance. In order for customers to feel comfortable, mall owners try to provide as safe an environment as possible.

The Security Director in a mall or shopping center is responsible for overseeing the safety of the mall, its employees, and customers. The Director develops and implements a mall safety and security plan. Some centers employ their own security department. Others contract out for the services of a security company.

The mall Security Director is expected to protect the mall and the mall's property. The individual hires security officers and trains and supervises them. He or she must explain the mall's policies and procedures to each officer.

Every mall has different days and times in which the center is busiest. The Security Director is in charge of scheduling the security staff in the most effective manner possible, and monitoring the activities in the mall to make sure the schedule is working properly.

While tenants are generally responsible for handling shoplifting incidents in their own store, the mall is expected to provide a security presence which will deter this crime. If there is a great deal of shoplifting occurring in the mall on Friday nights, for example, the Security Director may put more officers on duty that night.

Shrinkage is a big problem to stores in malls. Shrinkage is the loss of merchandise due to various means, the most prominent being shoplifting. Loss prevention is important. Shoplifters often go from store to store in a mall taking merchandise. The Security Director often develops seminars for mall employees to help them find ways to cut their shrinkage. He or she may also put together various classes on safety.

In some instances, the shrinkage in mall stores involves employees. The mall Security Director may be asked to hire undercover officers or involve the police in the investigation.

The mall Security Director usually has a good working relationship with the local law enforcement agencies. Usually, the mall security calls local law enforcement to arrest people for infractions as they themselves have very limited authority.

The mall Security Director is in charge of keeping the entire mall property safe. He or she may assign officers to patrol the inside of the mall as well as the outside of the property including the parking lot.

Shrinkage is not the only problem that might occur in a mall. There are a variety of potential disturbances and problems that might need to be addressed. The Security Director is in charge of handling these situations or assigning a security officer to take care of the problem. These problems might include calming loud or boisterous customers, evicting customers who are acting in a disorderly fashion, or helping in a medical emergency. Individuals must be able to handle emergency situations such as power outages, weather problems, and medical emergencies.

The Security Director often uses a two-way radio system to keep in contact with officers.

Additional duties of the Security Directors working in shopping centers or malls may include:

- Assuming duties of security officers
- Checking to make sure daily shift reports detailing occurrences are complete
- Handling traffic concerns going in and out of the mall
- Preparing reports for mall management on security and safety
- Making recommendations to mall management about security and safety concerns
- Formulating policies regarding safety
- Determining need for special safety programs

Salaries
Annual earnings for Security Directors working in shopping centers and malls can range from approximately $25,000 to $49,000 or more. Variables affecting earnings include the geographic location, size, and prestige of the shopping center as well as the experience, training, and responsibilities of the individual.

Employment Prospects
Employment prospects are poor for individuals seeking this position. As noted previously, many malls employ outside security firms instead of in-house people. The best prospects for employment in this area will be at large malls.

Advancement Prospects
Security Directors working in malls may advance their career in a number of ways. The most common is landing similar positions in larger, more prestigious malls. Others may climb the career ladder by striking out and starting their own security firms.

Education and Training
Education and training requirements vary for this type of position. While some malls require their Security

Directors to have a minimum of a high school diploma or the equivalent, most malls will prefer or require individuals to have a college background or degree.

Certain states may require individuals working in security to go through specified training programs. Some states may also require an annual in-service course to refresh or update officers in changes in the security field.

Any armed officer must go through a firearms training course. These usually involve both classroom instruction and a specified number of hours on the firing range.

Special Requirements
A clean police record and good moral character are essential. As previously noted, those who are armed usually also must be registered with their specific state to carry firearms.

Experience, Skills, and Personality Traits
The Security Director is required to have a great deal of experience. Many Security Directors started out in police work. Some are retired police officers. Others have experience in the military or other areas of civil service. There are also some individuals who obtained experience and worked themselves up to the top position from security departments in malls or working with outside security companies.

The Security Director working in a mall should have an array of skills. First and foremost, individuals need to be responsible people with good judgment. Leadership skills are vital. Interpersonal and customer relations skills are essential. Communications skills are mandatory.

Unions and Associations
Individuals may obtain information about possible licensing requirements from their state or local licensing commission.

Tips for Entry
1. Openings may be advertised in the classified sections of newspapers. Look under heading classifications such as "Malls," "Shopping Centers," "Security Directors," or "Mall/Shopping Center Security."
2. Check out openings on the Internet. Many malls have their own Web sites listing employment opportunities.
3. You might also find openings on the World Wide Web job sites. Start with the more popular ones such as www.hotjobs.com and www.monster.com. Then surf the Web looking for sites specifically geared towards the retail industry.
4. Contact mall management companies. As they usually handle more than one center, they may be aware of openings.

SECURITY OFFICER— SHOPPING CENTER/MALL

CAREER PROFILE

Duties: Patrol, inspect, and protect the shopping center and center property; enforce regulations; handle loss prevention

Alternate Title(s): Guard

Salary Range: $7.50 to $20.00+ per hour

Employment Prospects: Fair

Advancement Prospects: Fair

Best Geographical Location(s) for Position: Jobs may be located throughout the country

Prerequisites:

Education and Training—High school diploma or equivalent; on-the-job training; additional training may be required

Experience—Experience requirements vary

Special Skills and Personality Traits—Good judgment, responsible; interpersonal skills; leadership; people skills; communications skills; good moral character

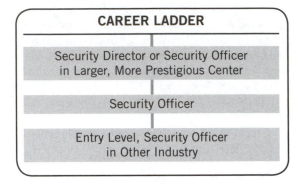

CAREER LADDER

Security Director or Security Officer in Larger, More Prestigious Center

Security Officer

Entry Level, Security Officer in Other Industry

Special Requirements—Clean police record; armed officers must be registered to carry firearms and state licensing may be required; may need to go through specified training program.

Position Description

It is essential that malls be as safe as possible. Security Officers are responsible for helping to keep malls safe for customers and mall tenants. Some centers employ their own security department. Others contract out for the services of a security company.

Security Officers are expected to protect the mall and the mall's property. Generally, Security Officers are uniformed and can be identified. On occasion, Security Officers may work "undercover." In these instances, they will not wear uniforms and will dress in plain clothes to blend in with the other shoppers.

Security Officers patrol the mall. They walk around the center and maintain a presence. Some Security Officers may also drive around the property to assure the safety of customers and mall employees in the parking lot. Security Officers may be assigned designated areas to patrol or may move around the mall during their shift. It is up to them to identify potentially dangerous situations and act in an effective manner. It is important to note that unless the Security Officer is also a licensed police officer he or she usually has limited legal authority.

Security Officers are expected to keep the peace. Individuals handle any disturbances within the shopping center, such as calming situations if customers become loud or boisterous. They may also be required to evict a customer who is acting in a disorderly fashion.

Loss prevention is a major problem in many malls. Security Officers are responsible for protecting against theft and vandalism. Individuals must be alert to everything going on around them. They must observe the actions and activities of both customers and employees. If they see a potential problem, they are expected to contact the police or other local law enforcement agency to handle the arrest.

Security Officers often use two-way radios to keep in contact with their supervisor. Individuals must be able to handle emergency situations such as power outages, weather problems, and medical emergencies which may occur.

Security officers are expected to file daily shift reports detailing occurrences and logging any incidents or accidents during their shifts. All unusual activities within the mall must be documented.

Additional duties of the Security Officers working in shopping centers or malls may include:

- Assisting lost children
- Checking to make sure store gates are down, doors are closed and locked
- Escorting mall employees to their vehicles after hours
- Answering customers' questions regarding the mall
- Giving directions to stores within the mall

Salaries

Earnings for Security Officers working in shopping centers and malls can range from approximately $7.50 to $20.00 or more per hour. Variables affecting earnings include the geographic location, size, and prestige of the shopping center as well as the experience, training, and responsibilities of the individual. Salaries may also differ depending on whether the individual is employed directly by the mall or working for a security company which is contracted by the mall.

In some cases, off-duty police officers work as Security Officers in their off hours. These individuals may earn upward of $30 or more per hour.

Employment Prospects

Employment prospects are fair for individuals seeking this position. Jobs can be located in malls and shopping centers throughout the country. As noted previously, individuals may be employed by malls directly or by security companies.

Advancement Prospects

Security Officers may advance their career in a number of ways. After obtaining experience, some individuals find similar positions in larger, more prestigious malls or with larger security companies. Others may climb the career ladder by becoming security supervisors or directors. Still others decide they enjoy security work and become trained police officers.

Education and Training

Education and training requirements vary from mall to mall. Generally, most malls prefer their Security Officers to have a minimum of a high school diploma or the equivalent. Depending on the situation, the mall may provide on-the-job training. Those working for security companies may go through similar training programs.

Certain states may require individuals working as Security Officers to go through a specified training program offered in the area. Some states may also require

an annual in-service course to refresh or update officers in changes in the security field.

Armed officers must go through a firearms training course. These usually involve both classroom instruction and a specified number of hours on the firing range.

Special Requirements

A clean record and good moral character are essential. Security officers who are armed usually also must be registered with the state in which the mall is located to carry firearms. As noted previously certain states may require security officers to go through a specified training program.

Experience, Skills, and Personality Traits

Entry-level positions may be open in some malls. Experience, however, working in private security, the military, or civil service police is useful. Security Officers need a multitude of skills. Individuals should be responsible people with good judgment. Interpersonal and customer relations skills are essential. Communications skills are mandatory.

Unions and Associations

There is no association specific to Security Officers working in malls or shopping centers. However, individuals may obtain information about possible licensing requirements from their state or local licensing commission.

Tips for Entry

1. There are some community colleges, vocational, and technical schools offering courses for security officers. These courses may be useful in career advancement.
2. Jobs may be advertised in the classified sections of newspapers. Look under classifications such as "Security Officer," "Security," "Guard," or "Mall/Shopping Center Security."
3. Stop in the mall's management office to see if you can fill out an employment application. Ask that your application be kept on file if there are no current openings.
4. Look in the yellow pages to check the names and addresses of security companies.
5. If your local mall utilizes the services of a security company, ask one of the officers to give you a contact name and phone number. Then call the company and make an appointment for an interview.

LEASING DIRECTOR—
MALL/SHOPPING CENTER

Position Description

The way mall and shopping center owners and management make money is by renting space to tenants. The person responsible for this function is the Leasing Director, but in some malls, the mall manager may handle the duties. Leasing Directors act as the mall owner's representative or agent.

Prospective tenants often contact malls to find out about rents, other charges, and availabilities. The Leasing Director may send out leasing packages to these individuals or may set up meetings to discuss pertinent information. If individuals are interested, the Director is expected to show spaces in the mall.

The Leasing Director must also seek out tenants who might be beneficial to the mall's tenant mix. The success of malls often depends on this. Just filling up stores does not always work, because people like to visit malls where they have a variety of shopping options. Having ten shoe stores, for example, with little else might not be the best mix to bring in the most shoppers.

In this position, the individual may be required to meet frequently with prospective tenants. He or she will answer questions and emphasize the selling points about the mall that are likely to be the most important to the tenant. For example, the Director may show sales figures, foot traffic reports, or advertising budgets.

Once tenants decide they might be interested in leasing space in the mall, the Leasing Director must negotiate a lease. There are a variety of areas to consider including rents, taxes, CAM (common area maintenance) charges, advertising charges, prepping of the space, length of the lease, options, and kick-out clauses. (A kick-out clause allows a tenant to leave without penalty if certain conditions are not met. For example, not meeting a specified amount of sales.) The Leasing Director usually has a degree of leeway to negotiate terms.

The Leasing Director is often the individual responsible for dealing with tenants after a lease has been executed when the tenants have a major complaint. Continual roof leaks, constantly dirty rest rooms, unkempt mall property, low foot traffic, or lack of mall advertising and promotion might all cause tenants to complain bitterly. The Leasing Director is expected to calm the tenants and deal with the problems. He or she may contact the mall manager, tenant relations director, marketing director, or public relations director to look into the problems and solve them. In some instances, the Leasing Director may authorize abatements to appease irate tenants.

The Leasing Director is in charge of tracking tenant leases and handling renewals. He or she may write letters, call, or personally visit tenants when leases are close to completion and need to be renewed. At times, the Leasing Director may renegotiate the lease. In other situations, the Director may just make sure the tenant picks up his or her option.

There is a great deal of paperwork connected with this job. The Leasing Director must make sure accurate records are kept. It is essential that the individual remember what was said at meetings, promised during phone calls, and negotiated. The Leasing Director must be sure leases are executed and signed by all parties.

Leasing Directors working for real estate developers or mall management companies may be responsible for handling the leasing of more than one mall.

Additional duties of Leasing Directors might include:

- Developing leasing packages
- Working with outside real estate agents
- Dealing with corporate leasing directors and agents
- Attending conventions and other leasing events
- Visiting other malls to seek out potential tenants

Salaries

Earnings for mall Leasing Directors can vary greatly starting at approximately $35,000 and going up to $125,000 or more. Earnings depend on the size, prestige, and geographic location of the property and number of properties the individual is responsible for leasing. Other variables include the experience, responsibilities, and education of the individual.

Leasing Directors often receive a salary plus commissions or percentages on the gross terms of the leases they write. In some situations individuals may receive bonuses based on increased rentals or the handling of extra projects.

Employment Prospects

Aggressive and effective Leasing Directors are always in demand. However it should be noted that every mall does not employ a Leasing Director. In smaller malls the mall manager often handles the leasing functions.

Individuals seeking this position may find employment throughout the country. Leasing Directors may be directly employed by malls or work for real estate developers, development companies, or property management companies.

Advancement Prospects

The most common method of career advancement for Leasing Directors is to find similar positions in larger, more prestigious malls, mall management companies,

or real estate developers. Some individuals strike out on their own and form leasing companies.

Education and Training

Educational requirements vary from mall to mall. While much of the training individuals receive is on the job, many employers prefer that individuals have some sort of real estate training. Others require it.

Most positions will also prefer or require the Leasing Director to hold a real estate agent or brokers license. In order to obtain this licensing, individuals must usually take and pass a written test as well as go through at least 30 hours of classroom instruction to become an agent or 90 hours of training to become a broker.

For those interested in a college degree, relevant majors might include real estate, business, public administration, finance, or related fields.

Professional and trade associations often offer helpful seminars and courses in all aspects of real estate.

Experience, Skills, and Personality Traits

Leasing Directors may begin their careers in a variety of ways. Some work as assistant leasing directors or in real estate in other industries. Others work in various aspects of mall administration either directly for a mall, a mall management company, or a real estate management company.

Leasing Directors should be assertive with an ability to deal with and work well with others. Individuals need to be good problem solvers who are energetic, detail oriented, and highly motivated.

Successful Leasing Directors have developed many contacts. This is helpful in bringing people to the table when looking for new tenants. The ability to negotiate well is essential.

Unions and Associations

Mall or shopping center Leasing Directors may be members of a number of associations providing career guidance and support. These include the National Association of Realtors (NAR), a local state real estate association, the International Council of Shopping Centers (ICSC), and the Institute of Real Estate Management (IREM).

Tips for Entry

1. Contact larger property management and real estate development companies to find out what internship and training programs they have available in this area.
2. There are a number of executive search firms dealing exclusively with jobs in shopping centers and malls.

3. Send your resume and a cover letter to retail property management companies, real estate development companies, and large malls.

4. Positions are often advertised in the classified sections of newspapers. Look under classifications including "Leasing Director," or "Mall Leasing Director," or "Shopping Center Leasing Director," and "Retail Leasing Director."

5. Openings are also advertised in trade journals such as *Value Retail News*.

6. Jobs in this field may be located on-line. Begin your search on some of the more popular job search sites such as the Monster board (www.monster.com) and Yahoo! HotJobs (www.hotjobs.com). Then surf the Web for sites specific to the retail or shopping center industries.

SPECIAL EVENTS COORDINATOR— MALL/SHOPPING CENTER

CAREER PROFILE

Duties: Plan, develop, and implement special events and promotions for mall or shopping center

Alternate Title(s): Special Events Manager; Events Coordinator

Salary Range: $25,000 to $40,000+

Employment Prospects: Fair

Advancement Prospects: Fair

Best Geographical Location(s) for Position: Jobs may be located throughout the country

Prerequisites:

Education and Training—Bachelor's degree preferred

Experience—Experience in special events, publicity, and/or public relations preferred

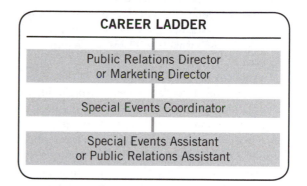

CAREER LADDER

Public Relations Director
or Marketing Director

Special Events Coordinator

Special Events Assistant
or Public Relations Assistant

Special Skills and Personality Traits—Creativity; detail oriented; imagination; innovation; communications skills; understanding of shopping center industry

Position Description

Most malls and shopping centers sponsor a variety of special events and promotions throughout the year in order to bring in potential shoppers, attract the attention of the media, and create goodwill in the community.

The Special Events Coordinator is responsible for helping to develop, create, and implement the special events and promotions in the mall. The individual is often expected to develop an annual calendar of events. This contains all the events and promotions planned for the coming year. While the calendar is subject to change, it gives tenants the opportunity to plan copromotions if they wish, and also helps them plan to have more staff when traffic may be busiest. For example, if the mall schedules a Washington's Birthday Sidewalk Sale, the stores must make sure they have merchandise marked down. If the mall is sponsoring a safe trick-or-treating night, store managers may need to put on more staff to deal with the crowds of children and their parents.

Promotions and events may be routine or may be more complex. Routine events might include things such as sidewalk sales, health fairs, community fairs, Santa's arrival, crafts shows, antiques shows, a safe Trick or Treat night, or fashion shows. More complex events might include how-to days, wine and cheese tastings, soap opera festivals, concerts in the parking

lot, museum exhibits, mall anniversary celebrations, or weddings in the mall.

Some events are developed and executed by the Special Events Coordinator, but others may require outside contractors. For example, the Coordinator may hire a carnival or circus promoter to set up in the mall or parking lot. He or she might put together crafts shows, antiques shows, or computer shows, or work with a promoter or agent to bring in events like puppet shows, beauty pageants, or petting zoos.

Many Special Events Coordinators work on events and promotions with cosponsors. These may include stores within the mall, car dealerships, radio or television stations, or newspapers. Some promotions may feature contests or sweepstakes giving away big prizes such as cars, jewelry, or money.

Depending on the structure of the mall, the Special Events Coordinator may be responsible for dealing with the community organizations. In many centers, mall management allows not-for-profit groups to set up in the hallways to raise funds, have bake sales, or recruit new members. In this case the individual may be expected to coordinate the groups, show them where to set up, and take care of any necessary paperwork.

When developing events and promotions the Special Events Coordinator takes a number of things into account. These include what events will bring the most shoppers into the mall, what it takes to execute the event, and how it figures into the budget.

Foot traffic is essential to malls. The more people walking around, the better the chance they will make purchases. Sometimes the purchases may not be immediate. In some cases, once an event brings in people to the mall, they see what is available and return when they need items.

The number of events the individual will be responsible for annually depends to a great extent on the size and structure of the center as well as its promotional budget. Events and promotions can be inexpensive or they might be very expensive. The best ideas in malls are sometimes the tried and true ones. However, the successful Special Events Coordinator must initiate innovative and creative events to supplement the standard routine events.

The Special Events Coordinator is expected to create a basic plan for the event, and develop and stick to a budget to complete the project. In some cases, the Special Events Coordinator may be responsible for handling the promotion and publicity for the events. In other cases, the individual will work with the public relations and advertising departments on these functions.

Generally, the mall Special Events Coordinator must be on hand for special events and promotions. This means, the individual may work on weekends or during evening hours.

Other duties of a mall Special Events Coordinator may include:

- Developing special events for mall employees
- Working on off-site events such as mall sponsorship of runs or marathons
- Obtaining proposals from outside vendors
- Supervising staff

Salaries
Earnings for Special Events Coordinators working in a retail environment range from approximately $25,000 to $40,000 or more. Factors affecting earnings include the specific retail store as well as its size, prestige, and location. Other variables include the education, experience, and responsibilities of the individual.

Employment Prospects
Employment prospects are fair for Special Events Coordinators, however, every mall does not have such a position. In some centers, the public relations director, marketing director, or community relations director, or a combination of the three, may be responsible for handling these functions.

Advancement Prospects
Advancement prospects are fair for Special Events Coordinators. Individuals might climb the career ladder by finding similar positions in larger or more prestigious malls. With education, experience, and training, individuals might also advance to become mall public relations or marketing directors.

Education and Training
While there are exceptions, individuals seeking positions in mall special event coordination are usually required to hold a bachelor's degree. Good majors include communications, public relations, English, liberal arts, advertising, business, journalism, or retail management.

Seminars and workshops in special events, promotions, public relations, publicity, and advertising are helpful.

Experience, Skills, and Personality Traits
Special Events Coordinators working in malls often receive experience as interns or assistants in the marketing, public relations, or special events office prior to their current position.

Successful Special Events Coordinators are creative, innovative, and have excellent communications skills. Individuals need to be extremely organized and detail oriented with the ability to deal calmly with stressful situations.

Unions and Associations
Special Events Coordinators working in malls might be associated with a number of associations and organizations providing professional support and educational guidance. These might include the Public Relations Society of America (PRSA), the International Council of Shopping Centers (ICSC), the National Retail Merchants Association (NRMA), or the National Retail Federation (NRF).

Tips for Entry
1. Contact the International Council of Shopping Centers and other organizations to see when and where they hold seminars or workshops in mall promotion and special events.
2. Look for an internship or a position as a special events assistant in a mall. This will give you great experience and get your foot in the door.

3. Positions may be located in the newspaper help wanted section. The Sunday classified section is usually the largest of the week. Look under headings such as "Special Events," "Special Events Coordinator," "Retail Opportunities," "Public Relations," "Marketing," "Promotion," or "Malls."

4. Job openings may also be listed in trade publications such as *Value Retail News*.

5. Jobs may also be located via the Internet. Start by checking out some of the more popular sites such as www.hotjobs.com.

DEPARTMENT STORES

STORE MANAGER— DEPARTMENT STORE

CAREER PROFILE

Duties: Handle day-to-day management of department store; oversee staffing needs of store; deal with customer service issues; make sure store is in compliance with safety issues; work with staff to help store meet sales and profit goals

Alternate Title(s): Manager

Salary Range: $35,000 to $150,000+

Employment Prospects: Good

Advancement Prospects: Fair

Best Geographical Location(s) for Position: Jobs may be located throughout the country

Prerequisites:

Education and Training—Training requirements vary; see text

Experience—Experience in retail management

CAREER LADDER

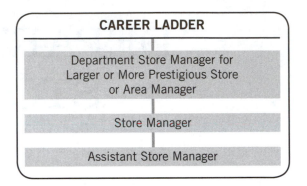

Department Store Manager for Larger or More Prestigious Store or Area Manager

Store Manager

Assistant Store Manager

Special Skills and Personality Traits—Problem solving skills; negotiation skills; communications skills; ability to deal well with people; management skills; administrative skills

Position Description

Department stores encompass a variety of sizes and types. Some are huge stores covering three floors or more. Others are smaller. Department stores may cater to average consumers offering discount merchandise or they may cater to upscale shoppers. No matter what type of store, each has a Store Manager.

The Department Store Manager has a great deal of responsibility. He or she is ultimately responsible for everything that happens within the store. The individual handles the day-to-day management of the department store. Within the scope of the job, the Manager has many different duties.

One of the main functions of the Store Manager is working with his or her staff to meet corporate sales and profit goals. Stores generally keep accurate records of sales figures on a daily, weekly, monthly, and annual basis. This information is used to help project profits. Based on these figures along with various other information, the corporate offices set sales goals. It is up to the Manager to try to find ways to meet these goals. This might include working with assistant managers, merchandise managers, buyers, operations people, and the corporate office as well as other store employees.

The Store Manager oversees the staffing needs of the store. In large department stores there may be a human resources department or manager handling these functions. However, the Store Manager will still usually oversee the hiring or termination of key executives within the store. In smaller department stores, the Manager may be responsible for staffing the store with the help of assistant managers. He or she may schedule job fairs or write and place help wanted ads for the newspaper or other media.

The working and customer climate of department stores often depends on the Store Manager. Those who can make a store a pleasant shopping environment for customers and a pleasant workplace for employees will be most successful.

The Department Store Manager also oversees a staff of assistant managers, department managers, merchandise managers, and other employees who help fulfill the duties of running the store. The Store Manager must be familiar with the workings of every department.

There are an array of laws, rules, and regulations which must be followed for health, legal, and safety reasons. It is the responsibility of the Store Manager to make sure all of these are adhered to. These may include making sure aisles are wide enough for wheelchairs to get through, merchandise isn't blocking exits, and fire extinguishers are inspected.

The Store Manager is also expected to make sure that all employment regulations are followed within the store. These might include things like following labor rules, making sure teenagers don't work more hours than their allotted time, or forms are filled out for tax purposes. While the individual may have others handling these tasks, the Manager still is responsible for overseeing the function.

Many department stores, especially chains, have weekly promotions and sales advertised in the local paper and fliers. These promotions, ads, and fliers are used to attract customers. While these are often handled by the corporate office of a chain, it is up to the Manager to make sure the specials and items advertised are on the shelves. The Manager is expected to make sure the merchandise is moved from the stockroom to the shelves so it is available. In instances where merchandise wasn't delivered to the store, the Manager must determine how to best handle the situation. In some stores, the Manager may decide to give rain checks to customers. In others, Store Managers may offer the customer comparable merchandise when items aren't available.

The Store Manager sets the tone for customer service in the store. Customer service is of utmost importance to keeping customers happy and satisfied. The Store Manager is expected to make sure the customer service of the store is up to par. While most department stores have customer service representatives and managers, there are always customers and situations that need extra special care and attention.

The Manager will usually be the one called when a customer has a problem no one else can handle or wants to handle. He or she is responsible for dealing with emergencies, crises, and any problems which crop up in the store during the day. He or she is expected to write reports on accidents or other incidents such as when employees or customers are hurt within the store or in the parking lot.

Most department stores have accounting departments or cash offices. As the Department Store Manager is ultimately responsible for overseeing all monies in the store, he or she usually works closely with the managers of these departments. He or she may go over reports of the day's receipts as well as weekly and monthly reports.

In some department stores the Manager may also be responsible for depositing the day's receipts in the bank or may accompany an assistant manager or other employee in this task. The Manager also may be expected to analyze other data as well to help determine what direction the store might take to increase profits.

Many chain department stores have similar layouts in each store. That means that the floorplans are much the same whether you are in a store in New York or Los Angeles. In many department stores, the Manager is responsible for making sure that the store layout is handled in accordance with corporate layout designs.

Additional duties of Department Store Managers may include:

- Representing the store at community events
- Handling emergencies and crises
- Handling loss prevention
- Terminating employees
- Recommending raises and promotions for employees

Salaries

Earnings for Department Store Managers can range from approximately $35,000 to $150,000 or more. Variables affecting earnings include the size, prestige, and geographic location of the department store. Other variables include the experience, responsibilities, and education of the individual. Generally, those with the highest salaries will have a great deal of responsibility and manage large stores. Some Store Managers may receive bonuses when sales meet or exceed goals.

Employment Prospects

Employment prospects are good for Department Store Managers. Positions are located throughout the country. Possibilities include large chains stores like Wal-Mart, K-Mart, Target, Kohls, J.C. Penney, Sears, Macy's, Dillards, Bloomingdales, and Nordstroms. Individuals may also find employment working in smaller department stores that are locally owned.

Advancement Prospects

The most common method of career advancement for Store Managers working in department stores is locating similar jobs in larger or more prestigious stores. Those working in chains may climb the career ladder by promotion to larger stores within the chain. Individuals may also advance their careers by becoming area managers or moving into other areas of corporate management.

Education and Training

Educational and training requirements vary from store to store. Generally larger stores and chains require their Managers to go through formal training programs which include both classroom and in-store training.

Many of the larger department store chains send their management recruits to these training programs which are often located at the company's corporate offices. Some stores will hire individuals who have no formal training, but who have worked their way up obtaining on-the-job training along the way.

Educational backgrounds of Department Store Managers vary too. While stores may not require individuals to hold anything above a high school diploma, they may prefer Managers with college backgrounds or degrees. Good majors include business, management, marketing, retailing, merchandising, communications, advertising, liberal arts, or related fields.

Experience, Skills, and Personality Traits

Department Store Managers are required to have experience in retail and management. Generally, individuals have worked the sales floor and have been department managers, group department managers, and assistant store managers prior to becoming Store Managers.

Managers must have a knowledge of management principles as well as a total understanding of the retail industry. Leadership skills, self-confidence, and decisiveness are essential. The ability to deal with and work well with people is mandatory. Individuals need to be good problem solvers who are energetic, detail oriented, and highly motivated.

Communication skills, both written and verbal, are necessary as well.

Unions and Associations

Individuals interested in learning more about careers in this field should contact the American Collegiate Retailing Association (ACRA), National Retail Federation (NRF) and the National Retail Merchants Association (NRMA).

Tips for Entry

1. Many larger department and chain stores offer management training programs. Contact the headquarters of these stores to find out about requirements.
2. Positions may be advertised in the classified sections of newspapers. Look under classifications including "Store Manager," "Retail Opportunities," "Department Stores," "Store Management," or "Management Opportunities."
3. Openings are also advertised in trade journals.
4. Jobs in this field may be located on the Internet. Begin your search on some of the more popular job search sites such as Monster board (www.monster.com) and Yahoo! HotJobs (www.hotjobs.com).
5. Check out the Web sites of retail chains. Many list openings.
6. Contact recruiters and executive search firms specializing in retail management positions.
7. Send your resume and a short cover letter to the corporate offices of chain and department stores.

ASSISTANT STORE MANAGER— DEPARTMENT STORE

Position Description

No matter the size of a department store or the clientele they hope to attract, most employ not only a manager, but one or more Assistant Managers. These individuals assist the store manager with the day-to-day management of the store. Specific responsibilities depend on the size and structure of the store.

The Assistant Manager works with the store manager to find ways to meet corporate sales and profit goals. He or she may work with the manager in reviewing daily, weekly, monthly, and annual sales figures. This information is often used to determine which days of the week generally require more sales staff, which promotions and special events work and which do not. The information is also used to help the corporate office set sales goals for the coming year.

The Assistant Store Manager will act in the capacity of the store manager when that individual is off duty. He or she may also work when the manager is on duty assisting with the various functions of the store.

The Assistant Manager is on the front line with both the customers and the staff. He or she may assist in the staffing needs of the store working with the manager or the human resources department. He or she may assist with the decisions concerning hiring key employees. The Assistant Manager may also be expected to terminate employees when required.

The individual is responsible for helping to make a pleasant workplace. He or she may assist in training programs or supervising trainers. Successful Assistant Managers know how to motivate employees to do their job well and provide excellent customer service.

Depending on the size and structure of the department store, the Assistant Manager may oversee department managers, merchandise managers, sales associates, cashiers, or stock people. He or she may offer suggestions to department managers regarding how to improve their departments and productivity.

The Assistant Manager often will be on the frontline checking to see if more cashiers are needed, if customers need help, or if any problems need to be solved. He or she will work with other store management in assuring health, legal, and safety rules, regulations, and laws are followed precisely. The individual will routinely check to see if aisles or entrances are blocked, spills are cleaned, and fire exits are free.

The Assistant Manager must also make sure the store and its rest rooms and parking lot are safe, clean, and orderly. In the event there are accidents, slips, and falls or other incidents, the individual will be expected to make written reports.

The Assistant Manager helps assure customer service in the store. In the event a customer isn't happy, the Assistant Manager may be called in to help resolve the problem. As he or she has more authority, the individual may offer customers solutions that more directly resolve their problem with the store.

The Assistant Manager and manager may share responsibility for going over reports of the day's receipts. They may work with the accounting department or cash office on this task. The individual may also accompany another employee when depositing the day's receipts in the bank.

Additional duties of Department Store Assistant Managers may include:

- Analyzing data to help determine what direction the store might take to increase profits
- Representing store at community events
- Handling emergencies and crises
- Handling loss prevention
- Helping set up the store according to corporate floorplans

Salaries

Annual earnings for Department Store Assistant Managers can range from approximately $26,000 to $53,000 or more. Variables affecting earnings include the size, prestige, and geographic location of the department store as well as the experience, responsibilities, and education of the individual.

Employment Prospects

Employment prospects are good for Department Store Assistant Managers. Many department stores may have two or more Assistant Managers on staff.

Positions are located throughout the country. Possibilities include large chains stores like Wal-Mart, K-Mart, Target, Kohls, J.C. Penney, Sears, Macy's, Dillards, and Bloomingdales. Individuals may also find employment working in smaller department stores owned by local merchants.

Advancement Prospects

The most common method of career advancement for Department Store Assistant Managers is promotion to store manager. Another way individuals climb the career ladder is to locate similar positions in larger or more prestigious department stores.

Education and Training

There are no hard-and-fast rules regarding education and training requirements for Department Store Assistant Managers. While not always required, a college degree or background is usually preferred and may give one applicant an edge over another. College may

also provide opportunities and experiences which the individual may not otherwise have. Good choices for majors might include retailing, merchandising, business, management, marketing, communications, advertising, liberal arts, or related fields.

Generally, larger department stores and chains have formal training programs for their key executives including managers and Assistant Managers. These programs include both classroom and in-store training. Smaller stores may have informal and on-the-job training.

Some stores will hire individuals who have no formal training, but have worked their way up obtaining on-the-job training along the way.

Experience, Skills, and Personality Traits

Department Store Assistant Managers are required to have experience both in retail and management. Prior to becoming Assistant Managers, most individuals will have worked on the sales floor as sales associates, as department managers, or group department managers. Some Department Store Assistant Managers have already managed smaller specialty stores or other retail outlets.

Assistant Managers should be self-confident individuals with an understanding of management principles. The ability to deal with and work well with people is mandatory. Individuals need to be good problem solvers who are energetic, detail oriented, and highly motivated.

Communications skills, both written and verbal, are necessary as well. An understanding and knowledge of the retail industry is also needed.

Unions and Associations

Individuals interested in learning more about careers in this field should contact the American Collegiate Retailing Association (ACRA), National Retail Federation (NRF) and the National Retail Merchants Association (NRMA).

Tips for Entry

1. One of the best ways to get into store management is by going through an executive training program. Many larger department and chain stores offer these management training programs. Contact the headquarters of stores to find out about requirements.
2. Many department stores post signs and posters touting their management career opportunities. Look for these at store entrances and in the customer service department. Don't forget to check out the human resources department.

3. Positions may be advertised in the classified sections of newspapers. Look under classifications including "Assistant Store Manager," "Retail Opportunities," "Department Stores," "Store Management," or "Management Opportunities."
4. Openings are also advertised in trade journals.
5. Contact recruiters and executive search firms specializing in management positions in retail.
6. Send your resume and a short cover letter to the corporate offices of chain and department stores.
7. Jobs in this field may be located on the Internet. Begin your search on some of the more popular job search sites such as Monster board (www.monster.com) and Yahoo! HotJobs (www.hotjobs.com). Then surf the net looking for sites geared towards the retail job market.

DEPARTMENT MANAGER— DEPARTMENT STORE

CAREER PROFILE

Duties: Supervise and coordinate activities of employees working in a department; assign duties to employees; train department workers; handle customer service within the department; prepare sales and inventory reports

Alternate Title(s): Toy Department Manager; Clothing Department Manager; Housewares Department Manager; Electronics Department Manager

Salary Range: $24,000 to $47,000+

Employment Prospects: Good

Advancement Prospects: Fair

Best Geographical Location(s) for Position: Jobs may be located throughout the country

Prerequisites:

Education and Training—Training requirements vary; see text

CAREER LADDER

Department Manager of Larger Department, Group Department Manager, or Assistant Store Manager

Department Manager

Department Manager Trainee or Floor Supervisor

Experience—Experience in retail management

Special Skills and Personality Traits—Leadership skills; communication skills; ability to deal well with people; management skills; administrative skills

---

Position Description

Department stores are made up of a number of departments, each selling different types of merchandise. Each of these departments has an individual called the Department Manager overseeing the area.

Depending on the specific store, departments might include: health and beauty; housewares; women's clothing; junior's clothing; children's clothing; men's clothing; boy's clothing; infants; small appliances; large appliances; electronics; books; office supplies; toys; jewelry; cards; gifts; bed and bath; cd's, tapes, videos; automotive; hardware; and house and garden. Different stores have different departments. They may also call departments by different names.

The Department Manager supervises and coordinates the activities of the employees in his or her department. He or she will assign tasks and duties to each individual so that the department is kept clean, well stocked, and orderly. For example, the Department Manager may assign one employee the task of putting out new merchandise. He or she may assign another the task of making sure that displays of merchandise are straightened at regular intervals during the day. Another may work at the register. One or all may work on the sales floor helping customers.

The Department Manager schedules lunch and dinner breaks for each employee in the department. This must be done so that the sales floor is always covered. Depending on the specific store, the individual may also be responsible for scheduling the work hours and vacations for employees in the department.

Another function of the Department Manager is training the employees. He or she may suggest more effective methods of selling or displaying merchandise. The individual also must explain store and department policies to employees.

The Department Manager may assist employees in completing difficult transactions. He or she also is expected to listen to customer complaints and try to resolve them. A successful Department Manager will know how to restore and promote goodwill by offering the best customer service possible to each customer.

When customers are returning merchandise, the Department Manager will often be the individual who examines it. The individual must determine if the merchandise is defective, used, or new and can be put back on the selling floor.

The Department Manager must keep track of merchandise that is selling. He or she may then be expected to order needed merchandise or give an order to the main office. The individual will also be responsible for preparing sales and inventory reports.

As merchandise comes in, the Department Manager will make sure that it is priced correctly and displayed in an attractive manner. Often, customers come in and ask for a product that the store doesn't carry. Other times the individual may see merchandise in other stores that his or her store doesn't have. The individual may then suggest to the buyer that the merchandise be added to the department's line.

Additional duties of Department Managers may include:

- Working on the sales floor
- Evaluating performance of department employees
- Handling loss prevention
- Helping set up the department displays

Salaries

Annual earnings for Department Managers working in department stores can range from approximately $23,000 to $47,000 or more. Variables affecting earnings include the size, prestige, and geographic location of the department store as well as the experience, responsibilities, and education of the individual. Some Department Managers may receive bonuses when sales meet or exceed goals.

Employment Prospects

Employment prospects are good for Department Managers. Positions are located throughout the country. Possibilities include large chains stores like Wal-Mart, K-Mart, Target, Kohls, J.C. Penney, Sears, Macy's, Dillards, Nordstroms, and Bloomingdales. Individuals may also find employment working in smaller department stores.

Advancement Prospects

Department Managers may climb the career ladder in a number of ways. The most common method of career advancement is to land a job as a Department Manager of a larger department or in a larger, more prestigious department store. This will result in increased responsibilities and earnings. Other Department Managers become group department managers.

After obtaining experience or training, some individuals may also land positions as assistant store managers.

Education and Training

There are no hard-and-fast rules regarding education and training requirements for Department Managers. There are many Department Managers who hold just a high school diploma. However, a college background or degree may give one applicant an edge over another and is often helpful in career advancement. College may also provide opportunities and experiences which the individual may not otherwise have. Good choices for majors might include retailing, merchandising, business, management, marketing, communications, advertising, liberal arts, or related fields.

As far as training is concerned, larger department stores and chains generally have formal training programs for their management personnel. These programs include both classroom and in-store training. Smaller stores may have informal and on-the-job training.

Experience, Skills, and Personality Traits

Some stores hire individuals who have no formal training, but have worked their way up obtaining on-the-job training along the way. Others recruit people who are graduating from college. Whichever way individuals are hired, they usually must have had retail and supervisory experience.

Department Managers should have a complete understanding of the workings of the retail industry as well as management principles. They should be self-confident individuals with the ability to deal with and work well with others.

Department Managers need the ability to work on multiple projects at one time without getting flustered. They should be detail oriented and highly motivated individuals with a great deal of energy. Customer service skills are mandatory. Communication skills are imperative.

Unions and Associations

Individuals interested in learning more about careers in this field should contact the American Collegiate Retailing Association (ACRA), National Retail Federation (NRF) and the National Retail Merchants Association (NRMA).

Tips for Entry

1. Most department stores promote from within. Get your foot in the door, learn everything you can, and move up the career ladder.
2. One of the best ways to get into a management position is by going through an executive training program. Many larger department and chain stores offer these management training programs. Contact the headquarters of stores to find out about requirements.

3. Many department stores post signs and posters touting their management career opportunities. Look for these at store entrances and in the customer service department. Don't forget to check out the human resources department.

4. Positions may be advertised in the classified sections of newspapers. Look under classifications including "Department Manager," "Department Store," or "Retail Opportunities." Jobs may also be advertised in ads for specific department stores.

5. Stop in to department stores and ask to fill out an application. Ask that it be kept on file if there are no current openings.

6. Surf the net. Start by checking out traditional job sites like monster.com and hotjobs.com. Then look for sites specific to the retail industry.

DIRECTOR OF PUBLIC RELATIONS— DEPARTMENT STORE

Position Description

One of the main functions of public relations is to help promote a positive name, image, and awareness of a business. With the abundance of different places to shop and in an effort to increase their market share, retail outlets like department stores try to do everything possible to promote their store in this manner.

The individual who handles this job for a department store is called the Director of Public Relations. Depending on the specific department store and its size structure, he or she may also be called the public relations director.

The Director of Public Relations for a department store is responsible for the development and implementation of all of the store's public relations campaigns. In some situations, such as when a department store is part of a large chain, the individual works in conjunction with either a senior director of public relations or vice president of public relations who are located in the store's corporate headquarters.

Depending on the size and structure of the department store, the individual may work with the store's marketing director, the in-house advertising department, or an advertising agency, as well as vendors promoting the store, its image, and events.

In addition to developing and implementing major PR campaigns, the Director of Public Relations is expected to handle day-to-day public relations functions for the department store. These might include writing press releases about events at the department store, celebrity appearances, or other special promotions. He or she may also be responsible for developing calendars of events and special promotions scheduled for the store as well as making sure that they are distributed to the media.

The Director of Public Relations is responsible for preparing feature stories, special-interest articles, and press releases for the news and other available media. It is essential that the individual have the ability to come up with unique hooks or angles that make the story or release interesting so it will grab the attention of the media.

An important function of the Director of Public Relations is having a good relationship with the media. He or she must constantly keep the media apprised of all store special events and promotions that they might want to cover. This may be done through press releases, a calendar of event entries, e-mails, or phone calls. The individual may work with the media to try to attain pre-event promotion, to cover the event as it occurs, and/or for post-event coverage.

Sometimes these events are in store. In other situations, the department store may lend its name as a sponsor of an event or cause. Department stores may work with local charities, sponsor events for not-for-profit organizations, host celebrity appearances, sponsor or cosponsor concerts or other cultural events, or do an array of other things. The idea is continually to work toward keeping the name of the store in the public's eye in a positive manner. One of the most well-known events sponsored by a department store is the Macy's Thanksgiving Day Parade held annually in New York City.

Special events may be designed for a number of different reasons. Some attract customers into the store while others may promote goodwill. Some may help create a better image for the store, while still others may simply get the store's name out to the public.

In addition to preparing articles and feature stories, the Director of Public Relations also arranges for members of the media to do these stories. As people tend to believe stories they read or hear more than advertisements, these articles can be immensely useful to creating a positive image for a department store.

The Director of Public Relations is often the official spokesperson for the department store. He or she may be asked to speak on radio, appear on television, or at press conferences.

The individual is responsible for fielding calls from the media. These calls might be to seek out general information regarding the department store or its events or promotions. At times, the media may have questions about other types of situations that are more negative such as potential or current employee strikes, accidents, or injuries. The Director of Public Relations must be able to deal effectively with the media in every situation, both positive and negative, always trying to improve the image of the department store.

Another essential function of the Director of Public Relations is crisis management. If and when there is a problem or crisis, the Director of Public Relations will be called upon to comment. He or she must find ways to handle the crisis in the best manner possible. As part of the job, the individual will often try to downplay the negatives of the crisis while highlighting the positive things being done to fix the problem.

The successful Director of Public Relations at a department store must maintain a good business rela-

tionship with the media at all times. In this way, he or she can help ensure that press releases will get placed in papers and special events are covered. Additionally, when there is a crisis or problem, the media may give the Director of Public Relations a fair chance to handle it before jumping on the story.

The Director of Public Relations at a department store is responsible for developing, planning, and implementing unique special events and promotions that help draw people into the store. These might include contests, sweepstakes, cooking demonstrations, fashion shows, celebrity appearances, product giveaways, etc. At times, the director may work with store vendors cosponsoring or promoting events. For example, a cookware company that has their product in the department store may be having a birthday and giving away prizes through each department store carrying their merchandise.

The Director of Public Relations may call the media to cover the event or develop promotions to coincide with the vendor's event. Depending on the size and structure of the specific department store, special events may be handled by a special event director or coordinator.

The Director of Public Relations may attend civic, community, or not-for-profit meetings on behalf of the department store. He or she may additionally be asked to serve on committees of these groups or act as a liaison between the store and the community group.

Other responsibilities of the Director of Public Relations at a department store include:

- Developing media lists
- Designing and developing promotional materials
- Attending vendor meetings
- Overseeing and managing staff

Salaries

Earnings for the Director of Public Relations at a department store can range from approximately $35,000 to $72,000 or more. Variables affecting earnings include the size, location, prestige, and popularity of the specific department store as well as the experience, responsibilities, and professional reputation of the individual.

Employment Prospects

Employment prospects are fair for those aspiring to work as the Director of Public Relations at a department store. Individuals may find opportunities throughout the country in large well-known department stores as well as smaller local department stores. The most opportunities will exist in areas hosting large numbers of department stores.

Advancement Prospects

Advancement prospects are fair for Directors of Public Relations at department stores. Individuals may climb the career ladder in a number of ways. Some advance their careers by locating similar positions in larger or more prestigious department stores resulting in increased responsibilities and earnings. Others may be promoted to marketing directors either in the same store or land a position in another department store. Still others strike out on their own and start their own public relations firm.

Education and Training

A minimum of a four-year degree is required for those seeking positions as Director of Public Relations at department stores. Good choices for majors include public relations, advertising, marketing, communications, journalism, business, or a related field. Courses, seminars, and workshops in public relations, marketing, special events, publicity, and promotion, as well as in the retail industry, will prove useful for both the informational value and the ability to make important contacts.

Experience, Skills, and Personality Traits

Experience requirements vary for Directors of Public Relations at department stores. Larger, more prestigious department stores generally prefer applicants to have a fair amount of experience handling public relations and publicity in retail or a related industry. Smaller department stores may have less stringent experience requirements.

Successful Directors of Public Relations are creative, innovative individuals who can think outside of the box. The ability to communicate well both verbally and on paper is critical. The ability to be persuasive is essential.

Individuals need to be organized, detailed-oriented people with the ability to multitask effectively without getting flustered. Excellent interpersonal skills are necessary. Those working in public relations need to be personalble individuals who really like dealing with others. The ability to deal effectively with the media is critical. An understanding of publicity, promotion, public relations, and marketing is necessary to be successful in this type of position.

Unions and Associations

Individuals interested in careers in this area may belong to the Public Relations Society of America (PRSA). This organization provides professional guidance, educational support, and other important information to members. They might also contact the National Retail Federation (NRF) for additional career information.

Tips for Entry

1. Many department stores post their openings on their Web site. Check it out.
2. Even if you don't see an opening, send your résumé and a short cover letter. You can never tell when a job opening will occur. If your résumé is there, you might get the call before someone else.
3. Don't forget to check out some of the more popular job search sites such as monster.com and hotjobs.com. Surf the net looking for other job sites that specialize in either retail or public relations jobs.
4. If you are still in college, contact department stores in which you are interested in working to find out if they have any internship possibilities.
5. Join the student group of the Public Relations Society of America. (PRSA). This trade association provides you with an array of services to help you develop your skills and make important contacts.
6. Positions may be advertised in the classified sections of newspapers under headings including "Public Relations," "Director of Public Relations," "Public Relations Director," "Department Store Public Relations Director," "Retail Opportunities," "Retail," etc. Don't forget to check out display advertisements listing one or more job openings of a particular retailer.
7. Contact executive recruiters specializing in either the public relations or the retail industry. Make sure you check ahead of time to see who pays the fee when you get the job—you or the employer.

COMPENSATION AND BENEFITS MANAGER—DEPARTMENT STORE

CAREER PROFILE

Duties: Oversee and coordinate employee wage, salary, and benefit programs in department store; supervise payroll and benefits office employees

Alternate Title(s): Payroll Manager; Benefits Manager; Compensation Manager

Salary Range: $33,000 to $55,000+

Employment Prospects: Fair

Advancement Prospects: Fair

Best Geographical Location(s) for Position: Jobs may be located throughout the country; large cities hosting more department stores offer more possibilities

Prerequisites:

    Education and Training—Educational requirements vary; see text

    Experience—Experience in human resources, benefits, or labor relations

CAREER LADDER

```
┌─────────────────────────────────────────┐
│ Compensation and Benefits Manager        │
│ in Larger, More Prestigious Store,       │
│ Director of Compensation and Benefits,   │
│ or Human Resources Manager               │
└─────────────────────────────────────────┘
                    ↑
┌─────────────────────────────────────────┐
│ Compensation and Benefits Manager        │
└─────────────────────────────────────────┘
                    ↑
┌─────────────────────────────────────────┐
│ Payroll Clerk or Benefits Coordinator    │
└─────────────────────────────────────────┘
```

Special Skills and Personality Traits—Communications skills; people skills; interpersonal skills; computer skills; patience; familiarity and understanding of compensation and benefits programs utilized in the industry

Position Description

Department stores generally have many employees working in an array of areas. Depending on their type of work, experience, and responsibilities, individual employees may receive various compensation packages. In order to recruit and retain employees many department stores also offer a variety of benefits in addition to earnings. The individual in charge of overseeing and directing the various compensation and benefit plans at a department store is called the Compensation and Benefits Manager.

He or she may also be called the compensation manager or payroll manager. The manager oversees the employees in the compensation and benefits or payroll office. Depending on the size and structure of the specific department store, the Compensation and Benefits Manager may supervise benefits coordinators, payroll clerks, compensation and benefits analysts, and benefit clerks.

In some stores, the Compensation and Benefits Manager may administer the health insurance and other benefit plans personally. In others, this task may be handled by a benefits coordinator.

Generally, department store employees meet with the Compensation and Benefits Manager during the hiring process. The manager discusses the type of compensation the employee will receive for the job. Some employees are paid on an hourly basis. Others are compensated with a set salary. The Compensation and Benefits Manager will explain to each employee whether he or she will be paid on a weekly or biweekly basis.

The Compensation and Benefits Manager also explains the benefits which are offered as part of the job to each employee. Depending on the store, benefits may include health insurance, life insurance, pension plans, profit sharing, child care, educational reimbursement, paid holidays, sick days, and vacations.

In many cases, employees may have questions regarding compensation or benefits. The Compensation and Benefits Manager may answer these questions him or herself or may refer employees to other employees working in the department for answers and assistance.

An important function of the Compensation and Benefits Manager is tracking employee evaluations, promotions, length of time they are in service, additional education, and training information. These factors are often used to determine employee raises. Raises are usually within the policy previously set by the department store.

Additional duties of the department store Compensation and Benefits Manager may include:

- Gathering information regarding salaries, wages, and benefits offered within the industry as well as the geographic area in which the department store is located
- Analyzing the store's compensation and benefits programs and making recommendations for new ones
- Assuring that employees meet the proper employment requirements
- Maintaining accurate files on employees and the compensation and benefits they receive

Salaries

Earnings for Compensation and Benefits Managers working in department stores range from approximately $33,000 to $55,000 or more annually. Factors affecting earnings include the size, structure, prestige, and geographic location of the specific department store. Other variables include the education, experience, and responsibilities of the individual.

Employment Prospects

Employment prospects for Compensation and Benefits Managers aspiring to work in department stores are fair. Positions may be located throughout the country. Areas hosting greater numbers of large department stores will offer the most opportunities.

Advancement Prospects

Compensation and Benefits Managers may climb the career ladder in a number of ways. Individuals may land similar positions in larger, more prestigious stores resulting in increased responsibilities and earnings. Compensation and Benefits Managers may also be promoted to directors of payroll and benefits. Those who have the education and experience may even become assistant directors or directors of human resources.

Education and Training

Educational requirements for Compensation and Benefits Managers vary from store to store. Many stores require or prefer individuals hold a degree in human resources, personnel management, labor relations, compensation and benefits, business management, or economics.

In some stores, experience is accepted in lieu of education. This is often the case when an individual has moved up the ranks in the compensation and benefits area.

Experience, Skills, and Personality Traits

Compensation and Benefits Managers should have experience in various areas of human resources, personnel administration, insurance administration, labor relations, benefits, and compensation. Individuals should have an understanding of insurance programs, retirement plans, labor relations, and wage and benefit trends.

Individuals should have excellent communications and interpersonal skills. Management, administrative, and supervisory skills are also needed. The ability to handle multiple projects at one time without becoming flustered is necessary.

Unions and Associations

Those interested in learning more about careers in this field should contact the International Foundation of Employee Benefit Plans (IFEBP) and the American Compensation Association (ACA). Individuals might also contact the National Retail Federation (NRF).

Tips for Entry

1. Jobs may be advertised in the classified sections of newspapers. Look under classifications such as "Compensation Manager," "Payroll Manager," "Retail Opportunities," "Department Stores," "Benefits and Compensation," "Benefits and Compensation Manager."
2. You might also look for jobs on the Internet. Many department stores now have Web sites listing their employment opportunities.
3. Send your resume and a short cover letter to department stores. Ask that your resume be kept on file if there are no current openings.
4. Contact the corporate offices of large chains and department stores to see who you might contact for this position in their local stores.
5. Department stores often promote from within. Get your foot in the door and move up the ranks.

PAYROLL CLERK— DEPARTMENT STORE

CAREER PROFILE

Duties: Ensure that department store employee paychecks are correct; calculate earnings and deductions; compute pay; maintain backup files; research payroll records

Alternate Title(s): Payroll Specialist; Payroll Technician; Compensation Clerk

Salary Range: $7.50 to $15.00+ or more per hour

Employment Prospects: Fair

Advancement Prospects: Fair

Best Geographical Location(s) for Position: Jobs may be located throughout the country; large cities will offer more possibilities

Prerequisites:

Education and Training—Educational requirements vary

CAREER LADDER

Payroll Supervisor, Payroll Manager, or Compensation Manager
Payroll Clerk
Payroll Clerk in other industry, Payroll Trainee or Entry Level

Experience—Accounting or payroll background preferred, but not always required

Special Skills and Personality Traits—Detail oriented; organized; ability to work accurately with numbers; data entry skills

Position Description

Department stores employ large numbers of workers. Each expects his or her paycheck to be correct. Payroll Clerks, who may also be referred to as payroll specialists, payroll technicians, or compensation clerks, help ensure that this happens.

Specific responsibilities of Payroll Clerks depend on the specific department store and the manner in which payroll is handled. Generally, Payroll Clerks input data regarding employees' pay, as well as maintaining and researching these records.

Payroll Clerks are responsible for calculating the earnings of the employee. This includes regular and overtime hours. They must also calculate deductions such as income tax withholding, social security, credit union payments, and insurance. This task is usually accomplished using computers.

Generally hourly employees in department stores punch time cards. At the end of the pay period, Payroll Clerks screen the time cards to make sure there are no calculating, coding, or other errors. Pay is then computed by subtracting allotments such as retirement, federal and state taxes, or insurance from the employee's gross earnings.

When a computer is used to perform these calculations, it will alert the payroll clerk to problems or errors in data. The individual can then adjust the errors.

In some situations, the department store utilizes the services of a payroll service. In these circumstances the clerk still must give the service the correct information.

Payroll Clerks may be expected to enter the correct data on checks, check stubs, and master payroll sheets or more commonly on forms for computer preparation of checks. Individuals are also expected to prepare and distribute pay envelopes.

Payroll Clerks may be called on by employees to correct problems in their checks or to explain calculations. These may include adjusting monetary errors or incorrect amounts of vacation time.

Other responsibilities of Payroll Clerks working in department stores may include:

- Performing additional clerical tasks
- Maintaining records of employee sick leave pay and nontaxable wages
- Typing, checking, and filing wage information forms
- Keeping wage and fringe benefit information on employees

Salaries

Earnings for Payroll Clerks working in department stores range from approximately $7.50 to $15.00 per hour or more. Factors affecting earnings include the experience, level of training, and responsibilities of the individual as well as the geographic location, size, and prestige of the specific department store.

Employment Prospects

Employment prospects for Payroll Clerks are fair. Large department stores may employ one or more people in this position. As noted previously, even department stores utilizing payroll services usually have at least one individual working in payroll.

Advancement Prospects

Advancement prospects for Payroll Clerks are fair. After obtaining additional experience and or training individuals may climb the career ladder by becoming payroll supervisors, payroll managers, or compensation managers.

Education and Training

Educational requirements for Payroll Clerks can vary from employer to employer. While some employers prefer a college or business school background, many employers will hire those with a high school diploma. While no specific training may be necessary, Payroll Clerks must have the ability to use adding machines, calculators, computers, and word processors. The ability to use office machinery may be self taught or learned in high school or business courses at vocational-technical schools, community colleges, or adult education.

Many department stores also offer on-the-job training, including payroll trainee positions.

Experience, Skills, and Personality Traits

Experience requirements vary from employer to employer. In many situations this is an entry-level position. Some employers, however, prefer or require experience or background in payroll.

Clerks should be detail oriented and organized. The most successful Payroll Clerks enjoy working with numbers. The ability to work accurately, and find and correct math errors is essential. Data entry skills are mandatory. Communications skills are helpful as well.

Unions and Associations

Individuals interested in pursuing a career in this field might also obtain additional information from the National Retail Federation (NRF) and the American Collegiate Retailing Association (ACRA).

Tips for Entry

1. Jobs may be advertised in the newspaper classified section under headings including "Payroll," "Payroll Specialist," "Payroll Clerk," "Payroll Technician," "Retail Opportunities," or "Department Store."
2. Send your resume and a short cover letter to department stores.
3. Many department stores also list openings on their Web site.
4. Contact the corporate offices of large chains and department stores to see who you might contact for this position in their local stores.
5. Check out openings online by visiting traditional job sites like monster.com and hotjobs.com. Then surf the net to find other job sites specializing in careers in the retail industry.

DIRECTOR OF HUMAN RESOURCES—DEPARTMENT STORE

Duties: Direct operations of human resources department; supervise and monitor department employees; develop and administer policies; recruitment; oversee employee relations

Alternate Title(s): Human Resources Manager; Human Resources Director; Personnel Director

Salary Range: $33,000 to $68,000+

Employment Prospects: Fair

Advancement Prospects: Fair

Best Geographical Location(s) for Position: Jobs may be located throughout the country; large cities will offer more opportunities

Prerequisites:

Education and Training—Bachelor's degree required or preferred

Experience—Extensive experience in human resources

CAREER LADDER

Director of Human Resources in Larger, More Prestigious Department Store, or VP of Human Resources

Director of Human Resources

Assistant Director of Human Resources or Personnel Manager

Special Skills and Personality Traits—Interpersonal skills; communications skills; management skills; knowledge of federal and state employment laws; detail oriented; organized

Position Description

Without employees, department stores couldn't function. Attracting, training, and retaining the best employees available is essential to the success of every department store.

The department handling a store's employees is called human resources. Depending on the specific store, it may also be referred to as the personnel or employment department.

At one time or another, everyone who is hired must go through the human resources department. The individual in charge of the department is called the Director of Human Resources. He or she has a very important position.

The director controls the operation of the department, and is responsible for planning, organizing, and managing everything that happens within it.

In large stores, the human resources director may oversee several areas. Each of these is headed by a manager specializing in a specific human resource activity. These might include employment, compensation, benefits, employee relations, and training and development. In smaller department stores, the human resources director may be responsible for handling all these on his or her own or with the help of one or more assistants.

The Director of Human Resources develops, writes, and administers policies. These policies have a direct impact on the employees who are hired and the manner in which they are expected to work. They also have a great impact on the store atmosphere and the way the department store functions.

The human resources director is responsible for strategic planning as it relates to human resources. The individual may develop programs designed to enhance training, provide internship opportunities, and create career development for employees within the department store or any of its sister stores.

Other duties of the Director of Human Resources working in a department store may include:

- Developing employee relations programs
- Working with negotiators during contract negotiations
- Overseeing special projects and promotional events such as job fairs to stimulate recruitment of potential employees
- Developing and coordinating personnel programs

Salaries

The Director of Human Resources working in department stores may earn between $33,000 and $68,000 or more annually. Factors affecting earnings include the geographic location, size, and prestige of the specific store as well as the education, experience, and responsibilities of the individual. Generally, those with the most education and experience working in larger stores will earn the highest salaries.

Employment Prospects

Employment prospects are fair for a qualified human resources director seeking employment in department stores. Those seeking jobs in this field may have to relocate to areas hosting great numbers of large department stores.

Advancement Prospects

Advancement prospects for the Director of Human Resources working in department stores are fair. Individuals might climb the career ladder by locating a similar position in a larger or more prestigious department store. Some find similar jobs in other industries. After obtaining a great deal of experience, some individuals move into positions as the vice president of Human Resources.

Education and Training

Most department stores today either require or prefer their Directors of Human Resources hold a minimum of a bachelor's degree. The best major is human resources. However, majors in other areas are often acceptable with work experience.

Additional courses, workshops, and seminars in human resources, labor relations, personnel, compensation, employee relations, and the retailing industry are very helpful. A graduate degree may give one applicant an edge over another.

Experience, Skills, and Personality Traits

A great deal of experience working in human resources and related areas is usually necessary for this type of position. Human Resources Directors usually have worked in the Human Resources department in various other positions. Many have been personnel directors or the director of human resources in areas other than retail.

Human Resources Directors should have supervisory and administrative skills. Writing and communications skills are also necessary. Individuals must have in-depth knowledge of all federal and state employment laws.

Unions and Associations

Those interested in learning more about careers in this field should contact the Society for Human Resources Management (SHRM). This organization provides professional guidance and support to its members.

Tips for Entry

1. Jobs may be advertised in the newspaper classified section under headings including "Human Resources," "Human Resources Director," "H.R. Director," "Retail Opportunities," or "Retail/Human Resources Director."
2. Send your resume and a short cover letter to department stores.
3. Many department stores have Web sites listing their openings.
4. Contact the corporate offices of large chains and department stores to see who you might contact for this position.
5. Contact an executive search firm specializing in retail and/or human resources.

HUMAN RESOURCES GENERALIST— DEPARTMENT STORE

CAREER PROFILE

Duties: Schedule preemployment job interviews; screen applicants; check references; evaluate applicants

Alternate Title(s): Human Resources Interviewer; Human Resources Coordinator

Salary Range: $8.00 to $18.00 + per hour

Employment Prospects: Fair

Advancement Prospects: Fair

Best Geographical Location(s) for Position: Jobs may be located throughout the country; large cities will offer more opportunities

Prerequisites:

Education and Training—Bachelor's degree required or preferred

Experience—Experience in recruiting, counseling, interviewing, or retail helpful

CAREER LADDER

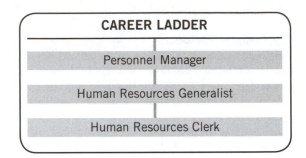

Personnel Manager

Human Resources Generalist

Human Resources Clerk

Special Skills and Personality Traits—Interpersonal skills; people skills; communications skills; interviewing skills; personable; objective; detail oriented

Position Description

Department stores employ many people. Prior to becoming employed, each individual must be recruited, screened, and interviewed. The Human Resources Generalist may have an array of duties depending on the specific job.

The Generalist, who also may be called an interviewer or human resources coordinator, greets applicants upon arrival at the department store's human resources department for the initial interview. He or she schedules and conducts preemployment job interviews with potential applicants. This determines their qualifications as well as if they match those of the job openings. The individual ascertains the skills, personality traits, education, and training of applicants. In this manner, the Human Resources Generalist determines other jobs for which the potential employee may be qualified.

There may be a number of people for each job opening. The Human Resources Generalist may be responsible for screening applicants to weed out those who do not have the proper qualifications or might not fit into the department store environment.

Other duties of the Human Resources Generalist may include:

- Assisting applicants with applications
- Checking references

- Handling administrative functions
- Developing and placing ads for employees in newspapers and magazines
- Assisting the human resources department with special projects

Salaries

Human Resources Generalists may earn between $8.00 and $18.00 or more per hour. Factors affecting earnings include the geographic location, size, and prestige of the specific department store as well as the experience, education, and responsibilities of the individual. Generally, those with the most education and experience working in larger stores will earn the highest salaries.

Employment Prospects

Employment prospects are fair for qualified Human Resources Generalists seeking employment in department stores. The most opportunities will be in areas hosting large numbers of department stores.

Advancement Prospects

Advancement prospects for Human Resources Generalists working in department stores are fair. Individuals may climb the career ladder in a number of ways. Some Human Resources Generalists obtain experience and locate similar positions in larger or more prestigious department stores. Others who have the proper education and training eventually may be promoted to different positions in the human resources department.

Education and Training

Department stores may prefer, but not always require, their Human Resources Generalists hold a college degree. Good majors include human resources, liberal arts, marketing, communications, and retail. However, majors in other areas are often acceptable with work experience.

Courses, workshops, and seminars in human resources, labor relations, personnel, compensation, employee relations, and the retailing industry are also helpful.

Experience, Skills, and Personality Traits

Experience working in human resources, recruiting, or vocational counseling is usually required. Prior to getting their job in the department store, many Human Resources Generalists have worked in public or private personnel offices or departments. Some have moved up the ranks in the human resources department of the store.

A knowledge and understanding of the retailing industry is necessary. Human Resources Generalists should be objective and articulate. Good communications skills and interviewing skills are essential. The ability to make people comfortable is useful.

Unions and Associations

Those interested in learning more about careers in this field might be members of the Society for Human Resources Management (SHRM). This organization provides professional support and guidance.

Tips for Entry

1. Jobs may be advertised in the newspaper classified section under headings including "Human Resources," "Human Resources Generalist," "H.R. Interviewer," "Retail Opportunities," or "Retail/Human Resources Generalist."
2. Send your resume and a short cover letter to department stores.
3. Many department stores have Web sites listing their openings.
4. Contact the corporate offices of large chains and department stores to see who you might contact for this position.
5. Get experience in this department by starting out as a secretary or administrative assistant.

TRAINING MANAGER— DEPARTMENT STORE

CAREER PROFILE

Duties: Develop and facilitate classes, seminars, workshops, and other training programs for employees; develop key management programs

Alternate Title(s): Training and Development Manager; Training Director

Salary Range: $27,000 to $58,000+

Employment Prospects: Fair

Advancement Prospects: Fair

Best Geographical Location(s) for Position: Areas hosting large numbers of department stores and chains

Prerequisites:

Education and Training—College degree preferred

Experience—Experience in training and development

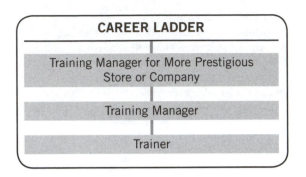

CAREER LADDER

Training Manager for More Prestigious Store or Company

Training Manager

Trainer

Special Skills and Personality Traits—Communications skills; interpersonal skills; employee relations skills; writing skills; ability to speak in public; creative; organized; motivating

Position Description

Department stores employ large numbers of employees. Training Managers are employed to develop programs for employees in a multitude of areas and a variety of subjects depending on the needs of the specific department store.

The Training Manager has a great deal of responsibility. The manager may facilitate all classes personally or work with a staff which may include a training coordinator and other trainers to handle this task.

The Training Manager works with the human resources director who writes and administers policies. These policies have a direct impact on the way employees are expected to work. The human resources director may, at his or her discretion, ask the Training Manager to develop programs designed to enhance training as well as providing internship opportunities within the store.

The Training Manager may develop and facilitate orientation programs for new employees. During orientation, employees will learn the policies of the department store, and the way they are expected to act on the job and react to difficult situations.

In some situations, the department store Training Manager may be expected to develop and put together an employee handbook discussing workplace policies and regulations. In others, the individual may work with other members of the human resources department on this task.

As department stores learn that success can be built on customer service, it is essential that each and every employee be trained to treat customers in a courteous and gracious manner. An important function of Training Managers in department stores is teaching employees what good customer service is and how it should be provided.

The Training Manager may offer classes for management in learning how to communicate with their employees. Other subjects covered in this type of class may include acceptable methods for disciplining employees and how to speak to subordinates without coming across abruptly. The individual may also develop classes for employees dealing with sexual harassment in the workplace and avoiding this problem.

The Training Manager may develop classes specific to certain jobs in the department store such as cashiers, salespeople, or customer service.

Other duties of the Training Manager may include:

• Creating and directing programs to teach department directors, managers, and supervisors methods of conducting training within their department

- Teaching department directors, managers, and supervisors proper procedures for interview techniques and handling employment reviews
- Training employees in team building so that managers, supervisors, and subordinates all work together

Salaries

Annual earnings for Training Managers working in department stores can range from approximately $27,000 and $58,000 or more. Factors affecting earnings include the geographic location, size, and prestige of the specific department store as well as the education, experience, and responsibilities of the individual.

Employment Prospects

Employment prospects for department store Training Managers are fair. The greatest number of opportunities will be in areas hosting large numbers of department stores. Certain department store chains employ a Training Manager in their main store or corporate office instead of one in each store. Note that not every department store employs a Training Manager. Some facilities utilize the services of the human resources director to handle the training functions as well.

Advancement Prospects

Training Managers working in department stores may advance their careers by locating a similar position in larger or more prestigious facilities. Individuals might also climb the career ladder by becoming an assistant director of human resources or director of human resources. These promotions usually require additional experience, training, and education.

Education and Training

Educational requirements vary from employer to employer. Generally department stores require or prefer individuals to hold a minimum of a bachelor's degree in human resources, communications, retail, or a related field. There are some department stores, however, which may accept individuals with a high school diploma and a background and experience in training, human resources, or the retail industry.

Experience, Skills, and Personality Traits

Experience working in training and development is almost always required. Additional experience in retailing may also be needed.

Training Managers must have excellent people and employee relations skills. They must also have both good verbal and written communication skills. The ability to speak effectively in front of groups of people is essential to success in this position.

Unions and Associations

Those interested in learning more about careers in this field should contact the American Society of Training Developers (ASTD) and the Society for Human Resources Management (SHRM).

Tips for Entry

1. Become either an active or affiliate member of the ASTD. This may give you the edge over another applicant with the same qualifications.
2. If you have experience in training, see if a position exists as a trainer. Get your foot in the door of the department store, obtain some experience, and climb the career ladder.
3. Openings are often advertised on the Internet. They may be located via the home pages of department stores. They may also be found by doing a search of department store job opportunities.
4. Positions may be advertised in the classified sections of newspapers. Look under classifications such as "Department Store Training Manager," "Training and Development Manager," "Retail Opportunities," or "Human Resources."
5. You may be asked to conduct an impromptu training presentation as part of your interview process. Develop a sample program ahead of time and rehearse before the interview.
6. Search out openings online. Start by checking out traditional job search sites such as the Monster board and Yahoo! HotJobs. Then surf the net for other sites specific to the retail industry to find other opportunities.

STOCK ROOM MANAGER

Duties: Oversee stock room; supervise and coordinate activities of stock room workers

Alternate Title(s): Stock Room Supervisor

Salary Range: $22,000 to $35,000+

Employment Prospects: Good

Advancement Prospects: Fair

Best Geographical Location(s) for Position: Jobs may be located throughout the country

Prerequisites:

Education and Training—On-the-job training

Experience—Experience working in stock room

Special Skills and Personality Traits—Supervisory skills; organized; ability to lift cartons of various weights and sizes

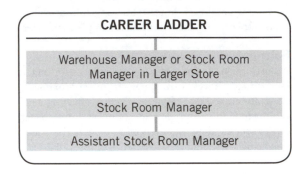

CAREER LADDER

Warehouse Manager or Stock Room Manager in Larger Store

Stock Room Manager

Assistant Stock Room Manager

Position Description

Department stores are filled with great amounts of merchandise. When merchandise is received it is unloaded and brought into the stock room. The stock room of a store is the area in which merchandise is checked in, priced, and stored until it is put out on the selling floor. The individual responsible for the stock room is called the Stock Room Manager.

The Stock Room Manager supervises and coordinates the activities of the stock room workers. He or she will assign duties to each worker so that the stock room is run effectively and efficiently.

The Stock Room Manager assigns workers to receive merchandise as well as inventory control. In many stores today, this is accomplished with the help of hand-held scanners and computers. UPCs (Universal Product Codes) which look like lines or bars are found on merchandise or merchandise tags and tickets. Once these bars are scanned, employees of the store or the Stock Room Manager can instantly find out what is and is not in stock.

The individual keeps records of merchandise received and merchandise returned. He or she is responsible for reviewing these records and determining any discrepancies. The Stock Room Manager must also be sure that procedures regarding returning defective merchandise are followed.

The Stock Room Manager is expected to organize the stock room. He or she may plan the layout of the stockroom, warehouse, and other storage areas. This is important so that merchandise can be stored both safely and so it can be located easily. When doing this, the Stock Room Manager must take certain factors into account, such as the amount of merchandise needed to be stored, the size and weight of the items, and the expected turnover time.

Additional duties of Stock Room Managers might include:

- Unpacking and repacking cartons of merchandise
- Checking inventory for specific items
- Scheduling workers for inventories
- Handling loss prevention in the storeroom area

Salaries

Annual earnings of Stock Room Managers can range from approximately $22,000 to $35,000 or more. Variables affecting earnings include the size and geographic location of the store and the experience and responsibilities of the individual.

Employment Prospects

Employment prospects for Stock Room Managers are good. Positions may be located throughout the country. The greatest number of openings are located in large areas hosting a great number of stores.

Advancement Prospects

The most common method of career advancement for Stock Room Managers is locating similar positions in larger department stores. This will result in increased responsibilities and earnings. Individuals may also find jobs as warehouse supervisors or managers.

Education and Training

Generally, Stock Room Managers have moved up the ranks and obtained their experience through the on-the-job training necessary to perform their job. Some stores might also provide more formal training programs.

Experience, Skills, and Personality Traits

Prior experience working in stock rooms is necessary. Supervisory experience is helpful. Stock Room Managers should be very organized people. Communications skills are useful as are computer skills.

Unions and Associations

Individuals may get additional career information by contacting the National Retail Federation (NRF).

Tips for Entry

1. Jobs are often advertised in the classified section of the newspaper. Look under headings such as "Stock Room Manager," "Stock Room," "Department Store," or "Retail Opportunities," Specific stores may also advertise a number of job opportunities.

2. There is often turnover in these positions. Stop in stores and ask the manager if you can fill out an application.

3. Remember to bring the names, addresses, and phone numbers of a few people you can use as references with you when applying for jobs. Make sure you ask people if you can use them as references BEFORE you use them.

4. Stores often call local labor offices to post these jobs. Remember to stop by your state employment office.

5. Stores often promote from within. Get your foot in the door, do a little bit extra, and climb the career ladder.

LOSS PREVENTION MANAGER— RETAIL

Position Description

Loss prevention is an important part of the retail industry and every store takes it seriously. While most people are honest, a great deal of theft still occurs in stores. This may encompass shoplifting by shoppers, as well as inside theft by store employees and others.

The Loss Prevention Manager is the individual responsible for developing a plan to control the shrinkage of store's inventory. Shrinkage is a tremendous problem to stores. Shrinkage is the loss of merchandise from various means, the most prominent being shoplifting. Loss prevention is very important to the bottom line of a store. Depending on the specific employment situation, the Loss Prevention Manager may have varied responsibilities.

The Loss Prevention Manager in a retail environment is responsible for overseeing the safety of the store, its employees, and customers. The individual is in charge of developing and implementing the store's safety and security plan. In some situations, the Loss Prevention Manager works for the corporate office of a chain or department store. In these cases, he or she will develop plans for all the stores in the chain.

It should be noted that some retail stores employ their own security department while others contract it out utilizing the services of a security company. However, one way or the other, most larger stores will still hire their own Loss Prevention Manager to oversee the security department.

The Loss Prevention Manager is responsible for recruiting, hiring, training, and supervising security guards for the store. It is essential that each guard know and understand the store's policies and procedures and is instructed in the ways to carry them out.

The Loss Prevention Manager is expected to recommend the type of security devices the store should utilize. These may include closed-circuit cameras, electronic security devices, security tags, and mirrors. The individual must also determine how many security guards are needed as well as if they should be undercover or uniformed. Undercover officers are often used to catch shoplifters as well as watching out for internal theft by store employees. Security guards are used to provide a security presence within the store.

The Loss Prevention Manager must develop procedures for handling shoplifting incidents within the store. These must follow legal procedures for stopping, searching, and holding suspected shoplifters. Generally, once a suspect is stopped, the local law enforcement agency is called in to make an arrest.

The Loss Prevention Manager may develop seminars for store employees to help them find ways to cut their shrinkage. However, in some instances, the shrinkage in retail stores is internal (involving employees). In these cases, the Loss Prevention Manager must utilize undercover officers or involve the police in the investigation. Internal shrinkage is often more difficult to find until stores conduct their inventory.

The Loss Prevention Manager may work with others in store management scheduling inventories and going over results. A large shrinkage, no matter what the reason, means people are not doing their jobs correctly.

The Loss Prevention Manager in many situations is also responsible for safety issues within the store. He or she may recommend policies regarding safety of employees, customers, and the handling of emergencies. The Manager may also develop and run seminars for store employees to help them find ways to make the store safer and more pleasant in which to shop.

The Loss Prevention Manager needs to develop policies on dealing with potential disturbances and problems such as calming loud or boisterous customers, evicting customers who are acting in a disorderly fashion, helping in a medical emergency, or dealing with lost children. The individual must be sure store employees know how to handle emergency situations such power outages, weather problems, and medical emergencies.

Additional duties of retail Loss Prevention Managers may include:

- Assuming duties of security guards
- Checking to make sure daily shift reports detailing occurrences in stores are complete
- Preparing reports for management on security and safety in store
- Making recommendations to store management about store security and safety concerns
- Formulating policies regarding safety and determining needs for safety programs

Salaries

Annual earnings for Loss Prevention Managers working in retail can range from approximately $26,000 to $68,000 or more. Variables affecting earnings include the geographic location, size, and prestige of the specific store as well as the number of stores for which the Loss Prevention Manager is responsible. Other factors affecting earnings include the experience, training, and responsibilities of the individual.

Employment Prospects

Employment prospects are fair for Loss Prevention Managers in the retail industry. Individuals may find employment in department stores and chain stores as well as specialty shops selling big ticket items. Positions may also be located with the corporate office of chains and department stores. The best prospects for employment will be in areas hosting a large number of retail stores.

Advancement Prospects

Loss Prevention Managers working in retail may advance their career in a number of ways. The most common method is finding similar positions in larger, more prestigious retail stores. This results in increased responsibilities and earnings. Individuals may also be promoted to the position of loss prevention director. Some might advance to positions such as vice president of Loss Prevention and Security. This type of position, however, is usually only found in the corporate office of chains and department stores. Others may climb the career ladder by striking out and starting their own security firms.

Education and Training

Education and training requirements vary for this type of position. While some retail stores require their Loss Prevention Managers to hold a minimum of a high school diploma, most stores will prefer or require individuals to have a college background or degree.

Certain states may require individuals working in security to go through specified training programs offered in the area. Some states may also require an annual in-service course to refresh or update officers in changes in the security field. The Loss Prevention Manager may fall into this category.

If the Loss Prevention Manager is armed when working, he or she must go through a firearms training course. These usually involve both classroom instruction and a specified number of hours on the firing range.

Classes, seminars, and workshops in loss prevention and retail loss prevention are helpful in keeping abreast of new techniques and strategies in this field.

Special Requirements

A clean record and good moral character are essential. Those who are armed usually also must be registered with their specific state to carry firearms.

Experience, Skills, and Personality Traits

The Loss Prevention Manager working in retail is required to have a great deal of experience in security, loss prevention, and retail. Some have worked as police officers or mall security directors prior to their current appointment. Others have experience in the military or other areas of civil service. There are also some individuals who obtained experience working in security and loss prevention and moved up the career ladder.

The Retail Loss Prevention Manager should have an array of skills. As in all other security and loss prevention positions, individuals should be responsible with good judgment. Leadership skills are important. Interpersonal and customer relations skills are essential. Communications skills are mandatory.

An understanding of the retail industry is necessary.

Unions and Associations

Retail Loss Prevention Managers may obtain additional information by contacting the National Retail Federation (NRF). Individuals may also obtain information about possible licensing requirements from their state or local licensing commission.

Tips for Entry

1. Openings may be advertised in the classified sections of newspapers. Look under heading classifications such as "Loss Prevention Manager," "Director of Loss Prevention," "Retail Opportunities," "Retail Security Director," "Retail Security Manager," or "Shrinkage Control Manager." Also look under specific store listings for job opportunities.

2. Jobs may be located on the Internet. Many retail stores have their own Web sites which list employment opportunities.

3. Don't forget to look on some of the World Wide Web job sites. Start with some of the more popular ones such as the Monster board (www.monster.com) and Yahoo! HotJobs (www.hotjobs.com) and go from there.

4. Contact the corporate office of chains and department stores. Send a short cover letter and your résumé inquiring about openings.

RECEIVING CLERK—DEPARTMENT STORE

Duties: Receive, unpack, and check in merchandise

Alternate Title(s): Stock Clerk

Salary Range: $7.50 to $9.50+ per hour

Employment Prospects: Good

Advancement Prospects: Fair

Best Geographical Location(s) for Position: Jobs may be located throughout the country

Prerequisites:

Education and Training—On-the-job training

Experience—No experience required

Special Skills and Personality Traits—Organized; ability to lift cartons of various weights and sizes

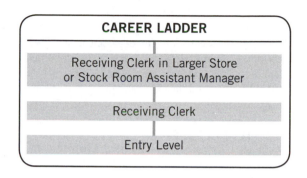

CAREER LADDER

Receiving Clerk in Larger Store or Stock Room Assistant Manager

Receiving Clerk

Entry Level

Position Description

Department stores, by definition, sell many different types of merchandise. This merchandise is delivered by trucks on a regular basis. Some stores have daily deliveries, others weekly or biweekly.

Deliveries of merchandise are received and put into the stock room until they can be inventoried and ticketed. While smaller stores may just employ stock clerks to handle stock room functions, larger department stores may have a number of different employees working in the stock room. These may include a stock room manager, ticketers, stock clerks, inventory clerks, and Receiving Clerks.

Receiving Clerks work in the stock room of the department store, unloading the merchandise off the truck. In some situations the truck driver will take the merchandise off the truck and place it on a loading dock. The Receiving Clerk must then move the merchandise from the loading dock to the store's stock room. Generally, when merchandise is delivered it comes with a delivery or shipping list, indicating exactly what merchandise is supposed to be in the delivery.

For example, the delivery might include 18 boxes. The Receiving Clerk must check to be sure each box is accounted for. Sometimes the delivery doesn't come in boxes. Clothing might come on racks. The Receiving Clerk must then count the dresses or jackets against the list. No matter what the merchandise or container, the individual must account for its delivery before a final acceptance. The Receiving Clerk will then sign the slip indicating that the merchandise has been delivered and accepted.

Boxes of merchandise usually come with packing lists telling what should be in each box. Packing lists may include information such as the number of items, the color, and the size. The list will also include the identification numbers corresponding to each piece of merchandise.

When unpacking each box, the Receiving Clerk is responsible for checking to see if any of the items are damaged or broken. The store is usually not responsible for paying for damaged merchandise. If the Receiving Clerk finds damaged goods, he or she will record the information. This will then be used when the store does a final accounting for payment.

Depending on the specific department store and its size and structure, Receiving Clerks may also fulfill some duties handled by others in the stock room of smaller stores. For example, individuals may scan incoming merchandise into the store's computer systems. Additionally, they may be responsible for ticketing or putting prices on merchandise. In other stockrooms this may be done by a ticketer or a stock clerk.

Additional duties of Receiving Clerks might include:

- Repacking merchandise and returning it to manufacturer

- Keeping records of merchandise which must be sent back
- Checking inventory for specific items
- Storing merchandise in correct area of store room
- Stocking shelves

Salaries

Receiving Clerks working in department stores earn between $7.50 and $9.50 per hour or more. Variables affecting earnings include the size and geographic location of the store and the experience and responsibilities of the individual.

Employment Prospects

Employment prospects for Receiving Clerks are good. Jobs may be located throughout the country. The greatest number of openings are located in areas hosting large department stores.

Advancement Prospects

This is an entry-level position. Advancement prospects are based, to a great extent, on individual career aspirations. Some Receiving Clerks may find similar positions at larger department stores resulting in increased responsibilities and higher earnings. With additional experience and training, the Receiving Clerk may climb the career ladder by becoming an inventory or stock room assistant manager.

Education and Training

Receiving Clerks generally do not need any specialized training. On-the-job training is often provided by the stock room manager or other stock room employees.

Most employers prefer to hire those who hold a high school diploma or the equivalent, or individuals who are still in school. However, there are many who will hire able people who are eager to work no matter what their educational background.

Experience, Skills, and Personality Traits

As noted previously, this is an entry-level position. No prior experience is needed. Receiving Clerks should be organized with the ability to keep good records. The ability to lift large boxes or heavy merchandise is necessary.

Unions and Associations

Individuals may get additional career information by contacting the National Retail Federation (NRF). Depending on the specific department store, Receiving Clerks may belong to house unions.

Tips for Entry

1. Jobs are located in the classified section of newspapers under headings such as "Receiving Clerk," "Stock Room," or "Retail Opportunities."
2. Specific stores may also list job openings in the classifieds.
3. There is a great deal of turnover in these positions. Visit the human resources department of stores and ask to fill out an application.
4. Remember to bring with you the names, addresses, and phone numbers of a few people you can use as references on your applications. Make sure you ask people if you can use them as references. BEFORE you use them.
5. Stores often call local labor offices to post these jobs. Remember to stop by your state employment office.

CUSTOMER SERVICE MANAGER— DEPARTMENT STORE

Position Description

Most department stores have customer service desks. These areas are set up so the store can handle various services for customers. The individual responsible for overseeing this area in the department store is called the Customer Service Manager.

It is the main function of the Customer Service Manager to make the shopping experience as pleasant as possible for every customer. He or she may offer suggestions to the store management regarding steps that can be taken to accomplish this goal. For example, customers may approach the Customer Service Manager to complain about dirty rest rooms. The individual will bring this to the attention of the store manager who will see that the situation is corrected.

The Customer Service Manager oversees the customer service department. He or she will not only determine how many individuals are needed at particular times in order to adequately cover the desk, but schedule them as well.

As part of the job, the Customer Service Manager is expected to train his or her staff. The individual may develop programs or work with the department store's training department.

The customer service area will usually handle returns and exchanges. The Customer Service Manager

sets policies for returns and exchanges. While many department store chains have policies set by the corporate office, the Customer Service Manager often has the authority to make exceptions. For example, even if the store has a 30-day return policy, the Customer Service Manager may override the policy for a customer if the merchandise has not been used and the individual has a receipt.

Many department stores offer an array of other customer services including gift wrapping, shipping, layaways, gift certificates, and personal shopping. The Customer Service Manager may oversee all of these areas.

Problems can vary tremendously in department stores. The Customer Service Manager must be adept at handling an array of situations in a calm and helpful manner. It is not uncommon in department stores for customers to lose their wallets, leave their purses in dressing rooms or rest rooms, and put bags of merchandise down and forget to take them. Customers may find large sums of money or jewelry that others have dropped by mistake or bags of merchandise that someone else has lost. The Customer Service Manager generally has a policy for handling these situations so customer service representatives know what to do.

Some situations are more stressful than others and need more understanding. Children often wander away from parents, husbands can't find wives, customers slip or fall, or other accidents may occur. The Customer Service Manager may assist the store manager or others in keeping everyone calm while following the store's procedures. Depending on the situation, he or she may be expected to call store management, security, or even the police when needed.

Additional duties of Customer Service Manager working in department stores may include:

- Handling special orders for customers
- Answering customers questions regarding store policies
- Calling other stores in the chain to look for merchandise for customers that may not be available in their specific store
- Answering phone inquiries regarding merchandise in the store

Salaries

Department store Customer Service Managers can have annual earnings ranging from approximately $26,000 to $49,000 or more. Variables affecting earnings include the size, prestige, and geographic location of the specific store as well as the experience, education, and responsibilities of the individual.

Employment Prospects

Employment prospects are fair for individuals seeking positions as Customer Service Managers in department stores. Jobs can be located throughout the country in a variety of types of stores ranging from discount chains to upscale department stores.

The greatest number of opportunities will be located in areas hosting large number of department stores.

Advancement Prospects

Department store Customer Service Managers climb the career ladder by locating similar position in larger or more prestigious stores. Depending on experience and training, some individuals advance their career by becoming either an assistant or full-fledged store manager.

Education and Training

Educational requirements vary from store to store. While a college background or degree is usually pre-ferred, it is not always required. College gives individuals the opportunity to gain experience and may be useful in career advancement. It may also give one applicant an edge over another who doesn't have a college degree. There are also many seminars, courses, and workshops in the area of customer service that will be useful in honing skills and may give one applicant an edge over another.

Experience, Skills, and Personality Traits

Customer Service Managers must possess the ability to make decisions quickly and effectively. Individuals should enjoy dealing with the public and have a pleasant personality. Interpersonal and customer relations skills are essential. The ability to lead others is necessary as well.

Customer Service Managers should have excellent written and oral communications skills. In addition to dealing with the public, individuals may be responsible for developing written policies, writing reports, and handling other paperwork.

Unions and Associations

Individuals interested in becoming department store Customer Service Managers can obtain additional information by contacting the National Retail Merchants Association (NRMA) and the National Retail Federation (NRF).

Tips for Entry

1. There are many seminars, workshops, and courses offered throughout the country in customer service. These are useful to hone skills, obtain new ideas, and make useful contacts.
2. Jobs may be advertised in the classified sections of newspapers. Look under classifications such as "Customer Service Manager," "Customer Service," "Retail Opportunities," or specific department store ads advertising multiple positions.
3. Many department stores today have Web sites where they advertise employment opportunities.
4. Trade journals also may advertise openings.
5. Stop by the human resources office of department stores to fill out an application.

CUSTOMER SERVICE REPRESENTATIVE— DEPARTMENT STORE

CAREER PROFILE

Duties: Handle returns and exchanges for customers; sell gift certificates; wrap gifts; provide information regarding stores and merchandise

Alternate Title(s): Customer Service Clerk

Salary Range: $7.50 to $15.00+ per hour

Employment Prospects: Good

Advancement Prospects: Fair

Best Geographical Location(s) for Position: Jobs may be located throughout the country

Prerequisites:

Education and Training—High school diploma or equivalent preferred

Experience—No experience necessary

Special Skills and Personality Traits—Pleasant personality; outgoing; interpersonal skills; people skills; communications skills

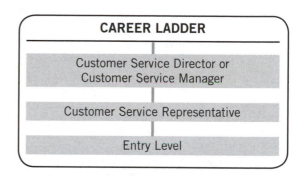

CAREER LADDER

Customer Service Director or Customer Service Manager

Customer Service Representative

Entry Level

Position Description

Most department stores have customer service areas where special services are provided for customers. These areas are usually centrally located in the store so customers can find them easily. The customer service area is staffed by Customer Service Representatives.

The Customer Service Representative's duties vary depending on the specific store, its structure, and the services provided. One of the main responsibilities of Customer Service Representatives is handling returns and exchanges for customers. The individual is expected to follow the store's policies regarding returns. He or she may issue a credit, return cash, or do an exchange depending on the customer's wishes. If there is a problem, the Representative must call the customer service manager or store manager to see if he or she can handle the difficulty.

The Customer Service Representative may answer customers' questions about store merchandise either in person or on the phone. He or she may direct individuals to a specific department to find merchandise they are seeking or give directions to the store's rest rooms, restaurants, elevators, or escalators.

Many department stores have special promotions to attract shoppers such as frequent buyer's clubs or senior citizen discounts. The Customer Service Representative may give out applications and prepare cards for customers so they can take advantage of these discounts and promotions. The individual might also offer customers sale flyers and advertised coupons.

Some department stores provide gift wrapping services either free or for a small fee. The representative may be expected to wrap customers' gifts in a neat and attractive manner.

Other stores offer shipping or delivery services for the convenience of customers. In these instances, the Customer Service Representative may be responsible for weighing items, packaging them for shipping, collecting monies, and getting the correct shipping information.

If a customer has a problem in the store, he or she usually will go to the customer service counter and speak to a Customer Service Representative. It is the responsibility of the individual to help the customer as much as possible. Problems can vary tremendously in department stores. Whether it is customers losing their wallets, someone finding a handbag in a dressing room, an angry shopper, or a child who has wandered away from his or her parents, the Customer Service Representative must be adept at handling any situation in a calm and helpful manner.

The Customer Service Representative may also sell gift certificates or gift cards and explain how they may be used and any conditions and limitations.

Additional duties of Customer Service Representatives may include:

- Holding merchandise for customers until they pick it up
- Checking with a department manager to see if specific merchandise is in stock
- Assisting lost children and others looking for each other in the store
- Making announcements on the public address system
- Answering phone inquiries regarding store hours or availability of merchandise

Salaries

Customer Service Representatives working in department stores can earn between $7.50 and $15.00 or more per hour. Variables affecting earnings include the geographic location, size, and prestige of the store as well as the experience and responsibilities of the individual.

One of the added perks of working in a department store is often an employee discount.

Employment Prospects

Employment prospects are good for Customer Service Representatives seeking employment in department stores. Almost every department store employs Customer Service Representatives. Most employ more than one.

Jobs can be located throughout the country. Possibilities include large chains stores like Wal-Mart, K-Mart, Target, Kohls, J.C. Penney, Sears, Macy's, Dillards, and Bloomingdales. Individuals may also find employment working in smaller department stores.

Customer Service Representatives may work full time or part time depending on the specific position.

Advancement Prospects

Advancement prospects for Customer Service Representatives working in department stores are fair. After obtaining experience, motivated individuals may move up to positions as assistant customer service managers or full-fledged customer service managers. They may, however, need to find positions in other stores.

Education and Training

Most stores prefer to hire Customer Service Representatives with a minimum of a high school diploma or the equivalent. However, there are also many stores that hire individuals who are still attending school.

Informal on-the-job training is usually provided for this position. Those seeking to advance their careers in retail may want to consider college.

Experience, Skills, and Personality Traits

This is usually an entry-level position. Most stores do not require experience.

The Customer Service Representative working in a department store should be an outgoing individual with a pleasant personality. He or she should be articulate with good customer service skills. Interpersonal and customer relations skills are essential. The ability to empathize with a customer who has a problem is a plus.

Unions and Associations

Individuals interested in learning more about careers in retail customer service can obtain additional information by contacting the National Retail Merchants Association (NRMA) and the National Retail Federation (NRF).

Tips for Entry

1. Jobs may be advertised in the classified sections of newspapers. Look under classifications such as "Customer Service Representative," "Customer Service Clerk," "Customer Service," or "Retail Opportunities." Specific stores may also advertise multiple jobs in an advertisement.
2. Stop in stores and ask to fill out an application. Request that it be kept on file if there are no current openings.
3. Local chambers of commerce or community colleges often offer hospitality and customer service seminars. These may be helpful in giving you the edge over another applicant.
4. There are also many seminars, courses, and workshops in the area of customer service which will be useful in honing skills and may give one applicant an edge over another.
5. Many department stores now have Web sites where they list employment opportunities. Some even allow you the opportunity to fill out an application on line.

GREETER

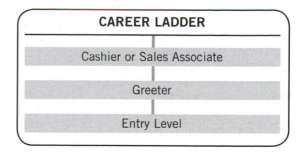

CAREER LADDER

Cashier or Sales Associate

Greeter

Entry Level

Position Description

Customers like to feel valued by the stores in which they shop. Many department stores employ people called Greeters to welcome customers as they enter a store.

The main function of Greeters is to make customers feel important when they walk into the store. They accomplish this by warmly welcoming customers, saying hello as the people walk through the door, and smiling.

Greeters may help customers get shopping carts to make shopping easier. They may also assist customers in getting wheelchairs or mobile shopping carts.

In some department stores, Greeters give children little toys, balloons, stickers, or coloring books. These products may be emblazoned with the store's logo. Greeters may also hand out flyers or store coupons to shoppers.

Greeters answer customers' questions as they enter the store. Customers may ask the Greeter the location of specific items in the store or where specific departments are located within the store. Customers may ask where rest rooms are or if the store has a baby changing area. Sometimes customers need to know where extra flyers or shopping baskets can be found. Others may be looking for the customer service or lay-a-way desk.

Depending on the department store, the Greeter may be responsible for tagging merchandise customers come into the store to return. The Greeter may stamp or tag the merchandise and then direct the individual to the customer service area for returns.

Additional duties of Greeters may include:

- Informing management when shopping carts are needed
- Thanking customers for visiting and wishing them well when they leave the store
- Keeping an eye out for people leaving the store without paying for merchandise

Salaries

Earnings for Greeters working in department stores can range from approximately $7.00 to $9.50 or more per hour. Variables affecting earnings include the geographic location, size, and prestige of the store, the specific days and hours the individual works, as well the experience and responsibilities of the individual. Earnings for Greeters are also dependent on the demand for employees in a given area.

Employment Prospects

Employment prospects are good for Greeters. Individuals may find work throughout the country.

One of the selling points for many people seeking this job is the flexibility of working hours. Individuals may work full time, part time, mornings, afternoons, evenings, weekdays, weekends, or holidays.

Advancement Prospects

Advancement prospects for Greeters are dependent to a great extent on the individual's career aspirations. Some people take jobs as Greeters while in school or on a part-time basis to augment other income. These individuals usually move on to other types of jobs depending on their training. Others may start out as Greeters and move into positions as sales associates or cashiers.

Education and Training

Generally, there are no educational requirements for Greeters. Most employers prefer people who have either a minimum of a high school diploma or are still in school. Individuals are trained on the job.

Experience, Skills, and Personality Traits

This is an entry-level position. No experience is required. Good interpersonal and customer relations skills are essential, as is a pleasant personality. Greeters are on their feet a good portion of the workday.

Unions and Associations

Greeters may get additional career information by contacting the National Retail Federation (NRF). Depending on the place of the employment, Greeters may belong to house unions.

Tips for Entry

1. There is a great deal of turnover in these positions. Stop in stores in which you are interested in working and ask to fill out an application.

2. Openings may be posted in store windows. Look for announcements stating "Greeters Wanted."

3. Jobs may be advertised in the classified sections of newspapers. Look under classifications such as "Greeters" or "Retail Opportunities," "Department Stores," or see the ads of specific department stores.

4. Remember to bring with you the names, addresses, and phone numbers of a few people you can use as references when filling out applications. Make sure you ask people if you can use them as references BEFORE you use them.

5. Stores often call local labor offices to post these jobs. Remember to stop by your state employment office.

STORES, CHAINS, SHOPS, AND BOUTIQUES

DISTRICT MANAGER

Duties: Oversee stores in district; oversee transfer of merchandise; assure stores in district are running properly; oversee key staffing positions; oversee merchandising in stores; work with staff to help store meet sales and profit goals

Alternate Title(s): District

Salary Range: $36,000 to $75,000+

Employment Prospects: Good

Advancement Prospects: Good

Best Geographical Location(s) for Position: Jobs may be located throughout the country

Prerequisites:

    Education and Training—Training requirements vary; see text

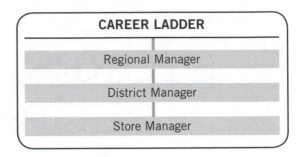

CAREER LADDER

Regional Manager

District Manager

Store Manager

Experience—Experience in retail management

Special Skills and Personality Traits—Management skills; problem solving skills; communications skills; organizational skills; ability to deal well with people; administrative skills

Position Description

Chain and department stores often have multiple outlets in locations from one end of the country to the other. To assure that all the stores are run properly, corporations divide the areas in which they are located into regions. Regions are overseen by regional managers. These regions are then divided into districts. Depending on the specific company, a district may have eight to 15 stores or more. Each district is overseen by an individual called a District Manager.

District Managers are responsible for overseeing all of the stores in a specific area or district. They are expected to make sure each store in the district is running properly.

The District Manager is ultimately responsible for everything that happens within the stores in the district. The individual communicates with each store on a regular basis. Many District Managers speak to their store managers daily. During these conversations, they check to see if there are any problems in the stores and make sure the day-to-day management is going well.

He or she will usually ask how sales are, about store traffic, and what merchandise is moving and what is not. The District, as he or she may be referred to, may ask about personnel issues or possible problems with the landlord or mall management.

If there are problems in any of the stores, the District Manager will offer suggestions to effectively deal with them. This may be handled on the phone or the

individual may visit the store to help deal with the situation.

The District Manager is the liaison between the corporate office and the store. He or she is responsible for communicating routine corporate policies to store managers as well as letting them know of any policy changes. For example, the corporate office may want customer returns handled in a certain manner. The District Manager must make sure all store managers are familiar with the policy and make sure they follow it. The individual may either send a written letter or fax or make a call to each store manager.

One of the main functions of the District Manager is working with his or her stores to make sure they meet corporate sales and profit goals. He or she may visit the store to motivate employees as well as to give them product information helpful in making sales. The individual may make suggestions about displays, merchandising, and other visual opportunities designed to attract the attention of potential customers.

What sells in one store may not sell in another. In many stores, the District Manager will supervise the transfer of merchandise that is not moving to a store where it might.

Stores generally keep accurate records of sales figures on a daily, weekly, monthly, and annual basis. This information is used to help project profits. Based on these figures, along with various other information, the corporate offices set sales goals. In many stores, the store manager is expected to call in or fax the daily figures to the District Manager.

The District Manager is often responsible for recruiting managers and assistant managers for his or her stores. He or she may write and place ads for the newspaper or other media, schedule interviews, and hire qualified individuals.

Many stores, especially chains, have weekly promotions and sales advertised in the local paper and flyers. These promotions, ads, and flyers are used to attract customers. The District Manager will make sure the store management in his or her district knows about the promotions so they can be run effectively.

The District Manager is often required to step in to handle a customer service problem when it can't be handled on the store level. A customer, for example, may have had a problem with a store manager and wants to deal with a person on a higher level. The District Manager, as everyone else in retail, constantly strives to make sure his or her store excels in customer service.

There is a great deal of traveling involved in this job. District Managers may work out of an office or one of the stores in their area. They may travel to visit stores three or four times a week. This is essential to make sure stores are merchandised properly, everything is going well, and all problems are taken care of immediately.

Additional duties of District Managers may include:

- Preparing new stores for opening
- Handling loss prevention
- Terminating key employees
- Recommending raises and promotions for key employees

Salaries

Earnings for District Managers can range from approximately $36,000 to $75,000 or more. Variables affecting earnings include the number of stores in the specific district, as well as the size, prestige, and geographic locations of each. Other variables include the experience, responsibilities, and education of the individual. Generally, those with the highest salaries will have a great deal of responsibility and oversee large districts.

Employment Prospects

Employment prospects are good for District Managers. Positions are located throughout the country. Employers may include chain and department stores, convenience stores, supermarkets, drug stores, and stores in specialty chains.

Advancement Prospects

District Managers may climb the career ladder in a number of ways. Some individuals find similar jobs with larger or more prestigious chains or retail outlets. Others are promoted to positions overseeing larger districts. Another common method of career advancement for District Managers is landing a job as a regional manager. These individuals oversee a number of districts.

Education and Training

Educational backgrounds of District Managers vary. There are many District Managers who hold a high school diploma and no higher education. There are others who have college backgrounds and degrees.

While stores may not require individuals to hold anything above a high school diploma, some may prefer District Managers with college backgrounds or degrees. Good majors include retailing, merchandising, business, management, marketing, communications, advertising, liberal arts, or related fields.

Training requirements vary from store to store. Some stores provide formal training programs. Others have on-the-job training.

Experience, Skills, and Personality Traits

District Managers usually have gone through the ranks getting experience as sales associates, assistant managers, and then store managers prior to their placement in current positions. Individuals need a complete knowledge of management principles as well as a total understanding of the retail industry. Leadership skills, self-confidence, and the ability to make decisions are essential. The ability to deal with and work well with others is necessary. Individuals need to be good problem solvers who are energetic, detail oriented, and highly motivated. Communications skills, both written and verbal, are necessary as well.

Unions and Associations

Individuals interested in learning more about careers in this field should contact the American Collegiate Retailing Association (ACRA), National Retail Federation (NRF), and the National Retail Merchants Association (NRMA).

Tips for Entry

1. Stores often promote from within. Get your foot in the door, learn everything you can, and move up the career ladder.
2. Many chains and department stores offer management training programs. Contact the

headquarters of these stores to find out about requirements.

3. Positions may be advertised in the classified sections of newspapers. Look under classifications including "District Manager," "Retail Opportunities," or "Management Opportunities." Look also in the ads of specific stores.

4. Jobs in this field, may be located on the Internet. Begin your search on some of the more popular job search sites such as Monster board (www.monster.com) and Yahoo! HotJobs (www.hotjobs.com). Then search for career sites specializing in the retail industry.

5. You might also check specific store Web sites. Many post job openings.

6. Contact recruiters and executive search firms specializing in management positions in retail.

7. Send your résumé and a short cover letter to the corporate offices of chain and department stores.

REGIONAL MANAGER—RETAIL

Duties: Oversee stores in region, coordinate the activities of district managers; assure stores in region are running properly; recruit and train district managers; work with key employees to help store meet sales and profit goals

Alternate Title(s): Regional

Salary Range: $46,000 to $100,000+

Employment Prospects: Good

Advancement Prospects: Good

Best Geographical Location(s) for Position: Jobs may be located throughout the country

Prerequisites:

Education and Training—Training requirements vary; see text

Experience—Extensive experience in retail management

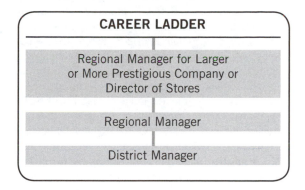

CAREER LADDER

Regional Manager for Larger or More Prestigious Company or Director of Stores

Regional Manager

District Manager

Special Skills and Personality Traits—Management skills; problem solving skills; communications skills; ability to work well with people; administrative skills; leadership skills

Position Description

The day-to-day management of a single retail store is handled by a store manager. Many retail stores have multiple outlets in locations from one end of the country to the other. In order to assure all the stores are run properly, corporate management divides the areas in which stores are located into regions. These regions are overseen by individuals called Regional Managers.

The Regional Manager oversees all the stores in the region. The Regional Manager is expected to coordinate the activities of the district managers in his or her region. The Regional Manager provides leadership and motivation and works with district managers and their stores to help each meet sales and profit goals.

The Regional Manager works with the corporate office to set both long- and short-term sales goals and strategies. These are based on a number of factors and information including prior sales figures. Stores generally keep accurate records of sales figures on a daily, weekly, monthly, and annual basis. These figures are usually called in or faxed to the district manager who in turn gets them to the Regional Manager.

The Regional Manager tracks the sales figures. If he or she sees sales slipping in one or more stores, the individual will call the district manager to see what the problem is and how it can be remedied.

Sales can decline for numerous reasons. For example, sales may be off for a simple reason such as bad weather, which may keep people off the roads. This will resolve itself as soon as the weather gets better. Sometimes, if there has been a big storm during a storewide scheduled promotion, the Regional Manager will suggest to corporate that the promotion be extended.

Sales may be off because a new competitor has just opened a store in the area. In this case, the Regional Manager may call the marketing department and recommend additional advertising, coupons, or promotions for a short period of time. On the other hand, sales may be off because a store in the region is not being managed properly or customer service is poor. The Regional Manager will work with the district manager straightening out the situation.

Regional Managers are responsible for overseeing all of the stores in his or her region. They are expected to make sure each store in the region is running properly. To do this, the individual communicates with each district manager on a regular basis.

The Regional Manager also works closely with district managers to identify and correct general management problems within stores in the region. This may include things such as improving traffic and merchandising matters, dealing with personnel issues, and handling any possible problems with the landlord or mall management.

The Regional Manager may visit stores with the district manager to deal with specific problems or to see first-hand how things are going. The individual is the liaison between upper corporate management and the district managers. He or she is responsible for communicating routine corporate policies and policy changes to district managers so they, in turn, can inform store managers.

In many cases, the Regional Manager will assist upper corporate management in the development of policies and policy changes. The Regional Manager often recruits district managers, and he or she may also assist the district managers in recruiting and hiring key personnel such as managers or assistant managers for stores in the region.

The Regional Manager may work with others in upper corporate management recommending merchandise, sales, or marketing programs.

Regional Managers travel a great deal in their job. Depending on the specific company and its structure, they may work out of a corporate office or out of one of the stores in their region. Regional Managers often travel to meet with their district managers as well as to visit stores in their region.

Additional duties of Regional Managers may include:

- Preparing new stores for opening
- Helping close stores in the chain
- Meeting or calling the landlord or mall management to discuss problems and complaints
- Terminating district managers or other key employees
- Recommending raises and promotions for district managers or other key employees

Salaries

Earnings for Regional Managers can range from approximately $46,000 to $100,000 or more. Variables affecting earnings include the number of districts and number of stores in the specific region, as well as the size, prestige, and geographic locations of each. Other variables include the experience, responsibilities, and education of the individual. Generally, those with the highest salaries will have a great deal of responsibility and oversee large regions.

Employment Prospects

Employment prospects are good for Regional Managers. Positions are located throughout the country. Employers may include chain and department stores, convenience stores, supermarkets, drug stores, and stores in specialty chains.

Advancement Prospects

Regional Managers may climb the career ladder in a number of ways. Some individuals find similar jobs with larger or more prestigious stores. Others are promoted to positions overseeing larger regions. Another method of career advancement for Regional Managers is landing a job as a director of stores.

Education and Training

Educational backgrounds of Regional Managers vary. There are many Regional Managers who hold a high school diploma and no higher education. There are others who have college backgrounds and degrees.

While some companies may not require individuals to hold anything above a high school diploma, some may prefer or require Regional Managers with college backgrounds or degrees. Relevant majors include retailing, merchandising, business, management, marketing, communications, advertising, liberal arts, or other related fields.

Training requirements also vary from company to company. Some companies provide formal training programs, while others have on-the-job training.

Experience, Skills, and Personality Traits

Regional Managers are required to have a great deal of experience in retail management. Most have gone through the ranks getting experience as sales associates, assistant managers, store managers, and regional managers prior to their current positions. Individuals need a complete knowledge of management principles as well as a total understanding of the retail industry. Leadership skills, self-confidence, and decisiveness are essential. The ability to deal with and work well with others is necessary. Individuals need to be good problem solvers who are energetic, detail oriented, and highly motivated. Communications skills, both written and verbal, are necessary as well.

Unions and Associations

Individuals interested in learning more about careers in this field should contact the American Collegiate Retailing Association (ACRA), National Retail Federation (NRF) and the National Retail Merchants Association (NRMA).

Tips for Entry

1. Contact recruiters and executive search firms specializing in management positions in retail.
2. Trade journals often advertise openings.
3. Retail companies like to promote from within. Get your foot in the door, learn everything you can, and move up the career ladder.

4. Many chains and department stores offer management training programs. Contact the headquarters of these stores to find out about requirements.
5. Positions may be advertised in the classified sections of newspapers. Look under classifications including "Regional Manager," "Retail Opportunities," or "Management Opportunities." Look also in the ads of specific stores.
6. Jobs in this field may be located on the Internet. Begin your search on some of the more popular job search sites such as the Monster board (www.monster.com) and Yahoo! HotJobs (www.hotjobs.com).
7. You might also check specific store Web sites. Many post job openings.
8. Send your resume and a short cover letter to the corporate offices of chain and department stores. Ask that your resume be kept on file if there are no current openings.

MANAGER—SPECIALTY OR CHAIN STORE

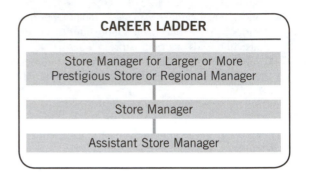

Position Description

While department stores are prevalent in this country, there are an array of other types of stores where people shop. These include specialty stores selling merchandise such as toys, fabrics, clothing, hardware, jewelry, luggage, electronics, books, plants, cosmetics, and gourmet foods, among other items. Each of these stores needs a Manager. In some stores, the owner may act as the Manager.

The Store Manager handles the day-to-day management of the store. His or her management techniques will have a direct impact on the success of the store.

Specific responsibilities will depend, of course, on the type of store the individual is managing. However, there are general duties all Store Managers must fulfill. As in all retail outlets, the Store Manager is expected to work with his or her staff to meet sales and profit goals.

The Store Manager is responsible for opening the store each day. This responsibility may be shared with other key holders such as the assistant manager or third key. Before the gates or doors are opened to the public, the Manager makes sure the store is ready. If the carpet or floor wasn't cleaned the night before, the Manager or his or her staff may vacuum. The individual must be sure the shelves, displays, and racks are stocked and neat. The Store Manager will also go

to the safe and take out cash to fill cash drawers with change for the day.

The Manager is expected to make sure all scheduled employees are present. If employees call in sick, the Manager is responsible for calling in replacement staff.

The Manager is responsible for the recruiting and training needs of the staff for the store. He or she may place ads, conduct interviews, and hire needed employees. The Store Manager is also expected to make sure that all employment regulations are followed within the store. These might include things like following labor rules, making sure teenagers don't work more hours than their allotted time, and forms are filled out for tax purposes. The Manager will recommend raises and promotions and is also expected to terminate employees.

The Store Manager must constantly strive to keep customers happy. The climate of the store is often dependent, to a great extent, on the Store Manager. Those who can make a store a pleasant shopping experience for customers and a pleasant workplace for employees will be most successful.

To accomplish these goals, the Manager must provide the best customer service possible. It is the responsibility of the Manager to train the rest of the staff to provide excellent customer service as well.

The Manager will usually be the individual called upon when a customer has a problem no one else can or wants to handle. He or she will always try to resolve customer complaints to the customer's satisfaction.

The Manager must make sure that the store is stocked with merchandise that customers want. If the store has sales and promotions, the Manager must be sure stock is available, and must keep abreast of what is selling and what is needed. When merchandise is low, the Manager may place an order personally or may inform the store's buyer or owner.

The individual is often responsible for accepting merchandise shipped to the store. He or she may also supervise its unpacking. At times, the Manager will also supervise the repacking of merchandise to send back to a manufacturer or to another store.

The Manager may design store windows and displays so that merchandise is attractively shown. In other cases, the individual may assign this duty to the assistant manager or another member of the staff.

The individual is expected to deal with any emergencies or problems within the store. These might include accidents or incidents in which either customers or employees are hurt. The individual may call paramedics or ambulances when needed. He or she will also be expected to file reports detailing incidents for store owners or insurance purposes.

The Manager is responsible for loss prevention. He or she must key an eye out for shoplifters as well as employee theft, and may work with local police agencies or private investigators.

The Store Manager is ultimately responsible for overseeing all monies in the store. He or she may go over the day's receipts as well as weekly and monthly reports. In many stores, the Manager must report daily figures to the corporate office or store owner.

At the end of the day, the Store Manager, an assistant, or key holder will be responsible for cashing out registers and counting the day's receipts. Depending on the specific store, the individual may either put the day's receipts in the store's safe or deposit it in the bank.

Some Store Managers develop and implement advertising campaigns, promotions, and special events. He or she may also write advertising copy, design ads, and place them in various media.

Additional duties of Store Managers may include:

- Assisting customers
- Representing the store at community events and organizations
- Handling emergencies and crises after hours
- Closing the store after hours
- Scheduling employees work hours
- Approving customers' returns

Salaries

Annual earnings for Store Managers can range from approximately $26,000 to $75,000 or more. Variables affecting earnings include the size, prestige, and geographic location of the specific store. Other variables include the experience, responsibilities, and education of the individual. Some Store Managers may also receive bonuses when sales meet or exceed goals.

Employment Prospects

Employment prospects are excellent for Store Managers seeking to work in retail. Positions are located throughout the country. There are an array of possibilities ranging from small boutiques to larger specialty stores, chains, franchises, and everything in between. Stores like Dress Barn, J. Crew, Petco, Rite Aid, Victoria's Secret, The Gap, Borders, and Barnes and Noble have locations nationwide.

Advancement Prospects

The most common method of climbing the career ladder for Store Managers is locating similar jobs in larger or more prestigious stores. Those working in chains may climb the career ladder by promotion to larger stores within the chain. Individuals also may advance their careers by becoming area managers or moving into other areas of corporate management.

Education and Training

Educational backgrounds of Store Managers vary. While stores may not require individuals to hold anything above a high school diploma, they may prefer Managers with college backgrounds or degrees. Good majors include retailing, merchandising, business, management, marketing, communications, advertising, liberal arts, or other related fields.

Chain stores often require their management recruits to go through their own formal training programs. These may be necessary even if a Manager has worked in the same position in a store outside of the specific chain. These programs train the individual in store policies and management techniques necessary to running the store effectively.

Experience, Skills, and Personality Traits

The most successful Store Managers work in stores where they have some knowledge or interest in the products or merchandise being sold. Most Managers have had experience on the selling floor as well as third keys and assistant managers prior to their current position.

Store Managers must be self-confident, enthusiastic leaders who are energetic, detail oriented, and highly motivated. They must know a great deal about the products and merchandise the store carries in order to be able to assist customers effectively. The ability to solve problems and make quick decisions is essential.

Customer service skills are vital for store management. The ability to deal with and work well with people is mandatory. Store Managers should also be articulate with good communications skills.

Unions and Associations

Individuals interested in learning more about careers in this field should contact the American Collegiate Retailing Association (ACRA), National Retail Federation (NRF) and the National Retail Merchants Association (NRMA).

Tips for Entry

1. Positions may be advertised in the classified sections of newspapers. Look under classifications including "Store Manager," "Retail Opportunities," "Store Management," or "Management Opportunities." Other positions may be advertised under specific store names.

2. Many chain stores offer management training programs. Contact the headquarters of these stores to find out about requirements.

3. Many stores now have Web sites where they also list employment opportunities.

4. Jobs may also be located on the Internet. Begin your search on some of the more popular job search sites such as the Monster board (www.monster.com) and Yahoo! HotJobs (www.hotjobs.com).

5. Contact recruiters and executive search firms specializing in management retail positions.

6. Send your resume and a short cover letter to the corporate offices of chain stores.

ASSISTANT MANAGER— SPECIALTY OR CHAIN STORE

CAREER PROFILE

Duties: Assist manager in daily operations; deal with customer service issues; assist customers; assist with loss prevention; work with staff to help store meet sales and profit goals

Alternate Title(s): Key holder

Salary Range: $22,000 to $48,000+

Employment Prospects: Good

Advancement Prospects: Good

Best Geographical Location(s) for Position: Jobs may be located throughout the country

Prerequisites:

    Education and Training—Training requirements vary

    Experience—Experience in retail management

CAREER LADDER

Store Manager

Assistant Store Manager

Third Key

Special Skills and Personality Traits—Problem solving skills; negotiation skills; communications skills; ability to deal well with people; management skills; administrative skills

---

Position Description

There are many different types of stores. Some might specialize in selling clothing, toys, accessories, fabrics, luggage, pet products, or gifts, among other things. Some may specialize in more niche markets such as gourmet teas, hair pieces, antique clothing, or music boxes. Some stores may be a part of chains or franchises. Others may be privately owned. Each of these stores has a manager. Most also have Assistant Managers.

These individuals are second in command in the store. They assist the store manager with day-to-day store operations. Assistant Managers also step in and assume the duties of the manager when he or she is off.

While there are similarities between the management of department stores and other types of stores, there are also differences. In smaller independent stores, for example, the Assistant Manager may have more generalized duties. He or she may work with the manager to buy merchandise. The individual may also assist with the store's accounting and bookkeeping functions.

Depending on the store, the Assistant Manager may be expected to help develop and implement advertising campaigns, writing copy, designing ads, and placing them. The individual might also help the manager develop promotions and special events to attract customers to the store.

In order for stores to stay in business they need to sell merchandise. Assistant Managers are expected to help motivate the staff to work to meet sales and profit goals.

The Assistant Manager may take turns with the store manager and the third key opening the store. Before the gates or doors are opened to the public, the individual works with other employees making sure the store is ready for customers. This might include checking to see if shelves, displays, and racks are neat and fully stocked, the floor is clean, and the registers have change.

The Assistant Manager may be required to fill in when other employees call in sick and replacement staff can't be located. The individual may assist the store manager in recruiting and training staff. He or she will work with the manager assuring that all employment regulations are followed within the store. These might include things like following labor rules, making sure teenagers don't work more hours than their allotted time, or filling out forms for tax purposes.

One of the main responsibilities of the Assistant Manager is making sure the store employees provide excellent customer service, and that shopping in the store is a pleasant experience. In the event a customer does have a problem or complaint, the Assistant Manager may be called to resolve it.

The Assistant Manager makes sure that merchandise sold during the day is replaced from the stock room at regular intervals. In this way displays always look filled and appear inviting to customers.

The individual is expected to deal with any emergencies or problems within the store when the manager is not available. These might include accidents or incidents in which either customers or employees are hurt. He or she will also be expected to file reports detailing incidents for store owners or insurance purposes.

The Assistant Manager works with others in the store on loss prevention. He or she must keep an eye out for shoplifters as well as employee theft. The Assistant Manager and the manager may work with local police agencies or private investigators.

Depending on who is working at the close of business, the Assistant Manager, manager, or third key will be responsible for cashing out registers and counting the day's receipts. One or more of these individuals may put the day's receipts in the store's safe or deposit it at a bank.

Additional duties of Assistant Store Managers may include:

- Assisting customers
- Handling emergencies and crises after hours when the manager is not available
- Closing the store after hours when manager is not on duty
- Assisting with the scheduling of employees work hours
- Approving customers' returns

Salaries

Annual earnings for Assistant Store Managers can range from approximately $22,000 to $48,000 or more. Variables affecting earnings include the size, prestige, and geographic location of the specific store. Other variables include the experience, responsibilities, and education of the individual. Some Store Managers may also receive bonuses when sales meet or exceed goals.

Employment Prospects

Employment prospects are good for Assistant Managers. Positions may be located throughout the country. There are an array of possibilities ranging from small boutiques to larger specialty stores, chains, franchises, and everything in between. Chain stores such as Dress Barn, J. Crew, Petco, Rite Aid, Victoria's Secret, The Gap, Borders, and Barnes and Noble have locations nationwide.

Advancement Prospects

Some Assistant Store Managers advance their careers by landing similar positions in larger or more prestigious stores. This results in increased responsibilities and earnings.

Another common method of career advancement for Assistant Managers is promotion to store manager. Those working in chains may climb the career ladder by promotion to larger stores within the chain.

Education and Training

Educational backgrounds of Assistant Managers vary. While stores may not require individuals to hold anything above a high school diploma, they may prefer Assistant Managers with college backgrounds or degrees. Good majors include retailing, merchandising, business, management, marketing, communications, advertising, liberal arts, or related fields. College is especially helpful for individuals seeking to advance their careers.

Chain stores often require their management recruits to go through their own formal training programs. These may be necessary even if the individual has worked as an Assistant Manager in a store outside of the specific chain. These programs train the individual in store policies and management techniques necessary to running the store effectively.

Experience, Skills, and Personality Traits

Assistant Managers are required to have experience working in a retail environment. Most have worked on the selling floor as well as been in third key positions.

Assistant Store Managers should be highly motivated, self-confident, and enthusiastic individuals. They should be detail oriented and have the ability to do multiple projects at one time. Customer service skills are essential. Good communications skills are mandatory.

Unions and Associations

Individuals interested in learning more about careers in this field should contact the American Collegiate Retailing Association (ACRA), the National Retail Federation (NRF) and the National Retail Merchants Association (NRMA).

Tips for Entry

1. Stores often post signs in their windows advertising openings for management positions.
2. You might also stop in stores and ask to fill out an application. Ask that your resume be kept on file if there are no current positions.
3. Positions may be advertised in the classified sections of newspapers. Look under classifications including "Assistant Store Manager," "Retail

Opportunities," "Store Management," or "Management Opportunities." Other positions may be advertised under specific store names.

4. Many chain stores offer management training programs. Contact the headquarters of these stores to find out about requirements.

5. Many stores now have Web sites where they also list employment opportunities.

6. Remember to check out corporate Web sites of chain stores as well.

THIRD KEY

CAREER PROFILE

Duties: Oversee small staff; assist customers; sell merchandise; open store; close store; cash out registers; handle deposits

Alternative Titles(s): Junior Assistant Manager

Salary Range: $8.00 to $18.00+ per hour

Employment Prospects: Excellent

Advancement Prospects: Excellent

Best Geographical Location(s) for Position: Positions located throughout the country

Prerequisites:

Education and Training—On-the-job training

Experience and Qualifications—Retail sales experience required

CAREER LADDER

Assistant Store Manager

Third Key

Sales Associate

Special Skills and Personality Traits—Management skills; customer service skills; sales ability; communications skills; pleasant attitude; money handling skills

Position Description

Retail establishments may have an array of supervisors and managers running the store. Depending on the size and structure of the establishment these might include managers, assistant managers, department managers, supervisors, and Third Keys.

The Third Key is an entry-level management position with varied duties depending on the organization. The Third Key may be in charge of overseeing staff. A Third Key may often work either on weekends or evenings when a manager or assistant manager is not on duty. During this time, the Third Key will supervise the staff. In this position, the Third Key may handle problems which might occur within the store. These might include unhappy or irate customers, accidents with customers or employees, shoplifters, or difficult merchandise returns.

The Third Key reports to the assistant manager and manager of the store. He or she may work full time or part time and usually will be expected to work evenings or weekends.

Depending on the store, managers, assistant managers, and Third Keys may hold the keys to the store. One of the responsibilities of the Third Key may be opening the store for business in the morning. To do this the individual unlocks the door, makes sure the store is straightened and ready to open, puts cash in the registers for change, and makes sure all scheduled employees are accounted for.

Conversely, the Third Key may be scheduled to close the store at the end of business hours. When doing this he or she must first make sure all customers are out of the store and then close the doors or pull the gate for the evening. The Third Key may be expected to cash out the registers, do cash counts and then prepare a deposit. Some stores may have safes where money is kept until a morning deposit. In other stores, only monies designated for change will be kept in a safe at night. The rest of the day's receipts must be dropped in a night deposit by the Third Key or another member of the management staff.

Before the Third Key leaves, he or she must make sure the store is ready to open the next day. He or she will work with other members of the staff putting back merchandise, vacuuming the store, and straightening displays in preparation for the next day's business.

Some Third Keys may be assigned to specific parts of the store or departments. The individual may, for example, be in charge of keeping display tables stocked and arranged attractively. This may need to be done a number of times a day as customers rifle through stock looking for merchandise.

Third Keys are also expected to assist customers. Like sales associates, they must determine the needs of customers to make each person feel comfortable whether they come in the store to browse or buy. Third Keys often take payment when customers decide on purchases.

The Third Key job is a stepping stone to a management position in retail. Other duties of Third Keys include:

- Stocking, pricing, and ticketing merchandise
- Displaying merchandise
- Training new employees
- Handling loss prevention
- Accounting for sales
- Handling returns

Salaries

Earnings for Third Keys range from approximately $8.00 to $18.00 or more per hour. Factors affecting earnings include the geographic location, size, prestige, and specific type of retail establishment. Other variables include the experience and responsibilities of the individual. A perk of the job for many individuals is often an employee discount in the store in which they work.

Employment Prospects

Employment prospects are excellent for Third Keys. Individuals may find positions throughout the country in a variety of retail establishments. Third Keys may work full time or part time, as well as various shifts.

Most stores employ Third Keys or the equivalent. Many employ more than one person in this position. As noted, this is an entry-level management position. There is a great deal of turnover as individuals climb the career ladder or move to other jobs.

Advancement Prospects

Advancement prospects are excellent for Third Keys. With experience or additional training, Third Keys often advance to positions as assistant store managers.

Education and Training

The Third Key usually receives on-the-job training at the store in which he or she works. Many stores also provide formal training programs.

Experience, Skills, and Personality Traits

Third Keys need retail sales experience. They usually start out as sales associates. Individuals should be reliable with management skills and the ability to supervise others.

They should be courteous, pleasant people with good customer service skills. Sales ability and money handling skills are essential.

Unions and Associations

Those interested in learning more about careers as sales associates can obtain information from the National Retail Merchants Association (NRMA) or the American Collegiate Retailing Association (ACRA).

Tips for Entry

1. Larger stores often have management training programs. If you are aspiring to a career in retail seek these out.
2. Jobs are often advertised in the classified sections of newspapers. Look under classifications such as "Retail," "Retail Opportunities," "Third Key," or "Management—Retail."
3. Many larger stores have job hotlines. These are frequently recorded updated messages listing job availability. Call stores directly to obtain their job hotline phone numbers, or check their ads.
4. Stop by the human resources department of larger stores to learn about job openings.
5. Stop in smaller stores and ask the manager if there are any openings or if you can fill out an application.
6. Many stores post "help wanted" signs in their store's windows.

SALES ASSOCIATE

Position Description

There are a variety of retail establishments of every size and type. These include department stores, specialty shops, grocery stores, convenience stores, newspaper and sundry shops, souvenir stores, kiosks, clothing stores, and boutiques and gift shops to name a few. No matter what they sell, every store and shop needs Sales Associates, also referred to as salesclerks.

Sales Associates assist customers, and determine the needs of each customer. Sales Associates must make every person who comes into the retail establishment feel comfortable whether they are just browsing or they want to buy. Customer service is extremely important in this job.

Sales Associates must know the stock in their store and be able to answer questions regarding merchandise. Individuals may offer suggestions to customers regarding purchase possibilities.

Once patrons decide what they want to purchase, Sales Associates may be responsible for taking payment. Individuals must know how to ring up purchases and make correct change if people are paying with cash. They also must know the proper procedure for accepting checks or processing credit card charges.

Sales Associates in some stores stock, price, and ticket merchandise. They are responsible for putting merchandise out in displays. Individuals also are expected to clean and to organize shelves as well as keep the shop or store neat and orderly.

Other duties of Sales Associates include:

- Handling loss prevention
- Accounting for sales
- Handling returns

Salaries

Salaries for Sales Associates may vary greatly. Many associates earn minimum wage. Others may be paid between $8.00 and $15.00 or more per hour. Factors affecting earnings include the geographic location, size, prestige, and specific type of retail establishment. Other variables include the experience and responsibilities of the individual. In some stores, Sales Associates may be paid a commission in addition to their hourly wage boosting their earnings.

One of the perks many Sales Associates enjoy is an employee discount in the store in which they work.

Employment Prospects

Employment prospects are excellent for Sales Associates throughout the country. One of the great things about working as a Sales Associate is the flexibility it affords. Sales Associates might work full time, part time, nights, weekends, or holidays. In addition to being a good career choice for those interested in retail, it is often an excellent opportunity for students or people looking for a second income.

Advancement Prospects

With experience and/or additional training, Sales Associates are often promoted to supervisory or managerial positions. Depending on career aspirations individuals might be promoted to third key, floor supervisor, or even assistant store manager.

Education and Training

Generally, Sales Associates receive on-the-job training. Depending on the specific employer, training might include how to help customers with sales, as well as how to use the cash register and credit card machines properly.

Experience, Skills, and Personality Traits

Experience requirements for Sales Associates vary. There are many entry-level positions in sales requiring no experience. Others may prefer or require some type of retail sales experience.

Sales Associates must be courteous, pleasant, and have good customer service skills. Sales ability and money handling skills are essential. The most successful Sales Associates enjoy being around people.

Unions and Associations

Those interested in learning more about careers as sales associates can obtain information from the National Retail Merchants Association (NRMA) or the National Retail Federation (NRF).

Tips for Entry

1. While retail experience is not always needed, it may be preferred. Include any prior retail experience on your job application or resume.
2. Jobs are often advertised in the classified sections of newspapers in areas hosting large department stores. Look under classifications such as "Retail," "Retail Opportunities," "Sales Associates," or "Salesclerks."
3. Many larger stores have job hotlines. These are frequently recorded updated messages listing job availability. Call stores directly to obtain their job hotline phone numbers, or check their ads.
4. Stop by the human resources department of larger stores to learn about job openings.
5. Feel free to stop in smaller stores to ask the manager if there are any openings or if you can fill out an application.
6. Look for help wanted signs in store windows.

BRAND MANAGER

Duties: Developing and implementing marketing campaigns for a specific brand; developing direction of specific brand; working with research and development (R&D) to develop new products within brand

Alternate Title(s): Product Manager

Salary Range: $35,000 to $150,000+

Employment Prospects: Good

Advancement Prospects: Good

Best Geographical Location(s) for Position: Positions located throughout the country

Prerequisites:

Education or Training—Bachelor's degree in marketing, advertising, communications, or related field

Experience—Marketing and branding experience necessary

Special Skills and Personality Traits—Creativity; ingenuity; motivation; ambition; ability to think outside the box; verbal and written communication skills; market research skills; analytical skills; interpersonal skills

CAREER LADDER

Senior Brand Manager, Senior Vice President in Charge of Branding, or Corporate Director of Marketing

↓

Brand Manager

↓

Assistant Brand Manager, Associate Brand Manager

Position Description

Large corporations are frequently composed of smaller companies or divisions that have their own brands. Disney, for example, is the parent company of ABC television and CNN. Mars, Inc., is the parent company of M&Ms, 3 Musketeers, Mars, Milky Way, and an array of others. Kraft has numerous brands under their umbrella, including Velveeta, Philadelphia Cream Cheese, and Kraft Salad Dressing.

The person in charge of developing and implementing marketing campaigns for a particular brand is called the Brand Manager. Brand management uses a variety of marketing techniques to increase a specific brand's value to consumers. This in turn increases the brand equity and worth which can mean millions of dollars to a company.

Brand Managers have a number of different responsibilities. Their main function is leading a company's specific brand through development, execution, and product strategy to increase product sales. They are responsible for developing a strong brand with high visibility.

Individuals are expected to develop both long- and short-term marketing plans for their brand. Within the scope of their job, Brand Managers may handle new products or existing products. Indviduals may work with the company's research and development team in developing new products for the brand or creating new features for one or more of the company's existing products.

Brand Managers work with various departments within the company to maximize promotion for the brand. These include the marketing, advertising, public relations, and art departments.

Brand Managers may use various types of campaigns to increase customers' awareness of their brand as well as maximizing the brand promotion. These can include broadcast and/or print advertising, point of purchase displays, public relations, promotions, sweepstakes and contests, Web promotion, e-mail blasts, and more.

Whether campaigns are aimed at television advertising, billboards, print ads, the Web, or packaging, Brand Managers must ensure brand consistency. This is essential so potential customers can easily identify the specific brand on a continuing basis.

The Brand Manager must develop budgets for his or her departments. In doing so, the individual determines how best to spend the monies allocated in order to increase sales. Should more monies go toward research? What about advertising? How about changing the packaging? The decisions of the Brand Manager can affect the bottom line of that brand.

Part of the responsibilities of the Brand Manager is to work with the research and development team. This is necessary for many reasons. Research might determine, for example, how products in the brand can be improved. Research often can help determine the feeling customers (or potential customers) have about a product. For example, do customers not like something about the product or brand? Do customers purchase a product once and then not again? If so the Brand Manager must determine the reason why, as well as what can be done to turn the problem around. As part of the job, Brand Managers must locate key markets and potential customers. Once that is done, the individual must find ways to reach those customers.

The Brand Manager is crucial to the success of a brand. The decisions he or she makes in this role can ultimately make the difference between a brand making it or falling between the cracks.

Additional responsibilities of Brand Managers may include:

- Launching a media blitz for a new brand campaign
- Coordinating public relations activities
- Monitoring and controlling advertising and promotions for the brand

Salaries

Earnings for Brand Managers can vary tremendously, ranging from $35,000 to $150,000 or more. Factors affecting earnings include the size, structure, prestige, and popularity of the specific company for which the Brand Manager works, as well as its geographic location. Other variables affecting earnings include the experience and responsibilities of the individual and his or her level in the organization.

It should be noted that in addition to base salaries, Brand Managers often also receive bonuses for meeting sales quotas as well as increased sales of the brand.

Employment Prospects

Employment prospects are good for qualified individuals seeking positions as Brand Managers. Jobs may be located throughout the country. Individuals may, however, need to relocate for a specific position. Positions are most often available in companies that host multiple brands. These might include companies that manufacture products, as well as those that provide services.

Advancement Prospects

Advancement prospects are good for talented Brand Managers. Those who have proven themselves may move up the corporate career ladder in a number of ways.

Some individuals are promoted to positions within their company, handling larger or more prestigious brands. This generally results in increased responsibilities and earnings. Others climb the career ladder by finding similar positions with larger, more prestigious companies. Still others become corporate marketing directors.

Education and Training

A minimum of a bachelor degree in marketing, advertising, communications, or a related field is required for positions in this area. Many Brand Managers also hold postgraduate degrees. Classes, seminars, and workshops in marketing, market research, branding, advertising, and related areas are helpful for both honing skills and making important contacts.

Experience, Skills, and Personality Traits

In order to become a Brand Manager, individuals need a fair amount of experience in marketing. Depending on the specific job, applicants may also need experience in brand management. There are a lot of brands. Finding ways to get the market share takes a lot of effort and ingenuity. In order to be successful, Brand Managers need to be highly motivated, ambitious individuals. Creativity and innovation are critical. It takes a lot of thinking outside the box to make a brand stand out among other brands.

As the Brand Manager needs to lead his or her team, there is a tremendous amount of communication necessary. Both excellent written and verbal communication skills are essential. The ability to do market research is vital, as is the ability to effectively analyze the results.

Brand Managers should be detail-oriented people with the ability to handle multiple tasks at once. Time management skills, the ability to prioritize tasks, and the ability to meet tight deadlines are critical.

Unions and Associations

Individuals interested in careers in this field might belong to a number of professional or trade associations that provide professional support and guidance. These include the American Marketing Association (AMA), the Direct Marketing Association (DMA), the Marketing Research Association (MRA), and the Advertising Research Foundation (ARF). Brand Managers may also belong to trade associations specific to the corporate area in which they work.

Tips for Entry

1. Corporate Web sites often list job openings. Visit the sites of companies for which you might be

interested in working. (A listing of selected companies can be located in Appendix VIII of this book.)

2. Even if you don't see a job opening, send your résumé and a short cover letter to the human resources department of any company in which you are interested in working. Ask that your résumé be kept on file even if there is no current opening. You can never tell when a job opportunity will occur. If your résumé is there, you might get a call before someone else.

3. Don't forget to surf the net for openings. Start by checking out popular job search sites such as those at www.monster.com, www.hotjobs.com, indeed.com, and simplyhired.com. Then go from there.

4. If you are still in college, either ask your adviser or contact a company yourself regarding internship opportunities. These are valuable for experience, as well as the important contacts you will make.

5. Positions may be advertised in the classified sections of newspapers under headings including "Brand Manager," "Product Manager," "Marketing," "Corporate and Industry," or in specific corporate company advertisements.

6. Contact executive recruiters specializing in executive jobs in marketing and brand management. Make sure you check ahead of time to see who pays the fee when you get the job—you or the employer. Generally, the hiring company pays the fee when they find applicants for jobs.

BUYER

CAREER PROFILE

Duties: Determine which products are best; find suppliers and vendors; negotiate lowest prices; award contracts

Alternate Title(s): Purchasing Professional

Salary Range: $27,000 to $75,000+

Employment Prospects: Good

Advancement Prospects: Good

Best Geographical Location(s) for Position: Jobs may be located throughout the country; large cities will offer more possibilities

Prerequisites:

    Education and Training—College degree preferred

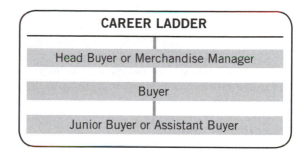

CAREER LADDER

Head Buyer or Merchandise Manager

Buyer

Junior Buyer or Assistant Buyer

Experience—Experience in buying or merchandising

Special Skills and Personality Traits—Self-confidence; leadership; communications skills; organization; ability to foresee trends

Position Description

Every time you walk into a store full of merchandise, you are seeing the work of a Buyer. The Buyer is the individual responsible for choosing the merchandise that is sold in the store. In some stores, especially smaller ones, the owner or manager assumes the responsibilities of the Buyer.

Responsibilities of Buyers can vary depending on the specific employment situation. Buyers may be responsible for buying the merchandise for an entire store or may be responsible for buying for one or more specific departments. A large department store may, for example, have a toy buyer, a women's clothing buyer, and a small appliance buyer. In large chains, Buyers of specific departments often are expected to buy merchandise for all of the chain's stores.

Buyers usually have a number of different vendors to choose from when selecting merchandise. They must evaluate and select vendors or suppliers based on a number of criteria. While price is important, it can not be used solely in choosing suppliers of merchandise. Other factors to be considered when choosing suppliers include the quality of the merchandise, availability, selection, and reliability of the vendor.

One of the Buyers most important functions is finding the correct merchandise. The individual may look for merchandise which is currently in demand as well as predict trends and seek out new merchandise which may be in demand in the future.

Depending on the situation, the individual may look for suppliers and vendors both domestically and inter-

nationally. Buyers find merchandise in a variety of ways. They may meet with vendors to look at merchandise in their own offices or may visit showrooms or factories. Individuals might review listings in catalogs, industry periodicals, directories, and trade journals. Buyers often research the reputation and history of suppliers to assure that they are reliable.

Buyers often must travel a great deal. Individuals may go on buying trips as well as attend meetings, trade shows, and conferences. Individuals also may visit vendors' plants and distribution centers, so they can examine products as well as assess the vendor's production and distribution capabilities.

The Buyer solicits bids from vendors to obtain the best prices for the merchandise. He or she must then price the merchandise so that it sells at the best markup possible. The Buyer must keep abreast of changes affecting the supply and demand for products. If products aren't selling he or she must mark down prices in an effort to move them and improve sales. The bottom line is to keep the store or department as profitable as possible.

Additional duties of Buyers might include:

- Studying sales record and inventory levels of current stock
- Working with the advertising department to create ad campaigns for specific merchandise
- Visiting the selling floor to assure products are displayed properly
- Meeting with sales staff to discuss new merchandise or trends in the marketplace

- Developing good working relationships with vendors
- Overseeing assistant buyers

Salaries

Annual earnings for Buyers can range from approximately $27,000 to $75,000 or more depending on a number of variables. These include the size, prestige, and geographic location of the specific employers as well as the experience, responsibilities, and education of the individual.

Employment Prospects

Employment prospects for Buyers are good. Individuals may find employment in a variety of retail or wholesale outlets throughout the country. These might include large retail organizations, small stores, department stores, specialty stores, or chain stores. The greatest opportunities will exist in areas hosting large numbers of retail and wholesale outlets.

Advancement Prospects

Advancement prospects for Buyers are good. After obtaining experience, Buyers may climb the career ladder by moving to a department managing a larger volume of merchandise resulting in increased responsibilities and earnings. An individual might also become a senior buyer, purchasing manager, or merchandising manager.

Education and Training

Educational requirements vary depending on the specific employer. While there are exceptions, most employers prefer to hire Buyers holding college degrees. Depending on the size of the organization, employers usually prefer to hire individuals with a minimum of an associate's or bachelor's degree.

Good majors for this type of career include business, retailing, merchandising, and marketing, among others. These are useful because many schools with majors in these fields work with employers on internship and placement programs. Once on the job, individuals often go through either formal or informal training programs.

Experience, Skills, and Personality Traits

Generally Buyers begin their careers as trainees, junior buyers, and assistant buyers. Some companies promote qualified employees to assistant buyer positions. Others recruit and train college graduates as assistant buyers. One way or the other, individuals must have experience for this position.

Buyers should be motivated, confident individuals with an interest in merchandising. They should be good at planning and decision making. Good judgment is essential. Successful Buyers need the ability to predict sales trends and anticipate consumer preferences.

Buyers should have good communications skills. The ability to deal with stress and pressure is necessary.

Unions and Associations

Buyers might belong to a number of associations including the American Collegiate Retailing Association (ACRA), American Purchasing Society, Inc. (APS) or the National Association of Purchasing Management, Inc. (NAPM). Individuals might also obtain additional career information from the National Retail Federation (NRF).

Tips for Entry

1. Make sure that you register with the placement office at your college. Retail recruiters often work with these placement offices.
2. Check out the Web sites of stores in which you're interested in working. Many have employment opportunities on the site.
3. Jobs can often be located on-line too. Look at some of the major sites such as www.hotjobs.com and www.monster.com. Then surf the net for career sites specific to the retail industry.
4. Positions are often advertised in the classified sections of newspapers under headings including "Retail Opportunities," "Retail," "Buyer," and "Purchasing Professional."

ASSISTANT BUYER

CAREER PROFILE

Duties: Assist buyer in determining which products are best; handle clerical duties; help buyer in locating suppliers and vendors; handle customer service

Alternate Title(s): Junior Buyer

Salary Range: $24,000 to $32,000+

Employment Prospects: Good

Advancement Prospects: Good

Best Geographical Location(s) for Position: Jobs may be located throughout the country; large cities will offer more possibilities

Prerequisites:

Education and Training—College degree and/or executive training program

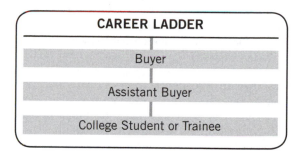

CAREER LADDER

Buyer

↑

Assistant Buyer

↑

College Student or Trainee

Experience—Experience requirements vary; see text

Special Skills and Personality Traits—Clerical skills; leadership; self-confidence; communication skills; organization; ability to foresee trends

Position Description

The job of buyers can be tremendous. Generally, they have one or more Assistant Buyers to help them handle their responsibilities. The Assistant Buyer may have varied depending on the specific employer and the structure of the company.

One of the best things about a job as an Assistant Buyer is the opportunity for the individual to watch the buyer do his or her job. From this experience, the Assistant learns the ropes. The individual starts out handling routine functions. He or she might, for example handle records and do clerical work. As part of that function, the Assistant might check that orders go out and verify that shipments come in.

As the individual gains more experience, he or she will be assigned projects with more responsibilities. The buyer may ask the Assistant to write special orders or reorders of merchandise which is selling well. As part of the job, the individual might also check on stock and keep the buyer appraised of the status of that stock. If something is selling particularly well, the Assistant must alert the buyer so more can be ordered. On the other hand, if something isn't moving, an alert by the Assistant can help the buyer decide to do price markdowns so the merchandise moves.

Gradually, the Assistant will learn more about dealing with vendors. He or she might sit in on meetings with vendors or accompany the Buyer on buying trips. The individual may also attend other meetings, trade shows, and conferences as well as visit vendors' plants and distribution centers. In this manner he or she can learn about examining products as well as assessing the vendor's production and distribution capabilities. It's essential at this point that the Assistant become familiar with consumer trends so he or she will begin to understand what types of merchandise will sell and what won't.

Depending on the situation, the Assistant may work with a buyer responsible for the merchandise for an entire store or may work with a buyer responsible for one or more specific departments. An individual working in a large department store may, for example, work as the assistant toy buyer, assistant children's clothing buyer, or assistant domestics buyer.

Sometimes the difference between merchandise selling and not selling is the way it is presented. Assistant Buyers often work closely with the store's salespeople to make sure merchandise is displayed attractively. Individuals may help the sales staff choose which merchandise should be presented in windows or on wall or stand-alone displays.

Additional duties of Assistant Buyers might include:

- Studying sales record and inventory levels of current stock to see what is selling and what is not
- Handling special orders for customers
- Visiting the selling floor to assure products are displayed properly
- Overseeing inventory counts

Salaries

Annual earnings for Assistant Buyers can range from approximately $24,000 to $32,000 or more depending on a number of variables. These include the size, prestige, and geographic location of the specific employer as well as the experience, responsibilities, and education of the individual.

Employment Prospects

Employment prospects for Assistant Buyers are good. Individuals may find employment in a variety of retail or wholesale outlets throughout the country. These might include large retail organizations, small stores, department stores, specialty stores, or chain stores. The greatest opportunities will exist in areas hosting large numbers of retail and wholesale outlets.

Advancement Prospects

Advancement prospects are good for motivated individuals. After obtaining experience, Assistant Buyers may climb the career ladder by becoming full-fledged buyers.

Education and Training

Educational requirements vary depending on the specific employer. While there are exceptions, most employers prefer to hire Assistant Buyers holding college degrees. Based on the size or the organization, employers usually prefer to hire individuals with a minimum of an associate's or bachelor's degree.

Appropriate majors for this type of career include business, retailing, merchandising, and marketing. These are useful because many schools with majors in these fields work with employers on internships and placement programs. Generally, once on the job, individuals go through either formal or informal training programs.

Experience, Skills, and Personality Traits

Assistant Buyers often start their careers on the sales floor. Many individuals have been recruited from colleges.

Assistant Buyers should be eager to learn. Individuals need to be motivated and confident with an interest in merchandising. Clerical skills are often necessary when assisting the buyer. Good communications skills are essential, as is the ability to deal with stress and pressure.

Unions and Associations

Assistant buyers might belong to a number of associations including the American Collegiate Retailing Association (ACRA), American Purchasing Society, Inc. (APS) or the National Association of Purchasing Management, Inc. (NAPM). Individuals might also obtain additional career information from the National Retail Federation (NRF).

Tips for Entry

1. Contact stores you are interested in working at to find out if they offer executive training programs.
2. Make sure that you register with the placement office at your college. Retail recruiters often work with these placement offices.
3. Check out the Web sites of stores where you're interested in working. Many have employment opportunities on the site.
4. Jobs can often be located on-line too. Look at some of the major sites such as www.hotjobs.com.
5. Positions are often advertised in the classified sections of newspapers under headings including "Retail Opportunities," "Retail," "Assistant Buyer," and "Junior Buyer."
6. Contact executive recruiters specializing in the retail industry. Make sure you check ahead of time to see who pays the fee when you get the job—you or the employer.

ADVERTISING DIRECTOR— RETAIL STORE

Position Description

In any given area, there are an array of stores from which customers can choose to shop. In order to attract potential shoppers, most retail stores advertise in some manner. The individual responsible for the advertising is called the Advertising Director.

Retail stores utilize advertising for a number of reasons. It helps people learn what a specific store carries. Advertising also lets customers know when products are on sale. Additionally, advertising helps put the name of a store in the public's mind and eye.

A retail store can carry just the right product that everyone wants at a lower price than their competitors. However, if no one knows it's available and few people are familiar with the store, the product will not sell. One of the functions of the Advertising Director is making sure this doesn't happen.

The Advertising Director plans, develops, and implements the advertising campaigns and individual ads for the store. Those working in the corporate offices of retail chains will be responsible for handling the advertising for the entire chain.

In smaller stores the Advertising Director may work alone or with the help of an assistant and perhaps a graphic designer. In larger stores or in the corporate office, the Advertising Director will work with a staff.

This might include an assistant advertising director, advertising assistants, graphic artists, art directors, copywriters, or producers.

The Advertising Director works closely with the store's marketing director. Together they plan the direction of the store's marketing and advertising campaigns.

The Advertising Director develops and plans the store's annual advertising budget. Depending on the store or chain, this may encompass weekly sales flyers, inserts in newspapers, print ads in newspapers and magazines, radio and television commercials, and billboards. Advertising may also include promotions, promotional merchandise, and other items used to draw attention to the store and its merchandise.

Today, many retail stores advertise on the World Wide Web utilizing banner ads and other advertisements. Additionally, many traditional retail stores now also have on-line stores. The Advertising Director must be able to advertise both effectively.

The Advertising Director must develop ad campaigns and single ads which are memorable and effective. Many stores such as K-Mart, Wal-Mart, and Target have continuing advertising themes carried through in their print, television, and Internet ads. This helps keep the name of the store in the public's mind. In many circumstances, the individual will develop ads and campaigns for the entire year. These may include advertising for holidays, promotions, special events, and sales programs.

Most stores feel that as long as they have people walking through and browsing, they will have shoppers. While these people may not make immediate purchases, they may buy at a later date. The Advertising Director works with the marketing, promotional, and public relations departments to develop ads and campaigns that will help make as many people as possible aware of what the store offers.

Depending on the size and structure of the specific retail store, the Advertising Director may be required to do copywriting, graphics, layout, and production for advertisements and commercials or may work with copywriters, graphic artists, and producers. He or she might also lay out rough ideas for advertisements and have the publication's or broadcast station's advertising department put the ad together. In some instances, the Advertising Director may also work with advertising agencies that handle some of these functions.

As part of the job, the Advertising Director is expected to decide what media to place ads in or on, specific sections of publications to have ads inserted and when to schedule broadcast commercials. He or she is responsible for making sure all advertisements and commercials have accurate copy and graphics and are mailed or delivered to the correct media before deadline.

Additional duties of the Advertising Directors may include:

- Developing and putting together weekly advertising flyers
- Tracking tear sheets, clippings, visual cuts, and audiotapes
- Checking bills for ad placement and authorizing payment
- Advertising special events and promotions store is hosting
- Working on cooperative ads or billboards with malls in which their stores are located

Salaries

Salaries for Advertising Directors can range from approximately $26,000 to $75,000 or more annually. Factors affecting earnings include the size and prestige of the specific store, as well as its geographic location. Other factors include the store's advertising budget and whether the individual is responsible for the advertising for one store or an entire retail chain. Other variables include the responsibilities, experience, and education of the individual.

In addition to a salary, some Advertising Directors also receive bonuses when there are sales increases in given sales periods.

Employment Prospects

Employment prospects are fair for Advertising Directors. Individuals may find employment throughout the country in a variety of retail outlets. These include small, midsized, and large stores, chain and department stores, supermarkets, convenience stores, and more.

Advancement Prospects

Retail Advertising Directors may climb the career ladder in a number of ways. Some individuals find similar positions in larger or more prestigious stores. Others may become directors of retail marketing. Still others may be promoted to the vice president of Advertising. There are also individuals who find positions in advertising agencies or become advertising directors in other industries.

Education and Training

Most employers require or prefer their Advertising Directors hold a minimum of a four-year college degree. Good choices for majors include advertising, business, journalism, public relations, retail, marketing, liberal arts, English, communications, and business.

Courses and seminars in advertising, copywriting, business, or retail management are also helpful.

Experience, Skills, and Personality Traits

Retail Advertising Directors should be creative people with an understanding of both advertising and the retail industry. Individuals are often asked to show their portfolio of ads and campaigns prior to being hired. These are used to illustrate talent to potential employers.

Advertising Directors working in retail need the ability to communicate well, both verbally and on paper. Experience working in advertising in the retail industry is usually required.

Individuals need the knowledge to develop both single ads and entire advertising campaigns which are successful and effective. The ability to work on multiple projects at one time and meet deadlines is essential.

Unions and Associations

Retail Advertising Directors may belong to a number of trade associations providing support and guidance.

These may include the American Advertising Federation (AAF), the Business/Professional Advertising Association (B/PAA) and the American Marketing Association (AMA). Individuals interested in this type of career might also contact the National Retail Federation (NRF) and the American Collegiate Retailing Association (ACRA) for additional information.

Tips for Entry

1. Join trade associations and attend their meetings and conventions. These are invaluable sources of information and networking opportunities.
2. Positions are often advertised in the classified sections of newspapers. Keep in mind the Sunday paper usually has the largest classified section. Look under headings including "Advertising," "Marketing," "Advertising Director," or "Retail Opportunities." Stores also often advertise a number of opportunities in a boxed classified ad.
3. Send your resume and a cover letter to specific retail stores as well as to their corporate offices. Ask that your resume be kept on file.
4. Larger chain stores often offer internship or summer jobs as assistants. Contact both stores in your area and corporate offices of chains to check into the possibilities.
5. Take seminars and courses in advertising, promotion, public relations, marketing, and publicity.
6. A good way to gain experience in advertising is to work in the advertising department of a local newspaper, magazine, or television or radio station.
7. Start working on your portfolio now. Make it diverse and full of your best work. As noted, a good portfolio can get you a job.

DIRECTOR OF REAL ESTATE—STORE

Duties: Find properties to locate stores; visit properties and sites to make appraisals and evaluations; do selections of stores within shopping centers; negotiate business terms and conditions

Alternate Title(s): Real Estate Director; Leasing Director

Salary Range: $37,000 to $150,000+

Employment Prospects: Fair

Advancement Prospects: Fair

Best Geographical Location(s) for Position: Jobs may be located throughout the country

Prerequisites:

Education and Training—Educational requirements vary

Experience—Experience working in real estate and leasing necessary

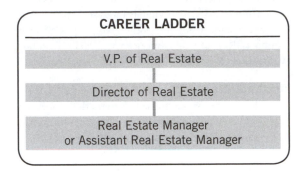

CAREER LADDER

V.P. of Real Estate

Director of Real Estate

Real Estate Manager
or Assistant Real Estate Manager

Special Skills and Personality Traits—Negotiating skills; problem solving skills; communications skills; ability to deal well with people; assertive

Special Requirements—Real Estate or Real Estate Brokers license may be required.

Position Description

There are many places retail stores can be located. These include indoor malls and shopping centers, outdoor strip centers, stand alone stores, and more. Many retail stores, most notably chains, employ Directors of Real Estate. These individuals, also known as leasing directors, are the people who are responsible for finding just the right locations for retail stores.

Within the scope of the job, the Director of Real Estate may have varied duties. His or her main function is to find the perfect location for the retail chain's stores. Depending on the size and structure of the real estate department, the individual may be assisted by one or more managers, assistants, and other staff members.

The Director of Real Estate is often contacted by the corporate office when they determine that they are interested in opening new stores in one or more geographic areas. The individual may also be responsible for scouting out new locations where stores might be viable. In some situations a leasing director from a mall may contact the store's Director of Real Estate.

The Director of Real Estate is expected to do extensive research on various locations. He or she often must go to look at properties and sites. The individual may visit malls or other centers to make an evaluation.

The Director of Real Estate may check out things such as the foot traffic, the condition of the mall, and how the management company cares for the property.

While at a mall, the Director of Real Estate may stop into mall stores and listen to comments by customers or employees. All this information helps him or her make an informed decision about the viability of a property for a new store.

Once the decision has been made that a store would be viable in a mall, the real estate director is responsible for selecting the specific store within the center.

The Director of Real Estate may contact mall leasing directors or real estate agents representing available properties, or management companies to find out about rents, other charges, and availabilities. The individual may ask for leasing packages or may set up meetings to discuss pertinent information. The real estate director may also visit the various locations to see the physical spaces.

Sometimes the Director of Real Estate may be contacted by malls which are interested in having the Director's stores in the mall. The Director of Real Estate may meet with mall management or other real estate people a number of times before a lease is signed. He or she may ask to see sales figures of other stores, foot traffic reports, or advertising budgets.

The Director of Real Estate negotiates leases. The business terms of the lease may include rents, taxes, CAM (common area maintenance) charges, advertising charges, preparation of the space, length of the lease, options, and kick-out clauses. (A kick-out clause is a clause in a lease whereby a tenant may leave without penalty if certain conditions are not met. For example, not meeting a specified amount of sales.) The director is expected to make the best deal possible for the store.

The individual may also negotiate for any necessary construction costs before the store can move in. This is especially important with chain stores which often have similar layouts in every location.

The Director of Real Estate must keep track of when leases are up for all his or her stores. In this way the individual can handle renewals or exercise any options available according to the lease agreement.

There is a great deal of paperwork in this job. The Director of Real Estate must keep immaculate records. He or she must make sure leases incorporate all negotiated points. The individual must also be sure all leases are executed and signed by all parties.

Additional duties of the Director of Real Estate for retail stores might include:

- Handling lease administration
- Working with real estate agents
- Dealing with mall management or landlords regarding problems in the mall or on the property
- Attending conventions and other leasing events

Salaries

Real estate directors working in retail stores and chains can earn between $37,000 and $150,000 or more. The tremendous range is dependent on a number of factors. Variables affecting earnings include the size, prestige, and geographic location of the property and number of properties the individual is responsible for leasing. Other variables include the experience, responsibilities, and education of the individual.

Employment Prospects

Employment prospects are fair for Directors of Real Estate in a retail chain environment. Individuals may find employment in the corporate offices of a variety of chain and other retail stores. These might include drug stores, department stores, supermarkets, clothing stores, furniture stores, or toy stores.

While jobs may be located throughout the country, individuals may need to relocate for specific positions.

Advancement Prospects

The most common method of career advancement for Directors of Real Estate is to find similar positions in larger, more prestigious companies. Another way an individual may climb the career ladder is to land a position as a vice president of real estate in the retail company. Many Directors of Real Estate strike out on their own and become leasing consultants or form their own leasing companies.

Education and Training

Educational requirements for Directors of Real Estate vary from store to store. Most retail chains today prefer individuals have a college background and degree. There are individuals in this position who hold law degrees or have majors in accounting, retail management, business, marketing, real estate, public administration, finance, liberal arts, or related fields.

While experience is the best teacher, many employers also prefer that individuals have some sort of real estate training. Others require it. Most positions will also prefer or require the Director of Real Estate to hold a real estate agent or broker's license. In order to obtain this licensing, individuals must usually take and pass a written test as well as go through at least 30 hours of classroom instruction to become an agent or 90 hours of training to become a broker.

Professional and trade associations often offer helpful seminars and courses in all aspects of real estate.

Special Requirements

As noted previously many employers prefer or require individuals in this position to either hold a real estate license or real estate broker's license.

Experience, Skills, and Personality Traits

The Director of Real Estate needs a great deal of experience for this position. Many individuals started out in real estate first as salespeople and then as brokers. Others have gone through training programs in retail environments. Some started out as assistant leasing administrators and obtained experience moving up the ranks.

Directors of Real Estate need to be highly motivated, energetic individuals. They should be pleasantly aggressive with the ability to deal with and work well with others. Individuals need to be good problem solvers and negotiators.

Unions and Associations

Directors of Real Estate working in retail chains may be members of a number of associations providing career guidance and support. These include the National Association of Realtors (NAR), local state real estate associations, the Outlet Retail Manufacturers Association (ORMA), the International Council of Shopping Centers (ICSC) and the Institute of Real Estate Management (IREM).

Tips for Entry

1. Many large chain stores offer internship and training programs in this area.
2. There are a number of executive search firms dealing exclusively with jobs in retail.
3. Send your resume and a cover letter to the corporate offices of large chain stores.
4. Positions are often advertised in the classified sections of newspapers. Look under classifications including "Leasing Director," or "Store Leasing Director," or "Retail Leasing Director," "Director of Leasing," or "Real Estate Director-Retail."
5. Openings are also advertised in trade journals.
6. Jobs in this field may be located on-line. Begin your search on some of the more popular job search sites such as the Monster board (www.monster.com) and Yahoo! HotJobs (www.hotjobs.com).

CASHIER

Duties: Take payment from customers for purchases; ring up sales; complete credit card transactions; give change to customers

Alternate Title(s): Clerk

Salary Range: $7.00 to $10.00+ per hour

Employment Prospects: Excellent

Advancement Prospects: Excellent

Best Geographical Location(s) for Position: Jobs may be located throughout the country

Prerequisites:

Education and Training—On-the-job training

Experience—Experience requirements vary

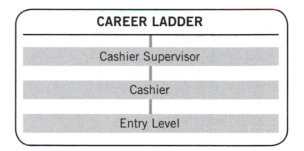

CAREER LADDER

Cashier Supervisor

Cashier

Entry Level

Special Skills and Personality Traits—Ability to use cash register; basic math skills; people skills; communications skills; good moral character

Position Description

Cashiers are the individuals responsible for taking the payment from customers for their purchases. Within the scope of the job, Cashiers may perform varied duties.

After customers choose the items they are interested in purchasing they bring them to a Cashier. The individual is expected to ring up the merchandise. This may be done in a variety of ways depending on the situation. Cashiers in grocery stores, for example, might scan the selected items over a special scanning device. Those working in other stores may scan the pricing label or manually punch in prices on a cash register. In some situations, the Cashier may ring up a price from a sales slip prepared by a salesperson. In performing this function, the individual may need to punch in certain codes to make sure correct taxes are charged.

After the Cashier rings up the customer's purchases, he or she informs the customer the amount that is due. The customer may pay the amount due in a number of different methods. These include cash, check, or a credit card.

If the customer chooses to pay in cash, the Cashier must make sure he or she gives the individual the correct amount of change. In the event the customer is paying by check, the Cashier is expected to follow the correct procedures. For example, the individual may need to take down identifying information from the customer's license or may need to get approval from a supervisor for accepting the check.

Many people pay with credit cards or debit cards. In these cases, the Cashier must complete the transac-

tions according to procedures. This may include getting approval from the credit card company for putting through the charge. The Cashier must also be sure the customer signs the credit card slip and that he or she gets a copy of the transaction.

At the end of his or her shift, the individual compares the totals on the cash register with the amount of currency in the register to verify balances. In doing this, he or she must take into account checks and charge slips.

Additional duties of the Cashiers may include:

- Processing refunds
- Taking layaways
- Performing the duties of a salesperson
- Packing merchandise

Salaries

Earnings for Cashiers working in retail environments can range from approximately $7.00 to $10.00 or more per hour. Variables affecting earnings include the geographic location, size, and prestige of the store as well as the experience and responsibilities of the individual. Earnings for Cashiers are also dependent on the demand for employees in a given area.

Employment Prospects

Employment prospects are excellent for Cashiers. Individuals may find work throughout the country in a variety of retail situations including department stores, convenience stores, grocery stores, boutiques, and stores selling every conceivable type of merchandise.

One of the perks for many people seeking this job is the flexibility of working hours. Individuals may work full time, part time, mornings, afternoons, evenings, weekdays, weekends, or holidays.

Advancement Prospects

Advancement prospects for Cashiers depend to a great extent on the individual's career aspirations. Some people take jobs as Cashiers while in school or on a part-time basis to augment other incomes. These individuals usually move on to other types of jobs depending on their training. Others interested in a full-time career in retail, may start out as Cashiers and move into sales positions or cashier supervisors.

Education and Training

Generally, Cashiers are trained on the job. Individuals will learn how to run cash registers and use charge card systems. Most employers prefer people who have a minimum of a high school diploma.

Experience, Skills, and Personality Traits

There are many entry-level positions available as Cashiers as well as those for experienced people. Individuals must have basic math skills with the ability to make change correctly. The ability to handle large sums of money is mandatory. Good interpersonal and customer relations skills are essential as is a pleasant personality. Cashiers are on their feet a good portion of the workday.

Unions and Associations

Cashiers may get additional career information by contacting the National Retail Federation (NRF). Depending on the place of the employment and the specific type of store, Cashiers may be members of unions.

Tips for Entry

1. There is a great deal of turnover in these positions. Stop in stores in which you are interested in working and ask to fill out applications.
2. Openings may be posted in store windows. Look for announcements stating "Cashier Wanted."
3. Jobs may be advertised in the classified sections of newspapers. Look under classifications such as "Cashiers," "Retail Opportunities," "Department Stores," or "Grocery Stores."
4. Remember to bring with you the names, addresses, and phone numbers of a few people you can use as references when filling out applications. Make sure you ask people if you can use them as references BEFORE you use them.
5. Stores often call local labor offices to post these jobs. Remember to stop by your state employment office.

TAILOR—CLOTHING STORE, DEPARTMENT STORE/BOUTIQUE

CAREER PROFILE

Duties: Alter clothing purchased in store to fit individual customers

Alternate Title(s): Seamstress; Alteration Tailor

Salary Range: $24,000 to $55,000+

Employment Prospects: Good

Advancement Prospects: Good

Best Geographical Location(s) for Position: Positions located throughout the country

Prerequisites:

Education and Training—Training requirements vary; see text

Experience and Qualifications—Experience in tailoring, dressmaking, sewing

Special Skills and Personality Traits—Fitting skills; tailoring skills; alteration skills; hand-sewing skills; machine-sewing skills; customer service skills; pleasant; communication skills

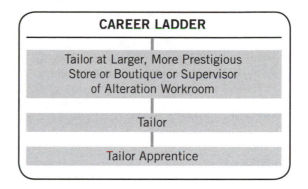

CAREER LADDER

Tailor at Larger, More Prestigious Store or Boutique or Supervisor of Alteration Workroom

Tailor

Tailor Apprentice

Position Description

Off-the-rack clothing often does not fit every body perfectly. Sometimes parts of an article of clothing may be too big, too small, too long, too short, or too tight. While there are some people who alter their own clothing and others who may use tailors off-site, many people prefer their clothing to fit correctly when they take it home from a store after a purchase. To handle this function, stores often employ Tailors.

An on-site Tailor is a customer service many customers appreciate. Tailors are coveted employees. A talented on-site Tailor can mean the difference between a customer shopping at one store or shopping at another with similar merchandise. Depending on the store, the service may be offered for a fee or free of charge to customers purchasing the store's clothing.

The main function of Tailors employed by stores is to alter clothing purchased at the store to fit the individual customer. When a customer decides to purchase an item, he or she will either go to the Tailor's office or the Tailor will go to the dressing room. He or she will then have the customer try on the garment. The Tailor may be asked perform a variety of alterations depending on what is needed and what the customer wants done.

For example, a woman may be purchasing a suit and need the skirt shortened and tapered, and the jacket's sleeves shortened. A man purchasing a suit may need the pants hemmed and buttons moved on the jacket. Individuals may need waistlines expanded or narrowed, collars or shoulders raised or lowered, or buttons changed.

Sometimes alterations are simple. Often they may be more complex. The Tailor must be capable of handling both. Some alterations are done using hand sewing. Others may be accomplished better by machines.

Once the individuals try on the articles of clothing, the Tailor will mark the alterations needed with tailor's chalk and pins. He or she may need to remove stitching from clothing by using a seam ripper or razor. In many instances, the individual will need to cut excess fabric, make the alterations, and resew the garment making sure the drape, style, and proportions are maintained.

A good Tailor knows and uses correct pressing techniques to finish his or her work. In this manner, the garment will appear fresh and finished. In some cases, the Tailor may work with an apprentice, supervising his or her work.

Customers may have an idea of what they want done or may ask the advice of the Tailor. Some people like things looser or tighter. The individual must be able to be communicate with customers so they know what the customer is looking for in fit. It is essential that the customer be pleased when the garment is done.

Other duties of on-site Tailors include:

- Repairing defective garments
- Repairing garments altered by people trying them on
- Replacing buttons or zippers
- Shortening or pressing drapes or other household accessories sold in the store
- Creating headpieces or accessories to go with clothing

Salaries

Salaries for Tailors can vary greatly. Full-time Tailors may have annual earnings ranging from $24,000 to $55,000 or more. Factors affecting earnings include the specific store size, prestige, and geographic location in which the individual is working. Other variables include the experience, responsibilities, and talent of the Tailor. If the individual is in an area with a shortage of Tailors, he or she can also command a higher salary.

In some stores, individuals may be paid a base salary plus a commission on fees charged to customers for tailoring.

Employment Prospects

Employment prospects are good for Tailors. The need for talented Tailors is greater than the number of qualified people available to handle the jobs. Individuals may find employment throughout the country both full time or part time.

Possible employment includes department stores, specialty clothing stores, and boutiques for men and women.

Advancement Prospects

Tailors generally climb the career ladder by locating similar positions at either larger, more exclusive, or more prestigious stores. Some Tailors advance their careers by becoming supervisors of alteration workrooms in large stores. Still others strike out on their own.

Education and Training

Many Tailors are self-taught. Others have attended classes, courses, and workshops or have gone through certificate programs in tailoring from vocational-technical schools. Some Tailors apprentice with experienced Tailors to learn the tricks of the trade. As a rule, if an individual can prove he or she can handle the job skillfully, there are no education or training requirements.

Experience, Skills, and Personality Traits

Tailors need experience handling a variety of alterations. No retail store wants a Tailor coming in and ruining an article of clothing a customer has purchased.

Tailors need a full working knowledge of hand- and machine-sewing techniques. They must be experts at tailoring, fitting techniques, and alterations. Customer service skills and communications skills are essential.

Unions and Associations

Those interested in learning more about careers as Tailors can obtain information from the National Retail Federation (NRF).

Tips for Entry

1. Try to find an experienced Tailor with whom you can apprentice. This will give you the best experience.
2. Jobs are often advertised in the classified sections of newspapers. Look under classifications such as "Retail," "Retail Opportunities," "Tailor," or "Seamstress."
3. Take as many classes, workshops, and seminars as you can. Each one will give you the opportunity to learn a new technique.
4. Contact the human resources manager of department stores to find if you can fill out an employment application. Ask that your application be kept on file. Check back frequently.
5. Don't forget to check out boutiques, men's clothing stores, wedding boutiques, and specialty stores for job possibilities.
6. Look for help wanted signs in store windows.
7. Check out opportunities online. Many stores put openings on their Web site. You might also find openings on job sites such as those at www.hotjobs.com or www.monster.com

BILLING MANAGER—DEPARTMENT OR SPECIALTY STORE

CAREER PROFILE

Duties: Oversee billing department; supervise billing clerks; look into errors and discrepancies on customer bills; handle customer service

Alternate Title(s): Billing Supervisor

Salary Range: $26,000 to $47,000+

Employment Prospects: Fair

Advancement Prospects: Fair

Best Geographical Location(s) for Position: Jobs may be located throughout the country; areas hosting many large department stores will offer more opportunities

Prerequisites:

Education and Training—Training requirements vary

Experience—Experience working in retail billing office necessary

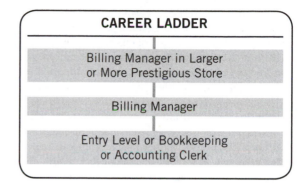

CAREER LADDER

Billing Manager in Larger
or More Prestigious Store

Billing Manager

Entry Level or Bookkeeping
or Accounting Clerk

Special Skills and Personality Traits—Aptitude for numbers; orderly; detail oriented; office skills; computer skills; communication skills; good judgment; customer relations skills

Position Description

Depending on a store's policies there are a number of methods customers can use to pay for merchandise. These include cash, checks, major credit cards, and store charge cards among others. Stores that have their own charge cards or allow customers to charge merchandise usually employ a Billing Manager.

When customers use store credit cards, they sign a slip promising to pay for their purchases. Some stores may not utilize store credit cards for charges. Instead, customers may just sign charge slips when making a purchase. Whatever the method of charges, the store must keep track of customer purchases and monies owed.

The Billing Manager has a number of different responsibilities depending on the size and structure of the store and the setup of the billing department. His or her main function is to oversee the billing department.

The Billing Manager coordinates and supervises the activities of the other employees in the department. These may include an assistant billing manager or supervisor, billing clerks, and sometimes credit clerks.

The Billing Manager trains each employee so he or she can accomplish assigned tasks. Today, most billing statements are computer generated. Some stores also utilize billing machines or special billing software to help prepare monthly statements. The individual may show employees how to run computer or billing machines as well as explain how to use the software effectively.

The Billing Manager must make sure billing clerks fully understand everything about monthly statements. This includes purchases, late charges, finance charges, and unpaid balances. It also includes customer discounts and credits of payments previously made. In some stores there are special codes for each charge. The Manager also must be sure the staff knows what each of these codes represents. This is essential when customers call to complain about errors on a bill. Sometimes there truly is an error. Other times, the customer may not understand how to read the monthly statement.

The Billing Manager assists billing clerks when they can not fully explain statements to customers. He or she is also called in when dealing with angry or irate customers. The Billing Manager often has the authority to take off a late charge or a finance charge on a customer's bill. He or she is always trying to find ways to keep the customer satisfied.

The Billing Manager is responsible for setting the tone for customer service in the billing department. It is essential to a store's success for everyone working there to make a customer feel that he or she is appreciated. This is especially important in the billing department where customers usually call when there is a problem. The Manager tries to teach the staff how to maintain a good relationship with each customer.

In some stores, the Billing Manager may be expected to supervise the monitoring of customers' payments to make sure they are updated. In other stores, this may be handled by the collection department.

Other duties of the Billing Manager may include:

- Writing letters and other correspondence regarding customers' bills
- Answering customers' questions regarding billings
- Developing policies for the billing department
- Recommending salary increases for department employees
- Recommending termination of employees

Salaries

Annual earnings for Billing Managers working in retail stores can range from approximately $26,000 to $47,000 or more. Variables affecting earnings include the geographic location, size, and prestige of the specific store as well as the experience, education, and responsibilities of the individual.

Employment Prospects

Employment prospects are fair for Billing Managers. Individuals may find jobs in both larger department stores and smaller local stores throughout the country.

Advancement Prospects

Billing Managers working in retail environments can climb the career ladder by landing similar jobs in larger or more prestigious stores. This results in increased responsibilities and earnings.

Education and Training

Educational requirements vary. Some stores require or prefer their Billing Managers to hold a college degree or at least have some college background. Other stores may hire individuals with a minimum of a high school diploma if they have experience and can illustrate that they can handle the job effectively.

Courses in bookkeeping, accounting, computers, and accounting software are helpful.

Experience, Skills, and Personality Traits

Billing Managers should like working with numbers. The ability to solve problems is needed. Individuals should be organized and detail oriented. Customer service skills and the ability to calm irate customers is necessary. Supervisory and leadership skills are also needed.

Unions and Associations

Billing Managers interested in working in retail environment may get additional career information by contacting the National Retail Federation (NRF).

Tips for Entry

1. Jobs may be advertised in the classified sections of newspapers. Look under headings such as "Billing Manager," "Retail Opportunities," "Billing Department," "Billing Supervisor," and "Department Store Opportunities." Positions may also be located in the ads of specific stores.
2. Visit the human resources office of larger stores to fill out an application. In smaller stores, ask to see the manager. Ask that your application be kept on file if there are no current openings.
3. Many larger chain stores have internship and training programs. Contact the corporate offices to find out about opportunities.
4. Department stores often promote from within. Get your foot in the door in the billing department, learn what you can, and climb the career ladder.
5. Check out store Web sites. Many post openings on their site.

BILLING CLERK—DEPARTMENT STORE OR SPECIALTY STORE

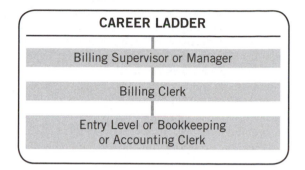

Position Description

Stores make money by selling merchandise to customers. Some customers pay for purchases using cash or checks. Others pay with major credit cards. Many stores also have their own credit cards.

Customers who use these store credit cards may receive special promotions or other considerations. When customers use store credit cards, the store keeps track of purchases. They then send bills to customers. Depending on the store and its structure, bills might be sent monthly or bimonthly.

Billing Clerks work in the billing department. The main function of these individuals is to produce the bills that are used to settle customers' accounts. Billing Clerks take information regarding the customer's purchases and input it into a computer system. They do this by reviewing charge slips to calculate the total amount due from a customer.

Today, most bills are computer generated. Many stores also utilize billing machines or special billing software to help Billing Clerks prepare monthly statements.

Billing Clerks must input information into the computer or billing machine. The individual must be sure the customer's name, address, and account number is correct. In addition to charges for purchases, there may be additional charges. These might include unpaid balances, late charges, and finance charges. Discounts and credits may also be added.

Once bills are prepared, they are printed out. At this point, the Billing Clerk often verifies them for accuracy. The individual is then responsible for sending them to the customer.

Even if bills are computer generated and checked for errors, there may be mistakes. When customers get bills they feel are wrong, they often become angry or irate and call the store to complain. The Billing Clerk is then responsible for checking the bill, trying to find the errors, and preparing a corrected bill. It is essential that the individual practice good customer service skills when speaking to unhappy customers so they feel they are important to the store.

Often the mistake is not a mistake at all. Instead, the customer may be upset about a bill carrying a finance charge he or she does not feel should be included. Perhaps the bill was held up in the mail or the customer forgot to make a payment. Whatever the situation, the Clerk tries to maintain a good relationship with the customer. He or she may, for example, take off the finance charge from a customer's bill or may refer the individual to the billing manager.

In some stores, the Billing Clerk may be expected to monitor customers' payments to make sure they are up to date. If they aren't, the individual may be required to call customers and issue a friendly reminder. In other stores, this may be handled by the collection department.

Many stores have codes for various categories on bills. For example, there may be one code for charges in the men's department, another for charges in the children's department, one for late charges, and yet another for finance charges. The Billing Clerk must be familiar with the codes and have the ability to explain them to customers.

Often customers may call the billing department because they don't understand their bill. Billing Clerks must be able to explain the bills to customers in an easy-to-understand manner.

Other duties of department store Billing Clerks may include:

- Printing out monthly billing and payment reports
- Writing letters and other correspondence regarding customers bills
- Answering customers' questions regarding billings

Salaries

Earnings for Billing Clerks working in retail stores can range from approximately $7.50 to $25.00 or more per hour. Variables affecting earnings include the geographic location, size, and prestige of the specific store as well as the experience and responsibilities of the individual.

One of the perks for individuals working in stores is that individuals often receive employee discounts.

Employment Prospects

Employment prospects are fair for individuals seeking this position. Jobs may be located in both larger department stores and smaller local stores throughout the country. Depending on the size and structure of the store, there may be one or more Billing Clerks on staff. Individuals may work full or part time.

Advancement Prospects

Billing Clerks working in retail may advance their career in a number of ways. After obtaining experience, individuals may take on additional duties or find similar positions in larger, more prestigious stores. Others may be promoted to billing managers.

Education and Training

Billing Clerks generally must hold a minimum of a high school diploma or the equivalent. Many larger department stores may prefer a college background or some business courses, but don't require it. Classes in bookkeeping, accounting, computers, and accounting software are helpful.

In some situations, the store will provide in-service training in the use of software programs or specific billing procedures used.

Experience, Skills, and Personality Traits

Billing Clerks should have a strong aptitude for numbers. Individuals need to be careful, orderly, and detail oriented. They should be comfortable using computers. There is often a lot of customer contact in this job. The ability to deal well with people is essential. Customer service skills are mandatory.

Unions and Associations

Billing Clerks interested in working in retail environment may get additional career information by contacting the National Retail Federation (NRF). Those working in department stores may belong to house unions.

Tips for Entry

1. Courses and workshops in billing, accounting, and bookkeeping techniques as well as billing software are helpful in making you more marketable.
2. Jobs may be advertised in the classified sections of newspapers. Look under classifications such as "Billing Clerk," "Department Store," "Billing Office," and "Retail Opportunities."
3. Visit the human resources office of larger stores to fill out an application. In smaller stores, ask to see the manager. Ask that your application be kept on file if there are no current openings.
4. Remember to bring with you the names, addresses, and phone numbers of a few people you can use as references when filling out applications. Make sure you ask people if you can use them as references BEFORE you use them.
5. Stores often call local labor offices to post these jobs. Remember to stop by your state employment office.

WINDOW DRESSER

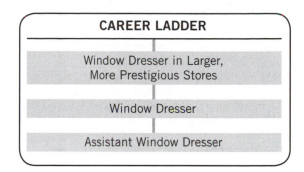

Special Skills and Personality Traits—Creative; artistic; sense of color and style; good aesthetic judgment

Position Description

People often wait with anticipation to see how well-known stores are going to decorate their windows for holiday seasons. Stores such as Saks Fifth Avenue and Bloomingdale's in New York City, for example, may have lines of people waiting to see annual holiday displays. Display windows may showcase products sold in stores as well as attract the attention of potential shoppers.

Every time someone passes by a store's display windows, they are viewing the work of a Window Dresser. In some cases, the person who handles this function may have additional duties, and dress the store's windows as part of his or her job.

Window Dressers are responsible for developing and designing store display windows. Depending on the specific store, they might display clothing and accessories, furniture, CD's, books, computers, software, or food items.

In some cases, the Window Dresser is responsible for creating fantasy windows designed to attract attention instead of just showcasing products sold.

In order to do their job, Window Dressers must know what the store wants to spotlight. The store may want certain products which are currently on sale highlighted in the window. Conversely, they might want to showcase unique products the store sells.

In order to put together aesthetically pleasing windows, the Window Dresser must keep in mind the size, shape, and color of items used in the display. To make the window display exciting, the individual may utilize products or items not sold by the store. The Window Dresser may use prefabricated display items to augment the window or may be responsible for constructing items of various materials. These might include items made of fabric, glass, paper, plastic, or wood, among other things. Sometimes, the Dresser may use items which have movement such as a moving mannequin to create innovative and exciting windows.

Window Dressers may also be responsible for developing interesting displays within the store as well as arranging showcases in a pleasing manner.

No matter what type of project the individual is working on, he or she may be expected to develop sketches ahead of time for approval by store management. These may be done freehand or may be done with the help of a computer.

Additional duties of Window Dressers might include:

- Making changes in window displays as needed
- Dressing mannequins for use in window displays or in displays in other parts of the store
- Adding prices and descriptive signs on backdrops, fixtures, and merchandise

Salaries

Earnings for Window Dressers range from approximately $25,000 to $58,000 or more. Factors affecting earnings include the size, location, and prestige of the specific employer as well as the experience, expertise, and talent of the individual.

Employment Prospects

While employment prospects for Window Dressers can be located throughout the country the greatest number of opportunities will be located in large metropolitan areas where there are more large retail stores. Smaller stores often have other employees handle the functions of the Window Dresser.

Window Dressers are used in a variety of types of stores including department stores, gift shops, furniture stores, and clothing stores. Individuals may be employed on staff or may freelance.

Advancement Prospects

Advancement prospects are difficult to determine. A great deal of advancement for Window Dressers is dependent on the talent, creativity, and aspirations of the individual. The most common method of career advancement for Window Dressers is locating similar positions in larger or more prestigious settings. Some Window Dressers strike out on their own.

Education and Training

Educational requirements for Window Dressers vary. Employers may require individuals to hold a college degree. Good majors include fine art, commercial art, or design. Employers will often hire talented individuals who have proven themselves in this line of work without a college background.

Experience, Skills, and Personality Traits

Some Window Dressers obtained experience putting together store windows and showcases and displays while working in sales. Others worked as assistant Window Dressers prior to their current job.

Successful Window Dressers are creative and artistic. They have a good sense of color, balance, and style. The ability to sketch, draw, and illustrate is helpful in putting together design ideas for windows. Good aesthetic judgment and an eye for detail are essential.

Unions and Associations

Window Designers may get additional information from the National Association of Schools of Art and Design (NASAD).

Tips for Entry

1. Openings may be advertised in the newspaper's classified section under headings including, "Window Dresser," "Window Designer," "Window Design," "Window Display," or "Retail Opportunities."
2. Visit department stores and large retail outlets to see if there are any openings in this area.
3. If you can't find a position right away in a retail outlet, check out design firms and interior design companies.
4. Take pictures of windows and displays you have worked on. Make sure you put together a portfolio of your best work.
5. Check for internships at design firms, interior design firms, department stores, and large retail outlets.

STOCK CLERK

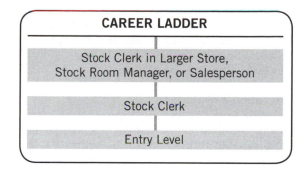

Position Description

Stock Clerks have a number of different responsibilities depending on the specific size and structure of the store in which they are working. Their main functions are receiving, unpacking, storing, and tracking merchandise.

Stock Clerks check the merchandise as it comes into the store. This is usually done in the stock room. They might check the number of items and the descriptions of each to be sure that they match packing slips. Individuals might also be responsible for inspecting goods for damage or spoilage.

Stock Clerks may be expected to track merchandise which has been received. They will keep records of merchandise which enters the stock room as well as merchandise that leaves. In many situations, Stock Clerks will be responsible for scanning items into computer systems so that the store knows what is in the inventory. This makes it easier to locate merchandise quickly and easily.

Stock Clerks sort, organize, and mark items with codes which identify the merchandise. This may include prices and stock or inventory control codes. This is often done with hand-held scanners connected to computers. This is necessary to keep inventories in stores up to date.

Stock Clerks bring merchandise to the sales floor and stock shelves and racks as needed. This may be done during store hours or after hours.

Most stores have stock rooms where extra merchandise is stored. Stock Clerks keep it organized until it is ready for display. They may place merchandise in bins, on floors, or on shelves, as well as organize merchandise in an orderly fashion.

In large stores, the Stock Clerk may be expected to handle more specific tasks such as inventory, receiving, or stocking shelves. In smaller stores, the individual will be expected to handle more general stocking duties.

Additional duties of Stock Clerks might include:

- Unpacking cartons of merchandise
- Repacking merchandise
- Checking inventory for specific items
- Handling the duties of a salesperson

Salaries

Stock Clerks earn between $7.00 and $8.50 or more per hour. Variables affecting earnings include the size and geographic location of the store and the experience and responsibilities of the individual.

Employment Prospects

Openings for Stock Clerks can be found throughout the country. The greatest number of openings are located in grocery stores and department stores. Large urban areas hosting a great many shopping centers, groceries, and warehouses will offer the most opportunities.

Advancement Prospects

This is an entry-level position. Advancement prospects are based, to a great extent, on the individual's career aspirations. Individuals may find similar positions at larger stores resulting in increased responsibilities and higher earnings. Others may climb the career ladder by becoming an inventory or stock room manager. Some people move into sales positions.

Education and Training

Generally there is informal on-the-job training provided by the employer. Most employers prefer to hire those who hold a high school diploma or the equivalent or those who are still in school. However, there are many who will hire able people who are eager to work no matter what their educational background.

Experience, Skills, and Personality Traits

As noted previously, this is an entry-level position. As a rule, no prior experience is needed. Stock Clerks should be organized people with stamina. Communications skills are helpful as are computer skills.

Unions and Associations

Depending on the type of store in which the individual works, Stock Clerks might be members of the United Food and Commercial Workers International Union or house unions. Individuals may also get additional career information by contacting the National Retail Federation (NRF).

Tips for Entry

1. There is a great deal of turnover in these positions. Stop in stores and ask the manager if you can fill out an application.
2. Remember to bring the names, addresses, and phone numbers of a few people you can use as references when filling out applications. Make sure you ask people if you can use them as references BEFORE you use them.
3. Look in the classified section of newspapers under heading classifications such as "Retail," "Retail Opportunities," "Stock Clerks," "Inventory Clerks," "Department Stores," or "Grocery Stores."
4. Many stores post job openings in windows. Visit your local mall, department store, or grocery store to check out possibilities.
5. Stores often call local labor offices to post these jobs. Remember to stop by your state employment office.

TRAINER—RETAIL

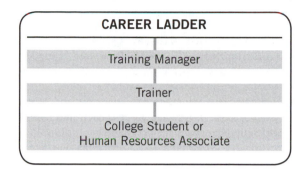

Special Skills and Personality Traits—Leadership skills; communications skills; interpersonal skills; employee relations; writing skills; public-speaking skills; creative; organized

Position Description

Trainers working in a retail environment are responsible for preparing and conducting training programs for the company's employees. Depending on the situation and the retail outlet, the individual may train employees to perform specific jobs, customer service skills, selling techniques, or the use of products and merchandise being sold.

Trainers may work under the direction of a human resources director, training manager, or store manager. They confer with management on training needs for the specific retail outlet. Once training needs are identified, the individual must formulate an outline for training sessions. These must include content as well as methods. Some Trainers use comedy in their presentations. Others are more straightforward. The Trainer will use the most effective methods to ensure employees understand the material and can put it to use.

Trainers may present material in a variety of formats. They may facilitate workshops or seminars, or give demonstrations. Some Trainers set up meetings and conferences or give lectures to present material. In some situations, Trainers also may work with employees on a one-on-one basis.

Trainers may prepare handouts, overheads, slides, or PowerPoint presentations to help employees absorb and understand needed skills. They may be expected to develop booklets or other training materials.

Trainers may be responsible for developing and facilitating programs for employees in a variety of subjects depending on the needs of the employer. For example, some stores may have Trainers conduct sessions for all new employees on providing excellent customer service. Other Trainers may be expected to work with employees on handling specialized skills.

Some Trainers may develop and facilitate orientation programs for new employees. During orientation, employees will learn the policies of the retail outlet. The orientation program may also explain to employees the way they are expected to act on the job and responses to difficult situations that are acceptable as well as unacceptable.

No matter the type of retail outlet, good customer service can mean the difference between success and failure. It is therefore essential that each and every employee treat customers in a courteous and gracious manner. An important function of Trainers is teaching employees what good customer service is and how it should be provided.

Trainers may offer classes for management in learning how to communicate with their employees. Other subjects covered in this type of class may include acceptable methods for disciplining employees and how to speak to subordinates without coming across abruptly. The individual may also develop classes for employees dealing with and avoiding sexual harassment in the workplace.

Trainers may also be expected to provide classes specific to certain jobs such as cashiers, salespeople, customer service, or call center representatives.

Other duties of the Trainers may include:

- Training employees in teamwork skills
- Facilitating programs to teach department directors, managers, and supervisors methods of conducting training within their department
- Teaching department directors, managers, and supervisors proper procedures for interview techniques and handling employment reviews

Salaries

Annual earnings for Trainers working in retail environments can range from approximately $25,000 to $60,000 or more. Factors affecting earnings include the geographic location, size, type, and prestige of the specific store. Other factors include the education, experience, and responsibilities of the individual.

Employment Prospects

Employment prospects are fair for Trainers working in retail environments. Individuals may find employment in either the local or corporate office of department stores, chains, or specialty stores. Other opportunities exist for Trainers in call centers or catalog houses.

It should be noted that not every retail outlet employs a Trainer. In many instances, a training manager, human resources director, or even the store manager may handle training functions.

Advancement Prospects

Trainers working in retail environments may advance their careers in a number of ways. Some locate similar positions in larger or more prestigious stores. Others climb the career ladder by becoming training managers. Still others may strike out on their own and become corporate training consultants.

Education and Training

Educational requirements vary from employer to employer. Most require or prefer individuals to hold a minimum of a bachelor's degree. Good majors for those interested in this field might include human resources, communications, retail, business, public relations, marketing, liberal arts, or a related field. There are also stores which may accept individuals with a high school diploma and experience in training, human resources, or the retail industry.

Individuals training employees in a special skill such as selling computers may be hired whatever their educational background as long as they have the ability to train people with easy to understand, effective methods.

Experience, Skills, and Personality Traits

Experience requirements vary. Generally experience in training and development is required or preferred. Additional experience in retailing also may be needed. Some employers will hire individuals out of college who have gone through internship programs.

Good Trainers have the ability to motivate others. They know how to explain things so they are easy to understand and remember.

Individuals should have excellent people and employee-relations skills. They must also have both good verbal and written communications skills. The ability to speak effectively in front of people is essential to this position.

Unions and Associations

Those interested in learning more about careers in this field should contact the American Society of Training Developers (ASTD) and the Society for Human Resources Management (SHRM).

Tips for Entry

1. Become either an active or affiliate member of the American Society of Training Developers (ASTD). This may give you the edge over another applicant with the same qualifications.
2. If you have the opportunity, go to some of the ASTD seminars and workshops. These are valuable for the learning opportunity as well as networking possibilities.
3. Openings are often advertised on the Internet. They may be located via the home pages of department stores, chains, specialty stores, call centers, and catalogs.
4. Positions may be advertised in the classified sections of newspapers. Look under classifications such as "Trainer," "Training and Development," "Retail Opportunities," or "Human Resources."
5. You may be asked to conduct an impromptu training presentation as part of your interview process. Develop a sample program ahead of time and rehearse before the interview.

PROMOTIONS MANAGER— RETAIL STORE

CAREER PROFILE

Duties: Develop, create, and implement promotions for retail store to attract shoppers and create advertising tie-ins

Alternate Title(s): Promotions Director

Salary Range: $27,000 to $55,000+

Employment Prospects: Fair

Advancement Prospects: Fair

Best Geographical Location(s) for Position: Jobs may be located throughout the country

Prerequisites:

Education and Training—Bachelor's degree preferred

Experience—Experience in promotions, advertising, marketing special events, publicity, or public relations preferred

Special Skills and Personality Traits—Creativity; detail oriented; imagination; innovation; communications skills; knowledge of retail industry

CAREER LADDER

Director of Marketing, Public Relations, or Advertising

Promotions Manager

Publicity or Promotion Assistant

Position Description

Many retail stores utilize a variety of promotions throughout the year to attract customers. The programs are designed to keep customers who have already shopped at the store as well as to bring in new ones.

Retail stores generally plan promotions well in advance. Generally, the Promotions Manager must prepare an annual calendar of promotions. In this way the advertising and marketing department will be able to adequately advertise and publicize the promotions.

Depending on the specific situation, Promotions Managers often plan the special sales stores have throughout the year. These may include, for example, seasonal sales such as January white sales, February president's birthday sales, "Spring Into Summer" sales, "July 4th blowouts," back to school sales, and Christmas sales.

Some promotions might utilize contests or sweepstakes. For example, stores might mail out keys to customers on their mailing list. The keys need to be brought in to the store be tried to see if they open a treasure chest full of money or prizes. Another promotion might advertise that every customer who visits the store can pick a key out of a receptacle and try to see if it starts a car. The customer whose key starts the car wins the automobile.

Promotions Managers might also use sweepstakes in which customers need only put their name, address, and phone number in a drop box to win prizes. Other promotions may encompass special sales, discount coupons, or percentage scratch-off cards. Some promotions are simple; others are more innovative and novel. Whichever type they are, they must have the potential of bringing more customers in to the store.

Promotions are often the result of brainstorming efforts of the Promotions Manager in conjunction with others in the promotions, marketing, public relations, special events, and advertisement departments. The Promotions Manager may develop promotional tie-ins. These may include copromotions with manufacturers of products sold in the store.

The individual handling promotions for a chain of gourmet food products may run chain-wide recipe contests using food items sold in the stores. After the contest has ended, the promotion may include having a tasting of the winning recipes in the store as well as a cookbook giveaway with the top recipe entries included. This type of promotion not only brings people into the store, but makes a lasting impression.

The Promotions Manager works with the community relations department developing promotions that help attract attention to the store as well as helping the community. The individual may, for example, put together programs such as the sponsorship of not-for-profit events or make donations in the store's name to worthwhile causes.

These promotions are used to help keep the store's name in the public eye. They are used for advertising as well as public relations and goodwill purposes.

The Promotions Manager is expected to develop a basic plan for promotions and their implementation. Depending on the structure of the company, this may be given to the director of marketing, advertising, or public relations for approval.

Other duties of the Promotions Manager working for a retail store or chain may include:

- Preparing a budget for promotions
- Working with the advertising department creating promotional ads and direct mail advertising pieces
- Developing marketing materials, including ads and brochures
- Developing promotions for the store's Web site

Salaries

Earnings for Promotions Managers working in retail stores or chains can range from approximately $27,000 to $55,000 or more. Factors affecting earnings include the specific retail store or chain for which the individual works as well as its size, prestige, and location. Other variables include the education, experience, and responsibilities of the individual.

Employment Prospects

Employment prospects are fair for Promotions Managers. Individuals may find employment in the corporate offices as well as local stores of a variety of chains and other retail outlets. These might include drug stores, department stores, supermarkets, clothing stores, furniture stores, or toy stores.

While jobs may be located throughout the country, individuals may need to relocate for specific positions.

Advancement Prospects

Advancement prospects are fair for Promotions Managers working in retail situations. Individuals may climb the career ladder by landing similar jobs in larger or more prestigious stores or chains. After obtaining experience, they might also be promoted to the director of either marketing, advertising, or public relations.

Education and Training

While there are exceptions, most retail chains and stores require Promotions Managers to hold a minimum of a bachelor's degree. Good majors include communications, public relations, marketing, advertising, business, journalism, retail management, English, liberal arts, or related fields. In some situations, work experience may be accepted in lieu of education.

Seminars and workshops in promotions, public relations, marketing, publicity, and advertising are helpful.

Experience, Skills, and Personality Traits

Promotions Managers are required to have experience in promotions, publicity, marketing, public relations, and advertising. This is often obtained through positions as assistants in publicity, promotion, public relations, marketing, or advertising. Any experience in retail is also useful.

Promotions Managers should be creative, detail-oriented, organized individuals. The ability to work on a variety of projects at one time without becoming flustered is essential.

Communications skills, both written and verbal, are mandatory, as is an understanding of the retail industry.

Unions and Associations

Promotions Managers working in retail may be members of a number of associations and organizations providing professional support and educational guidance. These might include the Public Relations Society of America (PRSA), the International Council of Shopping Centers (ICSC), the National Retail Merchants Association (NRMA) or the National Retail Federation (NRF).

Tips for Entry

1. Contact the International Council of Shopping Centers, the Public Relations Society of America and other organizations to see when and where they hold seminars or workshops in mall promotion and special events.
2. Positions may be located in the newspaper help wanted section. The Sunday classified section is usually the largest of the week. Look under headings such as "Promotions," "Promotion Manager," "Retail," "Retail Opportunities," or "Marketing."
3. Jobs may be advertised on retail store and chain Web sites.
4. Openings may also be listed or advertised in trade publications.
5. Look for an internship or a position as a promotions assistant in a retail store or chain. These will give you great experience and get your foot in the door.

ART DIRECTOR—RETAIL

Duties: Develop, design, and create advertisements for retail stores and outlets; design and create advertising sales flyers, posters, show cards, and promotional materials

Alternate Title(s): Advertising Art Director; Retail Art Director

Salary Range: $25,000 to $60,000+

Employment Prospects: Fair

Advancement Prospects: Fair

Best Geographical Location(s) for Position: Positions may be located throughout the country

Prerequisites:

Education and Training—Four-year degree in fine arts or commercial art required for some positions; others may not have any specific educational requirements

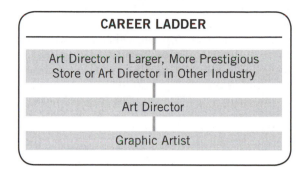

CAREER LADDER

Art Director in Larger, More Prestigious Store or Art Director in Other Industry

Art Director

Graphic Artist

Experience—Experience working in advertising or art department in any industry helpful, but not always required

Special Skills and Personality Traits—Creativity; artistic ability; understanding of retail advertising industry; knowledge of graphics, layout, paste-ups, photography, and typography

Position Description

The Art Director working in a retail outlet may work in a number of different job situations. He or she may work for small or large department stores, supermarkets, regional retail chains, or national retail chains. The Art Director might also work for a cataloger. This is a retail business that may or may not have an actual store but sells its products or services through catalogs. Art Directors may also work for on-line catalogs.

The individual's responsibilities vary depending on the size and structure of the retail outlet. The Art Director in the retail world may also be expected to perform the functions of an advertising director. In some stores he or she is also referred to as the Advertising Art Director.

In a small retail store the Art Director may be the only person in the art department. He or she may perform the tasks of a sketch and graphic artist, layout and mechanical person, or letterer. The owners of the store may offer their suggestions. The individual is then responsible for developing, creating, and in some cases actually placing the ads. The advertising Art Director may also be in charge of choosing the media in which to advertise.

In larger retail situations, the Art Director may supervise a staff of artists, layout and mechanical pre-

parers, and copywriters, or may work with outside or freelance people. He or she is still usually responsible for developing the advertising concepts and designing the ads.

The Art Director often designs the store posters and flyers used for advertising weekly specials and sales. He or she also designs and creates advertising show cards and counter signs. These are the cards or pieces seen on the countertops or windows or hanging from the ceiling advertising new products, price breaks, and sales specials. As these cards change frequently, the individual usually letters them by hand with markers, paint, or ink or electronically prints them with the use of a computer or other printing mechanism.

The Art Director designs promotional material for the retail store. Depending on the size and structure of the outlet, he or she may just do the designing or may be responsible for the development, writing the promotional copy, or creating the artwork.

Much of the artwork and advertising for large retail chains may be done by an advertising agency. However, the stores often put out local advertisements and catalogs. The Art Director may provide the layout and all graphics for these advertisements, sale flyers, and catalogs.

When creating advertisements, posters, flyers, show cards, and counter signs, the Art Director must make sure that everything used in advertising and promoting the store will retain a unified identity and image. This means that while every ad may be advertising a different weekly special, each must look somewhat like the others. Logos must remain the same and be in a similar position on each ad. The store name must always look the same. In this way, when customers read and see the ads and promotional materials they will automatically think of the store.

Additional duties of the Art Director may include:

- Working with outside printers
- Negotiating prices or getting bids for printing of large quantities of flyers and advertising sales pieces
- Performing functions of copywriter

Salaries

Earnings for the Art Director of the advertising department working in retail stores can vary greatly depending on the job. The range may begin around $25,000 and go up to $60,000 or more.

Generally, individuals with little experience or those working in smaller stores will earn less than their counterparts with more experience in larger, more prestigious stores and retail outlets.

Employment Prospects

Employment prospects are fair for individuals seeking this position. Jobs may be located throughout the country. More and more retail stores are following the current trend toward in-house advertising departments. As noted previously, individuals might find employment in a variety of settings including large department stores, supermarkets, regional retail chains, national retail chains, catalogs, or on-line catalogs and E-tailing Web sites.

Advancement Prospects

Prospects for career advancement for Art Directors working in the retail industry are fair. Individuals have a number of different options for moving up the career ladder. The most common is to become the Art Director for a larger, more prestigious store. An individual might advance his or her other career by becoming the advertising or art director in a large corporation, depending on his or her qualifications. The individual might also locate a position as an Art Director in an advertising agency.

Education and Training

Most employers in large retail stores, department stores, or chains will usually require an applicant to have a four-year college degree in fine arts or commercial art. Courses or seminars in advertising are a plus.

Smaller retail stores may or may not require a college degree. Certain stores may accept an applicant with art school training or even a self-taught individual who can demonstrate that he or she possesses the required skills.

Experience, Skills, and Personality Traits

Art Directors working in the advertising department of retail stores need a thorough understanding of the concepts of retail advertising and art. Individuals must be very creative and artistic to come up with concepts for advertisements as well as to design them and bring the ads to fruition. Individuals must be able to sketch, draw, paste up, lay out, put together mechanicals, and choose type. A great deal of this is done by computer today.

A portfolio or "book" made up of the individuals best work is usually necessary in order to show samples and illustrate skills.

Unions and Associations

Art Directors working in the advertising department in a retail setting do not usually belong to any bargaining union. They may, however, belong to a number of trade associations which offer professional guidance, education, and information. These might include the American Advertising Federation (AAF), the Art Director Club, Inc. (ADC), the One Club, the Society of Illustrators (SOI), the Graphic Artists Guild (GAG) and the American Institute of Graphic Arts (AIGA).

Tips for Entry

1. Start working on your portfolio now. A good portfolio can give you an edge over other applicants. In many instances, it can take the place of educational requirements. Make sure your portfolio includes some work relevant to the retail advertising field even if you have to do samples.
2. Join trade associations. Many have student memberships. Others offer critique sessions on improving your portfolio. All of them will help you make important contacts.
3. Many retail chain stores offer internships and training programs. Contact the company headquarters or ask the manager in your local store of the chain about whom to contact to get more information.
4. Obtain experience working in a newspaper advertising department. In addition to gaining experi-

ence you will make contact with local advertisers who might have a job opening down the line.

5. Positions are often advertised in the classified sections of the newspaper. Look under the classification headings of "Retail," "Art Director," or "Advertising."

6. Other positions may be located on career Web sites or specific store sites.

GRAPHIC ARTIST—RETAIL

CAREER PROFILE

Duties: Develop, design, and create graphics for advertisements for retail stores and outlets; design and create graphics for advertising sales flyers, posters, show cards, and promotional materials; design graphics for catalogs

Alternate Title(s): Graphic Designer; Artist

Salary Range: $23,000 to $48,000+

Employment Prospects: Good

Advancement Prospects: Good

Best Geographical Location(s) for Position: Positions may be located throughout the country

Prerequisites:

   Education and Training—Four-year degree in fine arts or commercial art required for some positions; others may not have any specific educational requirements

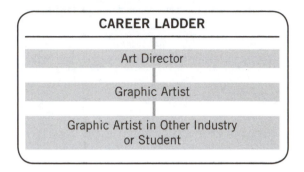

CAREER LADDER

Art Director

Graphic Artist

Graphic Artist in Other Industry or Student

Experience—Art and advertising experience helpful but not always required

Special Skills and Personality Traits—Creativity; artistic ability; understanding of retail advertising industry; knowledge of graphics, layout, paste-ups, mechanicals, typography, color, and photography; drawing and illustration skills

Position Description

Every retail advertisement in a magazine, store flyer, or catalog has usually been worked on by one or more Graphic Artists. These individuals, who may also be referred to as graphic designers or artists, are the ones who help make advertisements and other promotional pieces look visually attractive.

Graphic Artists working in retail settings may have a number of responsibilities depending on their specific job situation. Their main function is to design the graphics for the retail outlet's promotional material. In larger retail stores, individuals may work under the direction of the store's art director. In smaller stores where there is a one-person art department, the Graphic Artist may also act as the art director. Stores may employ one or more Graphic Artists depending on their size and structure.

Graphic Artists might develop and design the graphics for the retail store's advertisements. It is up to the Graphic Designer to develop graphics that are creative, innovative, appealing, and memorable.

Graphic Artists may design a retail catalog. Others may design weekly sales flyers, counter cards, display signs, or store signs. Depending on the situation, Graphic Artists might come up with store logos, designs for bags and other packaging, and virtually all printed promotional material.

When designing advertising and promotional pieces, logos, and packaging, the Graphic Artist generally tries to keep the image of the company prominently identified. The individual must keep the design of the product names, graphics, and logos closely tied together so that customers will relate the design to the company. In this way, customers who see the logo or name on anything will be able to identify the store, product, or brand easily.

Part of the job of the Graphic Artist may be choosing the kind and size of type to use in advertisements and other promotional material. He or she must choose typefaces as well as background colors.

The Graphic Artist must develop a layout for ads, flyers, or other promotional material. He or she also must design the graphics. Sometimes, Graphic Artists utilize photos. In other situations, the individual may draw, sketch, or use computer-generated graphics.

Graphic Artists often design and create advertising show cards and counter signs. These are the cards or pieces seen on the countertops or windows or hanging from the ceiling advertising new products, price breaks, and sales specials. As these cards change frequently, the individual usually letters them by hand with markers, paint, or ink or electronically prints them with the use of a computer or other printing mechanism.

Additional duties of a Graphic Artist may include:

- Designing the graphics and layout for on-line retailers
- Designing the graphics for other on-line sites
- Performing the functions of a copywriter

Salaries

Earnings for Graphic Artists working in retail can range from approximately $23,000 to $48,000 or more. Factors affecting earnings include the size, type, prestige, and geographic location of the specific retail company for which the individual works. Other variables include the talent, responsibilities, and experience of the individual.

Employment Prospects

Employment prospects are good for Graphic Artists seeking employment in the retail industry. Jobs may be located throughout the country. More and more retail stores are following the current trend toward in-house advertising departments. Individuals might find employment in a variety of settings including large department stores, supermarkets, regional retail chains, national retail chains, traditional paper catalogs, and catalogs on the Internet.

Advancement Prospects

Advancement prospects for Graphic Artists are dependent to a great extent on the talent of the individual as well as his or her career aspirations. Some Graphic Artists climb the career ladder by finding similar positions in larger or more prestigious retail companies resulting in increased responsibilities and earnings. Other individuals land jobs as art directors.

Education and Training

Experience requirements vary for Graphic Artists in the retail industry. Many employers require or prefer an applicant to have a four-year college degree in fine arts or commercial art, or an art school background. However, a good portfolio demonstrating the individual possesses the required skills can often land a job in lieu of education. Courses or seminars in advertising are a plus.

Experience, Skills, and Personality Traits

Graphic Artists should be very artistic individuals with a thorough understanding of the concepts of retail advertising and art. Creativity is essential in order to develop eye-catching ads or promotional material as well as to design them and bring them to fruition. Graphic Artists must be able to sketch, draw, paste up, lay out, put together mechanics, and choose type. A great deal of this is done by computer today. Therefore, computer skills and the ability to use appropriate software programs are mandatory.

A portfolio or "book" made up of the individual's best work is usually necessary in order to show samples and illustrate skills.

Unions and Associations

Graphic Artists working in the advertising department in a retail setting may belong to a number of trade associations which offer professional guidance, education, and information. These might include the American Advertising Federation (AAF), the Art Director Club, Inc. (ADC), the One Club, the Society of Illustrators (SOI), the Graphic Artists Guild (GAG) and the American Institute of Graphic Arts (AIGA).

Tips for Entry

1. Your portfolio can help you get a job. Start working on it now. A good portfolio can give you an edge over other applicants. In many instances, it can take the place of educational requirements. Make sure your portfolio includes some work relevant to the retail advertising field even if you have to do samples.
2. Join trade associations. Many have student memberships. Others offer critique sessions on improving your portfolio. All of them will help you make important contacts.
3. Many retail chain stores offer internships and training programs. Contact the company headquarters or ask the manager in your local chain store about whom to contact to get more information.
4. Positions are often advertised in the classified sections of the newspaper. Look under classification headings such as "Retail," "Graphic Artist," "Artist," "Graphic Designer," or "Advertising."
5. Other positions may be located on career Web sites or specific store sites.
6. Obtain experience working in a newspaper advertising department. In addition to gaining experience you will make contact with stores who might have a job opening in the future.

PERSONAL SHOPPER

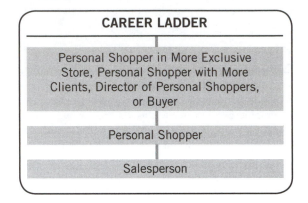

Position Description

Many stores have found that providing extra services increases customer loyalty, thus increasing sales and profit. These services can encompass a variety of areas such as free gift wrapping, delivery of merchandise, or tailoring. Personal Shoppers are another of those services.

Formerly only the most exclusive stores employed Personal Shoppers. Today, the service is becoming much more prevalent. Generally, the services of Personal Shoppers are free to the customer. The store makes its money by selling the items that the Personal Shopper has selected for the customer.

While some people love shopping, others find it stressful. Additionally, with many people's busy lifestyles today, some just don't have the time to "shop till they drop."

Personal Shoppers have a number of responsibilities depending on the structure of their department. Their main functions are offering customers individualized help and attention, and to make shopping a better and easier experience.

Personal shopping services vary from store to store. In many stores, the customers call the Personal Shopper to make an appointment. In others, customers may see the service advertised and visit the Personal Shopper at his or her office in the store. Some stores send Personal Shoppers and merchandise to the homes or offices of customers to make it easier for the individual to shop.

Depending on the store, Personal Shoppers may deal exclusively in one area such as clothing and accessories or with all the store's merchandise. The shopper must be not only familiar with the store's merchandise, but must know where it is located so he or she can find it quickly, so he or she can offer better advice to customers.

The Personal Shopper determines what the customer or client wants, and often has consultations with customers to learn their likes, dislikes, needs, and price range, as well as their sizes and lifestyles. Armed with the information, the Personal Shopper goes through the store choosing items to bring back to the customer.

The shopper brings back a variety of sizes and styles for the customer to try on, and often advises the client on how a garment or outfit looks. If the customer finds something he or she likes, they may buy it. If not, the Personal Shopper will look for something else. It is essential that the individual never make the customer feel obligated to buy something he or she doesn't like or want.

A major function of many Personal Shoppers is helping customers select gifts. Shoppers may, for example, often help select gifts for customers' business associates, family, or friends. One of the perks for customers is they only need give the Personal Shopper a list of people for whom they require gifts, a description of the recipients likes and dislikes or hobbies, and a price range. The individual can then choose a selection of possibilities for customer approval. In many instances the Personal Shopper performs yet another set of services to save the customer time, such as gift wrapping, enclosing cards, and delivering or mailing the gifts.

Most Personal Shoppers keep detailed information on steady customers including sizes, styles, fabrics and color preferences, previously purchased items, birthdays, and anniversaries. They also may keep similar information on the customer's business associates, friends, and family.

Other duties of Personal Shoppers may include:

- Helping customers coordinate outfits and accessories
- Helping customers coordinate home items
- Keeping abreast of new merchandise in the store
- Calling steady customers when new merchandise they might be interested in comes in

Salaries

Earnings for Personal Shoppers range from approximately $25,000 to $75,000 or more. Variables affecting earnings include the size, type, prestige, and geographic location of the store in which the individual works as well as the individual's experience, duties, and reputation in the field.

Personal Shoppers may be compensated in a number of different ways. Some may be paid a straight salary. Others may be paid a salary plus a commission on sales.

Employment Prospects

Employment prospects for Personal Shoppers are getting better every day. While this is a relatively new type of job, it is expanding quickly. Both male and female Personal Shoppers are in demand in a variety of retail establishments including department stores, boutiques, clothing stores, specialty shops, and gift shops.

Advancement Prospects

Personal Shoppers may climb the career ladder in a number of ways. Some individuals advance their careers by locating similar positions in larger or more prestigious stores resulting in increased responsibility and earnings. Others acquire supervisory positions. These might include becoming the director of the personal shopper department, a manager of a different department or in some cases, the store manager.

Some individuals become department buyers. Still others strike out on their own with personal shopping services.

Education and Training

Education and training requirements vary from position to position because of the newness of this job. Generally, most stores require individuals to hold a minimum of a high school diploma or the equivalent. Many prefer a college background or degree.

Good choices for majors for those aspiring to become Personal Shoppers include retailing, merchandising, or fashion. Seminars, workshops, and courses in fashion, color, accessorizing, merchandising, and retailing are helpful.

Experience, Skills, and Personality Traits

Personal Shoppers usually have worked in retail sales prior to garnering their positions. A background in retailing, merchandising, or fashion is needed.

Successful Personal Shoppers are pleasant people who enjoy working with and helping others. They have panache and a sense of style when selecting clothing, accessories, gifts, or anything else. Customer service skills are essential. Communications skills are mandatory.

Unions and Associations

Individuals may obtain information about a career in this field by contacting the National Retail Merchants Association (NRMA) and the American Collegiate Retailing Association (ACRA).

Tips for Entry

1. Look for an internship with a Personal Shopper in a department store or boutique.
2. Jobs may be advertised in the classified sections of newspapers. Look under headings such as "Personal Shopper," "Retail Opportunities," "Fashion Sales," "Salespeople," "Department Stores," or "Boutiques."
3. Sometimes jobs may not be advertised. You may have to create your own position. If you are currently working in a store that does not yet offer personal shopping services, suggest the idea to store management making sure you ask to be interviewed for the newly created position.
4. If you aren't working for the specific store you think might be open to this type of position, write a letter to the store manager or owner asking for an appointment to discuss the possibility. Make sure to include your resume.
5. Be sure to dress the part. You need to look stylish and well coordinated for this type of job.

SPECIAL EVENTS DIRECTOR—RETAIL STORE

CAREER PROFILE

Duties: Develop and implement special events and promotions for retail store

Alternate Title(s): Special Events Manager

Salary Range: $25,000 to $50,000+

Employment Prospects: Fair

Advancement Prospects: Fair

Best Geographical Location(s) for Position: Jobs may be located throughout the country

Prerequisites:

    Education and Training—Bachelor's degree

    Experience—Experience in special events, publicity, or public relations preferred

    Special Skills and Personality Traits—Creativity; detail oriented; imagination; innovation; communications skills

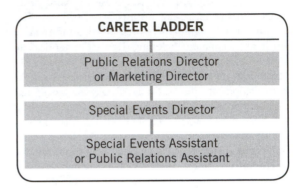

CAREER LADDER

Public Relations Director
or Marketing Director

Special Events Director

Special Events Assistant
or Public Relations Assistant

Position Description

Retail stores often have special events and promotions. One of the most well-known special events sponsored by a retail store is the Macy's Thanksgiving Day Parade.

Whether small or large, special events and promotions in retail have a purpose. Some may be designed to attract new customers. Others may enhance the image of the store as well as make it more visible. The Special Events Director formulates the special events in a retail store. He or she generally works in the store's marketing or public relations department. In some stores, the public relations director or marketing director handles the special events functions.

The Special Events Director must devise innovative ideas and then take them from inception through fruition. This must be done within a budget and a time frame.

The Special Events Director often works with store owners, management, public relations, and marketing staff to develop ideas. Special events will, of course, depend on the store. Depending on the situation and budget, events may be small or large and simple or complex. Some events may be industry specific and some may not.

For example, groceries and specialty food stores might hold events such as "Sampling Saturdays," where various food samples are put out for tasting; "Cooking with the Chefs," where chefs illustrate how to prepare dishes using products from the store; or a "Singles Meet and Greet," in the grocery aisles.

Clothing stores may put together fashion shows on or off site, spotlighting the store's clothing or a "Makeover Day" for customers. A furniture store might hold an indoor picnic to bring people into the store or might bring in an interior designer for the day to help customers learn how to decorate their home. Bookstores frequently bring in authors for book signings, workshops, and discussion groups. Department stores might do anything from having art exhibits to holding a concert in their parking lot or hosting a wedding in the public area of the store.

Some stores, like Macy's, sponsor events offsite. This helps the store in a number of ways. It helps build better public relations and good community relations. Off-site events may also obtain publicity and promotion for the store and bring their name to the public in a different manner than advertising can.

The Special Events Director may be responsible for implementing a certain number of events annually. For example, he or she may be expected to develop an event every week or every month. In other situations, the Special Events Director may be notified by the store's upper management when they want events developed. The individual must determine general information about the program. This may include things such as the time frame, proposed budget, and general purpose.

The goal of the Special Events Director is to develop an appropriate event with a novel, workable idea. The individual will brainstorm with other members of the store's management team or members of the public relations, marketing, advertising, or promotions department. The Special Events Director is then responsible for working out the details and writing a basic plan for the event. This includes devising a budget for the project.

After receiving approval, the Special Events Director moves forward and puts the idea into action. He or she often works with one or more assistants to help with the project.

Depending on the specific event the individual may be expected to locate people and items necessary to make the event a success. The Director may need to hire entertainers, talent, caterers, or customers. He or she may need to locate chairs, stages, promotional items, or other important items. Every detail of the entire event becomes the responsibility of the Special Events Director.

Depending on the specific store and its structure, the Special Events Director may be responsible for preparing press releases and other publicity on the upcoming event as well as post-publicity on portions of the programs that have already occurred. The Director may also be expected to call the media and arrange interviews, articles, feature stories, or photo opportunities. In other situations, the public relations department will handle these functions.

Some Special Events Directors are responsible for developing events for an entire chain of stores. This might occur when individuals work in the corporate department of chain stores. The Special Events Director in this circumstance must develop events that will work in multiple stores. An Easter egg hunt or the arrival of Santa Claus, for example, are universal events. In this case, the Special Events Director is often expected to oversee staff in other locations.

Other duties of the Special Events Director working in a retail environment may include:

- Developing special events for employees
- Devising budgets for special events
- Functioning as a public relations person
- Developing and placing advertisements for events
- Supervising staff
- Being present at events

Salaries
Annual earnings for Special Events Directors working in a retail environment can range from approximately $25,000 to $50,000 or more. Factors affecting earnings include the specific retail store as well as its size, prestige, and location. Other variables include the education, experience, and responsibilities of the individual.

Employment Prospects
Employment prospects are fair for individuals seeking this position. Jobs can be located in many retail stores throughout the country. As noted, every store does not have a Special Events Director. In some, the public relations or marketing director or even the store manager may be responsible for these functions.

Advancement Prospects
Advancement prospects are, to a great extent, dependent on the career aspirations of the individual. Some find similar positions in larger or more prestigious retail stores. Others move into handling special events for other industries.

Many Special Event Directors also climb the career ladder by acquiring positions as directors of marketing or public relations.

Education and Training
Individuals seeking positions in special events coordination should generally have a college degree. Good majors include communications, public relations, English, liberal arts, advertising, business, journalism, or retail management.

Seminars and workshops in special events, promotions, public relations, publicity, and advertising are helpful.

Experience, Skills, and Personality Traits
Experience working in special events, publicity, promotion, or retail management is usually required for a position like this. Many Special Events Directors were special events assistants or coordinators prior to their appointment.

Individuals should be creative and innovative with a good imagination. Excellent communications skills are necessary. An understanding of the retail industry is needed.

Special Events Directors should be detail oriented. The ability to deal well under stress is essential.

Unions and Associations
Special Events Directors working in retail might be associated with number of associations and organiza-

tions providing professional support and educational guidance. These might include the Public Relations Society of America (PRSA), Business/Professional Advertising Association (B/PAA), and the National Retail Merchants Association (NRMA) or the National Retail Federation (NRF).

Tips for Entry

1. Send a short cover letter and your resume to the corporate office of department or chain stores as well as specialty stores.
2. Positions may be located in the newspaper help wanted section. The Sunday classified section is usually the largest of the week. Look under headings such as "Special Events," "Special Event Director," "Retail Opportunities," "Public Relations," "Marketing," or "Promotion."
3. Job openings may also be listed in trade publications.
4. Contact large stores to see if they offer internships in this area.
5. Jobs may also be located on-line. Start by checking out some of the more popular sites such as www.hotjobs.com.

MYSTERY SHOPPER

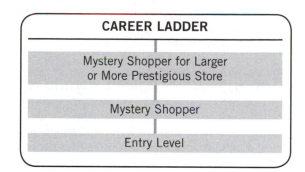

Position Description

The hope of retail establishments is that customers visiting their stores will have a pleasant shopping experience. It's difficult, however, to know how customers are really treated when the top managers aren't around. In order to find out how customers are treated by employees when they don't think anyone is watching, stores often hire Mystery Shoppers.

These individuals, also known as Secret Shoppers, provide store owners and upper management with a typical consumer's view of shopping in their establishment. In this manner, management can improve customer service and alleviate problems which may exist.

Mystery shopping is a great opportunity for individuals who love to shop. As an added bonus, they get paid for it. Mystery Shoppers can be male or female in virtually every age category from older high school students to senior citizens. Generally, jobs in this field are part time. However, there are some full-time positions available.

What does a Mystery Shopper do? He or she may have varied duties depending on the specific job. Mystery Shoppers are given assignments by their employer. For example, individuals may be asked to go to specific stores and be given a list of merchandise to purchase. The employer either gives the individual money for the purchases or reimburses him or her afterward.

While "shopping," the Mystery Shopper may be asked to check various situations within the store. These might include checking to see if and how employees greet customers, how they react and treat customers and if they are courteous. The Mystery Shopper may be responsible for checking to see if store policies and customer service standards are met, or how different problems are handled.

The Mystery Shopper might additionally be asked to check whether the store is clean and well stocked, rest rooms are clean, and aisles are wide enough. Most of this information is important to make sure store customer service standards are met. Other information may be needed to assure safety requirements are met.

After shopping and observing, the Mystery Shopper is expected to file a report of findings. Depending on the situation, the individual may write a general report or just be expected to fill out forms supplied by the employer.

Additional duties of Mystery Shoppers might include:

- Offering suggestions to employers regarding employees
- Tabulating information collected while shopping
- Visiting the selling floor to assure products are displayed properly
- Visiting the store with specific issues (such as returns) to see how they are handled by employees

Salaries

Salaries of Mystery Shoppers vary depending on the specific type of employment. Individuals working full time for a company specializing in mystery shopping might have annual salaries ranging from $23,000 to $35,000 or more. Mystery Shoppers working on a part-time basis might earn between $7.50 and $20.00 or more per hour. Additionally, some Mystery Shoppers get to keep their purchases.

Employment Prospects

Employment prospects for Mystery Shoppers interested in working on a part-time basis are good. Prospects for full-time employment are much more limited.

Individuals might find employment shopping in a variety of retail establishments including large department stores, chain stores, groceries, auto parts stores, cosmetic stores, drug stores, pharmacies, boutiques, or gift shops. Some Mystery Shoppers might even shop for cars. As noted previously, Mystery Shoppers might work in other industries in addition to retail. Individuals might be Mystery Shoppers in the hospitality industry, restaurants, hotels, travel, banking, insurance, or healthcare.

Some Mystery Shoppers work for mystery shopping companies. Others work for stores, chains, or retail establishments themselves.

Advancement Prospects

Advancement prospects for Mystery Shoppers are fair. The most common method of advancement in this type of job is by obtaining better assignments resulting in increased earnings. Some individuals may strike out on their own and open mystery shopping companies. This, however, is not common.

Education and Training

There are no specific educational requirements for Mystery Shoppers. Those working for companies specializing in mystery shopping may be provided with in-service training programs.

Experience, Skills, and Personality Traits

An important trait for the Mystery Shopper is the ability to "look the part." Individuals for the most part must look like "normal" shoppers in the specific store they're visiting. In some cases, however, Mystery Shoppers may be sent out to see how different groups are treated. For example, a store may want to see how employees treat senior citizen or minority shoppers.

Mystery Shoppers need good communications skills. The ability to be discreet is essential. A Mystery Shopper has no value to a company when everyone knows what he or she is doing in the store.

Unions and Associations

Individuals interested in pursuing a career in this field might also obtain additional information from the Mystery Shopping Providers Association (MSPA), the National Retail Federation (NRF) and the American Collegiate Retailing Association (ACRA).

Tips for Entry

1. Jobs may be advertised in the newspaper classified section under headings including "Mystery Shopper," or "Secret Shopper."
2. Contact large chains and department stores to see who in the organization you might contact regarding a position in this area. Sometimes it's human resources. Other times it might be another department.
3. Jobs can often be located on-line. Look at some of the major sites such as www.hotjobs.com.
4. Look for companies that specialize in mystery shopping. You might find them advertised in trade journals or via their own Web sites.

PRODUCT DEMONSTRATOR

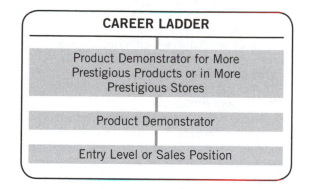

Position Description

Many stores have found that when products and merchandise are demonstrated they sell better. They therefore utilize the services of individuals called Product Demonstrators.

Demonstrators may work directly for stores or for manufacturers or other companies. Responsibilities differ depending on the specific employer and products, but their main function is to promote sales.

Individuals might demonstrate virtually any product, including but not limited to, food, cosmetics, appliances, or housewares.

An individual demonstrating a new ice cream product in a supermarket might scoop out various flavors and give samples and coupons to customers. If he or she is promoting a new kind of frozen pizza, he or she might bake it in a portable toaster, cut it into bite-size pieces, arrange them on plates and give out samples.

Individuals demonstrating cookware might prepare various foods in the cookware in front of customers. During this process, the individual may answer questions and illustrate the benefits of the new product.

Demonstrators working in the cosmetics department of a store might show individuals how to use the cosmetics the store sells. Often, the demonstrator utilizes the store's makeup to do a makeover on customers.

Individuals may be responsible for developing a mini sales pitch or may be given one.

Some demonstrators, such as those working in the cosmetics area of department stores, may also double as salespeople. Their function is to demonstrate merchandise and products to customers in stores and other outlets and to create an atmosphere conducive to sales.

In some situations, demonstrators may not only show new products to customers but record customer reactions as well. For example, did the customers like the new flavor of soda or did they dump half-filled cups into the trash? The demonstrator often is expected to write reports on consumer reactions to the products being demonstrated.

Additional duties of demonstrators might include:

- Giving out coupons for products being demonstrated
- Performing functions of sales associate
- Taking payments from customers for purchases
- Writing orders

Salaries

Earnings for demonstrators are dependent on a number of factors. These include the specific work situation and the type of product being demonstrated as well as the actual responsibilities, education, and experience of the individual.

Some demonstrators earn $7.00 an hour. Others earn $15.00 or more per hour. Some Demonstrators may also receive a commission on products sold.

Employment Prospects

Employment prospects for demonstrators are good. Individuals may find openings at a variety of retail outlets, department stores, specialty shops, and supermarkets throughout the country.

Some demonstrators work directly for specific companies and manufacturers demonstrating their products in various retail outlets.

Advancement Prospects

Advancement prospects for demonstrators are dependent to a great extent on an individuals specific career aspiration. Some individuals find more prestigious stores to work in or better products to demonstrate. Others strike out on their own selling products via home parties.

Education and Training

Educational requirements vary for demonstrators. Some employers prefer individuals have at least some college background if not a college degree. Others will hire individuals who have a high school diploma.

Once hired, employers often provide either formal or informal training programs. Individuals who are demonstrating specialized products may need more specialized training.

Experience, Skills, and Personality Traits

Experience requirements, like education, vary from employer to employer. In many situations this is an entry-level position. Some employers, however, prefer or require experienced employees.

Demonstrators should be well-groomed individuals. An enthusiastic, pleasant personality is helpful in this type of position. Good verbal communications skills are also necessary, as is the ability to repeat the same sales pitch over and over.

Unions and Associations

Individuals interested in pursuing a career in this field might also obtain additional information from the National Retail Federation (NRF), the American Collegiate Retailing Association (ACRA), the American Marketing Association (AMA) and the Direct Selling Association (DSA).

Tips for Entry

1. Jobs may be advertised in the newspaper classified section under headings including "Retail," "Retail Opportunities," "Demonstrator," "Product Demonstrator," "Cosmetics Demonstrator," "Food Demonstrator," or "Housewares Demonstrator."
2. Send your resume and a short cover letter to department stores, supermarkets, and other retail outlets.
3. You might also send your resume to the human resources directors of companies whose products you might be interested in demonstrating.
4. Contact the corporate offices of large chains and department stores to see whom you might contact in their local stores.
5. Get your foot in the door with a sales position. It might give you an edge over another applicant.

COMPARISON SHOPPER

Position Description

It is to the advantage of store owners and management to know as much as possible about what other similar stores are doing in their business. To accomplish this, many stores employ Comparison Shoppers who help stores get the edge over their competitors by gathering important information. This information will vary depending on the specific store.

Comparison Shoppers visit competing types of stores. They must do this in a discreet manner, fitting in with other customers. Individuals may have varied responsibilities depending on the job.

The Comparison Shopper may be given a list of items to view in competing stores. He or she may be asked to check the prices of the merchandise. This information is useful in helping the store become competitive in setting its prices. The individual may also be asked to compare the packaging of items to help the store set prices and package design.

The Comparison Shopper may be expected to check into policies of other stores. For example, he or she may purchase merchandise to see how the competitive store deals with returns. The individual might be asked to observe the number of cashiers or salespeople a store utilizes, the type of customer service they provide, or specific store policies they enforce.

Comparison Shoppers are often responsible for checking the types of merchandise sold in competing stores. If a competing store has the new toy, a new fashion, or fad and the other store does not, it can represent

a large loss of sales. Knowing what other stores have can give a store a tremendous edge. This information is also useful to help stores determine buying policies.

In many situations the Comparison Shopper actually buys the merchandise. It is then used to check not only price, but to compare quality. Individuals may visit more than one competitive store to gather information.

Once back at the office, the Comparison Shopper prepares reports of his or her findings. Depending on the situation, the individual may write a general report or just be expected to fill out forms supplied by the employer. This is an extremely important part of the job. This information is used by the employer to make better, more informed decisions on buying, pricing, and merchandising.

Additional duties of Comparison Shoppers might include:

- Checking that merchandise, price, and sales dates are accurately described in advertisement copy
- Checking to be sure merchandise advertised at a specific price by a competitor is available for customer purchase
- Comparing packaging of similar items in competitive stores

Salaries

Salaries of Comparison Shoppers working full time can range from approximately $21,000 to $26,000 or more depending on a number of variables. These include the size, type, prestige, and geographic location of the specific store. Other factors include the responsibilities, education, and experience of the individual.

Comparison Shoppers working on a part-time basis can earn between $7.00 and $12.00 or more per hour.

Employment Prospects

Employment prospects for Comparison Shoppers are fair and getting better every day. As more stores want the edge over their competitors, they will begin employing people in these positions.

Individuals might find employment in a variety of retail establishments including large department stores, chain stores, groceries, cosmetics stores, drug stores, pharmacies, or gift shops.

Advancement Prospects

Advancement prospects for Comparison Shoppers are dependent on the individual's career aspirations. With additional experience, training, or education individuals might move into positions as assistant buyers, merchandising assistants, or sales representatives.

Education and Training

Educational requirements vary for Comparison Shoppers. Some employers prefer individuals have at least some college background if not a college degree. Others will hire individuals who have a high school diploma. Good majors for those in college are marketing, merchandising, retailing, and liberal arts. Once hired, stores often provide either formal or informal training programs.

Experience, Skills, and Personality Traits

Experience requirements vary from employer to employer. Many stores have no experience requirements for this position. Others may prefer or require

individuals have some type of prior retail experience, such as sales.

The ability to be discreet is essential. Comparison Shoppers should be well groomed with the ability to "look the part." They should be able to walk into a store without attracting undue attention. They don't want to look like they're comparison shopping. Instead, they want to appear that they are "normal" shoppers in the specific store they're visiting.

Comparison Shoppers should be pleasant people with good verbal and written communication skills.

Unions and Associations

Individuals interested in pursuing a career in this field might also obtain additional information from the National Retail Federation (NRF), the American Collegiate Retailing Association (ACRA) and the American Marketing Association (AMA).

Tips for Entry

1. Jobs may be advertised in the newspaper classified section under headings including "Retail," "Retail Opportunities," and "Comparison Shopper."
2. Consider sending your resume and a short cover letter to department stores, supermarkets, and other retail outlets which might hire Comparison Shoppers.
3. You might also visit the human resources department of retail stores and groceries. Remember to dress appropriately when stopping by the human resources department as well as during any interviews.
4. Contact the corporate offices of large chains and department stores to see whom you might contact in their local stores.
5. Get your foot in the door with a sales position. It might give you an edge over another applicant.

STORE MANAGER— GROCERY/SUPERMARKET

CAREER PROFILE

Duties: Handle day-to-day management of supermarket; oversee staffing needs of supermarket; deal with customer service issues; make sure store is in compliance with health and safety regulations

Alternate Title(s): Supermarket Manager; Grocery Store Manager

Salary Range: $26,000 to $55,000+

Employment Prospects: Good

Advancement Prospects: Fair

Best Geographical Location(s) for Position: Jobs may be located throughout the country

Prerequisites:

Education and Training—Training requirements vary; see text

Experience—Experience in supermarket management

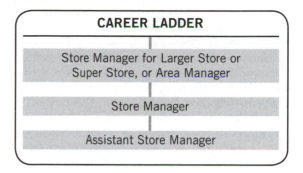

CAREER LADDER

Store Manager for Larger Store or Super Store, or Area Manager

Store Manager

Assistant Store Manager

Special Skills and Personality Traits—Problem solving skills; negotiation skills; communications skills; ability to deal well with people, management skills; administrative skills

Position Description

Grocery stores have changed over the years. Today, while there are still small corner groceries, most of us are more familiar with the large supermarkets, chains, and supercenters. These might encompass not only traditional groceries, but ready-made convenience food, pharmacies, bakeries, and more. The person in charge of overseeing the entire facility is known as the Store Manager.

The manager handles the day-to-day management of the entire store. Since he or she has many varied duties, the Store Manager generally has one or more assistant managers who help fulfill them.

The Store Manager must be familiar with all the departments in the store. He or she is ultimately responsible for all their activities, and must be sure the facility is kept clean, safe, and well-stocked.

As food spoilage can lead to illness and lawsuits, it is essential the Store Manager be sure that all food sold in the store is fresh. He or she may work with the various department managers to accomplish this task. Dates on merchandise such as dairy products, meats, or baked goods must be checked and expired food must be pulled off the shelves on a regular basis.

There are an array of laws, rules, and regulations which must be followed for health, legal, and safety

reasons. It is the responsibility of the Store Manager to make sure all of these are adhered to.

The Store Manager is responsible for staffing the store. If the store is new and just opening or if there are many job openings, the Store Manager may schedule a job fair to attract large numbers of potential employees. He or she may also write and place help wanted advertisements in the newspaper or other media. The manager will work with assistant managers in interviewing staff including department managers, customer service people, cashiers, baggers, and office staff. In some instances, the department managers will be responsible for interviewing employees for their department and making recommendations to the Store Manager.

The manager is also responsible for making sure employees are trained. He or she may accomplish this with the help of the assistant and department managers.

Supermarkets which are part of large chains usually have promotions such as loyalty programs, discount coupons, weekly flyers, and ads to attract and retain customers. These are handled by the corporate office. The manager must only make sure the specials and items advertised in fliers are on the shelves. In nonchain supermarkets, the manager may be responsible for developing these promotions or handling the store's advertising. The manager also may be expected to analyze other data as well to help determine what direction the store might take to increase profits.

Customer service is an important function of the Store Manager. A good Store Manager can make a big problem with a customer seem small. A Manager who is not customer service oriented can do just the opposite. Whether it's offering a customer a more expensive product when the one on sale isn't available, calling a company to find out about a recalled product, or opening up another checkout line so people don't have to wait, customer service is essential.

The manager will usually be the one called when a customer has a problem no one else can or wants to handle. He or she is responsible for dealing with emergencies, crises, and any problems which crop up during the day in the store. He or she is expected to write reports for accidents or other incidents such as when employees or customers are hurt within the store or in the parking lot.

The manager is responsible for overseeing all monies in the store. He or she may go over reports of the day's receipts as well as weekly and monthly reports. The individual may also be responsible for depositing the days receipts in the bank or may accompany an assistant manager or other employee in this task.

Additional duties of Store Managers in supermarkets and groceries might include:

- Terminating employees
- Recommending raises and promotions for employees
- Handling loss prevention
- Representing the store at community events
- Handling crises

Salaries

Earnings for Store Managers working in supermarkets range from $26,000 to $55,000 or more. Variables affecting earnings include the size, prestige, and geographic location of the supermarket. Other variables include the experience, responsibilities, and education of the individual.

Employment Prospects

Employment prospects are good for supermarket Store Managers. Positions are located throughout the country. Individuals may, however, have to relocate for a specific job.

Advancement Prospects

The most common method of career advancement for Store Managers working in supermarkets or groceries is for individuals to locate similar jobs in larger stores or the new superstores. Another way Store Managers climb the career ladder is by being promoted to positions such as area managers.

Education and Training

Educational and training requirements vary from store to store. Generally larger stores and chains require their Managers to go through formal training programs which include both classroom and in-store training. Some supermarkets will hire individuals who have no formal training, but have worked their way up obtaining on-the-job training along the way.

Educational backgrounds of supermarket Store Managers vary too. While stores may not require individuals to hold anything above a high school diploma, they may prefer managers with college backgrounds or degrees. Good majors include business, management, marketing, retailing, communications, advertising, liberal arts, or related fields.

Experience, Skills, and Personality Traits

Store Managers working in groceries and supermarkets need a great deal of experience. Most have gone through the ranks either starting out at the bottom and moving up or going through a management program. Store Managers may have been department managers and then assistant store managers prior to their appointment. The manager must have a knowledge of management principles as well as a total understanding of the retail grocery industry.

Leadership skills, self-confidence, and decisiveness are essential. The ability to deal with and work well with people is mandatory. Individuals need to be good problem solvers who are energetic, detail oriented, and highly motivated. Communication skills, both written and verbal, are necessary as well.

Unions and Associations

Supermarket Store Managers may get additional career information by contacting the Food Marketing Institute (FMI), the National Retail Merchants Association (NRMA), and the American Collegiate Retailing Association (ACRA).

Tips for Entry

1. Many larger supermarkets and chain stores offer management training programs. Contact the headquarters of these stores to find out about requirements.

2. Positions may be advertised in the classified sections of newspapers. Look under classifications including "Store Manager," "Supermarket Opportunities," "Grocery Stores," "Super Centers," "Store Management," "Store Manager-Food," or "Management Opportunities."

3. Openings are also advertised in trade journals.

4. Jobs in this field may be located on-line. Begin your search on some of the more popular job search sites such as the Monster board (www.monster.com) and Yahoo! HotJobs (www.hotjobs.com).

5. Contact recruiters and executive search firms specializing in management positions in supermarkets.

6. Send your résumé and a short cover letter to the corporate offices of supermarkets as well as to the local store.

7. As noted, you need experience in this position to move up. Get your foot in the door, get experience, and learn everything you can.

WRAPPER/BAGGER— GROCERY STORE/SUPERMARKET

CAREER PROFILE

Duties: Wrap merchandise for customers; put merchandise in bags or other packaging for customers; transport customers' purchases to their car

Alternate Title(s): Bagger

Salary Range: $7.00 to $8.00+ per hour

Employment Prospects: Excellent

Advancement Prospects: Excellent

Best Geographical Location(s) for Position: Jobs may be located throughout the country

Prerequisites:

    Education and Training—On-the-job training

    Experience—No experience required

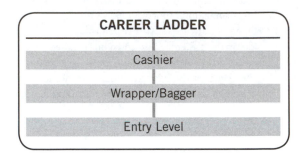

CAREER LADDER

Cashier

Wrapper/Bagger

Entry Level

Special Skills and Personality Traits—Ability to stand for extended periods of time; pleasant disposition; customer service skills

Position Description

Everyone needs groceries. Whether people do huge weekly shopping trips or just run into the store for a few items for dinner, Wrappers and Baggers make the whole process go quicker.

Wrappers, who are also referred to as Baggers, are the individuals responsible for packaging the merchandise customers purchase. As cashiers operate the cash register, scanning prices or ringing up purchases, they pass the merchandise to a Wrapper or Bagger. In many stores the cashier puts the merchandise on a moving belt as it is rung up. The Bagger then takes the merchandise and packs it for the customer. The individual may ask the customer if he or she prefers paper bags, plastic bags, or even boxes. The Bagger/Wrapper may use double bags if items are heavy.

The Bagger/Wrapper must be sure to package items carefully. He or she is expected to put heavier items on the bottom of bags and lighter or more fragile items on top. The individual must make sure that bags are not too heavy for customers to carry. He or she must also be sure bags are not so heavy they break when customers lift them out of their cart.

The Wrapper/Bagger may put items such as eggs and lightbulbs in separate bags so they don't break when boxes of laundry detergent or six-packs of soda roll on them. He or she may also put small items such as gum, candy, or batteries in separate bags. The individual might package frozen goods and other cold items together. This may help to keep them either frozen or cold until customers get their groceries home as well as making it easier to put them away.

Today, many grocery stores are superstores or supercenters. These stores sell groceries as well as a variety of other merchandise. In these cases, the Wrapper/Bagger may be responsible for packaging items other than those sold in traditional groceries.

After bagging the groceries and other merchandise, individuals are expected to put the bags into the customers' shopping carts.

Additional duties of Wrappers and Baggers may include:

- Carrying customers' packages to their car
- Checking prices for cashiers
- Putting merchandise which customers do not want to purchase back on shelves
- Collecting shopping carts from parking lot

Salaries

Earnings for Baggers and Wrappers working in grocery stores, supermarkets, or other retail establishments can range from approximately $7.00 to $8.00 or more per hour. Variables affecting earnings include the geographic location and size of the store as well as the demand for workers in the specific area.

Employment Prospects

Employment prospects are excellent for Baggers and Wrappers. Individuals may find work throughout the country.

One of the selling points for many people seeking this job is the flexibility of working hours. Individuals may work full time, part time, mornings, afternoons, evenings, weekdays, weekends, or holidays.

Advancement Prospects

Advancement prospects for Wrappers and Baggers are dependent to a great extent on the individual's aspirations. Some people take jobs as Baggers and Wrappers while in school, as a first job, or on a part-time basis to augment other incomes. These individuals can move on to other types of jobs depending on their training. Others may start out as Wrappers and Baggers and move into jobs as cashiers.

Education and Training

Baggers and Wrappers are trained on the job. Individuals will learn how to put items into bags so groceries don't get crushed and bags are not too heavy for customers to carry.

Experience, Skills, and Personality Traits

Jobs for Wrappers and Baggers are usually entry level and don't require any previous experience. Individuals should be able to stand on their feet for long periods of time. Good interpersonal and customer relations skills are essential as is a pleasant personality.

Unions and Associations

Wrappers and Baggers may be members of the United Food and Commercial Workers International Union or house unions. Individuals may get additional career information by contacting the National Retail Federation (NRF).

Tips for Entry

1. There is a great deal of turnover in these positions. Stop in stores where you are interested in working and ask to fill out applications. Ask that your application be kept on file if there are no current openings.

2. Remember to bring with you the names, addresses, and phone numbers of a few people you can use as references when filling in applications. Make sure you ask people if you can use them as references BEFORE you use them.

3. Jobs may be posted in store windows. Look for announcements stating "Baggers/Wrappers Wanted."

4. Jobs may be advertised in the classified sections of newspapers. Look under classifications such as "Baggers," "Wrappers," "Supermarket Opportunities," "Retail Opportunities," or "Grocery Stores."

5. Stores often call local labor offices to post these jobs. Remember to stop by your state employment office.

SALES MANAGER—AUTO SALES

CAREER PROFILE

Duties: Manage sales activities for automotive dealership; assist salespeople; recruit and hire sales staff, train salespeople; motivate salespeople; close deals

Alternate Title(s): Auto Sales Manager

Salary Range: $50,000 to $200,000+

Employment Prospects: Good

Advancement Prospects: Fair

Best Geographical Location(s) for Position: Jobs may be located throughout the country

Prerequisites:

    Education and Training—Educational requirements vary; see text

    Experience—Experience in auto sales

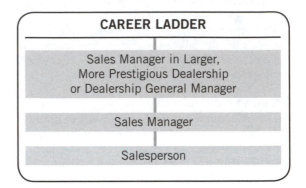

CAREER LADDER

Sales Manager in Larger, More Prestigious Dealership or Dealership General Manager

Sales Manager

Salesperson

Special Skills and Personality Traits—Management skills; administrative skills; motivation; selling skills; negotiating skills; interpersonal skills; communications skills; ability to work well with numbers

Position Description

Auto dealerships generally have a number of salespeople to help customers when buying cars. The Sales Manager holds an important job. He or she is responsible for leading the dealership's team of salespeople.

A good Sales Manager can mean the difference between success and mediocrity for both the dealership and its salespeople. The individual oversees the sales floor, and develops policies for managing it.

For example, the Sales Manager must determine how walk-ins are assigned to salespeople. (Walk-ins are customers who visit the dealership without being referred to a specific salesperson.) The Sales Manager also must determine how customers calling the dealership not asking for a specific person are assigned to salespeople.

Part of the job of the Sales Manager is recruiting and hiring the sales staff. The individual may develop and place help wanted ads in print or broadcast media. He or she may interview potential sales people. The Sales Manager may also set the work schedules for the sales staff.

One of the most important functions of a good Sales Manager is training the sales staff. The Sales Manager must make sure each salesperson knows as much as possible about each vehicle in order to sell it effectively. He or she may hold regular meetings to inform the sales staff about new cars, new options, and how vehicle features work.

The individual will also train salespeople on selling techniques utilizing policies of the dealership. The Sales Manager may provide training for the sales staff on a one-to-one basis or may be expected to develop formal group training programs.

Another important function of the Sales Manager is motivating the sales staff. Selling cars is not always easy. Every customer who walks in does not make a purchase. Most customers like to comparison shop. It is essential for all salespersons to remain upbeat and motivated. The Sales Manager needs to be effective in this task or he or she may lose salespeople.

When a customer comes in to purchase a car he or she may be indecisive. The Sales Manager often assists salespeople in closing deals or clinching the sale. He or she may explain the various options for obtaining a vehicle such as leasing, purchasing, and financing.

The Sales Manager must be a good negotiator. There is a great deal of negotiation in this type of job and it must be done in a polite and friendly manner to keep the customer.

While salespeople have some leeway in pricing vehicles, the Sales Manager has a great deal more. He or she usually has a great deal more experience in closing deals and may be more successful.

Other duties of car Sales Managers may include:

- Answering customers' questions regarding the dealership

- Handling paperwork
- Tracking weekly, monthly, and annual sales reports
- Ordering needed vehicles
- Arranging for financing
- Developing and setting up sales training programs
- Performing the duties of a salesperson

Salaries

Earnings for Sales Managers working in auto sales can range from approximately $50,000 to $200,000 or more. Factors affecting earnings include the specific dealership, size, location, and type of vehicles being sold.

Sales Managers may be compensated in a number of ways. These include either a straight salary, a low salary plus a high commission, or a higher salary and a lower commission. Commissions may be paid on vehicles sold by the dealership.

Earnings are dependent to a great extent on the aggressiveness, motivation, and sales ability of the individual. Earnings are also dependent on the type of vehicles sold. The more expensive the cars, the higher the commission paid.

Depending on the specific job, one of the perks that Automobile Sales Managers may receive in this line of work are demo cars to drive. Individuals also may receive liberal fringe benefit packages.

Employment Prospects

Employment prospects are good for individuals pursuing a career in this field. Every dealership is on the lookout for good Sales Managers who can motivate their sales staff. Jobs may be located throughout the country.

Advancement Prospects

Sales Managers working in auto sales may advance their career in a number of ways. Individuals may climb the career ladder by locating similar positions in larger or more prestigious dealerships. This would result in increased responsibilities and earnings. Others may be promoted to the position of dealership general manager.

Education and Training

While some dealerships may prefer applicants who have college backgrounds or degrees, most don't require it. Depending on the specific agency, individuals may be required to go through formal training programs or may go through less formal training or on-the-job training.

Any seminars, courses, or workshops in sales or motivation can be useful.

Experience, Skills, and Personality Traits

Prior to becoming Sales Managers, individuals usually have had a great deal of experience as auto salespeople. There are a lot of traits which make a good Automobile Sales Manager. Successful Sales Managers are reliable and loyal to their company, their salespeople, and their customers. Like salespeople, they must be good listeners, and have great selling and negotiating skills. The ability to motivate a sales staff is essential. Interpersonal and organizational skills are also necessary.

Unions and Associations

Those interested in learning more about careers in this field should contact the National Automobile Dealers Association (NADA).

Tips for Entry

1. Jobs may be advertised in the newspaper classified section under headings including "Auto," "Auto Sales," "Car Sales," "Truck Sales," or "Sales Manager—Auto."
2. Stop in to see auto dealers for which you might be interested in working. Ask to speak to the general manager.
3. Many auto dealerships have Web sites listing job openings.
4. Look for and take training programs, seminars, and workshops in selling and motivation.
5. You might also look for books and listen to tapes in these areas.

CAR SALESPERSON

CAREER PROFILE

Duties: Help customer determine which vehicle best suits individual's needs; accompany customer for test drives; provide customer with price of car

Alternate Title(s): Automobile Salesperson; Car Salesman; Car Saleswoman; Auto Sales Consultant; Salesman; Saleswoman; Sales Associate

Salary Range: $28,000 to $125,000+

Employment Prospects: Excellent

Advancement Prospects: Fair

Best Geographical Location(s) for Position: Jobs may be located throughout the country

Prerequisites:

Education and Training—Educational requirements vary

Experience—Experience requirements vary

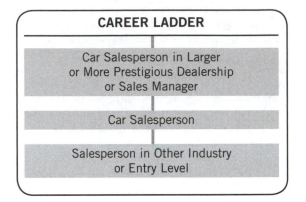

CAREER LADDER

Car Salesperson in Larger or More Prestigious Dealership or Sales Manager

Car Salesperson

Salesperson in Other Industry or Entry Level

Special Skills and Personality Traits—Sales skills; negotiation skills; interpersonal skills; communications skills; ability to work well with numbers; persuasive; driver's license

Position Description

Other than a home, the largest retail purchase many people make is their vehicle. The individual who sells these is called a Car Salesperson. He or she may also be referred to as a car salesman, car saleswoman, auto salesperson, or sales consultant, among other titles.

A Car Salesperson works for a car dealership. (In the context of this job, the word car will encompass all vehicles including automobiles, trucks, SUVs, etc.) He or she may work for a dealership selling new vehicles, used vehicles, or a combination of both.

The Car Salesperson is expected to greet potential customers when they walk into the dealership, and ascertain the type of vehicle in which the customer is interested. The salesperson determines the options that are important to the customer. Does the customer want an automatic transmission or standard? A sedan or two door? A luxury or an economy model? Does the customer plan on buying the car outright? How about financing? What about leasing? The salesperson sprinkles small talk into the conversation to put the customer at ease while gathering information. The more information the salesperson obtains, the better the opportunity to sell a car to a customer.

Salespeople encourage the customer to look at the car, and may bring the customer out to the car lot to show the various cars available. Salespeople also persuade customers to take a test drive, since customers who begin to take possession of a vehicle in their mind by driving it are more likely to make a purchase.

The salesperson explains why his or her dealership is better than others and outlines the perks of buying from that particular dealer. These may include free loaner cars when the customer's car is being serviced, discounted service rates for customers, and convenient service hours.

Throughout this process, the customer can be expected to come back to the same question. How much will the car cost? The salesperson must make the customer feel as if he or she is getting the best possible price. Depending on the structure of the dealership, the salesperson gives the customer a price or obtains a price from the sales manager. The price, of course, depends on the specific car and whether the customer is buying outright, leasing, financing, or trading in another vehicle. At times, the salesperson may have the customer talk to the sales manager to clinch the deal. He or she might additionally bring the customer to see the finance manager who can explain payment or lease terms.

The salesperson must be a good negotiator, and must be able to negotiate in a polite and friendly manner.

There are many dealers and options for people to select from when buying or leasing a vehicle. Some dealerships now offer "no haggle" pricing. Others may have prices set by Internet buying services. In these situations, it is even more important than ever for the Salesperson to be friendly and attentive to his or her customers.

Once a salesperson has closed a deal, he or she must complete a great amount of paperwork. The Salesperson makes sure contracts or sales agreements are signed and monies are correctly figured. In some dealerships, the salesperson also may arrange for auto registrations, licensing, etc.

The salesperson is responsible for making sure the vehicle is prepared for sale. When the customer comes in to take ownership, the salesperson is expected to take payment. He or she makes sure all transfers for the new vehicle and any trade-ins are signed. At this time, the salesperson shows the customer how all the features of the car work and covers any last-minute questions.

Other duties of a Car Salesperson may include:

- Answering customers questions regarding vehicles
- Selling extended warranties
- Selling additional options
- Following up after the car has been delivered to the customer to make sure they are happy and have no problems
- Arranging for financing

Salaries

Earnings for Car Salespeople vary tremendously. One of the greatest things about being a Car Salesperson is that the sky is the limit on earnings. Some individuals in this line of work make $28,000 and others earn $125,000 or more annually.

Salespeople may be compensated in a number of different ways. These include a straight salary, a commission on sales, or a combination of both. Earnings depend, to a great extent, on the aggressiveness, motivation, and sales ability of the individual. Earnings also depend on the type of vehicles sold. The more expensive cars are, the higher the commission for the salesperson.

The success of a Car Salesperson is in repeat business. Customers who feel they got the right vehicle at a fair price will not only come back for their next vehicle, but refer their friends, family, and business associates. Word-of-mouth referrals can increase a salesperson's income dramatically.

One of the perks that Car Salespeople may receive are demo cars to drive on their personal time. Individuals also may receive liberal fringe benefit packages.

Employment Prospects

Employment prospects for Car Salespeople are excellent. Dealerships are always on the lookout for aggressive, motivated salespeople. Individuals may find jobs throughout the country.

Depending on the situation, Car Salespeople may sell either new or used vehicles. Some sell both. Individuals may choose between jobs selling foreign or domestic vehicles.

Advancement Prospects

Advancement prospects for a Car Salesperson depend on the career aspirations of the individual. Some salespeople move up the career ladder by acquiring jobs as sales managers. Others enjoy the selling aspect of their job and want to stay in this type of position. These individuals may advance their careers by locating jobs in larger or more prestigious dealerships. The most common method of career advancement is selling more vehicles resulting in increased earnings.

Education and Training

There is usually no educational requirement for automobile salespeople. Some dealerships may prefer a college background, but they do not generally require it. Any seminars, courses, or workshops in sales will be useful. Once on the job, individuals will receive formal or informal training.

Experience, Skills, and Personality Traits

Experience requirements vary from dealership to dealership. While some employers require or prefer experience in auto sales, there are many who will hire motivated eager salespeople with no experience.

Good car salespeople are good listeners. They also know the right questions to ask potential buyers. The most successful Salespeople have great selling skills, negotiating skills, and interpersonal skills.

The ability to work well with numbers is essential. A clean driver's license is also needed.

Unions and Associations

Those interested in learning more about careers in this field should contact the National Automobile Dealers Association (NADA), the American Automobile Leasing Association (AALA), and the National Independent Automobile Dealers Association (NIADA).

Tips for Entry

1. Jobs may be advertised in the newspaper classified section under headings including "Auto,"

"Auto Sales," "Car Sales," "Truck Sales," "Sales-people," or "Auto Salesperson."

2. Stop in to see dealers you might be interested in working with. Ask to speak to the sales manager.

3. Many auto dealerships have Web sites listing job openings.

4. All sales experience is valuable in learning how to deal with the public.

5. Take advantage of any sales training programs you can find. These are motivational and help you hone your selling skills.

E-COMMERCE, MAIL ORDER, AND DIRECT RESPONSE SHOPPING

MARKETING DIRECTOR— WEB STORE

Duties: Develop and implement marketing plans and campaigns for company's Web site store or catalog; handle day-to-day marketing functions; plan and implement special events; oversee advertising and public relations program

Alternate Title(s): Internet Catalog Director of Marketing; Marketing Manager

Salary Range: $26,000 to $85,000+

Employment Prospects: Fair

Advancement Prospects: Good

Best Geographical Location(s) for Position: Jobs may be located throughout the country

Prerequisites:

Education and Training—College degree preferred, but not always required

Experience—Marketing, merchandising, publicity, public relations, advertising, and Internet experience necessary

CAREER LADDER

Marketing Director at Larger, More Prestigious Internet Site or Store

Web Store Marketing Director

Assistant Marketing Director or Marketing Director in Other Industry

Special Skills and Personality Traits—Creativity; good verbal and written communications skills; knowledge of retail industry; knowledge of consumer products; Internet savvy; marketing skills

Position Description

Today, many traditional retail outlets also have Web sites to showcase and sell their merchandise. These include department stores, specialty stores, chains and boutiques, catalogs, and even television shopping channels. There are also many companies selling merchandise on the Web that don't have traditional stores or catalogs and sell solely through the Web. Amazon.com is one of the better known of such sites.

There are thousands of Web sites on the Internet selling merchandise. It is increasingly becoming more important for retail as well as wholesale companies to have a presence on the Web. While some of these "stores" have names well known before their Internet presence, many do not. The Internet has made it possible for people in almost any part of the world to set up a store as small or large as they like on-line. No matter what the size, the site is available to the public. With so many sites available, how does an on-line store attract customers to their site? As in traditional retailing, an on-line store must market their site.

The Marketing Director of a retail Web site has a very important job. He or she finds ways to market the

site to potential customers. The manner in which this is done can mean the success or failure of an on-line retail store.

The Marketing Director develops the concepts and campaigns which will determine how the site will be marketed to potential shoppers. The individual determines the most effective techniques and programs to market the site and its products.

As part of this job, the Marketing Director plans and coordinates all of the site's marketing goals and objectives. How will people know the store is on-line? To whom will they market the site? What types of customers will they try to attract?

Marketing an on-line store is slightly different from marketing a traditional store. Customers for on-line stores can come from virtually anywhere in the world.

It is essential that the Marketing Director find ways to include the store's Web address in as many places as possible. In some situations, the store may have one or more traditional retail outlets. This often makes it easier to let people know of an on-line store.

The Marketing Director must be sure that the on-line store's Web site address is added to all television commercials, print advertisements, and packaging. This helps get the name and address of the web store in front of the public.

The Marketing Director's job becomes more challenging if the store's name isn't recognizable. In this case, he or she must find ways to bring the store to the public's attention. Marketing Directors may utilize a variety of programs to help attract shoppers and bring people to the store's site.

The Marketing Director must decide which of these programs and services are most viable for his or her specific audience. Often, Marketing Directors advertise the site. They may do this in print, television, or banner ads on other sites. Banner ads are the advertisements commonly seen on a Web site where an individual need only click on the banner to go to the site of the advertiser.

The Marketing Director often does research to obtain information about current and potential customers. He or she may prepare questionnaires or surveys to be placed on the site. In order to entice people to answer questionnaires, the Marketing Director may offer a gift, free shipping, or a percentage off on future orders.

Marketing Directors must devise innovate ideas to attract new visitors to the site. In many situations, on-line store Marketing Directors utilize sweepstakes and contests for this purpose. Once people log on to the on-line store site to enter the contest, the hope is they will return to the site to browse and buy. To accomplish this, many Marketing Directors run contests that customers can enter daily. This means customers may visit the site daily and see merchandise they want to purchase.

Another reason Marketing Directors of on-line stores use sweepstakes is to help build mailing lists. When people enter contests they must usually give their names, addresses, phone numbers, and email address. Additional information may be gathered as well which may be helpful in targeting shoppers to the site.

Marketing Directors also use contests to build lists for email newsletters. These newsletters are useful for informing customers about store specials, new merchandise, and promotions.

Promotions in traditional stores are designed to bring people in to browse and buy. Marketing Directors for on-line stores often utilize marketing efforts such as on-line coupons, offers of "buy one, get one for half price," or free shipping.

The Marketing Director who can come up with innovative and creative ideas might get the attention of journalists or others doing articles or stories on interesting Web sites. The individual may, for example, contact a television talk or news show to do a segment on an interesting product being sold on the site. Depend-

ing on which show a story ends up on, it can lead to thousands of Web site hits.

Depending on the size and structure of the site, the Marketing Director may work with an advertising and public relations director. In some situations, the Marketing Director may also be responsible for handling the public relations and advertising functions.

Additional duties of a web store Marketing Director might include:

- Supervising marketing, public relations, and advertising staff
- Developing marketing budgets
- Designing and developing marketing materials
- Conducting marketing research
- Developing and providing advertising content for site

Salaries
Annual earnings for Marketing Directors for on-line stores can range from approximately $26,000 to $85,000 or more. Variables affecting earnings include the size and prestige of the specific on-line store as well as the experience and responsibilities of the individual. Many on-line companies also offer stock options to their employees as part of their employment package.

Employment Prospects
Employment prospects are fair for this position. As more companies open on-line stores, prospects will improve. As Web stores can be located anyplace, jobs may be found throughout the country. Individuals who have a proven track record are most employable.

Advancement Prospects
Marketing Directors working in this industry have a number of options for career advancement. Some individuals get experience, prove themselves, and move on to positions at larger or more prestigious on-line stores. This results in increased responsibilities and earnings. Often, other on-line stores try to recruit the Marketing Director from a successful on-line store.

Other individuals move into positions as Marketing Directors for other types of Web sites or in other industries. Still others strike out on their own and start their own marketing firms.

Education and Training
Educational requirements vary for Marketing Directors working for on-line stores. Smaller or lesser known on-line stores may prefer a college degree, but not always require it. Generally larger, more prestigious, or better-known on-line stores will require their Marketing

Directors to hold a minimum of a four-year college degree. Good choices for majors include public relations, advertising, business, journalism, marketing, liberal arts, English, communications, and business.

Courses and seminars in marketing, public relations, publicity, promotion, the retail industry, and Web marketing are also helpful.

Experience, Skills, and Personality Traits

Marketing Directors in this industry must be Web savvy. Communications skills, both written and verbal, are essential. Individuals should be creative, innovative, ambitious, articulate, and highly motivated. Marketing Directors also need to be energetic with the ability to handle many details and projects at one time without getting flustered and stressed.

A knowledge of publicity, promotion, public relations, and advertising as well as research techniques is also necessary.

Unions and Associations

Marketing Directors may belong to a number of trade associations providing support and guidance. These might include the American Marketing Association (AMA), the Marketing Research Association (MRA), the Public Relations Society of America (PRSA), and Electronic Retailing Association (ERA).

Tips for Entry

1. Positions may be advertised in the classified ad section of newspapers. Look under headings including "Marketing," "Marketing Director," "Web Store," "On-Line Store," or "E-Tailing."

2. Send your resume and a cover letter to stores or sites in which you are interested in working. Ask that your resume be kept on file.

3. Join trade associations. These will help you in searching for internships, scholarships, and training programs in marketing.

4. Jobs may also be advertised in trade journals.

5. Look for jobs on-line. Check out sites such as those at www.hotjobs.com and www.monster.com to get started.

6. Take seminars and courses in marketing, promotion, public relations, publicity, and Web marketing. These will give you an edge over other applicants as well as helping you hone your skills and make valuable contacts.

WEBMASTER—ON-LINE STORE OR CATALOG

Position Description

Every day more companies are getting a presence on the World Wide Web. Retail businesses are no exception. Whether they are small retail companies aspiring to make it big or large companies who don't want to miss the boat with on-line sales, retail stores on the Internet are here to stay. An on-line store means a retailer can have customers around the corner or around the world.

In order to open an on-line store, a company must rent a space or location on the Web. This may be done by obtaining a host. The store pays the host for the right to place their store on-line on the host's space. In some instances, the store and the host are one.

In order for potential customers to find the store, it must have a Web address. This is the domain name. For example, the Web address of amazon.com is www.amazon.com. The Web address of the television shopping channel QVC is www.iqvc.com.

The individual responsible for putting together the Web site for the on-line store is called the Webmaster. The Webmaster's job is very important to the on-line retailer. His or her skill and talent can mean the difference between a Web store's success and failure.

Web stores are very much like traditional stores. If people don't go and visit, no one will buy anything. Traditional stores need foot traffic. Web stores need visitors. Every time an individual visits a Web page it is called a hit. Just as the more people who visit a store, the better the chance of sales, similarly, the more hits a Web store gets the better the chance of people buying. It is also essential that people not only visit a Web store, but revisit it on a consistent basis.

The Webmaster develops and creates the Web store site on the World Wide Web. He or she must design and program the on-line store site so it is exciting and easy to use. The Webmaster must be sure that the each Web page on the store site opens easy and quickly. If they don't, people often leave the site and surf to another location. This results in a loss of sales.

The Webmaster develops the site and adds pictures of products, animations, and other graphics. These are useful to help potential customers get a better idea of what the merchandise looks like as well as adding excitement to the various pages.

The individual may manipulate images to the proper size and format. This is necessary because if an image is too large it will slow down the loading of a Web page on an individual's computer. If an image is too small, a customer may not be able to see it clearly. The Webmaster must therefore know how many graphics to add and how to size them properly to make each page graphically pleasing, yet quick to open.

The Webmaster often develops a system for people to search for products on the store site. The easier it is for people to find what they are looking for, the better the chance of a sale. He or she may program pop-up windows, product compare features, shopping carts, secure payment systems, or other functions to make on-line shopping easier for the customer.

Developing and designing the Web store site is just one part of the job of the Webmaster. He or she is additionally responsible for the continued management and maintenance of the site.

In order to keep an on-line store site fresh and timely retailers often change the merchandise they are offering, update sale items, or have promotions to attract customers to their store site. Sometimes the on-line stores change content daily. The Webmaster must make ad changes and remove stale content.

Web sites are created in special languages so they can be displayed on the Internet. Text, for example, is converted into a language called HTML, or Hypertext Markup Language. Other languages may used as well. The Webmaster must know how to format the special languages.

Webmasters are expected to monitor the site continuously. Every time new content or a link is added, the individual must be sure everything on the site is working and all links are accurate.

Depending on the situation and the size of the on-line store, the Webmaster may work alone or may have one or more people working under his or her direction. He or she may also work with graphic designers and artists, photographers, copywriters, or editors.

Other duties of Webmasters for on-line stores include:

- Developing Web content
- Making sure the store site is user friendly
- Responding to inquiries from customers and other browsers having problems with the site
- Handling problems with the site
- Finding the best way to present information and graphics on the store site

Salaries

Annual earnings for Webmasters working for on-line retailers may vary from approximately $28,000 to $125,000 or more annually. Variables include the size and prestige of the specific retailer as well as the responsibilities, experience, and reputation of the individual.

Webmasters who have a proven track record for developing creative sites which attract attention will earn the highest salaries.

It should be noted that some retailers hire consultants to handle their Web site stores. These individuals may earn between $50 and $200 or more per hour.

Employment Prospects

Employment prospects are good for Webmasters seeking to work for on-line retailers and getting better every day. Depending on the experience of the individual, he or she might work for small start-up retailers or those that are well established.

Individuals may find positions with retailers who are currently on line, retailers who are planning an on-line presence and on-line catalogers. Jobs may be located throughout the country.

As a result of the nature of the job, some retailers may allow their Webmasters to telecommute all or part of the time. Individuals may also find part-time or consulting positions.

Advancement Prospects

Webmasters working for retailers with on-line stores can advance their careers in a number of ways. Those who build Web sites which consistently attract visitors will have no trouble climbing the career ladder. The most common method of career advancement for Webmasters is locating similar positions with larger or more prestigious retailers. This will result in increased responsibilities and earnings. Other Webmasters decide to strike out on their own and begin consulting firms.

Education and Training

Education and training requirements vary for Webmasters working for on-line retailers. Many Webmasters are self-taught. Some have taken classes. Others have college backgrounds or degrees in computers, programming, languages, graphics, web authoring, and the Internet. However it is learned, Webmasters must know HTML. It is also necessary to know other programming languages such as Cold Fusion, PERL, and Active Server Pages. It is helpful for those working on retail store sites to also know how to integrate databases.

Technology is constantly changing in this field. It is essential that Webmasters update their skills by self-study and/or classes, seminars, and workshops to keep up. Additional classes in understanding retail will also be helpful.

Experience, Skills, and Personality Traits

Experience requirements depend, to a great extent, on the size and prestige of the on-line store. Smaller on-line stores or those just starting up, may not require Webmasters with a great deal of experience as long as they illustrate that they can do an effective job. Larger, more prestigious on-line stores will generally want their Webmasters to have a proven track record and experience with retail sites.

Individuals must have a total competence with Web dynamics, HTML authorship, and other programming languages. While some graphics work is outsourced or done by graphic designers within the company, graphic talent is necessary.

Webmasters additionally need excellent communications skills, both verbal and written. Creativity is essential.

Unions and Associations

Individuals interested in learning more about careers in the field may obtain additional information by contacting the Internet Professionals Association (IPA) and the National Retail Federation (NRF).

Tips for Entry

1. Positions may be located in the classified section of newspapers. Look under heading such as "Webmaster," "Retail Opportunities," or "On-Line Store." Also look for ads under specific store and on-line store names.
2. Trade journals may also list openings.
3. Look for a job on-line. Start with the more popular job sites such as those at www.hotjobs.com and www.monster.com.
4. Check out the Web sites of stores and catalogs on-line. Many post job openings.
5. Get experience putting together Web sites for not-for-profit organizations or civic groups. Don't forget to add your name as the creator and Webmaster.

CUSTOMER SERVICE MANAGER— ON-LINE STORE OR CATALOG

Position Description

Web stores and catalogs, like other retail outlets must provide exemplary customer service in order to survive. While e-commerce is thriving, in order to be successful, web stores and catalogs must still remember the golden rules of retailing. "The customer is always right," and "The customer needs to feel valued and important."

Most web stores and on-line catalogs employ a Customer Service Manager or customer service representatives to handle any problems or difficulties customers may have shopping on the site. In smaller retail sites, the webmaster or store owner may handle these functions. However, larger sites and stores usually have at least one Manager and may have a number of customer service representatives.

While shopping on-line is convenient and, to many, the best way to make purchases today, to some the process is new and unfamiliar. People may be uncomfortable with putting their credit card on-line, worried about shipping dates, extra charges, returns, or an array of other problems. In a traditional store, a customer can pose a question and someone will answer face to face. In an on-line store, the question is often emailed to the customer service department. The Customer

Service Manager receives the email with the question and is expected to respond. Most of the time, this is done by email. In some cases, the Customer Service Manager will assign these duties to customer service representatives.

The Customer Service Manager handles a variety of situations ranging from technical difficulties to problems with returns. For example, a customer might email customer service when a web store link isn't working correctly. Another customer might email that he or she is having problems adding items to their shopping cart on the site. In these cases, the Customer Service Manager must contact the webmaster to check out the situations and see how quickly the situations can be resolved. The Customer Service Manager must also email customers to thank them for bringing problems to their attention and advise them of a solution.

Sometimes the problems the Customer Service Manager faces are not technical in nature or web specific. For example, a customer may have placed an order for merchandise and it didn't arrive in a timely manner. Understandably, the customer is irate and wants an answer. The Customer Service Manager may respond with an email apologizing and offer the customer something to make up for the trouble he or she experienced. Depending on the situation, this might be a discount on the order, free-shipping, or a gift certificate toward a future purchase. The Customer Service Manager may also send a letter through the mail to apologize.

Depending on the specific on-line store, customers may want more information on a product than is offered on the Web site. They may contact customer service to find out if additional colors are offered, when stock will be in, or warranty information. The Customer Service Manager or a subordinate will contact the buyers to get the information and e-mail back an answer.

Web-store customers generally want their queries answered in as immediate a fashion as possible. The Customer Service Manager must see that queries, questions, and problems are handled quickly. At the very least, the individual must email a note informing customers they are working on a solution. In many companies, this is automated.

Other duties of Customer Service Managers for on-line stores include:

- Overseeing customer service representatives
- Training customer service representatives
- Developing policies to handle customer service issues
- Working with other members of the on-line store development team to make sure the site is customer friendly
- Preparing reports on customer service inquires for the on-line store owners or management
- Handling difficult returns for customers
- Issuing credits or gift certificates to make up for unsatisfactory service

Salaries

Earnings for Customer Service Managers working for on-line stores can range from $25,000 to $48,000 or more annually. Variables include the size and prestige of the specific on-line retailer as well as the responsibilities and experience of the individual.

Employment Prospects

Employment prospects are good for Customer Service Managers interested in working for on-line stores. While jobs may be located throughout the country, individuals may need to relocate for the position.

Individuals may work for large established on-line stores and on-line catalogs as well as smaller retail sites which are just starting up.

Advancement Prospects

Customer Service Managers working with on-line stores may advance their careers by locating similar jobs at larger or more prestigious on-line retailers. This results in increased responsibilities and earnings. Some individuals may also become customer service directors with large on-line retailers.

Education and Training

Educational requirements vary. Generally, the more well known on-line retailers will require or prefer a college degree. Smaller or lesser known on-line stores may not have an educational requirement as long as individuals illustrate that they can handle the job.

College gives individuals the opportunity to gain experience and may be useful in career advancement. It may also give one applicant an edge over another who doesn't have a college degree.

Experience, Skills, and Personality Traits

Customer Service Managers need the ability to make decisions quickly and effectively. This is mandatory with on-line stores. As noted previously, because of the nature of electronic retailing, people expect an answer shortly after posing a question.

As so much of this job entails writing, it is essential for Customer Service Managers to have excellent written communications skills. An understanding of the retail industry, customer service, and the workings of the Internet are also necessary.

Unions and Associations

Individuals may be members of a number of organizations which provide career guidance and support. These include the Internet Professionals Association (IPA) and the Electronic Retailing Association. Additional career information may also be obtained by contacting the National Retail Federation (NRF).

Tips for Entry

1. Jobs may be advertised in the classified sections of newspapers. Look under classifications such as "Internet Opportunities," "On-line Opportunities," "On-line Retailing," "Customer Service Manager," or "E-Commerce Opportunities." Specific on-line stores may also list multiple jobs in an advertisement.
2. Visit the Web sites of on-line retailers. Many post job openings.
3. Look for a job on-line. Start with some of the better-known sites such as those at www.hotjobs. com and www.monster.com. Then search out other relevant job sites.

4. Make sure you are Internet savvy. If necessary, take a class at a local vocational-technical school or community college.

5. Seminars on Internet customer service will also be helpful. Many are offered throughout the country.

6. You might also stop at the library to get some books on customer service on the Internet and on-line retailing. The more you know, the better the job you can perform.

DIRECT RESPONSE COPYWRITER

Duties: Develop and write copy for direct response advertising; prepare copy for brochures, marketing pieces, etc.

Alternate Title(s): Copywriter

Salary Range: $24,000 to $100,000+

Employment Prospects: Good

Advancement Prospects: Good

Best Geographical Location(s) for Position: Positions located throughout the country

Prerequisites:

Education and Training—Bachelor's degree in advertising, business, journalism, public relations, marketing, liberal arts, English, communications, business, etc.

Experience—Experience as junior copywriter, trainee, or intern helpful

Special Skills and Personality Traits—Creativity; excellent writing skills; good command of the English language; knowledge and understanding of direct response copywriting

CAREER LADDER

```
Copy Supervisor or Copywriter at Large,
Prestigious Direct Response Agency

        ↑

Direct Response Copywriter

        ↑

Junior Copywriter or Trainee
```

Position Description

In addition to traditional retail stores, many products today are sold through direct response. One of the oldest forms of direct-response selling is the catalog. The newest are home shopping channels and infomercials, and other forms include direct mail as well as certain television or radio shows that are actually paid programming.

The individual responsible for writing and developing the copy for direct response advertising is called the Direct Response Copywriter. His or her main duty is writing copy for products generally sold through nontraditional retail outlets, and the exact duties of the job may vary among employers. The individual may write copy for print advertisements, sales letters, brochures, marketing pieces, copy for television or radio commercials, catalogs, or scripts for those selling products on home shopping channels or infomercials.

The Direct Response Copywriter may write simple copy such as headlines or may develop copy for entire mailings, advertisements or promotional packages. Direct Response Copywriters generally focus in on a specific group of people or market that may be interested in a product, and direct response pieces may be sent in the mail, advertised in a specialized publication, or seen during a televised program that targets these groups. Generally, the products being advertised can be ordered either by phone or mail.

Some Direct Response Copywriters, for example, may develop copy for literature sent in monthly credit card statements selling merchandise. This concept, often called piggy-backing, may offer merchandise at a discounted price for credit card holders. It is essential to the success of this type of selling that the Direct Response Copywriter develop ads and brochures that grab people's attention. The ad, letter, or sales piece must make people want to read it, pick up a phone or write out a check, and order the merchandise at that very moment. Successful Direct Response Copywriters develop ads that make a consumer want to take action immediately. In many situations, the Direct Response Copywriter inserts a coupon into the advertising or promotional piece in order to stimulate quick and immediate response. Direct response earned its name from this type of direct action.

One of the interesting things about the job of a Direct Response Copywriter is that the results of his or her work can be seen almost immediately. People may either order a product, call an "800" number and charge it for a purchase, throw a brochure away or ignore it completely. If a sales letter, commercial, or advertisement does not draw orders almost immediately, the Direct Response Copywriter may be asked to change it rapidly.

Depending on the specific employment situation, The Direct Response Copywriter may also be responsible for developing advertising and sales concepts. He or she may come up with an idea to use as the selling point such as the low price, a money back guarantee, the trial period, or the extra added value if the customer acts immediately.

Additional duties of Direct Response Copywriters may include:

- Preparing copy for web retail stores
- Doing research to gather information for copy
- Revising or rewriting copy that the copy supervisor may find unsatisfactory

Salaries

Earnings for Direct Response Copywriters can range from approximately $24,000 to $100,000 or more annually. Factors affecting earnings include the size and prestige of the specific employer, as well as the responsibilities, experience, education, and reputation of the individual. Those who have proved themselves will earn salaries towards the upper end of the scale.

Employment Prospects

Talented Direct Response Copywriters are always in demand. Individuals may find employment throughout the country in a variety of settings. These include small, mid-sized and large catalog companies, direct response agencies, retail web sites, direct television agencies, and manufacturers of products sold through direct response methods.

Advancement Prospects

Direct Response Copywriters who develop persuasive copy which shows results will have no trouble advancing their careers. Individuals may climb the career ladder by becoming copy supervisors or locate jobs at large direct response agencies.

Education and Training

Generally, employers prefer individuals hold a minimum of a four-year college degree. Good choices for majors include advertising, marketing, public relations, English, liberal arts, or communications.

Courses and seminars in advertising or copywriting are useful to hone skills.

Experience, Skills, and Personality Traits

Direct Response Copywriters should be very creative, with a flair for writing exciting, persuasive headlines and body copy. They need a way with words that can make people want to take action right away.

Excellent writing skills are mandatory. A complete working knowledge of word usage, grammar, and spelling is necessary. The ability to work on multiple projects at one time and meet deadline is essential.

Individuals are often asked to show their portfolio or "book" of their work prior to being hired. This book is used to illustrate talent to potential employers.

Unions and Associations

Direct Response Copywriters may belong to a number of trade associations providing support and guidance. These may include the American Advertising Federation (AAF), the Business/Professional Advertising Association (B/PAA), the American Marketing Association (AMA), and the Direct Marketing Association (DMA).

Tips for Entry

1. Join trade associations and attend their meetings and conventions. These are invaluable sources of information and networking opportunities.
2. Many associations have student memberships. Some of these also offer scholarships or internship opportunities.
3. Get experience in all facets of writing. This will help prepare you for your writing career.
4. Collect samples of direct response copy to see what might make you take action now. Practice writing your own copy for products.
5. Put together a portfolio of your writing samples. Include a variety of samples to illustrate your writing talents.
6. Positions are often advertised in the classified sections of newspapers. Keep in mind the Sunday paper usually has the largest classified section. Look under headings including "Direct Response," "Direct Mail," "Copywriter," or "Direct Response Copywriter." Companies may also advertise a number of opportunities in a boxed classified ad.

CATALOG COPYWRITER

CAREER PROFILE

Duties: Develop and write copy for catalogs

Alternate Title(s): None

Salary Range: $25,000 to $57,000+

Employment Prospects: Fair

Advancement Prospects: Fair

Best Geographical Location(s) for Position: The greatest number of positions will be in areas hosting catalogs

Prerequisites:

Education and Training—Bachelor's degree in advertising, business, journalism, public relations, marketing, liberal arts, English, communications, business

Experience—Experience as junior copywriter, trainee, or intern helpful

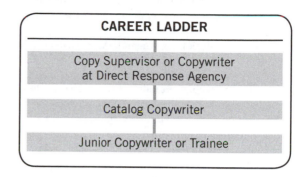

CAREER LADDER

Copy Supervisor or Copywriter at Direct Response Agency

Catalog Copywriter

Junior Copywriter or Trainee

Special Skills and Personality Traits—Creativity; excellent writing skills; good command of the English language; knowledge and understanding of catalog copywriting

Position Description

With today's busy lifestyles, more people than ever are catalog shopping. There are literally thousands of different catalogs selling everything from soup to nuts and masses of items in between. Some catalogs sell a variety of merchandise, much like a department store. Others sell specialty items such as crafts, clothing, toys, shoes, electronics, plants, gourmet food, jewelry, tools, vitamins, music, videos, and books.

Copywriters working for catalog companies have challenging jobs. Individuals must describe a product in few words in such a way that people are enticed to purchase it. A common saying in the advertising industry is "Sell the sizzle, not the steak." Catalog Copywriters must do the same. They must make products in the catalog seem exciting no matter what they are.

Successful Catalog Copywriters use descriptive terms so that those who read the copy can imagine seeing and feeling the product being described. They can often even make people imagine the smell and taste of a product. For example, a talented Copywriter might write the following blurb in a gourmet food catalog under a can of chocolate chip cookies. *"Double Decadent Chocolate-Chocolate Chip Cookies. Four dozen chewy, chocolaty, fresh baked, bite sized chocolate chip cookies. Each mouth-watering chocolate morsel is chock full of chips and covered in a crunchy chocolate coating. Tucked into a decorative collector's tin and wrapped separately for you to savor alone or share with a friend."*

One of the problems catalog shoppers often face is that they do not have the actual product in front of them to pick up and see. The more descriptive the words a Copywriter uses, the easier it is for a potential customer to imagine what a product will be like.

Catalog Copywriters are expected to write headline copy, as well as the body of the description for each product. The individual must be able to describe each product in just a few words. Although there are exceptions, this usually ranges from approximately thirty words to one hundred words per product.

In order to perform their job, Catalog Copywriters may read the product literature and look at photos as well as touch and feel the actual product. In this manner, the individual will better be able to describe the product. In some instances, the manufacturer of the product also provides some descriptive copy. The writer may use this as the basis of his or her copy. Generally, a picture will accompany the product in the catalog. The Copywriter must make sure the copy makes sense and relates to the accompanying photograph.

Some catalogs have hundreds of products. Each product sold in the catalog needs copy to describe it. Depending on the size and structure of the catalog, the individual may handle all the product copywriting duties or may work with one or more Copywriters. As a rule, copy must be approved by the catalog's copy supervisor. In some instances, the manufacturer of specific products may also need to approve copy.

It should be noted that many companies today also put their catalog on-line. Additionally, there are companies which solely have on-line catalogs. Catalog Copywriters may be responsible for handling the product copy for either variety.

Additional duties of Catalog Copywriter may include:

- Preparing copy for the catalog cover and back pages
- Doing research to gather information for copy
- Revising or rewriting copy that the copy supervisor may find unsatisfactory

Salaries

Earnings for Catalog Copywriters can range from approximately $25,000 to $57,000 or more annually. Factors affecting earnings include the size and prestige of the specific catalog as well as the responsibilities, experience, education, and reputation of the individual.

Employment Prospects

Employment prospects are fair for Catalog Copywriters. Individuals may find employment throughout the country. These include small, mid-sized, and large catalog companies. Additionally, there are increasing numbers of positions for Catalog Copywriters for on-line catalogs.

Advancement Prospects

Catalog Copywriters who consistently write persuasive copy will have no trouble advancing their careers. A common method of climbing the career ladder is landing a job with a larger or more prestigious catalog company. Some individuals advance their career by being promoted to copy supervisors. Still others locate jobs at advertising or direct-response agencies.

Education and Training

Most catalog companies prefer individuals hold a minimum of a four-year college degree. Relevant majors include advertising, marketing, public relations, English, liberal arts, and communications. Courses and seminars in advertising and copywriting are useful to hone skills.

Experience, Skills, and Personality Traits

Catalog Copywriters need to be very creative, with a flair for writing attention-grabbing, persuasive headlines and body copy. They need a way with words that can explain an item in an interesting manner with just a few words.

Excellent writing skills are mandatory. A complete working knowledge of word usage, grammar, and spelling is necessary. The ability to work on multiple projects at one time and meet deadlines is essential. Individuals are often asked to show their portfolio or "book" of their work prior to being hired. This book is used to illustrate talent to potential employers.

Unions and Associations

Catalog Copywriters may belong to a number of trade associations providing support and guidance. These may include the American Advertising Federation (AAF), the Business/Professional Advertising Association (B/PAA), the American Marketing Association (AMA), and the Direct Marketing Association (DMA).

Tips for Entry

1. Join trade associations and attend their meetings and conventions. These are invaluable sources of information and networking opportunities.
2. Get experience in all facets of writing. This will help prepare you for your writing career.
3. Collect samples of catalog copy to see what you might buy. Practice writing your own copy for products.
4. Put together a portfolio of your writing samples. Include a variety of samples to illustrate your writing talents.
5. Positions are often advertised in the classified sections of newspapers. Keep in mind the Sunday paper usually has the largest classified section. Look under headings including "Catalogs," "Catalog Copywriter," or "Copywriter." Catalogs may also advertise a number of opportunities in a boxed classified ad.
6. Send your resume and a cover letter to the corporate offices of companies at which you are interested in working. Ask that your resume be kept on file.

CALL CENTER REPRESENTATIVE

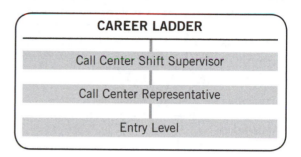

Position Description

A great deal of retailing is done through methods other than traditional store shopping. With today's busy lifestyles many individuals also shop on the Internet, buy from catalogs, or make purchases from infomercials or television shopping channels. Those who shop on the Web may just need to point and click to make a purchase. Those buying from catalogs or television often pick up a telephone and place their order.

Call Center Representatives are the individuals who answer the telephone calls from potential customers and take the orders. Depending on where they work, they may also be referred to as order entry operators, call center associates, or customer representatives. Some retailers farm out their order taking to huge call centers. Others have their own employees handling orders.

The Call Center Representative may answer questions and provide information regarding the company and it's products. The individual is expected to answer the phone in a pleasant and friendly manner.

The first contact many people have with the company they are calling is with the Call Center Representative. If he or she sounds unfriendly, the customer may be taken aback and not place an order.

The individual may greet customers and thank them for calling. The representative will then ask the customer how he or she can be of assistance. The Call Center Representative answers customer's inquiries to the best of his or her knowledge.

In some situations, the customer may want some information on a product or a price or may want to check availability. The Call Center Representative must be as helpful as possible. He or she often will punch information such as an item number or key word into a computer. In this manner the representative may be able to check availability, descriptions, and prices.

Once customers have decided what they want to purchase, the Call Center Representative will take the order. In some situations, the Call Center Representative will ask the individual for some information. This might, for example, include a customer's name, address, phone number, the code on the back of a catalog, a customer number, item numbers, colors, or sizes. This information is generally input into a computer.

The representative must obtain information on the customer's method of payment. Will he or she be sending a check? Is the item being shipped C.O.D.? Is a credit card being used? The representative will total the order including merchandise and any shipping, handling, and taxes and inform the customer of the final price. At this time the Call Center Representative will process the order and also let the customer know when the order should arrive.

The more familiar a Call Center Representative is with the products the company sells the better. In some situations, the representative may suggest products for customers or give explanations of merchandise.

A great deal of the success of companies selling products ordered by customers via the telephone is based on good customer service skills. Call Center Representatives who are good at their job are usually pleasant and helpful in making customers feel good about calling.

Additional duties of the Call Center Associates may include:

- Promoting the company's products
- Informing customers about current specials and promotions
- Giving customers phone number or addresses for additional customer service or contact information
- Handling customer service issues
- Searching the database for merchandise for which customers don't have item numbers

Salaries

Call Center Representatives earn hourly wages ranging from approximately $7.00 to $19.00 or more. Variables affecting earnings include the geographic location and size of the specific company for which the individual works as well as his or her experience and responsibilities. In some companies, individuals working overnight shifts or weekends will earn higher wages than those working more traditional hours and workdays.

Employment Prospects

Employment prospects are good for Call Center Representatives. While jobs may be located throughout the country, the most opportunities will be found in areas hosting large call centers. Individuals may work full time or part time.

Advancement Prospects

Advancement prospects are fair for Call Center Representatives. After obtaining experience, motivated individuals may advance their careers by acquiring positions as shift supervisors or call center managers.

Education and Training

Most employers require individuals to hold a minimum of a high school diploma or the equivalent. However, there are many Call Center Representatives who are still in school.

Generally, training is provided on the job. In some companies, formal training programs are provided to Call Center Representatives.

Experience, Skills, and Personality Traits

This is usually an entry-level job. While experience may give one applicant an edge over another, it is not generally required.

Call Center Representatives need a pleasant speaking voice and a good phone manner. Excellent customer service skills are mandatory. Computer skills are essential.

Unions and Associations

Individuals interested in learning more about careers in this field may obtain information by contacting the National Retail Federation (NRF) and the American Wholesale Marketers Association (AWMA).

Tips for Entry

1. Openings may be advertised in the classified sections of newspapers. Look under heading classifications such as "Call Centers," "Call Center Opportunities," "Catalog Opportunities," "Television Shopping Opportunities," "Call Center Representative," "Order Entry Operator," "Call Center Associate," or "Customer Representative." You might also look under ads for specific catalog companies, television shopping channels, or the mail order division of retail stores.
2. Check out openings on the Internet. Many call centers, catalogs, and television shopping channels have their own Web sites listing employment opportunities.
3. You might also find openings on the World Wide Web's job sites. Start with the more popular ones such as www.hotjobs.com and www.monster.com. A new site, www.abracat.com, is easy to use and has many job openings in all industries by geographical area.
4. Contact call centers, retail stores with mail order outlets, catalog companies, and television shopping channels. Ask to fill out an application.

TELEVISION SHOPPING CHANNELS

TELEVISION SHOPPING CHANNEL SHOW HOST

CAREER PROFILE

Duties: Presenting products on television shopping channel in interesting, persuasive, and credible manner; educating viewers on how to use products

Alternate Title(s): Program Host, Show Host

Salary Range: $70,000 to $500,000+

Employment Prospects: Poor

Advancement Prospects: Fair

Best Geographical Location(s) for Position: Positions located in areas hosting television shopping channels; three premier channels are located in West Chester, Pa., Tampa, Fla., and Eden Prairie, Minn.

Prerequisites:

Education and Training—Education requirements vary; on-the-job training

Experience—Experience in retail, sales, television, acting, or journalism helpful, but not always required

CAREER LADDER

```
Television Shopping Channel Show Host
for More Prestigious Television Shopping
Channel, Television Shopping Show Host
with Better Time Slot, or More Popular
Television Shopping Channel Show Host
```

```
Television Shopping Channel Show Host
```

```
Host Trainee
```

Special Skills and Personality Traits—Ability to speak to the camera; excellent verbal and written communications skills; creativity; personable; soft sales skills; understanding of the industry; sincere; believability; good listener; energetic

Position Description

Over the past few years television shopping has exploded into a very popular way to shop. These stations sell everything from clothing to housewares, gourmet food to beauty products, tools to gems and jewelry, electronics to toys, gadgets to gismos, and everything in between.

Some watch these stations for entertainment, others watch for company, and of course people watch them to shop. There are currently three major television shopping channels—QVC, HSN, and ShopNBC. Additionally there are an array of lesser-known local and cable shopping channels.

Television shopping originated in Clearwater, Fla., when during a break in a radio show, the owner of the station asked the on-air radio talk show host to sell a box of can openers to his listeners after the break. The show talk show host complied and described the can openers to his listeners in such a compelling manner that he ended up selling over 100 can openers in under an hour.

The owner of the station saw the business potential and launched the country's first shopping channel, initially on a local Tampa cable station and then the nationwide channel, the Home Shopping Network. The first-ever television shopping channel host was that very same radio talk show host, Bob Cirosta. Cirosta, the pioneer of television shopping, went on to sell over 75,000 products in 20,000 hours of live airtime during his career.

As a result of his successes, many now have the opportunity to be a Television Shopping Channel Show Host as well. The main responsibility of a Television Shopping Channel Show Host is presenting products to viewers. He or she may present alone, with another host, or may work with a guest presenter. Depending on the product, this might be the creator of the product, a manufacturer's representative, or even a celebrity guest.

Whether alone or with the help of a guest, the Television Shopping Channel Show Host is expected to introduce the product to viewers. In order to pique interest, he or she may start with a question asking viewers if they have a specific problem or telling them about a solution to a potential problem that the product can solve.

As part of the presentation, the Television Shopping Channel Show Host tells the viewers the name of the product, its price, and the product number. The individual may explain the value of the product by giving details of the price competing retailers would be selling the same product for or discussing extras that the shopping network is including.

The Television Shopping Channel Show Host is responsible for explaining the features of each product as well as demonstrating its ease of use. He or she may go over colors, sizes, pricing options, and more. During the presentation, the Television Shopping Channel Show Host must be sure to sound sincerely excited about the product.

A successful presentation will generally educate viewers on various aspects of the product being sold by covering the 5 Ws. These include: who, what, when, where, and why. For example, who is the product for? What does it do? When should it be used? Where should it be used? And why should it be used? Effective presentations also cover why the product is unique. It is essential in the selling process to get viewers thinking what the product will do for them; how it will improve their life or at least make it easier. The Television Shopping Channel Show Host may say, for example, "Don't go out in the cold and struggle with crowds. You can shop with us from the comfort of your living room, cuddled in a quilt and enjoying a hot cup of coffee."

If the product is being demonstrated by models showing fashion or jewelry, the Television Shopping Channel Show Host may point out various features of the product on the model and ask the model to turn this or that way to illustrate a specific feature of a garment.

The Television Shopping Channel Show Host is expected to explain the various qualities of each product as well as to illustrate why someone couldn't do without it. The individual may offer viewers various ideas on how and when the product could be used. For example, "You might wear this to the office and then take the jacket off, add some jewelry and heels and wear it out to dinner." Or, "Consider buying more than one, save on your shipping and handling, and you'll have a gift for that unexpected guest on Christmas."

In order to be effective, Television Shopping Channel Show Hosts must have the ability to use a *soft* sell. What that means is that the presentation should not sound like someone selling popcorn at a ball game. Instead, the presentation should be in a manner that someone would speak to a good friend.

It is essential for Television Shopping Channel Show Hosts to have full knowledge of each product. In order to get this information, the individual may meet with manufacturer's reps, developers of the product, buyers, or producers. He or she may also read product manuals or bring the product home to use it for a period of time before presenting it.

Individuals must have the ability to maintain an interesting patter, continually making sure the product presentation is exciting and appealing. As television shopping is live, there is no room for dead space while the host tries to think of what he or she wanted to say. During the course of the presentation, the Television Shopping Channel Show Host may take calls from viewers who either have purchased the product previously, just bought the product, or want to ask a question regarding the product. As most callers have never been on the air, the Television Shopping Channel Show Host must make each caller feel comfortable. He or she also must be able to end the call in a pleasant manner, be a good listener, and be engaged.

Before a Television Shopping Channel Show Host even gets on the air, he or she has work to do. Individuals may meet with buyers or manufacturer's reps to learn everything there is to know about the product and its competition.

Most hosts do extensive preparation before a show getting ready for each presentation. While it might look like the individual is just *talking* about a product off the top of his or her head, he or she often prepares by rehearsing so the presentation will be interesting and well organized. Television Shopping Channel Show Hosts work with producers who communicate with them via an earpiece. The producer may, for example, say that a certain color of a product is selling out or how many of which size of a product are left. Some people can get used to this "voice in their ear" easily. For others it is very disconcerting.

Some hosts specialize in certain areas such as fashion, beauty, electronics, gems, crafts, or cooking. This can often make shows much more interesting as individuals can offer tidbits of information. A host, for example, may be a certified gemologist and discuss what powers some think various gems possess.

Other responsibilities of Television Shopping Channel Show Hosts might include:

- Going on trips with buyers
- Traveling for remotes
- Attending industry meetings, conferences, and conventions

Salaries

Earnings for Television Shopping Channel Show Hosts can vary tremendously. There are some individuals who earn approximately $40,000 and others who earn $500,000 or more annually. Factors affecting earnings include the size, structure, prestige, and popularity of the specific shopping channel, as well as the experience, responsibilities, professional reputation, and popularity of the host.

Individuals working for small local cable shopping channels will earn salaries at the lower end of the scale. Those who are working for one of the larger, more popular shopping channels who have a proven track record and a following will have earnings at the higher end of the scale.

Employment Prospects

Employment prospects are poor for individuals seeking positions as Television Shopping Channel Show Hosts. There are a limited number of television channel shopping channels and a limited number of positions.

Individuals may find opportunities with one of the more popular television shopping channels such as QVC, HSN, or ShopNBC by attending open casting calls held throughout the year by the specific channels or by sending in videos directly to stations. Other opportunities may include local shopping channels and smaller cable shopping channels. As television shopping becomes more popular, additional stations will also being to emerge.

Those with the right look and personality as well as the ability to look into a camera and *talk* to viewers in a believable manner so viewers can't resist buying a product will have an easier time entering the profession.

Advancement Prospects

Advancement prospects for Television Shopping Channel Show Hosts are fair once the individual gets a foot in the door. He or she may climb the career ladder by obtaining a better time slot or becoming a show host for a larger, more prestigious television shopping channel. After obtaining some experience, many individuals are able to build a large following that allows them to negotiate higher earnings.

Some individuals move into other areas of the industry. There have been Television Shopping Channel Show Hosts such as Mike Rowe, the star of Discovery Channel's popular show *Dirty Jobs,* who became stars of their own television shows. Others start their own line of products and become successful vendors for one or more of the television shopping channels.

Education and Training

While television shopping channels want their hosts to be as well rounded as possible, generally they do not require a college degree. That is not to say that a college degree might not be preferred.

Some Television Shopping Channel Show Hosts have college degrees and others do not. Those who have degrees have them in an array of diverse areas including telecommunications, retail, business, teaching, radio, and everything in between. Most television shopping channels have their own training programs. These programs teach effective methods of selling on air. They also teach how to treat guests, answer customer questions, deal with phone calls and testimonials, policies, and so on. Some shopping channels pair new hosts with established hosts who mentor them through the learning process. Classes, seminars, and certifications in a specific field will often help the marketability of an individual.

Experience, Skills, and Personality Traits

Prior to Television Shopping Channel Show Hosts being hired as full-fledged hosts, they often go through a host trainee period lasting from three to nine months. During this time, the individual learns all about the company's products and policies as well as how to be the best host possible.

They can come from a variety of backgrounds. These include retail and wholesale, sales, acting, television news, other areas of television and radio, public relations, teaching, and almost every area in between.

Some Television Shopping Channel Show Hosts are experts in certain fields, such as gemology, electronics, computers, cooking, crafts, or fashion to name a few. Experience in a specific field can often give one applicant an edge over another with similar credentials. Hosts need to be comfortable in front of a camera in addition to having the ability to speak into the camera. They should be well spoken, poised individuals with excellent written and verbal communication skills. Good listening skills are critical. Successful hosts are likeable, personable, enthusiastic, and have the ability to share information in a credible and believable manner.

No one wants to watch a Television Shopping Channel Show Host hawk a product. As noted previously, soft sales skills are essential for this type of presentation. Individuals who can convey information to the television audience in a manner much like they would be talking to a friend will be more successful.

Unions and Associations

Individuals interested in a career in this field should contact the Electronic Retailing Association (ERA) as well as the various television shopping networks to get additional information. Depending on the specific employer and the background of the individual, Television Shopping Channel Hosts may belong to a number of different unions including AFTRA (American Federation of Television and Radio Artists) or SAG (Screen Actors Guild) among others.

Tips for Entry

1. Check out the Web sites of the various television shopping networks to see if and when they are hosting open casting calls or host searches.
2. Openings are often listed on television shopping channel Web sites.
3. Openings are also often listed on popular job search sites such as those at monster.com, hotjobs.com, and indeed.com.
4. If you don't see anything about a open casting calls or host search, don't despair. Consider checking out the employment section of television shopping channels in which you are interested in working, getting information on where to send a video of yourself presenting a product, and taking action.
5. Watch successful hosts to see what techniques work when presenting products on the air.
6. Take a product you are acquainted with, do some research so you know everything there is to know about it, and practice presenting it. Do the presentation in front of friends or family to get constructive criticism. Then make a three- or four-minute video to send to the shopping channels.

BUYER—TELEVISION SHOPPING CHANNEL

CAREER PROFILE

Duties: Shopping for products in specific category to sell on television shopping channel; working in partnership with vendors, merchandise planners, programming managers, etc., developing product selection in specific merchandise category; developing proprietary brands; negotiating prices

Alternate Title(s): None

Salary Range: $32,000 to $85,000+

Employment Prospects: Fair

Advancement Prospects: Fair

Best Geographical Location(s) for Position: Positions located in areas hosting television shopping channels; three premier channels are located in West Chester, Pa., Tampa, Fla., and Eden Prairie, Minn.; other channels may be located throughout the country in areas hosting local and cable television shopping channels

Prerequisites:

Education and Training—Bachelor's degree in business, management, fashion, merchandising, or a related area

Experience—Experience in buying and product development

CAREER LADDER

Buyer for Larger, More Prestigious Television Shopping Channel; Buyer for Larger Department at Television Shopping Channel; or Director or Manager of Buying of Specific Merchandise Area

↑

Buyer—Television Shopping Channel

↑

Assistant Buyer

Special Skills and Personality Traits—Negotiating skills; ability to forecast trends; verbal and written communications skills; creativity; personable; organized; understanding of the retail industry; understanding of electronic retailing; energetic; ability to multitask; detail oriented; understanding of trends; computer skills

Position Description

Television shopping, also known as electronic retailing, showcases a variety of products in a wide array of merchandise areas. In order to entice viewers to tune in and call to make a purchase, these channels need to be selling up-to-date and innovative merchandise. Finding just the right merchandise to sell is an essential part of the bottom line of all retail outlets, and television shopping channels are no exception. The individuals who do this job are called buyers.

Buyers hold an important position in the television shopping industry. They need to not only find the perfect merchandise, but negotiate great prices so people will be willing to buy it as well as paying for shipping and handling.

A Buyer Television Shopping Channel works in the merchandising department. Individuals are responsible for specific categories of merchandise. These might include broad categories such as clothing, jewelry, beauty,

kitchen, home, electronics, toys, gifts, crafts, leisure and fitness among others. Within each of these categories there are subcategories. For example, fashion subcategories might include accessories, handbags, shoes, careerwear, outerwear, and more. Electronics might include areas like phones, cameras, computers, and peripherals, etc. Jewelry might be separated into fashion and fine jewelry, silver, gold, and gems. Within each of these subcategories, there might even be additional subcategories such as specific vendors or proprietary brands.

Buyers work with merchandise planners, programming managers, and others on the television team as well as vendors to develop the perfect product selection. It is essential in doing this to come up with products that will be exciting, can be presented well, priced competitively, and irresistible.

Buyers deal with salespeople, manufacturers, wholesalers and inventors to find the new merchandise viewers see on television shopping channels everyday. Individuals may deal with both established vendors and new vendors to find fresh and innovative products. In some cases, shopping channels hold competitions or other events to locate vendors with new innovative products. Sometimes individuals meet with vendors at the television channel headquarters. In other situations, the individual goes on buying trips to visit suppliers or find new vendors in various locations throughout the country or the world, or to trade shows, expos, and exhibitions.

Buyers must have the ability to identify new products that will be successful. Every product does not sell well on television. Electronic retailing lends itself to selling products that can be presented, demonstrated, and explained easily on television. These products may solve everyday problems many of us have or simply make life easier. Some may be unique; other may not be sold in any other retail outlet. Once merchandise is found, Buyers need to determine how popular it will be so they can accurately determine the number of pieces to buy. Depending on the product and the shopping channel, this might be 1,000 pieces, 1,000,000 pieces, or more. Size and color must also be determined. If the Buyer is working in fashion, he or she must know the range of sizes that sell best and colors that are proven. Similarly, in the jewelry area, they must know what type of jewelry sells best to their customers, popular sizes, and/or gems. The best prices and terms from vendors must be negotiated. Television shopping channels commonly have one or more special values every day that are supposed to be an extraordinary price and product. For example, QVC has a "Today's Special Value" while HSN has "Today's Special." In order to make these a really good value to customers, Buyers must first locate a very special product that appeals to a wide audience and then negotiate the best prices and terms possible from the featured vendor. This generally can be accomplished by purchasing huge quantities of the product that are then featured prominently in shows during the day.

Individuals write orders for vendors to fill for products that they purchase. In addition to placing initial orders, they also write special orders or reorders of merchandise that is selling well or has sold out. They must keep appraised of the status of stock and products that sell particularly well. In this manner, they can determine what products are popular and what should be reordered and what will not be ordered again.

Buyers often watch the shows where products they have purchased are presented. By doing this they can hear comments from customers, hearing what customers want and what they like (or dislike) about the products. They can also get ideas for future purchases. Buyers must keep up with not only the number of product returns from a vendor, but the reasons. If too many products are returned because merchandise is defective, the individual may look for a new vendor to supply a similar product.

An interesting part of the job is actually developing proprietary product lines. These lines essentially mean that the television shopping channel can cut out the middleman. In essence the shopping channel creates a line of clothing, cookware, housewares, foods, etc., that is only available on the specific shopping channel. When doing this the Buyer may meet with manufacturers of known brands and negotiate deals where they will manufacture products similar to theirs or with specific features under a product line name created by the shopping channel. QVC, for example, has created their own line of cookware called Cooks Essentials, their own line of luxury bed linens called Amadeus, and their own lines of casual clothing called Sports Savvy and Denim and Company to name just a few.

As part of their job, Buyers often work with people in other departments. These may include individuals in quality control, the legal department, merchandising managers, planners, programming managers, and vendors. Together they work toward developing new shows or ideas for the television shopping channel as well as making sure every product is of the highest quality.

Buyers working at television shopping channels often have the unique opportunity of seeing how well their product choices are doing—almost instantaneously. Today's technology means that as soon as a product is presented on television, sales can be tracked. Seeing a product sell out in a matter of minutes can be very gratifying for a Buyer, as can great customer reviews.

Other responsibilities of Buyers working at a television shopping channel might include:

- Attending vendor meetings
- Sourcing new vendors for product and show ideas
- Developing special values
- Studying sales record and inventory levels of current stock to see what is selling and what is not
- Overseeing and managing staff
- Leading focus groups

Salaries

Earnings for Buyers working at television shopping channels can range from approximately $32,000 to $85,000 or more. Variables affecting earnings include the size, location, prestige, and popularity of the specific shopping channel as well as the experience and responsibilities of the Buyer. Other factors affecting earnings include the level the individual is in the organization as well as his or her professional reputation.

Employment Prospects

Employment prospects are fair for individuals seeking positions as Buyers for television shopping channels. While there are only a limited number of channels, each merchandise area generally has a number of buyers.

Individuals may find opportunities with one of the more popular television shopping channels such as QVC, HSN, or ShopNBC or one of the local shopping channels or smaller, lesser-known cable shopping channels. Opportunities are also available at shopping channels in other countries.

Advancement Prospects

Advancement prospects for Buyers at television shopping channels are fair. Individuals may climb the career ladder in a number of ways. Some advance their careers by becoming buying managers or directors for a specific merchandise area. Others become merchandise managers. Still others find similar positions at larger, more prestigious television shopping channels resulting in increased responsibilities and earnings.

It is important to note that advancement prospects often depend on the career aspirations of the Buyer. There have been Buyers at television shopping channels who have become program hosts and others who have created their own lines and become vendors themselves. It all depends on what the individual wants to do.

Education and Training

A college degree is generally required for Buyers working at television shopping channels. Good majors include business administration, marketing, management, fashion merchandising, or related areas. Individuals may additionally go through executive training programs either at the shopping channel or while employed by another company. These programs help individuals learn how to become Buyers through on-the-job training. It should be noted that while a college degree is required for most positions, experience may be accepted in lieu of education. Individuals will find reading trade and consumer publications in the buying area in which they are working to be very useful in keeping up with trends.

Experience, Skills, and Personality Traits

Buyers aspiring to work at television shopping channels need a good amount of experience. This might be obtained by working as an assistant buyer at a shopping channel or a buyer in another area of retail. Experience in product development will also be helpful.

The ability to predict trends is critical in buying. Successful Buyers have the innate sense of knowing what will be popular before it is. They have that special ability to project what colors will be hot, what products will be hot, and what people just won't be able to resist.

Negotiating skills are essential to Buyers. Finding the perfect products and not knowing how to or being able to comfortably negotiate will seriously hurt the bottom line of the electronic retailer.

Buyers should be creative individuals with an understanding of both the retail and electronic retailing industries. Good communications skills, both verbal and written, are necessary. Buyers should be organized, detailed-oriented individuals with the ability to multi-task effectively.

Computer skills are necessary.

Unions and Associations

Individuals interested in careers as Buyers for television shopping channels can contact the National Retail Federation (NRF). They might also want to contact the Electronic Retailing Association (ERA). Buyers might additionally belong to trade associations specific to the area of merchandise they are purchasing. For example, Buyers responsible for fashion or footwear may belong to the American Apparel and Footwear Association (AAFA), Fashion Group International (FGI), and the International Textile and Apparel Association (ITAA).

Tips for Entry

1. Check out the Web sites of the various television shopping networks. Most list openings.
2. Even if there isn't an opening, send your résumé and a short cover letter. You can never tell when a job opening will occur. If your résumé is there, you might get a call before someone else.
3. Openings are often listed on popular job search sites such as the Monster board, Yahoo! HotJobs, and Indeed.
4. If you are still in college, contact one of the major electronic retailers to find out if they have any intern openings.
5. Positions may be advertised in the classified sections of newspapers under headings including "Retail Opportunities," "Retail," "Electronic Retailing," "Buyer," etc. Don't forget to check out display advertisements listing one of more job openings of a particular retailer.
6. Contact executive recruiters specializing in the retail industry. Make sure you check ahead of time to see who pays the fee when you get the job—you or the employer.

FASHION STYLIST—TELEVISION SHOPPING CHANNEL

CAREER PROFILE

Duties: Selecting and coordinating merchandise, styles, jewelry, and accessories for models to wear during on-air presentations; creating image for models

Alternate Title(s): Stylist

Salary Range: $28,000 to $65,000+

Employment Prospects: Fair

Advancement Prospects: Fair

Best Geographical Location(s) for Position: Positions located in areas hosting television shopping channels; three premier channels are located in West Chester, Pa., Tampa, Fla., and Eden Prairie, Minn.; other channels may be located throughout the country in areas hosting local and cable television shopping channels.

Prerequisites:

Education and Training—Education requirements vary; see text

Experience—Experience working with a stylist may be required or preferred

CAREER LADDER

```
Fashion Stylist for Larger, More Prestigious
Television Shopping Channel, Television
Shopping Channel Fashion Stylist
Supervisor, or Stylist in Other Industry
            |
Fashion Stylist—Television Shopping
Channel
            |
Stylist in Other Industry
```

Special Skills and Personality Traits—Fashion sense; verbal communications skills; creativity; personable; organized; understanding of the retail industry; understanding of television cameras and lighting; energetic; ability to multitask; detail oriented; understanding of fashion and trends

Position Description

Television shopping has exploded over the past few years. While catalogs and even the Internet to some extent give people the ability to see a photo of a product, television shopping gives them the opportunity to really see what a product looks like and what it can do. While some people watch television shopping channels for the entertainment value and others watch for company, the largest number of people who watch television shopping channels do it to shop.

Television shopping channels present a wide variety of products. In order to entice people to not only watch, but to buy products, shopping channels put a lot of effort into making sure products are showcased in a positive manner.

To do this, the shopping network may build various sets to emulate rooms such as kitchens, living rooms, bedrooms, home offices, garages, etc., so it looks more realistic when presenting products. They also have specific sets built so fashions, jewelry, and beauty products can be showcased effectively.

Models are often also used during on-air presentations to help display and showcase products in a more natural manner. When presenting fashion and jewelry, models help viewers actually see products on a "live" person. This makes it easier to imagine how it will look on them. Similarly, models are frequently used for beauty shows featuring makeup and hair products as well. Models may also be used in live shows such as those featuring fitness products, home goods, and other housewares.

The individual responsible for the supervision of the models during the live production of shows is called the Fashion Stylist. The stylist is ultimately in charge of creating the on-air image of the models. Fashion Stylists assure that the models seen during on-air presentations look the best they can while making sure the company's products are showcased most effectively. To do this, they coordinate the image of models during on-air presentations so that their attire and accessories complement the products being sold. Fashion Stylists select and coordinate all merchandise, styles, jewelry, and accessories that models wear during fashion and jewelry presentations as well as any other on-air presentations where models are used.

To do this, the individual is given a list of the products that will be presented during an on-air presentation of a specific show. He or she is then responsible for coordinating wardrobe pieces and accessories for each model to wear. As models generally present a number of different items during a program, the stylist is usually responsible for creating a number of different looks. Additionally, in certain programs such as those that feature fashions, there may be three or four models. The stylist is responsible for styling each of them.

In some cases, the stylist may coordinate outfits for a model from a number of pieces being presented in the specific show. In others, he or she may coordinate pieces not only from the particular show but from other items that shopping channel offers. The individual may, for example, have one model wear a skirt, jacket, and blouse that are all products in the show. The stylist may have another model wearing a jacket that is in the show with a pair of jeans that are not. Yet another model may be asked to wear the jacket with a dress that is not even sold on the shopping channel. The idea is to showcase the products being sold, illustrating how they can be worn in a variety of situations.

The stylist must always accessorize each outfit. That means choosing just the right shoes, jewelry, scarves, hosiery, purses, etc. The idea is to create a look that viewers see and hopefully want.

The stylist must always keep the products being featured in mind when choosing styles for models to wear. If the stylist is working on dressing models for a high-end jewelry show with a lot of necklaces and pendants, he or she might choose a classic solid color gown with an open neckline instead of wearing a button-down blouse with a busy pattern. If models are part of an outerwear show full of coats, they must be accessorized with boots, hats, scarves, and gloves.

Successful stylists working for television shopping channels need the ability to create a variety of looks that viewers want to identify with. When this happens, viewers will hopefully have a difficult time resisting the urge to pick up the phone and buy. Sometimes a stylist dresses a model using an accessory such as a scarf in an interesting way that viewers may not have thought of. The stylist may use the scarf as a traditional scarf or may twist it and knot it in such a manner that it looks like a necklace. Viewers who might not even have considered buying the scarf might then call in and order it.

The stylist may also develop a "look" for models to wear when they are part of beauty shows. The stylist will often create a different image for models to wear during demonstrations for each different beauty vendor. Depending on the situation, the Fashion Stylist may work with a hair stylist or suggest the way models should wear their hair during a presentation. Similarly, there may be a makeup artist on staff or the stylist may suggest a certain look for the model's makeup. In some cases, the shows that the models are appearing in are not fashion, jewelry, or beauty oriented. Instead they may be fitness shows or programs focusing on housewares or other goods. In these situations, the stylists may work toward creating an image for models that will be consistent with the products being sold. For example, if a model is appearing in a show featuring sheets or bedding, the stylist may dress him or her in pajamas, a robe, and slippers. Stylists often have assistants who help them perform their duties by making sure clothing is clean, steaming it so it looks perfect, and helping dress the models. Fashion Stylists may work with a variety of additional people including buyers, vendors, and often even the designers to learn what type of image they want the models to convey when presenting their products. In this manner, the stylist can coordinate the image of the models and insure each product presentation is as effective as possible.

It is essential that the stylist create a "look" that is consistent with the image both the vendor and the channel wants and which will complement the products being sold. To do this, the stylist must be aware of the demographics of the viewers of the channel. What that means is that even if the current trend is crop tops and minidresses, if the demographics of the particular channel indicate that viewers would not generally wear fashions like that, the stylist cannot dress models in crop tops and minidresses. What many successful stylists do in situations like this is find a way to incorporate current trends and styles in a manner that takes viewers' tastes into mind.

It is essential that stylists continually keep up with new styles, colors, and trends in the fashion world. In order to accomplish this, he or she must read fashion magazines, attend fashion shows, and go to other events to stay in the loop.

Other responsibilities of Fashion Stylists working at a television shopping channel might include:

- Going on trips with buyers
- Going shopping to find items such as accessories, shoes, or complementary fashions necessary to create the perfect look and image

- Traveling for remotes
- Assisting models with hair and/or makeup

Salaries

Earnings for Fashion Stylists employed by television shopping channels may vary greatly. There are some individuals who earn approximately $28,000 and others who earn $65,000 or more. Variables affecting earnings include the size, location, prestige, and popularity of the specific shopping channel as well as the experience, responsibilities, and professional reputation of the individual.

Employment Prospects

Employment prospects are fair for individuals seeking positions as stylists at television shopping channels. There are a limited number of television channel shopping channels and a limited number of positions. Individuals may find opportunities with one of the more popular television shopping channels such as QVC, HSN, or ShopNBC or one of the local shopping channels or smaller, lesser-known cable shopping channels.

Advancement Prospects

Advancement prospects for Stylists at television shopping channels are fair. Individuals may climb the career ladder by becoming stylist supervisors. Some individuals advance their career by locating similar positions at a larger or more prestigious shopping channel. This generally results in increased responsibilities and earnings. Some individuals also become stylists in other industries or start their own stylist consultation business.

Education and Training

Education and training requirements vary for Fashion Stylists working at television shopping channels. Some employers require or prefer individuals to hold a degree in fashion, merchandising, or a related area. Others will accept experience in lieu of education. Stylists often receive on-the-job training by working as an assistant or apprentices to other stylists either at a shopping channel or in another industry.

Experience, Skills, and Personality Traits

Experience as a stylist is required for this position. Some individuals obtain this experience as assistants, apprentices, or even interns. Others have worked as stylists in industries other than television shopping. Stylists should be creative individuals with a great fashion sense. An understanding of fashion as well as television cameras and lighting is essential. Successful stylists have an innate sense of what will look good. They know how to pull together not only an outfit, but a total look. Verbal communication skills are needed for this type of job. Stylists should be personable people who like to work with others. The ability to multitask is vital. During an on-air presentation, there may be three or four models continually changing outfits. Individuals should additionally be detailed oriented and organized. An understanding of fashion, colors, and trends is critical.

Unions and Associations

Individuals interested in a career as a Fashion Stylist might want to contact the Association of Image Consultants International (AICI) or the Association of Stylists and Coordinators (ASC).

Tips for Entry

1. Check out the Web sites of the various television shopping networks. Most list openings.
2. Even if there isn't an opening, send your résumé and a short cover letter. You can never tell when a job opening will occur. If your résumé is there, you might get a call before someone else.
3. Openings are also often listed on popular job search sites such as those at monster.com, hotjobs.com, and indeed.com.
4. Consider taking some extra classes, workshops, and seminars on fashion trends, styling, and television lighting. In addition to picking up some new information, you might make some good contacts.

PRODUCT INFORMATION COPYWRITER—TELEVISION SHOPPING CHANNEL

CAREER PROFILE

Duties: Writing product descriptions for merchandise sold on television shopping channels and on their Web sites

Alternate Title(s): Copywriter

Salary Range: $35,000 to $70,000+

Employment Prospects: Fair

Advancement Prospects: Good

Best Geographical Location(s) for Position—Positions located in areas hosting television shopping channels; three premier channels are located in West Chester, Pa., Tampa, Fla., and Eden Prairie, Minn.; other channels may be located throughout the country in areas hosting local and cable television shopping channels

Prerequisites:

Education and Training—Bachelor's degree in communications, journalism, English, marketing, advertising, or related field

CAREER LADDER

```
Television Shopping Channel Senior
Copywriter
         |
Product Information Copywriter—
Television Shopping Channel
         |
Copywriter in Other Industry, Journalist, or
Position in Public Relations or Advertising
```

Experience—Professional writing experience necessary

Special Skills and Personality Traits—Excellent writing skills; creativity; good command of the English language; strong computer skills; detail oriented; ability to prioritize and manage time

Position Description

When television shopping first began, the only way to view it was on cable television. Today, in addition to watching it on TV, individuals can simply stop by the channel's Web site. They then have the option of watching the broadcast via the Internet or browsing through the products on the Web site.

Television shopping channels have thousands and thousands of different products in a wide array of areas. As potential buyers can't see the actual product, pick it up and feel it, or see the box or packaging, it is essential that the product is described as fully as possible. This description is then used on the Web site, on cards hosts refer to when presenting the product, or as descriptions when products are previewed on air.

The individuals who write these descriptions are called Product Information Copywriters. This is an important job at a television shopping channel. The descriptions that are written can mean the difference between someone wanting a product and actually purchasing it or simply passing it by.

Product Information Copywriters must write clear, concise, informative, and persuasive descriptions of products. They must be compelling, attention grabbing, and interesting. Additionally, they must write copy that gives details in which potential purchasers might be interested. When writing product descriptions, the Product Information Copywriter may do a bit of research. He or she may go over the information from the buyers as well as working with merchants and vendors. At times, it may be necessary for the Product Information Copywriter to check with the shopping channel's legal department to assure that claims made about a specific product are truthful and honest. Often shopping channel buyers or vendors may provide the Product Informaton Copywriter with information about a product. The individual may incorporate this information into the product description while enhancing it. The Product Information Copywriter may use the 5 W's when writing copy. *Who* is the product for; *What* is it and what makes it unique; *When* can it be used; *Where* can it be used; and *Why* should someone buy it. It is often helpful when writing the product description for the individual to determine what makes the product unique and how it is different from similar products.

The individual may include additional information in the description such as the manufacturer, care instructions, and the country in which the product was made. He or she may also include materials the product is made of, sizes, measurements, colors, and so on. The product copy may also include simple wording on how to use the product. Television shopping channels continually bring in products both for on-air presentations and for on their Web site. Product Information Copywriters often work under tight deadlines handling the high volume of product descriptions needed for all the new products that are added to the inventory each week.

Depending on the specific shopping channel and its structure, Product Information Copywriters may write the copy for product descriptions for all merchandise categories or may be assigned a specific category or area of products. Individuals may also be assigned to write the product information for on-air product presentations, for the television shopping channel Web site, or for both.

Additional responsibilities of Product Information Copywriters working at television shopping channels may include:

- Proofreading copy
- Revising and rewriting copy
- Ensuring consistency in product information copy

Salaries

Earnings for Product Information Copywriters working at television shopping channels can range from approximately $35,000 to $70,000 or more. Variables affecting earnings include the size, location, prestige, and popularity of the specific shopping channel as well as the experience and responsibilities of the individual. Other factors affecting earnings include the level the individual is in the organization, as well as his or her professional reputation.

Employment Prospects

Employment prospects are fair for individuals seeking positions as Product Information Copywriters for television shopping channels. While there are only a limited number of channels, each hires a good number of people for these type of positions. Individuals may find opportunities with one of the more popular television shopping channels such as QVC, HSN, or ShopNBC or one of the local shopping channels or smaller, lesser-known cable shopping channels.

Opportunities may be full time or part time. In some situations, individuals may also be hired to be on-call. This means that when the television shopping channel has extra work, they may use on call employees. In other situations, there may be positions in which individuals can telecommute part of the time.

Advancement Prospects

Advancement prospects for Product Information Copywriters at television shopping channels are good. Individuals may climb the career ladder in a number of ways. Some individuals find similar positions with larger, more prestigious television shopping channels resulting in increased responsibilities and earnings. Others are promoted to head up the product information copywriting of their specific merchandise area or become senior copywriters at the television shopping channel. Still others are promoted to editors overseeing the other copywriters. There are some Product Information Copywriters working for television shopping channels who also locate positions handling copywriting in other industries.

Education and Training

A minimum of a bachelor's degree is required for those aspiring to work as Product Information Copywriters at television shopping channels. Good choices for majors include advertising, marketing, communications, public relations, English, or a related field. Individuals will find classes, seminars, and workshops in copywriting, advertising, and related areas helpful.

Experience, Skills, and Personality Traits

Product Information Copywriters working at television shopping channels generally are required to have professional writing experience. This may be obtained through jobs as journalists or positions in public relations or advertising or copywriting in another industry. Product Information Copywriters working at television shopping channels should possess excellent writing skills and a good command of the English language. Individuals need a working knowledge of grammar, spelling, word usage, and punctuation. The ability to effectively multitask is essential. Product Information Copywriters need to be detail-oriented, organized people who can prioritize and meet tight deadlines. It should be noted that before being hired, some employers require an applicant to complete a writing test to illustrate his or her competency in writing.

Unions and Associations

Individuals interested in careers in this field might belong to a number of professional or trade associations that provide professional support and guidance. These include the Business/Professional Advertising Association (BPAA), the Direct Marketing Association (DMA), and the American Marketing Association (AMA). They might also contact the National Retail Federation (NRF) and the Electronic Retailing Association (ERA) for additional career information.

Tips for Entry

1. Shopping channel Web sites list many of their job openings. Check them out.
2. Send your résumé and a short cover letter to the human resources department of television shopping channels asking about openings. You can never tell when a job opportunity will occur. If your résumé is there, you might get a call before someone else.
3. Don't forget to check for opening on popular job search sites such as those at monster.com and hotjobs.com, as well as job search sites specific to the retail and copywriting industries.
4. If you are still in college, contact one of the major electronic retailers to find out if they have any internships in the copywriting area. If they don't, ask if one can be put together.
5. Positions may be advertised in the classified sections of newspapers under headings including "Copywriter," "Television Shopping Channel," "Electronic Retailing," "Product Information Copywriter," etc. Don't forget to check out boxed display advertisements listing one of more job openings of a particular shopping channel.
6. Contact executive recruiters specializing in copywriting. Make sure you check ahead of time to see who pays the fee when you get the job—you or the employer.
7. Put together a portfolio of your best writing samples. Include a variety of samples to illustrate your writing talents. When you go on an interview, bring your portfolio with you.
8. Look at products sold on television shopping channels and practice writing product descriptions.

WEB SITE CONTENT PRODUCER— TELEVISION SHOPPING CHANNEL

Position Description

When television shopping first began in the 1970s, no one could imagine that the Internet would be what it is today; no one could imagine the sales it could generate. Fast forward to the new millennium and the Internet is a viable force in the retail industry. It should be no surprise then that today television shopping channels, like most other retailers, have their own Web sites.

Web sites give television shopping channels a presence on the Web. This is essential for all retail businesses, and television shopping channels are no exception.

When television shopping channels first started their Web sites they did so to support the television shopping channel and offer people another option in buying. Today, however, television shopping Web sites are more integrated with the television broadcast. People can watch the live broadcast on the Web site, view products that have just been presented, take part in Web chats, and more.

Television shopping channels have an easier time than some other retailers making people aware that they have a Web site because they have the ability to constantly promote their Web site on air. Getting people to visit the site, however, is only half the battle. Finding ways to get them to visit on a regular basis is the challenge.

Television shopping channels have found that one way to make their Web sites more interesting so that visitors will want to keep coming back is to create supplementary content in addition to their product information.

The individuals who help create this additional content are called Web Site Content Producers. Their main function is to develop interesting and unique content for the shopping channel Web site. In this position, Web Site Content Producers are responsible for conceptualizing, developing, and maintaining content so that the site will attract and retain visitors on a regular basis. It is hoped that while there, visitors may see something they want and place an order.

Web Site Content Producers are responsible for researching and writing engaging stories and articles in a variety of areas and categories. Their job is similar to a combination of a print journalist and editor. In an attempt to engage visitors keep hem on the site longer as well as returning on a regular basis, Web Site Content Producers may use a variety of techniques. This includes developing stories and articles for the Web site on a variety of subjects that may be of interest to visitors. For example, content producers may create a section on the site focusing on the television channel show hosts. It might include bios, host interviews, their recommendations about product or gift ideas, and so on.

Similarly, content producers may develop a section on what is hot in fashion, trends in home decorating, or even recipes using cookware sold on the channel. The sky is the limit for savvy content producers as long as the content fits with the channel's corporate culture.

The Web Site Content Producer may develop e-mail text, videos, and photos for inclusion on the site. Television shopping channels, like other retailers, have learned that people want to be part of a community. The individual may develop Web chats, blogs, and forums in order to get visitors involved in the site. In this manner, visitors start feeling that they are part of the television shopping channel community. This in turn often makes visitors look forward to going to the site to see what others are saying as well as participating themselves.

Depending on the size, structure, and extent of the shopping channel Web site, there may be more than one content producer. Different content producers may be assigned to handle host blogs, product blogs, beauty forums, fashion forums, cooking forums, new product forums, and so on. Still other content producers may be responsible for stories and news about the shopping channel, special events, and new products. It all depends on how comprehensive the shopping channel wants the content of the Web site to be.

Depending on the structure of the specific shopping channel Web site, there may be an executive Web Site Content Producer responsible for overseeing the work of all the other content producers as well as on-call copywriters, freelancers, and graphic artists. These individuals are also expected to edit the articles given to them by other content producers or writers working under their direction and then giving them to the Webmaster to put online. There might also be senior Web Site Content Producers who may be responsible for overseeing the work of the other content producers working in their subject area.

The individual may be responsible for interviewing people such as celebrity guests, vendors, or inventors of new products featured on the shopping channel. He or she will then develop pieces for the Web site. The content producer may also be expected to arrange for photos and obtain other information to make the online stories interesting.

One of the exciting things about the Internet is that it can be interactive. With this in mind, the content producer may develop surveys, questionnaires, or other pieces to involve those visiting the site. These might be stand-alone questionnaires or integrated into on-air production. The individual might additionally create Web chats, blogs, and forums that are onetime events or hosted on a regular basis.

In some instances, one or more of the interactive sections of the site may be related to promotions or special happenings on the channel. For example, the shopping channel may have an hourlong show debuting a hot recording artist's new CD complete with the star giving an on-air mini-concert. Web site visitors may be asked to give their opinions or thoughts of the new CD and within minutes their words can help generate excitement.

The Web Site Content Producer is often responsible for finding pictures, animation, and other graphics to make the content more appealing. He or she may utilize the services of graphic artists, photographers, or others to accomplish this task. The individual may work with the Webmaster to find images that are appropriate and will look good but not affect the ease of opening the site. In order to keep the site fresh, Web Site Content Producers may be responsible for daily updates.

Other duties of Web Site Content Producers working at television shopping channels include:

- Staying up-to-date with shopping channel events, premier shows and product launches
- Responding to inquiries from people who visit the site
- Finding the best way to present information and graphics
- Handling Webcams and chats
- Working with the Web site marketing manager in handling online contests and promotions
- Monitoring blogs and user comments to insure appropriate content

Salaries

Annual earnings for Web Site Content Producers working at television shopping channels can range from approximately $29,000 to $75,000 or more annually. Variables include the location, size, and prestige of the shopping channel as well as the importance it puts on its Web site. Other variables influencing earnings include the responsibilities, experience, and professional reputation of the individual.

Employment Prospects

Employment prospects are fair for Web Site Content Producers working at television shopping channels. While there are only a limited number of channels, each generally has a number of people in this position. Unless individuals live in an area hosting a television shopping channel, they will generally need to relocate for a job. Individuals may find opportunities with one of the more popular television shopping channels such as QVC, HSN, or ShopNBC or one of the local shopping channels on smaller, lesser-known cable shopping channels.

One of the interesting things about being a Web Site Content Producer is that due to the nature of the job, some employers may allow individuals to telecommute all or part of the time. Individuals may also find part-time or consulting positions.

Advancement Prospects

Web Site Content Producers working for television shopping channels may advance their careers in a number of ways. Individuals responsible for a specific area of a Web site may be promoted to a position as a senior content producer. Senior content producers may be promoted to executive content producers.

Individuals may also find similar positions at one of the larger or more prestigious shopping channels resulting in increased responsibilities and earnings. Some Web Site Content Producers find similar positions in other industries.

Education and Training

Television shopping channels generally require their Web Site Content Producers to hold a minimum of a four-year college degree. Good choices for majors include journalism, communications, English, public relations, marketing, or liberal arts. Courses, workshops, and seminars in public relations, writing, promotion, and journalism, as well as the retail and electronic retailing industries, will be helpful in honing skills and making new contacts. While it may not be required, individuals who know HTML (a programming language) may have a leg up on other candidates.

Experience, Skills, and Personality Traits

The larger, more prestigious shopping channels that put a great deal of importance on their Web site will generally seek out individuals who have a proven track record. Depending on the specific position, they may require the individual to have a minimum of three years' experience creating, editing, and/or managing Web content.

Writing and editing experience will be useful, no matter what the capacity. The ideal candidate will be innovative, organized, and creative with great communications skills and Internet savvy. An excellent command of the English language is needed for this type of position. An understanding of the retail and electronic retail industries is helpful.

Web Site Content Producers should have the ability to multitask and work under pressure without getting flustered. People skills are mandatory in this type of position.

Unions and Associations

Individuals interested in learning more about careers in the field may obtain additional information by contacting the Internet Professionals Association (IPA), the National Retail Federation (NRF), and the Electronic Retailing Association (ERA).

Tips for Entry

1. Television shopping channels generally post their openings on their Web site. Look for the section of the Web site which says "employment opportunities" or "careers."
2. Positions may be located in the classified section of newspapers. Look under headings such as "Web Site Content Producer," "Web Site Content Manager," "Electronic Retailing," "Web sites," and "Web Careers." Don't forget to look at boxed display ads for specific television shopping channels advertising more than one job.
3. This is the perfect type of job to look for online. Start with some of the more popular job sites such as those at www.hotjobs.com and www.monster.com and then go from there.
4. Jobs openings may also be located on career sites specific to the retail and electronic retailing industries.
5. Get as much experience writing as you can. If you are still in school, get involved in your school newspaper and/or Web site.
6. Look for internships at television shopping channels. These will give you on-the-job training, experience, and the opportunity to make important contacts. Contact the human resources departments of television shopping channels to see what they offer.
7. Consider a part-time job for a local newspaper to get some writing experience and to build up your contacts.
8. Send your résumé and a short cover letter to the human resources department of television shopping channels. Ask that your résumé be kept on file, if no current openings exist.

CUSTOMER SERVICE REPRESENTATIVE—TELEVISION SHOPPING CHANNEL

Position Description

Today people have more choices than ever choosing where they want to shop. What sets retailers apart, to a great extent, is the level of customer service they provide. Television shopping channels pride themselves on offering some of the best customer service in retail. The people who provide the day-to-day customer service at television shopping channels are called Customer Service Representatives. These individuals are the liaison between customers and the shopping channel. Their actions and the manner in which they handle calls can often mean the difference between a customer having a bad shopping experience and a customer having a good experience.

While television shopping channels may host a small number of traditional retail outlets, the majority of their sales are generated directly from the television channel and their Web site. What this means is that as a rule, customers don't have the opportunity to have face-to-face contact with those at the shopping channel. When customers have a problem, they contact the shopping channel either by calling a toll-free number or e-mailing via the Internet.

Customer Service Representatives are responsible for interacting with customers, providing information in response to inquiries about products or services, and handling and resolving complaints.

Customers may call customer service for a number of reasons. They may want to ask questions about a product or may want to know the status of an order. They may also have a problem or concern that they want resolved. At the beginning of each call, the Customer Service Representative identifies the customer assuring that he or she has the customer's correct name, address, and phone number. Once that is accomplished, the Customer Service Representative must determine the reason for the call. With that done, the Customer Service Representative is expected to resolve the situation accordingly. Television shopping channels use a complex computer system to access the information that they need. This includes product information, numbers, prices, and, in many cases, dates on which products have been presented or will be presented in the future. It also includes customer information on orders that have been placed and on returns.

If a customer is simply looking for information on a product, the Customer Service Representative will look through the database of products to find the needed product information. He or she will then give the information to the customer including the product number, price, and product description. In some cases, customers require additional information. They may want information on the warranty of a certain product. They may want to contact a manufacturer and need the phone number. The Customer Service Representative is expected to do some research and find the number or other information requested. Sometimes customers have not received orders that were placed and call to check the status of their order. The Customer Service Representative will first check to see when the order was placed and how it was shipped. He or she then tracks it either through a UPS, FedEx, or post office tacking number. In rare circumstances, the order may be lost or not shipped. The Customer Service Representative will ask the customer if he or she wants the order resent or a credit. Customers may contact customer service because they receive wrong orders or one of the products in their order came broken or defective. The Customer Service Representative is expected to ask the customer about his or her preference in resolving the issue. He or she may offer to replace the items or give a refund or a credit to the customer. In some cases, he or she may offer the customer additional compensation such as a company gift certificate to make up for the inconvenience.

Customers may call customer service to complain about products that they ordered which did not meet their expectations or were not as advertised during the presentation. The Customer Service Representative may apologize to the customer for the inconvenience, offer a refund or replacement, and then have the merchandise picked up so the customer doesn't have to ship it back him or herself.

Customers often call customer service because they have billing issues or have returned merchandise and have not received the proper credit. Customer Service Representatives are expected to obtain the information from the customer and then straighten out the issue while explaining it to the customer. In some situations, customers may call to complain about an array of other issues, ranging from inappropriate comments on air to bad experiences they had when ordering. The Customer Service Representative must apologize for the situation and then attempt to make the customer happy. The individual often simply listens and tells customers that he or she understands. In this manner, customers feel that their comments have been heard and are valued. The Customer Service Representative may also take the customer's comments and send them via e-mail to the corporate office for review. In many cases the Customer Service Representative will ask the corporate office to respond to the customer either by phone or a letter. On rare occasions, customers may be upset about a variety of things that may or may not be related to the shopping channel. They may call up yelling, ranting, and raving. The Customer Service Representative is expected to stay calm, try to get to the root of the problem, and then come up with a satisfactory resolution. The idea is to have the customer hang up happy. It is essential that Customer Service Representatives always make customers feel valued. Successful Customer Service Reps never tell customers they are wrong. Instead, they listen attentively and try to find an effective resolution so that when customers hang up the phone, they feel satisfied.

Customer Service Representatives must be aware of all company policies and procedures. Despite that, however, they must know when they have leeway to make a decision on handling a problem and when a customer issue needs to be escalated to a supervisor for resolution. Depending on the specific shopping channel and its structure, Customer Service Representatives may work various shifts including mornings, afternoons, nights, and weekends.

In complex situations, Customer Service Representatives may be required to take the information from a customer and then get back to them with a resolution. In doing this, the Customer Service Representative will be able to do some research, come up with a resolution, and then get back to the customer either via a phone call, letter, or e-mail.

Other responsibilities of Customer Service Representatives working at a television shopping channel might include:

- Placing orders for customers
- Canceling orders for customers
- Following up with customers to resolve issues
- Handling administrative tasks to complete customer interactions
- Issuing credits and gift certificates

Salaries

Annual earnings for Customer Service Representatives working full time at television shopping channels can range from approximately $24,000 to $37,000 or more.

Variables affecting earnings include the size, location, prestige, and popularity of the specific shopping channel as well as the experience and responsibilities of the Customer Service Representative. Other factors affecting earnings may include the specific shifts the individual works.

Employment Prospects

Employment prospects are good for individuals seeking positions as Customer Service Representatives for television shopping channels. Individuals may find opportunities with one of the more popular television shopping channels such as QVC, HSN, or ShopNBC at their headquarters or at call centers located throughout the country. Individuals my also find employment at one of the local shopping channels or smaller, lesser-known cable shopping channels.

Advancement Prospects

Advancement prospects for Customer Service Representatives working at television shopping channels are fair. The most common method of career advancement for individuals is being promoted to a position of shift supervisor. Others climb the career ladder by finding positions as customer service coordinators. Some get their foot in the door, obtain some experience, and move into corporate positions in customer service.

Education and Training

Those seeking positions as Customer Service Representatives for television shopping channels need a minimum of a high school diploma. A college degree will be helpful to those aspiring to advance their careers in the customer service area or television shopping. Individuals generally receive on-the-job training. Classes, seminars, or workshops in customer service techniques will be useful.

Experience, Skills, and Personality Traits

Experience requirements vary for Customer Service Representatives at television shopping channels. Some positions are entry level. Others require applicants to have experience in some other area of customer service

or problem resolution. As customer service is so important to the bottom line of television shopping channels, it is essential that the Customer Service Representatives employed by the channel provide the best service possible. It is therefore critical that the individual have exemplary customer service skills. Customer Service Representatives must be self-motivated with the ability to multitask effectively. Problem-solving and good-listening skills are essential as are good verbal and written communication skills.

Customer Service Representatives need to be empathetic individuals who are calm and even-tempered. The ability to easily deal with others under challenging circumstances is a plus. Individuals should be organized and detail oriented. Computer skills and phone skills are a must.

Unions and Associations

Individuals interested in positions as Customer Service Representatives may want to contact the Electronic Retailing Association (ERA) and the National Retail Federation (NRF) to learn more about careers in this field.

Tips for Entry

1. Most television shopping networks post openings on their Web site. Check them out.
2. Even if there isn't an opening, send your résumé and a short cover letter. You can never tell when a job opening will occur. If your résumé is there, you might get a call before someone else.
3. Don't forget to surf the net in your job search. Start with popular job search sites such as those at monster.com and hotjobs.com and go from there.
4. Positions may be advertised in the classified sections of newspapers in areas hosting television shopping channels or their call centers. Look under headings such as "Customer Service," "Electronic Retailing," "Television Shopping Channel," "Customer Service Representative," etc. Don't forget to check out boxed display advertisements listing one of more job openings from a specific television shopping channel.

WHOLESALE

SALES MANAGER—WHOLESALE

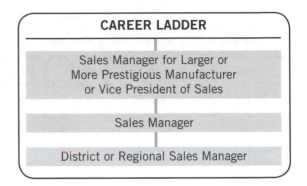

CAREER LADDER

Sales Manager for Larger or More Prestigious Manufacturer or Vice President of Sales

Sales Manager

District or Regional Sales Manager

Position Description

Wholesalers sell a large amount of products to other companies who in turn sell them to consumers. Merchandise includes, but is not limited to, food, clothing, pharmaceuticals, office equipment, computers, cosmetics, machinery parts, hardware, electronics, automobile parts, exercise and sports equipment, and furniture. Wholesale companies often hire salespeople or manufacturer's representatives to sell their products to retailers or other consumers.

Sales Managers working in the wholesale industry are the individuals responsible for managing the activities of a company's sales staff. Within the scope of their job, they have many responsibilities. The Sales Manager recruits and hires the sales staff and other key employees. In others, the human resources department will handle the recruiting function. However, the Sales Manager may still do final interviews of sales staff.

Depending on the specific product, there may be many areas and avenues in which a company can sell their products. A clothing company may, for example, sell their merchandise to department stores, chain stores, boutiques, specialty stores, and catalogs from coast to coast as well as other countries. Without the direction of the Sales Manager, the sales staff might go on their own, haphazardly selling wherever they chose and without any clear sales plan.

The Sales Manager separates geographic areas into territories. Sizes of territories depend on the specific company and the products they sell. A territory for one manufacturer might include the entire Northeast. For another, a territory might be southern New Jersey. Whatever the size of the territory, the Sales Manager is responsible for assigning territories to each sales representative. In many instances, the Sales Manager may work with district managers who also handle some of these functions.

Sometimes, the Sales Manager may also assign specific types of accounts to sales representatives. For example, the Sales Manager working for a photocopy machine manufacturer may assign one representative all the corporate business accounts in an area and another all the office supply stores and other retail outlets in the same area.

The Sales Manager will assign leads to the sales representatives or to the district manager who will handle the task. Leads are calls or other correspondence which come in to the company from potential buyers. For example, a company may manufacture a product which was shown on television. A spurt of business occurs. Stores may start calling the manufacturer because they want to carry the product. The sales staff must respond to these requests. The Sales Manager must see to it that it happens quickly.

The Sales Manager is expected to assist the manufacturers' sales representatives and the district managers in their job. He or she is in place to help them succeed. No matter what type of products are being sold, the main function of the representative is to interest buyers and purchasing agents in their merchandise.

Some representatives pick right up on this task. Others need help. The Sales Manager may accompany new representatives on sales calls to current company client as well as prospective buyers to show them the ropes. The Manager may also go with the representative to visit clients in their places of work or set up sales meeting in other locations when the representative needs some assistance clinching a big sale.

One of the most important functions of a good Sales Manager is training the sales staff. In order to be able to sell effectively, the Sales Manager must make sure each representative knows as much about the manufacturer's products as possible. He or she may hold regular meetings to inform the representatives about new merchandise or the use of products.

The individual will also train representatives and salespeople on selling techniques utilizing policies of the manufacturer. The Sales Manager may provide training for the sales staff on a one-on-one basis or may be expected to develop formal group training programs. This may be the case, even if there is a formal training program provided by the manufacturer.

Sales Managers may help their sales staff develop a strong sales pitch, give representatives information on the company's products or even information on the competitors products. This is essential so that the sales representatives are knowledgeable about the strengths and weakness of their merchandise and competing products in the marketplace.

The Sales Manager works closely with the marketing manager. He or she must be aware of any promotions or specials the company is running. The individual must then communicate the pricing of products and any specials to the sales staff. This may occur in regular sales meetings.

The Sales Manager is responsible for handling a great deal of paperwork. He or she must keep records of what is selling and what is not as well as tracking orders, invoices, and bills. Individuals might also be responsible for developing sales letters or brochures to new or established accounts.

The Sales Manager is expected to set goals for the sales staff. He or she must be aware of how representatives are performing and meeting quotas. An important function of the Sales Manager is motivating the sales staff. Selling any product is not always easy. Every meeting does not always culminate in a sale. It is essential for representatives to remain upbeat and motivated. The Sales Manager needs to be effective in this task or he or she may lose his or her sales staff.

The Sales Manager may run sales meetings for representatives and other employees to review sales performance, product development, sales goals, and profitability.

Sales Managers are also expected to attend conferences and conventions on behalf of the manufacturer to meet new clients and discuss product developments.

Additional duties of Sales Managers in wholesale industry might include:

- Answering questions about new products and merchandise
- Addressing concerns of clients
- Providing advice to clients on increasing sales
- Developing sales letters, product literature, and pricing sheets
- Recommending raises and promotions or terminating sales staff

Salaries

Annual earnings for Sales Managers working in the wholesale industry can vary greatly ranging from approximately $35,000 to $250,000 or more. Variables include the specific manufacturer for which the individual works, its size, location, and prestige as well as the types of products being sold. Other factors affecting earnings include the experience, reputation, and responsibilities of the individual. In some instances, the Sales Manager will receive a commission on sales as well as his or her salary. He or she might also receive bonuses for outstanding sales.

Employment Prospects

Employment prospects for Sales Managers in the wholesale industry are good. Prospects are best for individuals who have a proven track record. Positions can be located throughout the country, although the most opportunities will be in areas hosting large numbers of manufactures.

Advancement Prospects

Advancement prospects are fair for individuals in this line of work. The most common method of climbing the career ladder for Sales Managers is landing similar jobs at larger or more prestigious manufacturers. This leads to increased responsibilities and earnings. Some Sales Managers advance to positions as vice presidents of sales.

Education and Training

Educational requirements vary from company to company. A college degree or background may be preferred, but is not always required. A degree may give one applicant an edge over another who doesn't possess one.

Many companies send their Sales Managers to formal training programs. These programs help individuals learn new methods of motivating employees, selling new techniques, and may offer a different spin on sales strategies. Programs may also help Sales Managers learn more about the company's products.

Experience, Skills, and Personality Traits

Sales Managers are usually required to have a great deal of selling experience. Individuals must have a complete knowledge of the products being sold by the manufacturer.

Leadership skills are mandatory. The ability to motivate others is essential in this type of job. Successful Sales Managers are confident, assertive individuals. Communication skills, both written and verbal, are necessary. The ability to train others is helpful.

Unions and Associations

Sales Managers working in the wholesale industry may belong to a number of organizations providing professional support and guidance. These include Sales and Marketing Executives International (SMEI), the Manufacturers' Agents National Association (MANA), the American Management Association, the American Wholesale Marketers Association (AWMA), or associations specific to the products being sold.

Tips for Entry

1. Jobs as Sales Managers can often be located on-line. Start with some of the more well-known sites such as www.monster.com and www.hotjobs.com.

2. Positions are often advertised in the classified sections of newspapers under heading including "Sales Manager," "Wholesale-Retail Opportunities," "Wholesale Opportunities," "Wholesale Sales," or "Retail Opportunities." You might also look under industries specific to the products you are interested in representing.

3. Sunday's papers usually have the largest classified section. Most companies try to have their help wanted ads run on a Sunday.

4. If you are interested in working with a specific manufacturer or wholesaler, check to see if they have a Web site. Many companies today have Web sites featuring job opportunities.

5. Visit www.hoovers.com to get Web sites for specific companies as well as basic information on what various companies sell. Hoovers also often has information regarding specific names of people to send resumes in a company.

6. The yellow pages are a wealth of information in your job search. Check them to find the names, addresses, and phone numbers of manufacturers in your area.

7. Take classes, seminars, and workshops in selling techniques and motivation to give you an edge over other applicants. These classes are also useful in giving you ideas to motivate your sales force.

DISTRICT MANAGER—WHOLESALE

CAREER PROFILE

Duties: Supervise and coordinate the activities of sales representatives in the district; train sales staff; assist sales staff in meeting district's sales goals; motivate sales staff; handle paperwork

Alternate Title(s): Territory Manager

Salary Range: $33,000 to $85,000+

Employment Prospects: Good

Advancement Prospects: Fair

Best Geographical Location(s) for Position: Jobs may be located throughout the country; large cities will offer more possibilities

Prerequisites:

Education and Training—Educational requirements vary; see text

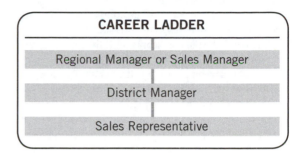

Experience—Experience in wholesale sales

Special Skills and Personality Traits—Sales ability; aggressiveness; ability to handle multiple projects; administrative skills; organization; communication skills; ability to motivate others

Position Description

Wholesale companies may manufacture merchandise or purchase it from manufacturers. They then sell the products to other companies who in turn sell them to consumers. Merchandise can include, but is not limited to, food, clothing, pharmaceuticals, office equipment, computers, cosmetics, machinery parts, hardware, electronics, automobile parts, exercise and sports equipment, or furniture.

Wholesale companies often have a sales staff responsible for selling the company's products to retailers or other consumers. This staff may be headed by a sales manager. Depending on the size and structure of the company, the sales staff may include salespeople, manufacturers representatives, regional managers, and District Managers.

It is not uncommon for wholesale companies to sell their merchandise throughout the country. This means that sales forces will be required in a number of different areas or districts. In order to assure all sales districts are run properly, areas of the country are often divided into regions, which are overseen by regional managers. These regions are then divided into districts or territories. Each district is then overseen by an individual called a District Manager.

District Managers manage all of the accounts in a specific area or district. They are expected to make sure each account or business in the district is serviced by salespeople.

Whether retail or wholesale, all customers want to feel important. They need to know they are being taken care of by the companies with which they are doing business. Not doing so can lead to a loss of sales. The District Manager makes sure clients are satisfied.

He or she may assign salespeople to call or visit established accounts. It is important to wholesale companies to constantly look for new business. The District Manager often works with salespeople and representatives to develop new clients.

District Managers often recruit and hire representatives and other sales staff for their districts. In some situations, the human resources department of the company or the sales manager may handle the recruiting function. However, the district manager may still take part in final interviews of his or her sales staff.

District Managers assign specific territories to each sales person and representative. In this manner, salespeople are not repeating their efforts calling on clients or ignoring the needs of others.

The District Manager may assign leads to the sales representatives in his or her district. Leads are calls which come in to the company from potential buyers. For example, a retail store may call the manufacturer of a line of dresses in which they have an interest.

The District Manager is expected to assist the sales staff in his or her district with their jobs. He or she is there to help them succeed. The individual may accompany new representatives on sales calls to current company client as well as prospective buyers to show them the ropes. The individual may also go with the representative to visit clients in their places of work or set up sales meetings in other locations when the representative needs some help clinching a big sale.

The District Manager works with the sales manager in training the sales staff. Some companies also have a trainer who develops and runs programs. The manager works with each member of the sales staff either one on one or as a group making sure each knows as much about the manufacturer's products as possible. He or she may hold regular meetings to inform the representatives about new merchandise or the use of products.

The individual communicates with each salesperson on a regular basis. During these conversations, the manager will check to see if there are any problems with any accounts and make sure each is being taken care of. He or she will usually need to know how sales are going.

The District Manager must keep accurate records of sales figures on a daily, weekly, monthly, and annual basis. This information is used to help the company project profits. Based on these figures, along with various other information, the corporate office sets sales goals. In many situations, the sales representatives are expected to call in or fax sales figures to the District Manager on a daily or weekly basis.

The District Manager works with the sales staff in his or her district to make sure they meet corporate sales and profit goals. He or she may hold meetings with staff to motivate them as well as giving them product information helpful in making sales.

The District Manager is the liaison between the corporate office and his or her sales staff. He or she is responsible for communicating routine corporate policies as any policy changes. For example, the corporate office may want new customers to fill in a credit report before credit is issued. The District Manager must make sure all sales representatives know the policies and be sure they are being followed.

The District Manager often handles a customer service problem when it can't be handled by the sales representative. A customer, for example, may need additional credit and want to deal with it on a higher level.

The District Manager handles a great deal of paperwork. He or she must keep records of what is selling and what is not, as well as tracking orders, invoices, and bills.

The District Manager must be aware of how representatives are performing and meeting quotas. The individual will constantly work to motivate the sales staff. Selling a product is not always easy. Every meeting does not culminate in a sale. It is essential for a sales staff to remain upbeat and motivated. The District Manager needs to be effective in this task or he or she may lose his or her staff.

District Managers are also expected to attend conferences and conventions on behalf of the manufacturer to meet new clients and discuss product developments.

Additional duties of District Managers might include:

- Answering questions about new products and merchandise
- Addressing concerns of clients
- Providing advice to clients on increasing sales
- Assisting sales manager in running sales meetings
- Recommending raises and promotions or terminating sales staff

Salaries

Annual earnings for District Managers working in the wholesale industry can vary greatly, ranging from approximately $33,000 to $85,000 or more. Variables include the specific manufacturer for which the individual works, its size, location, and prestige as well as the types of products being sold. Other factors affecting earnings include the experience, reputation, and responsibilities of the individual. In some instances, the District Manager will receive a commission on sales as well as his or her salary. He or she might also receive bonuses for outstanding sales.

Employment Prospects

Employment prospects are good District Managers interested in working in the wholesale industry. Prospects are best for individuals who have a proven track record. Positions can be located throughout the country although the most opportunities will be in areas hosting large numbers of manufacturers and wholesalers.

Advancement Prospects

Advancement prospects are fair for individuals in this line of work. The most common method of climbing the career ladder for District Managers is by landing similar jobs at larger or more prestigious manufacturers. This leads to increased responsibilities and earnings. District Managers may also advance to positions as regional managers or even sales managers.

Education and Training

Educational requirements vary. In many companies, experience is accepted in lieu of education. A college degree or background may be preferred, but is not always required. However, a college degree may give one applicant an edge over another who doesn't have one. Good majors include marketing, retailing, merchandising, business, management, communications, advertising, liberal arts, or related fields.

Once hired, many companies send their District Managers through formal training programs. These programs help individuals learn new methods of motivating employees, new selling techniques, and may offer a different spin on sales strategies. Programs may also help District Managers learn more about the company's products.

Experience, Skills, and Personality Traits

District Managers are usually required to have a great deal of selling experience. Individuals must have a complete knowledge of the products being sold by the manufacturer.

Leadership and management skills are mandatory. The ability to motivate others is essential. The ability to deal well with others is necessary. Communications skills, both written and verbal, are also necessary. The ability to train others is helpful.

Unions and Associations

District Managers working in the wholesale industry may belong to a number of organizations providing professional support and guidance. These include Sales and Marketing Executives International (SMEI), the Manufacturers' Agents National Association (MANA), the American Management Association, the American Wholesale Marketers Association (AWMA), or associations specific to the products being sold.

Tips for Entry

1. Positions as District Managers can often be located on-line. Start with some of the more popular sites such as www.monster.com and www.hotjobs.com.

2. Positions are often advertised in the classified sections of newspapers under headings including "District Manager," "Wholesale-Retail Opportunities," "Wholesale Opportunities," or "Wholesale Sales." You might also look under industries specific to the products you are interested in representing.

3. Sunday's paper usually has the largest classified section. Most companies try to have their help wanted ads run on a Sunday.

4. If you are interested in working with a specific company, check to see if they have a Web site. Many companies have Web sites featuring job opportunities.

5. Visit www.hoovers.com to get Web sites for specific companies as well as basic information on what various companies sell, and information regarding specific names of people to send resumes to a company.

6. The yellow pages are a wealth of information in your job search. Check them to find the names, addresses, and phone numbers of manufacturers in your area.

7. Take classes, seminars, and workshops in selling techniques and motivation to give you an edge over other applicants. These classes are also useful in giving you ideas to motivate your sales force.

8. Contact larger companies to see if they have internship programs.

MARKET RESEARCHER— MANUFACTURER

Duties: Perform market research to determine potential sales of new products; research demographics, pricing, packaging, and promotion of products produced by manufacturers; retailers; tabulate results; write reports

Alternate Title(s): Market Analyst, Product Analyst; Market Research Specialist

Salary Range: $28,000 to $70,000+

Employment Prospects: Good

Advancement Prospects: Fair

Best Geographical Location(s) for Position: Jobs may be located throughout the country; the greatest number of opportunities will exist in areas with large numbers of manufacturers

Prerequisites:

    Education and Training—Bachelor's degree

Experience—Experience performing surveys and tabulating results

Special Skills and Personality Traits—Excellent written and verbal communication skills; analytical mind; ability to solve problems; math skills; familiarity with statistics; computer skills

Position Description

Manufacturers do a great deal of research prior to developing products. Without performing this research they might produce something that does not meet the needs of the market or the population. Manufacturers also perform market research to assure proper pricing, competitive stature of their product, and that specific product targets are included.

Manufacturers employ individuals called Market Researchers to handle this job. The Market Researcher determines the need, interest, and willingness of a given market to pay for specific products. For example, a Market Researcher at a pharmaceutical manufacturer might research the needs of an arthritis drug which could be taken every other day instead of daily. The Market Researcher at a record company might research the willingness of the marketplace to purchase compilation CDs of their artist's greatest hits. The Market Researcher working for a food manufacturer might research the amount the general population might pay for specialty or convenience food items. Depending on the manufacturer and the specific project, the Market Researcher may also do research on types of packaging, product names, or advertising.

This is an interesting job. Market Researchers have the opportunity to talk to people, get their ideas, and help a manufacturer determine if a product can succeed in the marketplace.

Market Researchers research the market conditions in various areas to determine the potential sales of the manufacturer's product. The Researcher may also determine the type of words that potential customers might look for in the company's advertisements. Would the word "convenience" sell a product better than the words "cooks quickly?" How about the words "may reduce the risk of cancer" on a food product?

As part of the job, the Market Researcher uses a number of research techniques. The individual might develop a survey or questionnaire to find the answers to questions. Depending on the specific company and what is being manufactured, the questionnaires might ask about a person's age, gender, and income level. It may ask about potential buyers' shopping habits and preferences.

The Market Researcher may execute questionnaires and surveys on the phone or visit various areas to personally interview various groups of individuals. He or she may personally handle this function or have it done by research assistants.

The Market Researcher may send questionnaires and surveys in the mail offering free samples or other incentives for people to respond. Today, a great deal of market research by manufacturers is also done on the Internet. Many companies find it easier to get people to answer questions by holding on-line sweepstakes offering prizes. With this method the survey or questionnaire is put on-line as part of the entry form. At the end of the sweepstakes period, the manufacturer has the results of the questionnaire.

The Market Researcher may also use data from many sources including information compiled by federal, state, and local agencies as well as private sources. The individual may put together focus groups and panels of consumers to test products. He or she may also conduct consumer buyer surveys, audits, and new product sales surveys.

Once the Market Researcher performs surveys and questionnaires and other research, he or she must analyze the results. The individual is then expected to write a report on his or her findings. The manufacturer will then decide if there is a market for the product, pricing strategies, name possibilities, target markets, and potential advertising mediums.

Additional duties of Market Researchers working for manufacturers might include:

- Putting together focus groups to determine the need for a product
- Supervising research assistants
- Working with a manufacturer's advertising agency
- Working with the manufacturer's development team on new products

Salaries

Annual earnings of Market Researchers working for manufacturers can range from approximately $28,000 to $70,000 or more. Factors affecting earnings include the size, structure, and prestige of the manufacturer as well as the education, experience, and responsibilities of the individual.

Employment Prospects

Employment prospects for Market Researchers are good. Positions may be located throughout the country. However, the greatest number of openings are located in areas hosting large numbers of manufacturers.

Advancement Prospects

Advancement prospects for Market Researchers working for manufacturers are fair. The most common method of career advancement is landing a similar job with a larger or more prestigious manufacturer. Individuals may also climb the career ladder by being promoted to positions of research supervisor or director.

Education and Training

Generally, the minimum educational requirement for a position in this field is a bachelor's degree. Some employers may require a graduate degree. Classes in business, statistics, marketing, advertising, or behavioral sciences will be useful for a career in this field. A doctorate is helpful for career advancement.

Experience, Skills, and Personality Traits

Market Researchers should be excellent problem solvers with good analytical minds. The ability to perform math skills and familiarity with statistics are essential.

Communications skills, both oral and written are necessary. An understanding of people and their behavior is mandatory. Computer skills are also needed.

Unions and Associations

Market Researchers may learn more about this career by contacting the Council of American Survey Research Organizations (CASRO).

Tips for Entry

1. The better your education, the better the job you can get in this field. If you can, earn a master's degree. Some companies will pay for your continuing education.
2. Jobs are often advertised in the classified section of the newspaper. Look under headings such as "Research Analyst," "Market Researcher," "Manufacturing Opportunities," or "Market Research." Specific companies may also advertise a number of job opportunities in one advertisement.
3. Sunday's paper usually has the largest classified section. Most companies try to have their help wanted ads run on a Sunday.
4. Contact manufacturers to see if they have any internships in this area. Once in, learn everything you can.
5. Send your resume and a short cover letter to manufacturers you are interested in working with and inquiring about openings.
6. If you are interested in working for a specific manufacturer, check to see if they have a Web site. Many companies now have Web sites featuring

job opportunities. Check the appendix for some of the larger manufacturers.

7. Visit www.hoovers.com to get Web sites for specific companies as well as basic information on what various companies sell.

8. The yellow pages are a wealth of information in your job search. Check them to find the names, addresses, and phone numbers of manufacturers in your area.

CONSUMER AFFAIRS MANAGER— MANUFACTURER/WHOLESALER

Duties: Supervise the consumer affairs department; oversee the activities of customer services and consumer affairs staff; assist consumers in solving problems with company's products.

Alternate Title(s): Consumer Affairs Coordinator

Salary Range: $26,000 to $58,000+

Employment Prospects: Fair

Advancement Prospects: Fair

Best Geographical Location(s) for Position: Positions located throughout the country

Prerequisites:

Education and Training—Bachelor's degree

Experience—Experience working in consumer affairs, customer relations, customer service, or public relations necessary

Special Skills and Personality Traits—Ability to remain calm; good interpersonal skills; communications skills; writing skills; empathy; supervisory skills; people skills

CAREER LADDER

Consumer Affairs Director or Director of P.R. or Marketing

Consumer Affairs Manager

Consumer Affairs Assistant Manager or Customer Relations Representative

Position Description

Manufacturers and wholesalers, as other businesses, like to keep their customers happy and satisfied. Many employ Consumer Affairs Managers to handle these customer service and consumer affairs issues. The Consumer Affairs Manager supervises and coordinates the consumer affairs, customer services and customer-relations services of the manufacturer or wholesaler's company. The individual may have varied duties, depending on the specific company for which he or she works.

First and foremost, the Consumer Affairs Manager makes sure customers are satisfied with the company's products. The manufacturer or wholesaler may, for example, have an "800" number set up for customers to call. The Consumer Affairs Manager and his or her staff resolves any complaints or problems customers may have. The Consumer Affairs Manager often supplies customers with useful information about the company's products. In some cases, the Consumer Affairs Manager develops pamphlets, leaflets, or other literature for this purpose. In other cases, he or she may train customer service representatives on methods to answer questions and provide information.

The Consumer Affairs Manager may have additional duties when a manufacturer has a product recall or other similar problem. He or she may, for example,

develop literature to explain the recall procedures to customers. The individual might also train customer service representatives in dealing with frightened or angry consumers. It is always important to find ways to maintain customer confidence in the company as well as to alleviate any additional problems which may occur.

The Consumer Affairs Manager often works with the company's public relations department and others in upper management. Together they create corporate policies as they relate to consumers. It is essential that the Consumer Affairs Manager understand and have the ability to explain these policies to consumers and customer service representatives.

The Consumer Affairs Manager trains customer service representatives or develops the training program with the company's training manager. He or she may be expected to develop training manuals for the customer service representatives as well as others in the company dealing with the public.

The individual sets the policies on how consumer letters and calls should be handled, answered, and taken care of. The Consumer Affairs Manager must explain to each representative what information should be taken from each consumer when they call and how to maintain files.

Generally, the Consumer Affairs Manager will not handle routine calls from customers. However, he or she will often deal with phone calls, letters, or emails from extremely upset, "difficult" consumers. The individual also handles calls regarding major consumer problems, such as a customer suggesting that a lawsuit will ensue unless he or she is satisfied.

Sometimes the situation is easily resolved. The consumer may only want need to vent his or her frustration with an employee of the company they have a complaint with. One of the important functions of the Consumer Affairs Manager is being able to calm people down so that problems can be resolved.

Additional duties of Consumer Affairs Managers may include:

- Preparing copy for the company's Web site regarding consumer affairs
- Developing and writing consumer oriented materials such as leaflets, booklets, flyers
- Preparing consumer newsletters.

Salaries

Annual earnings for Consumer Affairs Managers working for manufacturers or wholesalers can range from approximately $26,000 to $58,000 or more annually. Factors affecting earnings include the size and prestige of the company as well as the responsibilities and experience of the individual.

Employment Prospects

Employment prospects are fair for Consumer Affairs Managers seeking employment with manufacturers or wholesalers. Most mid-sized and larger companies have someone in this position on staff. Positions may be located throughout the country. More opportunities will be available in areas hosting greater numbers of manufacturers and wholesalers.

Advancement Prospects

Advancement prospects are fair for Consumer Affairs Managers. Some individuals advance their careers by locating similar positions with larger, more prestigious manufacturers or wholesalers. Others may climb the career ladder by becoming the director of consumer affairs or the director of public relations or marketing.

Education and Training

Generally, employers prefer individuals hold a minimum of a four year college degree. Good choices for majors include public relations, marketing, advertising, English, communications, liberal arts, business administration or a related field.

Experience, Skills, and Personality Traits

Experience working in consumer affairs, customer service or public relations is usually necessary. Often individuals have gone through internships as well.

Supervisory skills are essential in this position. Good interpersonal skills are also necessary. The ability to deal well with subordinates, superiors and customers is needed.

Individuals must have a great deal of empathy for others and be able to keep people calm when they are upset and irate. Communication skills, both verbal and written are mandatory.

Unions and Associations

Consumer Affairs Managers may be members of the Society of Consumer Affairs Professionals (SOCAP). This organization provides professional guidance and support to its members. Individuals may also be members of the Public Relations Society of America (PRSA), Women in Communications Inc. (WICI), or private and voluntary consumer organizations.

Tips for Entry

1. Join SOCAP and take advantage of their membership opportunities. Go to meetings, get their literature and make important contacts.
2. Jobs may be located on-line at company Web sites. Many manufacturers and wholesalers list job openings on their Web site. Use the listing in the appendix to get you started.
3. Job openings may also be located in the classified section of newspapers. Look under headings such as "Consumer Affairs Manager," "Consumer Affairs," "Manufacturing Opportunities," "Wholesaling Opportunities," "Customer Service," "Customer Relations," or "Public Relations."
4. Get experience working in consumer affairs by volunteering your time to work with consumer organizations. This gives you valuable hands-on experience and looks good on your resume.
5. Get more experience by working as a customer service or customer relations representative. Learn what you can and climb the career ladder.

WHOLESALE SALES REPRESENTATIVE

Position Description

Wholesale Sales Representatives are the individuals responsible for selling a company's products to manufacturers, distributors, retail establishments, government agencies, and other institutions. Individuals might also be called Sales Representatives. The difference between Wholesale Sales Representatives and Manufacturer's Representatives is that Wholesale Representatives usually work solely for a wholesaler.

Wholesale Sales Representatives may work in any industry selling a variety of products. These might include raw materials, wholesale food, clothing, pharmaceuticals, office equipment, computers, cosmetics, machinery parts, electronics, automobile parts, exercise and sports equipment, or furniture.

No matter what type of products the Wholesale Sales Representative sells, the main function of the individual is to interest manufacturers and purchasing agents in their merchandise. Wholesale Sales Representatives are expected to make sales calls to current clients as well as prospective buyers. They may visit clients at their place of work or set up sales meetings in other locations.

The Wholesale Sales Representatives must learn the needs of the customer and then show him or her how the wholesaler's specific product can help meet those needs. There is often a great deal of competition in this field. As a result, the Wholesale Sales Representative must be aware of the unique qualities of the merchandise his or her company sells. In this manner, the Wholesale Sales Representatives can be more effective in the selling process. For example, the individual may work for a company that wholesales a variety of exercise equipment. The Representative must know everything about not only his company's exercise equipment, but that of the competitors. Individuals must have the ability to speak knowledgeably discussing the strengths and weakness of their products and others in the marketplace.

Depending on the specific company and the products the individual is selling, he or she may show the client samples or pictures in a catalog of merchandise offered. It is essential for Wholesale Sales Representatives to develop a strong sales pitch to sell their merchandise.

It is the responsibility of the Wholesale Sales Representative to supply each client with a pricing formula for merchandise. He or she will explain the different price breaks depending on the amount purchased by the customer. The Wholesale Sales Representative is expected to answer any of the customer's questions.

If all goes well, the Wholesale Sales Representative will then close the sale. The individual is expected to take and write up the customers order. At this point, he or she may explain payment options or provide shipping dates.

The Wholesale Sales Representative must keep in contact with clients to make sure merchandise has arrived, is satisfactory, and there are no problems with the order. He or she will also try to get reorders by determining the quantity of products which have been sold since the last sales call. Many Wholesale Sales Representative make regular scheduled calls to make sure they don't lose reorders.

Wholesale Sales Representatives might work from their office, making appointments and sales calls by telephone. Today, many make calls on their cell phones while enroute to other appointments.

Wholesale Sales Representatives also make sales calls in person visiting established accounts or making cold calls to potential new customers.

It is important for the individual to look constantly for new business and new accounts. He or she often does this by making cold calls to new prospects. The Wholesale Sales Representative may also get referrals from satisfied customers.

Wholesale Sales Representatives often are expected to attend trade shows, conferences, and conventions to meet other people from their industry as well as clients. They may also attend company sponsored sales meetings to review sales performance, product development, sales goals, and profitability.

Additional duties of Wholesale Sales Representatives might include:

- Keeping accurate records of orders, invoices, and bills
- Developing and sending sales letters or brochures to new or established accounts
- Addressing concerns of clients
- Visiting established accounts

Salaries

Earnings for Wholesale Sales Representatives can vary greatly ranging from approximately $23,000 to $150,000 or more annually. Variables include the specific wholesaler for which the individual works, the product being sold and the sales territory which is assigned. Other factors affecting earnings include the experience of the Representative as well as his or her sales ability, motivation, and aggressiveness.

There are a number of different methods by which Wholesale Sales Representatives may be compensated. Individuals might receive a straight salary, a commission, or a combination of the two. Individuals also may receive bonuses for outstanding sales. In many cases the Wholesale Sales Representative additionally receives a company car or a car allowance.

Employment Prospects

Employment prospects for Wholesale Sales Representatives are excellent. Those who are aggressive and motivated should have no problem finding a job. Positions are plentiful and can be located throughout the country although the most opportunities will be in areas hosting large numbers of wholesale companies.

Advancement Prospects

Advancement prospects are excellent for aggressive and motivated Wholesale Sales Representatives. There are a number of options for climbing the career ladder in this field. The most common is locating similar positions with a larger or more prestigious wholesaler. Individuals might also stay in the same company and get better territories. Some Wholesale Sales Representatives move into supervisory and management positions.

Education and Training

Educational and training requirements vary depending on the specific company and the product line. Some companies just require their Representatives to hold a high school diploma while others prefer or require a college background or degree. If the wholesaler is selling a product which is technical in nature such as computers or software, any technical knowledge the individual has will be useful.

Companies often have formal training programs for new employees as well as continuing programs for those with more experience. These programs help motivate employees and offer new ideas and selling techniques.

Other companies offer informal training with managers or supervisors helping employees learn sales techniques and policies. Some Representatives learn the trade by accompanying more experienced individuals on calls in the field.

Experience, Skills, and Personality Traits

Background and experience requirements Wholesale Sales Representatives vary. Experience selling in either the retail or wholesale industry may be preferred. However, there are often entry-level jobs available.

Successful Wholesale Sales Representatives like to sell. They are confident, assertive, motivated individuals with sales ability. Communications skills are essential. Wholesale Sales Representatives should have the ability to work well both independently and as part of a team. People skills are mandatory.

Depending on the specific job, the individual may be required to hold a valid driver's license.

Unions and Associations

Wholesale Sales Representatives may belong to a number of organizations providing professional support and guidance. These include the Sales and Marketing Executives International (SMEI), the American Management Association (AMA), the American Wholesale Marketers Association (AWMA), or associations specific to the products being sold.

Tips for Entry

1. Contact wholesalers with your resume and a short cover letter. Ask about openings for Wholesale Sales Representatives.
2. Jobs can often be located on-line. Start with some of the more popular sites such as www.monster.com and www.hotjobs.com.
3. Positions are often advertised in the classified sections of newspapers under heading including "Wholesale Sales Representative," "Wholesale Opportunities," "Wholesale Sales," "Sales Representative," or "Sales Representatives." Also check out manufacturers' ads, where they might advertise more than one job opening.
4. If you are interested in working with a specific wholesaler, check to see if they have a Web site. Many company Web sites now list job opportunities.
5. Visit www.hoovers.com to get Web sites for specific wholesalers as well as basic information on what various companies sell.
6. Take classes, seminars, and workshops in selling techniques and motivation to give you an edge over other applicants.

SALES TRAINER—WHOLESALE

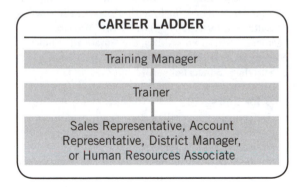

Position Description

Wholesalers, distributors, and manufacturers may employ an array of salespeople to move their products to the retail market. These may include sales representatives, manufacturers' representatives, account representatives, account managers, sales managers, district managers, or regional and territory managers.

In order to assure the staff be as effective as possible, many companies hire Sales Trainers. These individuals are responsible for preparing and conducting training programs for the company's sales staff. Depending on the situation and the specific company the individual may train employees to perform specific jobs, customer service skills, selling techniques, or the use of products and merchandise being sold.

Sales Trainers in this setting may work under the direction of a human resources director, training manager, or sales manager. They confer with management on training needs for the specific company. Once training needs are identified, the individual must formulate an outline for training sessions. These must include content as well as methods. Some Trainers use comedy in their presentations. Others are more straightforward. Many Sales Trainers develop programs with role playing and games which help employees absorb material as well as retain it. The

Trainer will use the most effective methods to ensure employees understand and can put the material presented into use.

In many situations, companies hire sales representatives or account representatives who may have limited experience either selling or selling the specific product. The Sales Trainer must be sure the representatives know how to sell and use the specific product, how to deal with the clients for those products, and what the products can and cannot do. A pharmaceutical company, for example, may hire representatives to sell their products to hospitals and other health care facilities. A lack of knowledge on the part of any of the sales force could lead to possible injury, death, or malpractice suits.

The Trainer also develops methods of teaching sales strategies. Selling can be a difficult job in the best of circumstances. Trainers must find ways to help motivate a sales staff even when sales are not going well.

Trainers may present material in a variety of ways. They may facilitate workshops or seminars, or give lectures or demonstrations. In many cases, manufacturers who hire Trainers have them give general training sessions to new employees as well as on-going sessions to seasoned employees.

Depending on the company, Trainers may have the capability to set up training sessions as part of sales conferences or trade shows. In some situations, Trainers may also work with employees on a one-on-one basis.

Trainers may be responsible for preparing handouts, overheads, slides, or PowerPoint presentations to help employees absorb and understand needed skills. They additionally may be expected to develop booklets or other training materials.

In many cases, Trainers working for manufacturers or other wholesalers may be responsible for developing materials to help the sales staff understand how to use and sell new products when they are launched.

Trainers may be responsible for developing and facilitating programs for employees in a multitude of areas and a variety of subjects depending on the needs of the specific manufacturer or wholesaler. For example, companies may have Trainers conduct sessions for all employees on dealing with providing customer service for established accounts. Other Trainers may be expected to work with employees on handling specialized skills. For example, a Trainer working with a software manufacturer will need to prepare training programs on working with the software in order for salespeople to have the ability to sell it effectively.

Many companies have routine orientation for new employees. In these cases, Trainers may be expected to develop and facilitate orientation programs. During orientation, the Trainer must explain company policies as well as acceptable and unacceptable behavior on the job.

Some Trainers working for manufacturers, distributors, and other wholesalers may offer management classes to teach methods for communicating with their employees. This is essential in retaining employees. Other subjects covered in this type of class may include acceptable methods for disciplining staff and how to speak to subordinates without coming across abruptly. The individual may also develop classes for employees dealing with and avoiding sexual harassment in the workplace. This is especially important to a sales staff who must go out and sell in various locations and businesses.

Trainers may also be expected to provide classes specific to certain jobs. Other duties of Trainers working for wholesalers, manufacturers, and distributors may include:

- Training employees in team building
- Preparing development programs for sales staff
- Facilitating programs to teach department directors, managers, and supervisors methods of conducting training within their department
- Teaching department directors, managers, and supervisors proper procedures for interview techniques and handling employment reviews

Salaries

Annual earnings for Trainers working for wholesalers, manufacturers, and distributors can range from approximately $29,000 to $58,000 or more. Factors affecting earnings include the geographic location, size, and type of the specific company as well as the education, experience, and responsibilities of the individual.

Employment Prospects

Employment prospects are good for trainers working for wholesalers, distributors, and manufacturers. The greatest number of positions will be located in areas hosting a lot of industry and many manufacturers.

Advancement Prospects

Trainers may advance their careers in a number of ways. The most common is to locate similar positions in larger or more prestigious companies. Another method of climbing the career ladder for a Sales Trainer is being promoted to the position of training manager. Some Trainers strike out on their own and become corporate training consultants.

Education and Training

Educational requirements vary. Most require or prefer individuals to hold a minimum of a bachelor's degree. Good majors for those interested in this field might include human resources, communications, retail, business, public relations, marketing, liberal arts, or a related field. There are some companies who may accept individuals with a high school diploma and a background and experience in training and human resources. Other companies may hire an individual without an educational background who has worked in sales management and has the ability to train others.

Experience, Skills, and Personality Traits

Experience requirements vary. Generally experience in training and development is required or preferred. Sales experience may also be needed. Some employers will hire individuals out of college who have gone through internship programs.

Good Trainers have the ability to motivate others. They know how to explain things in an easy-to-understand and easy-to-remember manner.

Sales Trainers need exemplary people and employee relations skills. Good verbal and written communication skills are also necessary. The ability to speak effectively in front of people is essential to this position. An understanding of the products being sold is mandatory to prepare programs.

Unions and Associations

Those interested in learning more about careers in this field should contact the American Society of Training Developers (ASTD), the Society for Human Resources Management (SHRM), Sales and Marketing Executives International (SMEI), the Manufacturers' Agents National Association (MANA), the American Management Association, the American Wholesale Marketers Association (AWMA) or associations specific to the products being sold.

Tips for Entry

1. Experience as a sales representative for a manufacturer or distributor is helpful in understanding the sales process.
2. Become either an active or affiliate member of the American Society of Training Developers (ASTD). This may give you the edge over another applicant with the same qualifications.
3. If you have the opportunity, go to some of the ASTD seminars and workshops. These are valuable for the learning opportunity as well as networking possibilities.
4. Openings are often advertised on the Internet. They may be located via the home pages wholesalers, distributors, or manufacturers.
5. Positions may be advertised in the classified sections of newspapers. Look under classifications such as "Trainer," "Training and Development," "Wholesale Opportunities," or "Human Resources." Also look at specific company advertisements.
6. You may be asked to conduct an impromptu training presentation as part of your interview process. Develop a sample program ahead of time and rehearse before the interview.
7. Send your resume and a short cover letter to wholesalers, distributors, and manufacturers. Inquire about openings and an interview. Get started by contacting some of the companies listed in the appendix.

MANUFACTURER'S REPRESENTATIVE

Position Description

Manufacturer's Representatives market a company's products to wholesale and retail establishments, government agencies, and other institutions. Individuals might also be called sales representatives.

Manufacturer's Representatives work in any industry selling a variety of products, including both retail and wholesale food, clothing, pharmaceuticals, office equipment, computers, cosmetics, machinery parts, electronics, automobile parts, exercise and sports equipment, furniture, and so on. No matter what type of products the Manufacturer's Representative sells, their main function is to interest wholesale and retail buyers and purchasing agents in their merchandise. Manufacturer's Representatives make sales calls to current clients as well as prospective buyers. They may visit clients at their place of work or set up sales meetings in other locations.

The Manufacturer's Representative must learn the needs of the customer and then show him or her how their specific product meets those needs. The individual may show the client samples or pictures in a catalog of merchandise he or she has to offer.

Successful Manufacturer's Representatives develop a strong sales pitch to sell their merchandise. Individuals must have the ability to discuss the strengths and weaknesses of their products and others in the marketplace. It is essential that the Manufacturer's Representative

know everything there is about not only his or her company's products but those of competitors. In this way, the individual can explain and emphasize the unique qualities of his or her specific merchandise in comparison to similar products sold by others.

The Manufacturer's Representative is expected to give pricing schedules for merchandise, answer questions, and then hopefully close a sale. At this point, the Manufacturer's Representative will take and write up orders.

The representative must keep in contact with clients to make sure merchandise has arrived, is satisfactory, and that there are no problems with the order. He or she will also try to get reorders by determining the quantity of products which have been sold since the last sales call.

At times, the Manufacturer's Representative might work from his or her office, making appointments and sales calls by telephone. At other times, the individual might make sales calls in person visiting established accounts or making cold calls to potential new customers.

It is essential that the Manufacturer's Representative keep abreast of new merchandise and the changing needs of their customers. Individuals often are expected to attend trade shows where new products are showcased. They might also attend conferences and conventions to meet other sales representatives and clients and discuss new product developments. Companies often sponsor sales meetings to review sales performance, product development, sales goals, and profitability.

There is a fair amount of office work in this type of position. Individuals might be responsible for developing and sending sales letters or brochures to new or established accounts. It is also necessary for the Manufacturer's Representative to keep accurate records of orders, invoices and bills.

Additional duties of Manufacturer's Representatives might include:

- Answering questions about new products and merchandise
- Addressing concerns of clients
- Providing advice to clients on increasing sales
- Visiting established accounts
- Writing sales letters and sending product literature and pricing sheets to customers
- Representing a company's products on television shopping channels such as QVC or HSN

Salaries

Earnings for Manufacturer's Representatives vary greatly ranging from approximately $24,000 to $125,000 or more annually. Variables include the specific company for which the individual works, the product being sold, and the sales territory which is assigned. Other factors affecting earnings include the experience of the Representative as well as his or her sales ability, motivation, and aggressiveness.

There are a number of different ways Manufacturer's Representatives are compensated. Individuals might receive a straight salary, a commission, or a combination of the two. Manufacturer's Representatives might also receive bonuses for outstanding sales. In many cases the Manufacturer's Representative additionally receives a company car or a car allowance.

Employment Prospects

Employment prospects for Manufacturer's Representatives are excellent. Those who are aggressive and motivated should have no problem finding a job. Positions are plentiful and can be located throughout the country although the most opportunities will be in areas hosting large numbers of manufacturers.

Advancement Prospects

Advancement prospects are excellent for aggressive and motivated Manufacturer's Representatives. There are a number of options for climbing the career ladder in this field. The most common is locating similar positions with larger or more prestigious companies. Individuals might also stay in the same company and get better territories. Some Manufacturer's Representatives move into supervisory and management positions.

Education and Training

Educational and training requirements vary depending on the specific company and the product line. Some companies just require their representatives to hold a high school diploma while others prefer or require a college background or degree.

Companies often have formal training programs for new employees as well as continuing programs for those with more experience. These programs help motivate employees and offer new ideas and selling techniques.

Other companies offer informal training with managers or supervisors helping employees learn sale techniques and policies. Some representatives learn the trade by accompanying more experienced individuals on calls in the field.

Experience, Skills, and Personality Traits

Background and experience requirements for Manufacturer's Representatives vary. Experience selling in either the retail or wholesale industry may be preferred. However, there are often entry-level jobs available.

Successful Manufacturers' Representatives are confident, assertive, motivated individuals with sales ability. Communications skills are essential. Manufacturer's Representatives need the ability to work well both independently and as part of a team. Depending on the specific job, the individual may be required to hold a valid driver's license.

Individuals must have a great deal of patience and perseverance. Sales don't always happen overnight.

Unions and Associations

Manufacturer's Representatives may belong to Sales and Marketing Executives International (SMEI), the Manufacturers' Agents National Association (MANA), or associations specific to the products they are selling. Individuals may also obtain additional career information from the Manufacturer's Representatives Educational Research Foundation.

Tips for Entry

1. Jobs can often be located on-line. Start with some of the more popular sites such as www.monster.com or www.hotjobs.com.
2. Send your resume and a short cover letter to manufacturers in your area.

3. Positions are often advertised in the classified sections of newspapers under heading including "Manufacturer's Representative," "Manufacturer's Rep," "Wholesale Opportunities," "Wholesale Sales," "Retail Opportunities," or "Sales Representatives." You might also look under industries specific to the products you are interested in representing.

4. If you are interested in working with a specific company, check to see if they have a Web site. Many companies have Web sites featuring job opportunities.

5. Visit www.hoovers.com to get Web sites for specific companies as well as basic information on what various companies sell.

6. You might also check product packaging to obtain the address of a specific product you are interested in selling.

7. The yellow pages can be a wealth of information in your job search. Check them to find the names, addresses, and phone numbers of manufacturers in your area.

8. Take classes, seminars, and workshops in selling techniques and motivation to give you an edge over other applicants.

TRADE SHOW REPRESENTATIVE— WHOLESALE

Duties: Represent manufacturer or wholesaler at trade shows and conventions; demonstrate products; staff the booth; take orders for products.

Alternate Title(s): Trade Show Representative; Trade Show Sales Representative

Salary Range: $25,000 to $100,000+

Employment Prospects: Good

Advancement Prospects: Fair

Best Geographical Location(s) for Position: Jobs may be located throughout the country; areas hosting large numbers of manufacturers and wholesalers will offer more possibilities

Prerequisites:

Education and Training—Educational requirements vary; see text

Experience—Experience dealing with the public is helpful

Special Skills and Personality Traits—Sales ability; articulate; people skills; organization; detail oriented; communication skills; ability to travel

Position Description

Manufacturers and wholesalers sell their products to retailers who in turn sell them to consumers. Manufacturers' representatives and other salespeople often make sales calls to current clients as well as prospective buyers. They may visit clients at their place of work or set up sales meetings in other locations. Sometimes clients visit manufacturers' or wholesalers' showrooms to place orders for merchandise. Another common way of selling merchandise is through trade shows.

Trade shows are events where companies have booths and showcase their products. Companies may spotlight new items at these shows as well as current inventory. Customers, or in this case retailers, visit the show to see a variety of products all in one location. Trade shows may run from one day to four or five days depending on the specific event.

Trade Show Representatives work for the wholesaler or manufacturer and act as their representatives in the field. Their main function is to help sell the company's product. Depending on the specific industry, there may be many different trade shows held in cities from coast to coast. Shows may also be held in other countries. As part of the job, the Trade Show Representative

is expected to travel to the different locations where events are being held.

Trade shows traditionally are set up with convention style booths in which companies create their own space. In this space they may include things such as product displays, merchandise, literature, signs, giveaways, promotional material, computers, or audiovisual equipment. Before a Trade Show Representative leaves the company's main office, he or she must be sure arrangements have been made to have everything shipped to the venue as well as shipped back or on to the next trade show.

Once at the venue, the Trade Show Representative is expected either to set up the booth or to oversee the set up. He or she may also work with union personnel present in many venues during the setup and break down.

The Trade Show Representative's main function during a show is attracting people to the booth and talking to them about the company's products. In this manner, the Trade Show Representative can interest potential customers.

The Trade Show Representative must know as much as possible about the manufacturer's products. He or she often spends a great deal of time before trade shows with company salespeople, technicians, and marketing people to obtain this information. The Trade Show Representative may read company literature and marketing pieces, or view commercials, ads, and videos to make him- or herself familiar with the merchandise and the company.

Depending on the structure of the company, the individual may work with one or more Representatives or salespeople at the show. Sometimes, if the show is very large and considered important in the industry, the company may also send others from upper management including the marketing manager and sales manager.

The Trade Show Representative arrives at the trade show before it opens to the public. Once retailers begin to come in, the Representative is expected to work the booth, demonstrate the merchandise, and answer questions from prospective customers.

Depending on the specific situation, some Trade Show Representatives may be responsible for taking orders for merchandise. Others might just take names, addresses, and phone numbers and set up meetings for company sales people.

Trade Show Representatives often meet with prospective clients after show hours to explain products in more detail or to help create good business relationships. Often manufacturers and wholesalers host informal get-togethers, cocktail parties, or receptions for potential clients after hours as well. The Trade Show Representative is expected to be on hand at these events, acting as host and setting up sales meetings, appointments, and presentations.

Additional duties of Trade Show Representatives working in the wholesale industry might include:

- Making travel and lodging arrangements for staff attending show
- Making sure trade show promoter has provided all equipment and space for which the company has contracted
- Breaking down booths at conclusion of trade show
- Answering questions about new products and merchandise
- Representing company during media interviews in areas where trade show is being held

Salaries

Annual earnings for Trade Show Representatives working for manufacturers in the wholesale industry can range from approximately $25,000 to $100,000 or more. Variables include the specific company for which the individual works as well as the experience and responsibilities of the individual.

Trade Show Representatives whose main responsibility is staffing a booth or demonstrating a product will earn the lower salaries. Those who have more responsibility or those who sell will have earnings at the higher end of the pay scale. Some Representatives also receive commissions on sales in addition to their base salary.

Employment Prospects

Employment prospects for Trade Show Representatives in the wholesale industry are good. Most companies attend trade shows on a regular basis and need individuals for this position. The greatest opportunities will exist in areas hosting large numbers of manufacturers and wholesalers. It is important to note that some companies utilize freelance Trade Show Representatives.

Advancement Prospects

Advancement prospects are dependent, to a great extent, on an individual's career expectations. Some people love the life of being on the road. They enjoy traveling and they can't think of a better career than working trade shows. These individuals will most likely climb the career ladder by landing jobs with larger or more prestigious companies. Others move into positions in marketing or sales.

Education and Training

Educational requirements vary. A college degree or background may be preferred, but is not always required. A degree may give one applicant an edge over another who doesn't have one.

Good majors to consider for positions in this field include sales, marketing, business, advertising, public relations, and communications.

Experience, Skills, and Personality Traits

Trade Show Representatives spend a great deal of time on the road. People in this field must like to travel and not mind "living out of a suitcase."

Individuals should be neat, articulate, and personable with excellent communication skills. The most successful Trade Show Representatives have pleasant personalities mixed with sales skills.

Unions and Associations

Depending on their duties and the industry in which the individual is working, he or she may be a member of industry specific associations. The Trade Show Representative may also be a member of a number of other organizations providing professional support and guidance including the Public Relations Society of America (PRSA), the Sales and Marketing Executives International (SMEI), the Manufacturers' Agents National Association (MANA), and the American Wholesale Marketers Association (AWMA).

Tips for Entry

1. Jobs as Trade Show Representatives can often be located on-line. Start with some of the more prevalent sites such as www.monster.com and www.hotjobs.com.

2. Positions are often advertised in the classified sections of newspapers under heading including "Wholesale Opportunities," "Wholesale-Retail Opportunities," "Trade Show Representative," "Wholesale Sales," "Marketing Opportunities," or "Sales." You might also look under industries specific to the products you are interested in representing.

3. Sunday's paper usually has the largest classified section. Most companies try to have their help wanted ads run on a Sunday.

4. If you are interested in working with a specific company, check to see if they have a Web site. Many companies have Web sites featuring job opportunities.

5. Visit www.hoovers.com to get Web sites for specific companies as well as basic information on what various companies sell. Hoovers also often has information regarding specific names of people in a company to whom to send resumes.

6. The yellow pages are a wealth of information in your job search. Check them to find the names, addresses, and phone numbers of manufacturers/wholesalers in your area.

7. Many wholesalers and manufacturers have freelance or part-time positions for Trade Show Representatives. Visit the human resources department to find out about possibilities. Often a part-time position leads to a full-time opportunity.

8. Get some experience by working as a freelance Trade Show Representative. Contact trade show companies to find out when and where they are holding events. Ask for a list of exhibitors. Send your resume and a short cover letter asking about possibilities.

9. You might also contact convention bureaus or convention managers of hotels to find out what trade shows are coming in. Contact their trade show manager to find a list of exhibitors.

RACK JOBBER

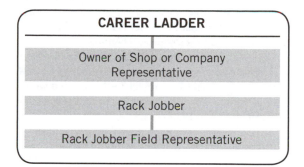

Position Description

Rack Jobbers offer merchandise that is not covered by existing inventory to retail stores. Rack Jobbers may be representatives of manufacturers or wholesalers or may be the manufacturer or wholesaler themselves.

Rack Jobbers are granted shelf space in retail stores for their merchandise. Rack Jobbers may bring in a variety of merchandise depending on the company they represent. Many of the record, book, and cosmetic displays seen in supermarkets, department stores, automotive shops, discount stores, and drug stores are put together by Rack Jobbers.

It is the responsibility of the Rack Jobber to select the products to display and sell in a section of someone else's store or market. He or she receives the space in return for either a rental fee, a leasing fee, a percentage of sales, or a combination of both.

The job of a Rack Jobber is much like that of owning a retail store. However, the merchandise is in a space that hopefully already draws a stream of customer traffic. The Rack Jobber may have a space in more than one store.

The Rack Jobber buys merchandise from a distributor or wholesaler. Since he or she has limited space it is impossible to stock everything. Instead, the individual will stock the merchandise customers are most likely looking for.

Rack Jobbers offer stores the opportunity to have a specific department without the risk. For example, a convenience store may not want to pay the expense for a compact disc, cassette, and videotape department. The Rack Jobber gives the store a department and merchandise. If something doesn't sell, the Rack Jobber takes it back. This is a no-risk situation for the store's management.

After selecting merchandise, the Rack Jobber makes sure it gets to the store. He or she must also make sure that merchandise is displayed properly. The display must be eye catching and draw potential customers. In this way they will see merchandise and hopefully make a purchase.

It is the responsibility of the Rack Jobber to periodically come into the store and take inventory. At this time, he or she will take back merchandise which isn't moving, and bring in "hot" sellers. Those selling CDs and tapes, for example, might bring in those by artists who have top twenty hits. As the "Top 20" changes, so will the merchandise. In some cases, such as where the Rack Jobber is selling perishable merchandise, he or she may have to return to the store more often to bring in fresh merchandise. This might be the case, for example, when a Rack Jobber is representing the manufacturer of baked goods.

Depending on the situation, the Rack Jobber must either hire a staff of salespeople (if it is a lease situation) or train and supervise members of the store's existing staff who will be working in the specific department. In this instance, the Rack Jobber may pay a rental fee or percentage to the store. In other instances, the Rack Jobber will just provide the merchandise and it will be run through the store's register when sold.

The Rack Jobber often will visit the store managers of established accounts. He or she will also look for new businesses in which to put merchandise. The individual must constantly keep the stores happy and satisfied or they will not renew their contracts.

Additional duties of Rack Jobbers might include:

- Answering questions about new products and merchandise
- Addressing concerns of clients
- Providing advice to salespeople on increasing sales
- Keeping accurate records of merchandise inventory and sales from his or her space
- Supplying the store with advertising and promotional material to help sell the merchandise

Salaries
Annual earnings for Rack Jobbers can range from approximately $26,000 to $75,000 or more depending on a number of factors. These include the size and prestige of the wholesaler or distributor with whom the individual is working, the specific product, how much is sold, and the type of salary received.

Rack Jobbers may be paid in the form of a straight commission or may be guaranteed a salary against a commission.

Employment Prospects
Employment prospects are fair for Rack Jobbers. Rack Jobbers may work for themselves or for wholesalers or distributors. There are many stores and shops that want departments serviced by Rack Jobbers. An individual may take over an entire rack jobbing operation or be a field representative.

Advancement Prospects
Advancement prospects are fair for individuals in this line of work. The most common method of climbing the career ladder is by increasing the size of an individual's business by broadening the base of the operation.

As Rack Jobbers meet and work closely with distributors of companies, they often make a large number of contacts. These individuals often offer the Rack Jobber a position in the distribution department of their company. Some Rack Jobbers strike out and open their own stores.

Education and Training
Generally, there is no specific educational background required to be a Rack Jobber or to work for one other than having a high school diploma. However, a college background or courses in business, merchandising, marketing, and related fields will be useful in honing skills and making contacts.

Experience, Skills, and Personality Traits
Rack Jobbers usually experience selling in both the retail and wholesale industries. Individuals must have a complete knowledge of the products being sold.

Management, organization, and communications skills are essential to the success of Rack Jobbers. Salesmanship and assertiveness are also useful.

Unions and Associations
Rack Jobbers may belong to a number of organizations providing professional support and guidance. These include Sales and Marketing Executives International (SMEI), the Manufacturers' Agents National Association (MANA), the American Management Association, the American Wholesale Marketers Association (AWMA), or associations specific to the products being sold.

Tips for Entry
1. Positions as Rack Jobbers can often be located on-line. Start with some of the more popular sites such as www.monster.com and www.hotjobs.com.
2. Positions are often advertised in the classified sections of newspapers under headings including "Rack-Jobber," "Wholesale-Retail Opportunities," "Wholesale Opportunities," "Wholesale Sales," or "Rack Jobber Field Representative."
3. Sunday's paper usually has the largest classified section. Most companies try to have their help wanted ads run on a Sunday.
4. If you are interested in working with a specific company, check to see if they have a Web site. Many companies have Web sites featuring job opportunities.
5. Visit www.hoovers.com to get Web sites for specific companies as well as basic information on what various companies sell.
6. The yellow pages are a wealth of information in your job search. Check them to find the names,

addresses, and phone numbers of manufacturers in your area.

7. Many major department stores around the country have departments serviced by Rack Jobbers. Contact the store and ask. Then contact the Rack Jobber and ask for a job as a clerk or sales associate in that department.

8. You might also visit drug stores, supermarkets, or convenience stores to determine their Rack Jobbers. Get addresses and phone numbers so you can send a resume and set up an interview.

PURCHASING MANAGER— WHOLESALE

CAREER PROFILE

Duties: Acquire products, material, intermediate goods, machines, supplies, and other items used in the production of a final product; find suppliers and vendors; negotiate lowest prices; solicit bids; award contracts.

Alternate Title(s): Industrial Purchasing Manager

Salary Range: $28,000 to $78,000+

Employment Prospects: Fair

Advancement Prospects: Fair

Best Geographical Location(s) for Position: Jobs may be located throughout the country; large cities and areas with a great many manufacturers and industry will offer more possibilities

Prerequisites:

Education and Training—College degree preferred

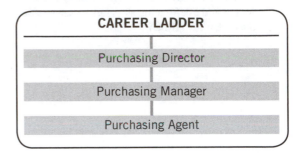

Experience—Experience in buying and purchasing

Special Skills and Personality Traits—Negotiation skills; leadership; communication skills; organization; planning skills; decision making skills

---

Position Description

There is a chain of supply in the production of merchandise. First it must be manufactured and then sold to wholesalers or distributors. These companies then sell the merchandise to retail outlets for the public to buy. In some cases, the manufacturer is also the wholesaler and/or the distributor.

In order to manufacture merchandise and products, raw materials and machinery are often needed by the manufacturer. The individual responsible for overseeing the acquisition of these products is called the Purchasing Manager.

Responsibilities of Purchasing Managers can vary depending on the specific employment situation. Purchasing Managers may buy product materials, intermediate goods, machines, supplies, and other materials used in the production of a final product. In some cases, individuals may specialize in a certain type of purchasing. For example, they may specialize in machinery or supplies. Others may specialize in wood, lumber, steel, plastic, or fabric materials.

Depending on the type of products the manufacturer sells, the Purchasing Manager may be expected to obtain goods ranging from the actual raw materials (such as wood), to fabricated parts or the machinery needed to complete the process.

Purchasing Managers usually have a number of different vendors to choose from when selecting materials. As part of their job, they must evaluate and select vendors or suppliers based on a number of criteria. While price is important, it can not be used solely in choosing suppliers of merchandise. Other factors to be considered when choosing suppliers include the quality of the merchandise, availability, selection, and reliability of the vendor.

It is essential to the success of a manufacturer to have the correct materials on hand when needed for a project. Not doing so can hold up manufacturing, which can have a serious impact on sales.

Depending on the size and structure of the manufacturer, Purchasing Managers may supervise and oversee the work of one or more purchasing agents. In others, he or she may work alone.

In some companies, the Purchasing Manager is expected to work on product development. This is because the Purchasing Manager is the one in the organization who often is best able to forecast which materials will be most available, cost effective, and acceptable in relation to production standards.

The Purchasing Manager may seek suppliers and vendors both domestically and internationally. Individuals find supplies in a variety of ways. They may meet with vendors to look at merchandise in their own offices or may visit warehouses, showrooms, or factories. Individuals might review listings in catalogs, industry periodicals, directories, and trade journals. Purchasing Managers often research the reputation and history of suppliers to assure that they are reliable in their business dealings.

Some Purchasing Managers must travel a great deal. Individuals may go on trips to purchase supplies as well as attending meetings, trade shows, and conferences. Many Purchasing Managers may also visit vendors' plants and distribution centers. In this manner they can examine products as well as assess the vendor's production and distribution capabilities.

The Purchasing Manager solicits bids from vendors to obtain the best prices for the best merchandise. A difference of even one cent per item can make a huge difference in the final cost of a product to a manufacturer. Once the Purchasing Manager obtains bids and analyzes them, he or she will award contracts.

In some instances, the Purchasing Manager may seek bids for contractors to handle certain parts of a manufacturing job. Because these might be long-term contracts, the Purchasing Manager must choose a suitable supplier.

It is mandatory to the success of the Purchasing Manager to have a good business relationship with suppliers. He or she may be expected to work out any problems and handle customer service issues.

Additional duties of Purchasing Managers might include:

- Supervising supply contracts
- Developing bid forms
- Handling quality control of materials
- Developing good working relationships with vendors

Salaries

Annual earnings for Purchasing Managers can range from approximately $28,000 to $78,000 or more depending on a number of variables. These include the size, geographic location, and specific employer as well as the experience, responsibilities, and education of the individual.

Employment Prospects

Employment prospects for Purchasing Managers are good. Individuals may find employment with a variety of manufacturers. The greatest opportunities will exist in areas hosting large numbers of manufacturers.

Advancement Prospects

Advancement prospects for Purchasing Managers are fair. Some individuals find similar positions with larger manufacturers. This results in increased responsibilities and earnings. After obtaining experience, other individuals may climb the career ladder by becoming Purchasing Directors.

Education and Training

Educational requirements vary depending on the specific employer. While there are exceptions, most employers prefer their Purchasing Managers hold a minimum of a four-year college degree.

Once on the job, individuals often go through either formal or informal training programs. Voluntary certification is available through the National Association of Purchasing Management and the American Purchasing Society.

Experience, Skills, and Personality Traits

Purchasing Managers need a great deal of experience in purchasing and often have started out as purchasing agents.

Individuals should be self-confident with the ability to make decisions. They should have a complete knowledge of the products they are purchasing and the industries they are working with. Good communications skills and the ability to deal with stress and pressure are necessary.

Unions and Associations

Purchasing Managers might belong to a number of associations including the American Purchasing Society, Inc. (APS) or the National Association of Purchasing Management, Inc. (NAPM). Both these organizations provide certification programs, professional support, and career guidance.

Tips for Entry

1. Contact the American Purchasing Society, Inc. (APS) and the National Association of Purchasing Management, Inc. (NAPM). Ask about certification requirements.
2. Jobs often can be located on-line too. Look at some of the major sites such as www.hotjobs.com and www.monster.com.
3. Positions are often advertised in the classified sections of newspapers under heading including "Wholesale Opportunities," "Manufacturing Opportunities," "Industry," "Purchasing Professional," "Purchasing Manager," or "Purchasing."
4. Send your resume and a short cover letter to manufacturers and inquire about internships or training programs. Contact manufacturers in your local area or some of those listed in the appendix of this book.

WAREHOUSE MANAGER— WHOLESALE MANUFACTURER OR DISTRIBUTOR

Duties: Oversee management of warehouse or distribution center; supervise and coordinate activities of warehouse workers; organize the receiving, storing, and shipping of merchandise and goods

Alternate Title(s): Distribution Warehouse Manager

Salary Range: $28,000 to $78,000

Employment Prospects: Good

Advancement Prospects: Fair

Best Geographical Location(s) for Position: Jobs may be located throughout the country; the greatest number of opportunities will exist in areas with large numbers of manufacturers or distributors

Prerequisites:

Education and Training—Educational requirements vary; see text

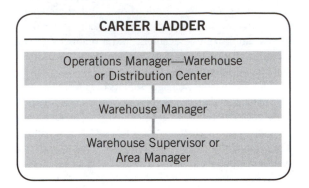

CAREER LADDER

Operations Manager—Warehouse or Distribution Center

Warehouse Manager

Warehouse Supervisor or Area Manager

Experience—Experience working in warehouse and/or distribution center

Special Skills and Personality Traits—Supervisory skills; organization; time management skills

Position Description

Manufacturers must store the merchandise they make so that it can be transported to distributors. Once received, the distributor must store the merchandise until it is sold to retailers or other consumers. Both manufacturers and distributors utilize warehouses to store these goods. The individual responsible for overseeing the warehouse is called the Warehouse Manager. He or she works under the direction of the warehouse operations manager.

The Warehouse Manager holds an important position in the supply chain of goods. He or she helps plan and prepare for the management of the warehouse. If the individual works for a distributor he or she will be in charge of the distribution center warehouse. Depending on the specific facility, he or she will be responsible for receiving, storing, and sending out stock from the warehouse. Within the scope of the job, he or she has additional responsibilities.

The Warehouse Manager supervises and coordinates the activities of the workers in the facility. Depending on the specific situation, this may include traffic workers, loading and unloading workers, clerks, area supervisors, and more. He or she will assign duties to

each worker so that the warehouse is run effectively and efficiently.

Depending on the type of goods, merchandise may be stored in a number of ways. It is up to the Warehouse Manager to determine the best method. Sometimes it may be on pallets. Other times it may be stored in areas called cages. If the merchandise or goods are perishable, such as certain food items, they must often be stored in cold areas, refrigerated storage, or huge freezers.

A great deal of machinery and equipment may be used within the warehouse. It is the responsibility of the Warehouse Manager to be sure all machinery is working and available. If there is a problem with machinery, he or she is responsible for reporting it immediately and making sure it is repaired. Failure to do so may result in a backup moving merchandise in, out, or around the facility.

A major function of the Warehouse Manager is assuring that all employees know how to use equipment properly. He or she must also be sure that employees practice safety methods and rules when working in the warehouse. Failure to do this might result in accidents injuring employees and/or damaging merchandise.

The Warehouse Manager assists in the planning of the distribution chain. He or she is responsible for assuring the quality of merchandise that comes in and leaves the warehouse. For example, if a distribution center brings in a truckload of frozen foods and they are not kept frozen at all times, the food will be spoiled.

The Warehouse Manager coordinates the receipt of goods coming into the warehouse as well as those leaving the facility. He or she makes sure all merchandise is accounted for. This is often done with the help of scanners and computer equipment used by receiving and shipping clerks and workers depending on whether merchandise is coming in or leaving the facility.

The Warehouse Manager orders and schedules deliveries of packaging and raw materials as needed. This is necessary in order to ship merchandise out of the facility.

The individual must keep accurate records of stock received and merchandise which is returned. He or she reviews these records and determines any discrepancies. The Warehouse Manager must also be sure that procedures regarding returning defective merchandise are followed.

In some cases, the Warehouse Manager may drive a forklift him- or herself helping to move merchandise. In other situations, the Warehouse Manager will just oversee employees handling these tasks.

Additional duties of a Warehouse Manager might include:

- Communicating with management
- Supervising the loading and unloading of bulk merchandise and goods on pallets
- Overseeing inventory control
- Hiring and terminating employees who do not perform satisfactorily
- Organizing and planning daily activities
- Receiving orders for goods
- Handling complaints regarding the warehouse

Salaries

Annual earnings of Warehouse Managers working for manufacturers or distributors can range from approximately $28,000 to $78,000 or more. Variables affecting earnings include the specific employer, the size, and geographic location of the warehouse and the experience and responsibilities of the individual.

Employment Prospects

Employment prospects for Warehouse Managers are good. Positions may be located throughout the country.

The greatest number of openings are located in large areas hosting large numbers of manufacturers and distribution centers.

Advancement Prospects

The most common method of career advancement for Warehouse Managers is locating similar positions for companies with warehouses. This will result in increased responsibilities and earnings. Individuals may also climb the career ladder through promotion to operations manager of a warehouse or distribution center.

Education and Training

Educational requirements vary. Some companies require or prefer individuals to hold a college degree. Other companies will hire individuals without a college degree or background who have moved up the ranks and prove they can handle the job. A college degree will help individuals move up the career ladder. Good possibilities for majors include operations, logistics, materials management, or related fields.

There are also trade schools and colleges which have certificate programs in warehouse work.

Experience, Skills, and Personality Traits

Prior experience working in a warehouse is needed as is supervisory experience. Warehouse Managers need to be detail oriented, organized individuals with excellent time management skills. Good verbal and written communications skills are also necessary. Interpersonal skills are needed. Computer skills are necessary. The ability to remain calm is essential.

Unions and Associations

Warehouse Managers may be members of the American Wholesale Marketers Association (AWMA) or associations or associations specific to the products and merchandise in their warehouse.

Tips for Entry

1. Jobs are often advertised in the classified section of the newspaper. Look under headings such as "Warehouse Manager," "Warehouse," "Distribution Center," "Wholesale Opportunities," or "Distribution Center Manager." Specific companies may also advertise a number of job opportunities in one advertisement.
2. Sunday's paper usually has the largest classified section. Most companies try to have their help wanted ads run on a Sunday.
3. Get your foot in the door and get experience. Learn what you can and move up the career ladder.

4. Contact manufacturers, wholesalers, and distributors. Send your resume and a short cover letter inquiring about openings.
5. If you are interested in working for a specific manufacturer or distributor, check to see if they have a Web site. Many companies now have Web sites featuring job opportunities. Check the appendix for some of the larger manufacturers.
6. Visit www.hoovers.com to get Web sites for specific companies as well as basic information on what various companies sell.
7. The yellow pages are a wealth of information in your job search. Check them to find the names, addresses, and phone numbers of manufacturers in your area.

EXECUTIVE DIRECTOR, RETAIL OR WHOLESALE TRADE ASSOCIATION

Duties: Oversee operations of trade association; manage business affairs of organization; implement programs; develop budgets

Alternate Title(s): Association Executive, Trade Association Director.

Salary Range: $26,000 to $95,000+

Employment Prospects: Fair

Advancement Prospects: Fair

Best Geographical Location(s) for Position: Positions located throughout country

Prerequisites:

Education or Training—Most positions require or prefer minimum of four-year college degree

Experience—Experience with public relations, grant writing, and administration

Special Skills and Personality Traits—Management skills; grant writing skills; fund-raising skills; creativity; personable; excellent verbal and written communications skills; understanding of the retail and/or wholesale industries

CAREER LADDER

```
┌─────────────────────────────────────┐
│ Executive Director of Larger, More  │
│ Prestigious Retail or Wholesale     │
│ Trade Association or Trade           │
│ Association in Other Industry        │
└─────────────────────────────────────┘
                 ▲
┌─────────────────────────────────────┐
│ Executive Director, Retail or        │
│ Wholesale Trade Association          │
└─────────────────────────────────────┘
                 ▲
┌─────────────────────────────────────┐
│ Trade Association Assistant          │
│ Director, Public Relations Director, │
│ Grant Writer, or Administrator,      │
│ Journalist, etc.                     │
└─────────────────────────────────────┘
```

Position Description

Both the retail and wholesale industries have a large number of trade groups, associations, and organizations geared at promoting their particular segment of the industry. These trade associations cover a wide array of areas including those that deal specifically with the various industries as well as their employees, employers, educators, equipment, regulatory issues, and more.

The individual in charge of overseeing the operations of these groups is called the Executive Director. In some instances, he or she may also be called the trade association director. Trade associations are generally not-for-profit organizations. The main function of the Executive Director is to manage the affairs of the organization. Responsibilities can vary greatly depending on the specific organization, its mission, size, structure, prestige, and budget. In smaller organizations, the Executive Director may handle everything, perhaps with the help of volunteers. In larger trade associations, the Executive Director may have a staff and assistants to help handle the various duties and responsibilities that are part of the job.

The Executive Director works with the board of directors of the organization to establish the direction that the trade association will go. The individual is also expected to determine what types of programs the association will undertake. The Executive Director is heavily involved in the budget and finances of the organization. As part of the job, the individual is responsible for the preparation of an annual budget. Depending on the size and structure of the organization, this may be difficult because in many cases, these organizations work with limited budgets.

Depending on the specific association and its size and structure, the Executive Director may be responsible for fund-raising. The individual may develop, implement, and execute one or more special events and projects during the year to raise needed money. These events may include dinners, membership drives, auctions, galas, golf tournaments, etc. Some of the fund-raising events may be simple while others are much more elaborate. In large associations, there often is a fund-raising director who works under the direction of the director handling this function.

Grants are an important source of funds trade associations frequently use to sustain themselves. The Executive Director is responsible for locating these grants that may come from federal, state, or local agencies, and/or from private industry. He or she must then write and prepare the grant application. If the individual is successful in securing a grant, he or she must then make sure that all rules and regulations of the grant are adhered to. In some associations, instead of handling grants, the Executive Director oversees a grant writer and administrator who handle these tasks.

Public relations and advertising are important to every trade association. The Executive Director is expected to either personally handle or oversee the association's public relations and advertising campaigns. This may include public relations and advertising efforts directed toward the public as well as internally within the organization's membership.

As part of this responsibility, press releases, calendar schedules, and newsletters must be developed and prepared. In addition, brochures, leaflets, and booklets may be developed and designed to promote the organization. In smaller organizations, the Executive Director may handle these tasks him or herself. In larger organizations, the Executive Director is responsible for overseeing the public relations and publications department and staffers.

Depending on the specific trade association and its mission, education may be another important function of the organization. In some cases, this may be to educate the public. In others education is geared toward the association members regarding issues related to the organization. The Executive Director is expected to develop programs that help with this task. This might include literature, campaigns, events, seminars, and so on.

A large responsibility for the Executive Director of trade associations in the retail and wholesale industries is scheduling conferences, conventions, and other educational and networking activities. The Executive Director is expected to either handle these activities and events or delegate the duties to a committee or conference coordinator. These conventions, conferences, and meetings are the organization's opportunity to promote the association, get its mission out, give members a chance to network, and provide education.

The Executive Director of the trade association must be the champion of the organization. He or she is expected to attend meetings and events on behalf of the association. This may include industry events as well as community meetings. The individual will often be the liaison between the association and community groups frequently serving on boards of community and civic organizations. Many trade associations depend on the help of volunteers within their membership. The Executive Director is responsible for coordinating the efforts of all volunteer groups and committees within the association membership.

Other responsibilities of the Executive Director of a retail or wholesale industry trade association might include:

- Developing new membership drives and handling membership applications and renewals
- Assisting with lobbying efforts
- Supervising staff
- Dealing with issues significant to the association's mission
- Attending industry meetings, conferences, and conventions on behalf of the association

Salaries

Earnings for Executive Directors of retail or wholesale industry trade associations can range from $26,000 to $95,000 or more depending on a number of factors. These include the size, structure, prestige, and budget of the specific trade association. Other factors affecting earnings include the responsibilities, professional reputation, and experience of the individual. Executive Directors of large, prestigious associations within the retail and wholesale industries will earn more than their counterparts working for smaller, lesser-known groups.

Employment Prospects

Employment prospects are fair for individuals seeking positions as Executive Directors of retail or wholesale trade associations. Whether a product or service, most every segment of the retail and wholesale industries has its own trade association.

While trade associations are located throughout the country, there is a large concentration in major metropolitan areas such as New York, Chicago, Boston, and Washington, D.C. It should be noted, that individuals may need to relocate for positions. Individuals may find opportunities in small, midsize, or large trade associations in organization headquarters or local chapters.

Advancement Prospects

Advancement prospects for Executive Directors of trade associations in the retail and wholesale industries are fair. Advancement is generally dependent to a great extent on the level the individual is currently in his or her career. The Executive Director of a smaller retail or wholesale trade association may climb the career ladder by finding similar positions at larger or more prestigious organizations. The Executive Director may also climb the career ladder by successfully building his or her trade association into a larger, more prestigious organization. In these situations, he or she will often have increased responsibilities and earnings. Some Executive Directors also advance their careers by moving into similar positions in larger or more prestigious associations outside of the retail or wholesale industries. There are others who move into corporate positions in the specific area of the industry in which they were involved.

Education and Training

Education and training requirements vary for Executive Directors in retail and wholesale industry trade associations. Most large associations require or prefer their applicant to have a minimum of a four-year college degree. There are, however, smaller associations that may accept an applicant with an associate's degree or even a high school diploma if it is coupled with experience. Courses, seminars, and workshops in fund-raising, grant writing, public relations, business, management, and presentation skills will be useful in honing skills and making new contacts.

Experience, Skills, and Personality Traits

Experience requirements depend to a great extent on the size, structure, and prestige of the specific trade association. Individuals seeking positions with large, prestigious associations generally are required to either have a minimum of two to three years' experience working with trade associations in some manner or working at a corporate job within the specific area of the industry in which the association targets. Experiences in public relations, journalism, grant writing, and working with not-for-profit organizations will also be helpful.

Individuals in this position need to be well spoken with excellent written and verbal communication skills. An understanding of grant writing is usually necessary as is the ability to develop and adhere to budgets. People skills are essential. Those who are creative and visionaries for the particular trade association will be especially successful in this type of job. Management and supervisory skills are crucial. An understanding

and knowledge of the specific area of the industry that the association serves is essential.

Unions and Associations

Individuals interested in careers as Executive Directors of retail or wholesale trade associations may want to contact the Center for Association Leadership. They should also join other professional associations representing the specific area of the retail or wholesale industry in which they are interested in working.

Tips for Entry

1. Get experience working with not-for-profit organizations by volunteering with a local civic or community organization.
2. Openings may be listed on the Web sites of specific retail and wholesale trade associations.
3. Consider sending your résumé and a short cover letter to trade associations in which you are interested in working. A listing of trade associations with addresses in located in the back of the book.
4. Network as much as you can in the industry. Go to conferences, conventions, and educational seminars and workshops to meet industry insiders.
5. Offer to do the publicity or fund-raising for a local not-for-profit organization. It doesn't matter if the organization is related to the retail or wholesale industry or not. If you can do publicity or fund-raising for one organization, you can do it for any type of group.
6. Read trade publications. They often advertise openings.
7. Don't forget to surf the net. Check out traditional job search sites like monster.com and hotjobs. com. Then look for other job sites.
8. Look for job openings in the classified section of newspapers. Heading titles might be under key words such as "Trade Association," "Trade Association Executive Director," "Executive Director," "Retail Trade Association," or "Association Executive." Jobs may also be advertised under the name of the specific retail or wholesale associations.

APPENDIXES

I. Degree and Non-Degree Programs
- A. Four-Year Colleges and Universities Offering Majors in E-Commerce
- B. Four-Year Colleges and Universities Offering Majors in Apparel and Accessory Marketing
- C. Four-Year Colleges and Universities Offering Majors in Public Relations
- D. Four-Year Colleges and Universities Offering Majors in Advertising
- E. Two-Year Colleges and Universities Offering Majors in Retailing

II. Trade Associations, Unions, and Other Organizations

III. Directory of Chain Stores

IV. Directory of Department Stores

V. Directory of Supermarkets/Groceries

VI. Directory of Catalog Companies

VII. Directory of Television Shopping Channels

VIII. Directory of Manufacturers and Other Companies

APPENDIX I
DEGREE AND NONDEGREE PROGRAMS

A. FOUR YEAR COLLEGES AND UNIVERSITIES OFFERING MAJORS IN E-COMMERCE

Although possession of a college degree does not guarantee a job, many people feel that it is in their best interest to pursue an education after high school to learn additional information, gain new skills, and make important contacts. A degree or background in higher education may give one person an edge over another who doesn't continue his or her schooling.

The following is a listing of selected four year schools offering majors in public relations. They are grouped by state. School names, addresses, phone numbers, Web addresses, and e-mail addresses are included when available.

The author does not endorse any one school over another. Use this list as a beginning. Check the reference section of libraries or guidance counseling centers for additional schools offering degrees in this field

ALABAMA

University of South Alabama
307 University Boulevard
Mobile, AL 36688
Phone: (251) 460-6141
E-mail: admiss@usouthal.edu
http://www.usouthal.edu

ARIZONA

University of Phoenix
4615 East Elwood Street
Mail Stop AA-K101
Phoenix, AZ 85040
Phone: (480) 557-3303
Fax: (480) 643-1020
E-mail: evelyn.gaskin@phoenix.edu
http://www.phoenix.edu

CALIFORNIA

Dominican University of California
50 Acacia Avenue
San Rafael, CA 94901
Phone: (415) 485-3204
Fax: (415) 485-3214
E-mail: enroll@dominican.edu
http://www.dominican.edu

Mt. Sierra College
101 East Huntington Drive
Monrovia, CA 91016
Phone: (888) 486-9818
http://www.mtsierra.edu

National University
11255 North Torrey Pines Road
La Jolla, CA 92037
Phone: (800) 628-8648
Fax: (858) 541-7792
E-mail: dgiovann@nu.edu
http://www.nu.edu

University of La Verne
1950 Third Street
La Verne, CA 91750
Phone: (800) 867-4858
Fax: (909) 392-2714
E-mail: admissions@ulv.edu
http://www.ulv.edu

University of Phoenix–Bay Area Campus
4615 East Elwood Street
Mail Stop AA-K101
Phoenix, AZ 85040
Phone: (480) 557-3303
Fax: (480) 643-1020
E-mail: evelyn.gaskin@phoenix.edu
http://www.phoenix.edu

University of Phoenix–Sacramento
4615 East Elwood Street
Mail Stop AA-K101
Phoenix, AZ 85040
Phone: (480) 557-3303
Fax: (480) 643-1020
E-mail: evelyn.gaskin@phoenix.edu
http://www.phoenix.edu

COLORADO

Colorado Technical University - Colorado Springs
4435 North Chestnut Street
Colorado Springs, CO 80907
Phone: (719) 598-0200

Colorado Technical University - Denver
5775 Denver Tech Center Boulevard
Greenwood Village, CO 80111
Phone: (303) 694-6600

University of Phoenix– University of Phoenix– Denver Campus
4615 East Elwood Street
Mail Stop AA-K101
Phoenix, AZ 85040
Phone: (480) 557-3303

Fax: (480) 643-1020
E-mail: evelyn.gaskin@phoenix.edu
http://www.phoenix.edu

DELAWARE

Delaware State University
1200 North DuPont Highway
Dover, DE 19901
Phone: (302) 857-6351
Fax: (302) 857-6908
E-mail: gcheatha@desu.edu
http://www.desu.edu

DISTRICT OF COLUMBIA

University of Phoenix–Washington D.C. Campus
4615 East Elwood Street
Mail Stop AA-K101
Phoenix, AZ 85040
Phone: (480) 557-3303
Fax: (480) 643-1020
E-mail: evelyn.gaskin@phoenix.edu
http://www.phoenix.edu

FLORIDA

Florida Institute of Technology
150 West University Boulevard
Melbourne, FL 32901
Phone: (321) 674-8030
E-mail: admission@fit.edu
http://www.fit.edu

University of Phoenix–Central Florida Campus
4615 East Elwood Street
Mail Stop AA-K101
Phoenix, AZ 85040
Phone: (480) 557-3303
Fax: (480) 643-1020
E-mail: evelyn.gaskin@phoenix.edu

Stetson University
Unit 8378, Griffith Hall
DeLand, FL 32723
Phone: (386) 822-7100
Fax: (386) 822-7112
E-mail: admissions@stetson.edu
http://www.stetson.edu

University of Phoenix–University of Phoenix–Central Florida Campus
4615 East Elwood Street
Mail Stop AA-K101
Phoenix, AZ 85040
Phone: (480) 557-3303
Fax: (480) 643-1020
E-mail: evelyn.gaskin@phoenix.edu
http://www.phoenix.edu

University of Phoenix–University of Phoenix–Jacksonville Campus
4615 East Elwood Street
Mail Stop AA-K101
Phoenix, AZ 85040
Phone: (480) 557-3303
Fax: (480) 643-1020
E-mail: evelyn.gaskin@phoenix.edu
http://www.phoenix.edu

GEORGIA

University of Phoenix–Atlanta Campus
4615 East Elwood Street
Mail Stop AA-K101
Phoenix, AZ 85040
Phone: (480) 557-3303
Fax: (480) 643-1020
E-mail: evelyn.gaskin@phoenix.edu
http://www.phoenix.edu

University of Phoenix–University of Phoenix–Columbus, GA Campus
4615 East Elwood Street
Mail Stop AA-K101
Phoenix, AZ 85040
Phone: (480) 557-3303
Fax: (480) 643-1020
E-mail: evelyn.gaskin@phoenix.edu
http://www.phoenix.edu

HAWAII

University of Phoenix–University of Phoenix–Hawaii Campus
4615 East Elwood Street
Mail Stop AA-K101
Phoenix, AZ 85040

Phone: (480) 557-3303
Fax: (480) 643-1020
E-mail: evelyn.gaskin@phoenix.edu
http://www.phoenix.edu

IDAHO

University of Phoenix–University of Phoenix–Idaho Campus
4615 East Elwood Street
Mail Stop AA-K101
Phoenix, AZ 85040
Phone: (480) 557-3303
Fax: (480) 643-1020
E-mail: evelyn.gaskin@phoenix.edu
http://www.phoenix.edu

ILLINOIS

DePaul University
1 East Jackson Boulevard
Chicago, IL 60604
Phone: (312) 362-8300
E-mail: admission@depaul.edu
http://www.depaul.edu

Westwood College-Chicago Du Page
7155 Janes Avenue
Woodridge, IL 60517
Phone: (630) 434-8244
http://www.westwood.edu

University of Phoenix–University of Phoenix–Chicago Campus
4615 East Elwood Street
Mail Stop AA-K101
Phoenix, AZ 85040
Phone: (480) 557-3303
Fax: (480) 643-1020
E-mail: evelyn.gaskin@phoenix.edu
http://www.phoenix.edu

INDIANA

University of Southern Indiana
8600 University Boulevard
Evansville, IN 47712
Phone: (812) 464-1765
Fax: (812)465-7154
E-mail: enroll@usi.edu
http://www.usi.edu

**University of Phoenix–
University of Phoenix–
Indianapolis Campus**
4615 East Elwood Street
Mail Stop AA-K101
Phoenix, AZ 85040
Phone: (480) 557-3303
Fax: (480) 643-1020
E-mail: evelyn.gaskin@phoenix.edu
http://www.phoenix.edu

KANSAS

Friends University
2100 West University Street
Wichita, KS 67213
Phone: (316) 295-5512
E-mail: sexson@friends.edu
http://www.friends.edu

LOUISIANA

**Southern University and
Agricultural and Mechanical
College**
PO Box 9901
Baton Rouge, LA 70813
Phone: (225) 771-2430
Fax: (225) 771-2500
E-mail: tracie_abraham@subr.edu
http://www.subr.edu

**University of Phoenix–
University of Phoenix–
Louisiana Campus**
4615 East Elwood Street
Mail Stop AA-K101
Phoenix, AZ 85040
Phone: (480) 557-3303
Fax: (480) 643-1020
E-mail: evelyn.gaskin@phoenix.edu
http://www.phoenix.edu

MARYLAND

**University of Phoenix–
University of Phoenix–
Maryland Campus**
4615 East Elwood Street
Mail Stop AA-K101
Phoenix, AZ 85040
Phone: (480) 557-3303
Fax: (480) 643-1020

E-mail: evelyn.gaskin@phoenix.edu
http://www.phoenix.edu

MASSACHUSETTS

**University of Phoenix–
University of Phoenix–
Central Massachusetts
Campus**
4615 East Elwood Street
Mail Stop AA-K101
Phoenix, AZ 85040
Phone: (480) 557-3303
Fax: (480) 643-1020
E-mail: evelyn.gaskin@phoenix.edu
http://www.phoenix.edu

MICHIGAN

Western Michigan University
1903 West Michigan Avenue
Kalamazoo, MI 49008
Phone: (269) 387-2000
http://www.wmich.edu/admissions

**University of Phoenix–West
Michigan Campus**
4615 East Elwood Street
Mail Stop AA-K101
Phoenix, AZ 85040
Phone: (480) 557-3303
Fax: (480) 643-1020
E-mail: evelyn.gaskin@phoenix.edu
http://www.phoenix.edu

**University of Phoenix–
University of Phoenix–
Metro Detroit Campus**
4615 East Elwood Street
Mail Stop AA-K101
Phoenix, AZ 85040
Phone: (480) 557-3303
Fax: (480) 643-1020
E-mail: evelyn.gaskin@phoenix.edu
http://www.phoenix.edu

MISSOURI

**Maryville University of Saint
Louis**
13550 Conway Road
St. Louis, MO 63141
Phone: (314) 529-9350

Fax: (314) 529-9927
E-mail: admissions@maryville.edu
http://www.maryville.edu

**University of Phoenix–
University of Phoenix–
Kansas City Campus**
4615 East Elwood Street
Mail Stop AA-K101
Phoenix, AZ 85040
Phone: (480) 557-3303
Fax: (480) 643-1020
E-mail: evelyn.gaskin@phoenix.edu
http://www.phoenix.edu

**University of Phoenix–
Springfield, MO Campus**
4615 East Elwood Street
Mail Stop AA-K101
Phoenix, AZ 85040
Phone: (480) 557-3303
Fax: (480) 643-1020
E-mail: evelyn.gaskin@phoenix.edu
http://www.phoenix.edu

University of Phoenix–St. Louis
4615 East Elwood Street
Mail Stop AA-K101
Phoenix, AZ 85040
Phone: (480) 557-3303
Fax: (480) 643-1020
E-mail: evelyn.gaskin@phoenix.edu
http://www.phoenix.edu

NEVADA

**University of Phoenix–
University of Phoenix–Las
Vegas Campus**
4615 East Elwood Street
Mail Stop AA-K101
Phoenix, AZ 85040
Phone: (480) 557-3303
Fax: (480) 643-1020
E-mail: evelyn.gaskin@phoenix.edu
http://www.phoenix.edu

**University of Phoenix–
University of Phoenix–
Northern Nevada Campus**
4615 East Elwood Street
Mail Stop AA-K101
Phoenix, AZ 85040

Phone: (480) 557-3303
Fax: (480) 643-1020
E-mail: evelyn.gaskin@phoenix.edu
http://www.phoenix.edu

NORTH CAROLINA

University of Phoenix–Charlotte, NC Campus

4615 East Elwood Street
Mail Stop AA-K101
Phoenix, AZ 85040
Phone: (480) 557-3303
Fax: (480) 643-1020
E-mail: evelyn.gaskin@phoenix.edu
http://www.phoenix.edu

University of Phoenix–Raleigh, NC Campus

4615 East Elwood Street
Mail Stop AA-K101
Phoenix, AZ 85040
Phone: (480) 557-3303
Fax: (480) 643-1020
E-mail: evelyn.gaskin@phoenix.edu
http://www.phoenix.edu

NEW YORK

Clarkson University

Holcroft House
P.O. Box 5605
Potsdam, NY 13699
Phone: (315) 268-6480
Fax: (315) 268-7647
E-mail: admission@clarkson.edu
http://www.clarkson.edu

OHIO

University of Akron

East Buchtel Avenue
Akron, OH 44325
Phone: (330) 972-6427
Fax: (330) 972-7022
E-mail: admissions@uakron.edu
http://www.uakron.edu

University of Phoenix–University of Phoenix–Cincinnati Campus

4615 East Elwood Street
Mail Stop AA-K101

Phoenix, AZ 85040
Phone: (480) 557-3303
Fax: (480) 643-1020
E-mail: evelyn.gaskin@phoenix.edu
http://www.phoenix.edu

University of Phoenix–University of Phoenix–Cleveland Campus

4615 East Elwood Street
Mail Stop AA-K101
Phoenix, AZ 85040
Phone: (480) 557-3303
Fax: (480) 643-1020
E-mail: evelyn.gaskin@phoenix.edu
http://www.phoenix.edu

University of Phoenix–University of Phoenix–Columbus, OH Campus

4615 East Elwood Street
Mail Stop AA-K101
Phoenix, AZ 85040
Phone: (480) 557-3303
Fax: (480) 643-1020
E-mail: evelyn.gaskin@phoenix.edu
http://www.phoenix.edu

OKLAHOMA

Bacone College

2299 Old Bacone Road
Muskogee, OK 74403
Phone: (918) 781-7342
http://www.bacone.edu

Northwestern Oklahoma State University

709 Oklahoma Boulevard
Alva, OK 73717
Phone: (580) 327-8545
Fax: (580) 327-8699
E-mail: wmadair@nwosu.edu
http://www.nwosu.edu

OREGON

University of Phoenix–University of Phoenix–Portland Campus

4615 East Elwood Street
Mail Stop AA-K101
Phoenix, AZ 85040
Phone: (480) 557-3303
Fax: (480) 643-1020

E-mail: evelyn.gaskin@phoenix.edu
http://www.phoenix.edu

PENNSYLVANIA

DeSales University

2755 Station Avenue
Center Valley, PA 18034
Phone: (610) 282-1100
E-mail: admiss@desales.edu
http://www.desales.edu

Harrisburg University of Science and Technology

304 Market Street
Harrisburg, PA 17101
Phone: (717) 901-5101
Fax: (717) 901-3110
E-mail: Connect@HarrisburgU.net
http://www.harrisburgu.net

Messiah College

Box 3005
One College Avenue
Grantham, PA 17027
Phone: (717) 691-6000
Fax: (717) 691-2307
E-mail: admiss@messiah.edu
http://www.messiah.edu

Philadelphia University

School House Lane and Henry Avenue
Philadelphia, PA 19144
Phone: (215) 951-2800
Fax: (215) 951-2907
E-mail: admissions@PhilaU.edu
http://www.PhilaU.edu

Thiel College

75 College Avenue
Greenville, PA 16125
Phone: (724) 589-2172
Fax: (724) 589-2013
E-Mail: admissions@thiel.edu
http://www.thiel.edu

University of Pennsylvania

1 College Hall, Levy Park
Philadelphia, PA 19104
Phone: (215) 898-7507
E-mail: info@admissions.ugao.upenn.edu
http://www.upenn.edu

University of Phoenix–
University of Phoenix–
Philadelphia Campus
4615 East Elwood Street
Mail Stop AA-K101
Phoenix, AZ 85040
Phone: (480) 557-3303
Fax: (480) 643-1020
E-mail: evelyn.gaskin@phoenix.edu
http://www.phoenix.edu

University of Phoenix–
Pittsburgh, PA Campus
4615 East Elwood Street
Mail Stop AA-K101
Phoenix, AZ 85040
Phone: (480) 557-3303
Fax: (480) 643-1020
E-mail: evelyn.gaskin@phoenix.edu
http://www.phoenix.edu

SOUTH CAROLINA

Winthrop University
701 Oakland Avenue
Rock Hill, SC 29733
Phone: (803) 323-2191
http://www.winthrop.edu

SOUTH DAKOTA

**Colorado Technical University
- Sioux Falls**
3901 West 59th Street
Sioux Falls, SD 57108
Phone: (605) 361-0200

TENNESSEE

King College
1350 King College Road
Bristol, TN 37620
Phone: (423) 652-4861
Fax: (423) 652-4727
E-mail: admissions@king.edu
http://www.king.edu

TEXAS

Texas Christian University
TCU Box 297013
2800 South University Drive, #112
Fort Worth, TX 76129
Phone: (817) 257-7490

Fax: (817) 257-7268
E-mail: frogmail@tcu.edu
http://www.tcu.edu

University of North Texas
Box 311277
Denton, TX 76203
Phone: (940) 565-3190
Fax: (940) 565-2408
E-mail: undergradadm@unt.edu
http://www.unt.edu

**University of Phoenix–
University of Phoenix–
Dallas Campus**
4615 East Elwood Street
Mail Stop AA-K101
Phoenix, AZ 85040
Phone: (480) 557-3303
Fax: (480) 643-1020
E-mail: evelyn.gaskin@phoenix.edu
http://www.phoenix.edu

**University of Phoenix–
University of Phoenix–
Houston Campus**
4615 East Elwood Street
Mail Stop AA-K101
Phoenix, AZ 85040
Phone: (480) 557-3303
Fax: (480) 643-1020
E-mail: evelyn.gaskin@phoenix.edu
http://www.phoenix.edu

VIRGINIA

Champlain College
163 South Willard Street
Burlington, VT 05401
Phone: (802) 860-2727
Fax: (802) 860-2767
E-mail: admission@champlain.edu
http://www.champlain.edu

**University of Phoenix–
Richmond, VA Campus**
4615 East Elwood Street
Mail Stop AA-K101
Phoenix, AZ 85040
Phone: (480) 557-3303
Fax: (480) 643-1020
E-mail: evelyn.gaskin@phoenix.edu
http://www.phoenix.edu

University of Phoenix–
University of Phoenix–
Northern Virginia Campus
4615 East Elwood Street
Mail Stop AA-K101
Phoenix, AZ 85040
Phone: (480) 557-3303
Fax: (480) 643-1020
E-mail: evelyn.gaskin@phoenix.edu
http://www.phoenix.edu

WASHINGTON

**University of Phoenix–
Washington Campus**
4615 East Elwood Street
Mail Stop AA-K101
Phoenix, AZ 85040
Phone: (480) 557-3303
Fax: (480) 643-1020
E-mail: evelyn.gaskin@phoenix.edu
http://www.phoenix.edu

Washington State University
PO Box 641067
Pullman, WA 99164
Phone: (509)335-5586
Fax: (509) 335-4902
E-mail: admiss2@wsu.edu
http://www.wsu.edu

WEST VIRGINIA

Mountain State University
Beckley, WV 25802
Phone: (304) 929-4636
http://www.mountainstate.edu

**Westwood College–Atlanta
Northlake**
2220 Parklake Drive
Atlanta, GA 30345
http://www.westwood.edu

WISCONSIN

**University of Phoenix–
Wisconsin Campus**
4615 East Elwood Street
Mail Stop AA-K101
Phoenix, AZ 85040
Phone: (480) 557-3303
Fax: (480) 643-1020
E-mail: evelyn.gaskin@phoenix.edu
http://www.phoenix.edu

B. COLLEGES AND UNIVERSITIES OFFERING MAJORS IN APPAREL AND ACCESSORY MARKETING

A college degree or background does not guarantee a job, but often gives an applicant an edge in marketability and advancement prospects, as well as providing experience not otherwise available.

The following is a listing of selected four-year schools offering majors in apparel and accessory marketing. They are grouped by state. School names, addresses, phone numbers, Web addresses, and e-mail addresses are included when available.

The author does not endorse any one school over another. Use this list as a beginning. Check the reference section of libraries or guidance counseling centers for additional schools offering degrees in this field.

CALIFORNIA

The Fashion Institute of Design & Merchandising
919 South Grand Avenue
Los Angeles, CA 90015
Phone: (800) 624-1200
Fax: (213) 624-4799
http://www.fidm.edu

COLORADO

The Art Institute of Colorado
1200 Lincoln Street
Denver, CO 80203
Phone: (303) 837-0825
Fax: (303) 860-8520
:http://www.artinstitutes.edu/denver

FLORIDA

The Art Institute of Tampa
Parkside at Tampa Bay Park
4401 North Himes Avenue
Tampa, FL 36614
Phone: (813) 873-2112
Fax: (813) 873-2171
http://www.artinstitutes.edu/tampa

GEORGIA

The Art Institute of Atlanta
6600 Peachtree Dunwoody Road, N.E.
100 Embassy Row
Atlanta, GA 30328
Phone: (770) 394-8300
Fax: (770) 394-0008
http://www.artinstitutes.edu/atlanta

Clayton State University
2000 Clayton State Boulevard
Morrow, GA 30260
Phone: (678) 466-4115
Fax: (678) 466-4149
E-mail: csu-info@clayton.edu
http://www.clayton.edu

MONTANA

The University of Montana
Missoula, MT 59812
Phone: (406) 243-6266
Fax: (406) 243-5711
E-mail: admiss@umontana.edu
http://www.umontana.edu

OHIO

Bluffton University
1 University Drive
Bluffton, OH 45817
Phone: (419) 358-3254
Fax: (419)358-3081
E-mail: admissions@bluffton.edu
http://www.bluffton.edu

PENNSYLVANIA

Philadelphia University
School House Lane and Henry Avenue
Philadelphia, PA 19144
Phone: (215) 951-2800
Fax: (215) 951-2907
E-mail: admissions@PhilaU.edu
http://www.philau.edu

RHODE ISLAND

University of Rhode Island
14 Upper College Road
Kingston, RI 02881
Phone: (401) 874-7000
E-mail: admission@uri.edu
http://www.uri.edu

SOUTH CAROLINA

The Art Institute of Charleston
24 North Market Street
Charleston, SC 29401
Phone: (843) 727-3500
Fax: (843) 727-3440
http://www.artinstitutes.edu/charleston

TENNESSEE

The Art Institute of Tennessee-Nashville
100 Centerview Drive
Nashville, TN 37214
Phone: (615) 874-1067
Fax: (615) 874-3530
http://www.artinstitutes.edu/nashville

TEXAS

The Art Institute of Houston
1900 Yorktown Street
Houston, Texas 77056
Phone: (713) 623-2040
Fax: (713) 966-2797
http://www.artinstitutes.edu/houston

C. FOUR-YEAR COLLEGES AND UNIVERSITIES OFFERING MAJORS IN PUBLIC RELATIONS

A degree or background in public relations is helpful in many jobs in the retail and wholesale industries. A college background may give an applicant an edge in marketability and advancement prospects, as well as providing experience not otherwise available.

The following is a listing of selected four year schools offering majors in public relations. They are grouped by state. School names, addresses, phone numbers, Web addresses, and e-mail addresses are included when available.

The author does not endorse any one school over another. Use this list as a beginning. Check the reference section of libraries or guidance counseling centers for additional schools offering degrees in this field.

ALABAMA

Alabama State University
915 South Jackson Street
Montgomery, AL 36104
Phone: (334) 229-4291
E-mail: mpettway@alasu.edu
http://www.alasu.edu

Auburn University
202 Martin Hall
Auburn University, AL 36849
Phone: (334) 844-4080
E-mail: admissions@auburn.edu
http://www.auburn.edu

Spring Hill College
4000 Dauphin Street
Mobile, AL 36608
Phone: (251) 380-3030
Fax: (251) 460-2186
E-mail: admit@shc.edu
http://www.shc.edu

University of Alabama
Box 870132
Tuscaloosa, AL 35487
Phone: (205) 348-5666
Fax: (205) 348-9046
E-mail: admissions@ua.edu
http://www.ua.edu

ARIZONA

Grand Canyon University
3300 West Camelback Road
Phoenix, AZ 85017
Phone: (800) 486-7085
E-mail: admissionsground@gcu.edu
http://www.gcu.edu

Northern Arizona University
PO Box 4084
Flagstaff, AZ 86011
Phone: (928) 523-5511
E-mail: undergraduate.admissions@nau.edu
http://www.nau.edu

ARKANSAS

Harding University
Box 12255
Searcy, AR 72149
Phone: (501) 279-4407
Fax: (501) 279-4129
E-mail: admissions@harding.edu
http://www.harding.edu

John Brown University
200 West University Street
Siloam Springs, AR 72761
Phone: (479) 524-7454
Fax: (479) 524-4196
E-mail: dcrandal@jbu.edu
http://www.jbu.edu

CALIFORNIA

California State Polytechnic University
3801 West Temple Avenue
Pomona, CA 91768
Phone: (909) 869-3210
http://www.csupomona.edu

California State University, Chico
400 West First Street
Chico, CA 95929
Phone: (530) 898-4879
Fax: (530) 898-6456
E-mail: info@csuchico.edu
http://www.csuchico.edu

California State University, Dominguez Hills
1000 East Victoria Street
Carson, CA 90747
Phone: (310) 243-4696
Fax: (310) 217-6800
http://www.csudh.edu

California State University, Fresno
5150 North Maple Avenue
Fresno, CA 93740
Phone: (559) 278-6115
Fax: (559) 278-4812
E-mail: yolandad@csufresno.edu
http://www.csufresnu.edu

California State University, Fullerton
PO Box 6900
800 North State College Boulevard
Fullerton, CA 92834
Phone: (714) 278-2370
E-mail: admissions@fullerton.edu
http://www.fullerton.edu

California State University, Hayward
25800 Carlos Bee Boulevard
Hayward, CA 94542
Phone: (510) 885-3248
Fax: (510) 885-3816
E-mail: adminfo@csuhayward.edu
http://www.csuhayward.edu

Chapman University
One University Drive
Orange, CA 92866

Phone: (714) 997-6711
Fax: (714) 997-6713
E-mail: admit@chapman.edu
http://www.chapman.edu

Pacific Union College
One Angwin Avenue
Angwin, CA 94508
Phone: (707) 965-6425
Fax: (707) 965-6432
E-mail: enroll@puc.edu
http://www.puc.edu

Pepperdine University
24255 Pacific Coast Highway
Malibu, CA 90263
Phone: (310) 506-4392
Fax: (310) 506-4861
E-mail: admission-seaver@
    pepperdine.edu
http://www.pepperdine.edu

San Diego State University
5500 Campanile Drive
San Diego, CA 92182
Phone: (619) 594-6886
Fax: (619) 594-1250
E-mail: admissions@sdsu.edu
http://www.sdsu.edu

San Jose State University
One Washington Square
San Jose, CA 95192
Phone: (408) 924-1000
E-mail: contact@sjsu.edu
http://www.sjsu.edu

**University of Southern
    California**
University Park
Los Angeles, CA 90089
Phone: (213) 740-1111
E-mail: admitusc@usc.edu
http://www.usc.edu

COLORADO

Colorado State University
Fort Collins, Colorado 80523
Phone: (970) 491-6909
E-mail: admissions@colostate.edu
http://www.colostate.edu

Johnson & Wales University
8 Abbott Park Place
Providence, RI 02903
Phone: (977) 598-3368
Fax: (303) 256-9333
E-mail: den.admissions@jwu.edu
http://www.jwu.edu

CONNECTICUT

Quinnipiac University
Hamden, Connecticut 06518
Phone: (203) 582-8600
Fax: (203) 582-8906
E-mail: admissions@quinnipiac.
    edu
http://www.quinnipiac.edu

DELAWARE

Delaware State University
1200 North DuPont Highway
Dover, DE 19901-2277
Phone: (302) 857-6351
Fax: (302) 857-6908
E-maill: gcheatha@desu.edu
http://www.desu.edu

University of Delaware
Newark, DE 19716
Phone: (302) 831-8123
Fax: (302) 831-6905
E-mail: admissions@udel.edu
http://www.udel.edu

DISTRICT OF COLUMBIA

American University
4400 Massachusetts Avenue, NW
Washington, D.C. 20016
Phone: (202) 885-6000
Fax: (202) 885-1025
E-mail: afa@american.edu
http://admissions.american.edu

FLORIDA

Barry University
11300 N.E. Second Avenue
Miami Shores, FL 33161
Phone: (305) 899-3000
E-mail: admissions@mail.barry.edu
http://www.barry.edu

**Florida Agricultural and
    Mechanical University**
Tallahassee, FL 32307
Phone: (850) 599-3796
E-mail: admissions@famu.edu
http://www.famu.edu

Florida Southern College
111 Lake Hollingsworth Drive
Lakeland, FL 33801
Phone: (800) 274-4131
E-mail: fscadm@flsouthern.edu
http://www.flsouthern.edu

Florida State University
Tallahassee, FL 32306
Phone: (850) 644-2525
E-mail: admissions@admin.fsu.
    edu
http://www.fsu.edu

University of Florida
PO Box 114000
Gainesville, FL 32611
Phone: (352) 392-3261
E-mail: freshman@ufl.edu
http://www.ufl.edu

University of Miami
PO Box 248025
Coral Gables, FL 33124
Phone: (305) 284-2211
E-mail: admission@miami.edu
http://www.miami.edu

University of Tampa
401 West Kennedy Boulevard
Tampa, FL 33606
Phone: (813) 253-6211
Fax: (813) 254-4955
E-mail: : admissions@ut.edu
http://www.ut.edu

GEORGIA

Georgia Southern University
Forest Drive, Statesboro, GA 30460
Phone: (912) 681-5391
Fax: (912) 486-7240
E-mail: admissions@
    georgiasouthern.edu
http://www.georgiasouthern.edu

Paine College
1235 15th Street
Augusta, GA 30901
Phone: (706) 821-8320
E-mail: tinsleyj@mail.paine.edu
http://www.paine.edu

Shorter College
315 Shorter Avenue
Rome, GA 30165
Phone: (706) 233-7319
Fax: (706) 233-7224
E-mail: admissions@shorter.edu
http://www.shorter.edu

University of Georgia
212 Terrell Hall
Athens, GA 30602
Phone: (706) 542-3000
E-mail: undergrad@admissions.
   uga.edu
http://www.uga.edu

HAWAII

Hawaii Pacific University
1164 Bishop Street
Honolulu, HI 96813
Phone: (808) 544-0200
E-mail: admissions@hpu.edu
http://www.hpu.edu

IDAHO

Northwest Nazarene University
623 Holly Street
Nampa, ID 83686
Phone: (208) 467-8000
Fax: (208) 467-8645
E-mail: admissions@nnu.edu

University of Idaho
PO Box 444264
Moscow, ID 83844
Phone: (208) 885-6326
Fax: (208) 885-9119
E-mail: carolynl@uidaho.edu
http://www.uidaho.edu

ILLINOIS

Bradley University
1501 W. Bradley Avenue
Peoria, IL 61625

Phone: (309) 676-7611
E-mail: admissions@bradley.edu
http://www.bradley.edu

Columbia College Chicago
600 South Michigan Avenue
Chicago, IL 60605
Phone: (312) 344-7130
Fax: (312) 344-8024
http://www.colum.edu

Greenville College
315 East College Avenue
Greenville, IL 62246
Phone: (618) 664-7100
Fax: (618) 664-9841
E-mail: admissions@greenville.edu

Illinois State University
Normal, IL 61790
Phone: (309) 438-2181
Fax: (309) 438-3932
E-mail: ugradadm@ilstu.edu
http://www.ilstu.edu

Lewis University
One University Parkway
Romeoville, IL 60446
Phone: (800) 897-9000
E-mail: admissions@lewisu.edu
http://www.lewisu.edu

McKendree University
701 College Road
Lebanon, IL 62254
Phone: (618) 537-6833
Fax: (618) 537-6496
E-mail: : inquiry@mckendree.edu
http://www.mckendree.edu

Monmouth College
700 East Broadway
Monmouth, IL 61462
Phone: (309) 457-2140
Fax: (309) 457-2141
E-mail: admit@monm.edu

Quincy University
1800 College Avenue
Quincy, IL 62301
Phone: (217) 228-5210
E-mail: admissions@quincy.edu
http://www.quincy.edu

Roosevelt University
Chicago Campus
430 South Michigan Avenue
Chicago, IL 60605
Phone: 877-APPLY-RU
http://www.roosevelt.edu

INDIANA

Ball State University
2000 University Avenue
Muncie, IN 47306
Phone: (765) 285-8300
E-mail: askus@bsu.edu
http://www.bsu.edu

Goshen College
1700 South Main Street
Goshen, IN 46526
Phone: (574) 535-7535
Fax: (574) 535-7609
E-mail: lynnj@goshen.edu
http://www.goshen.edu

Purdue University
475 Stadium Mall Drive
Schleman Mall
West Lafayette, IN 47907
Phone: (765)494-1776
Fax: (765) 494-0544
E-mail: admissions@purdue.edu
http://www.purdue.edu

University of Southern Indiana
8600 University Boulevard
Evansville, IN 47712
Phone: (812) 464-8600
E-mail: enroll@usi.edu
http://www.usi.edu

IOWA

Clarke College
1550 Clarke Drive
Dubuque, IA 52001
Phone: (563) 588-6300
E-mail: admissions@clarke.edu
http://www.clarke.edu

Coe College
1220 First Avenue, NE
Cedar Rapids, IA 52402
Phone: (319) 399-8500

Fax: (319) 399-8816
E-mail: admission@coe.edu
http://www.coe.edu

Drake University
2507 University Avenue
Des Moines, IA 50311
Phone: (515) 271-2011
E-mail: admitinfo@acad.drake.edu
http://www.drake.edu

St. Ambrose University
518 West Locust Street
Davenport, IA 52803
Phone: (563) 333-6300
E-mail: admit@sau.edu
http://www.sau.admissions

University of Northern Iowa
Cedar Falls, IA 50614
Phone: (319) 273-2281
Fax: (319) 273-2885
E-mail: admissions@uni.edu

Wartburg College
100 Wartburg Boulevard
P.O. Box 1003
Waverly, IA 50677
Phone: (319) 352-8264
Fax: (319) 352-8579

KANSAS

Fort Hays State University
600 Park Street
Hays, KS 67601
Phone: (785) 628-5830
E-mail: tigers@fhsu.edu
http://www.fhsu.edu

MidAmerica Nazarene University
2030 East College Way
Olathe, KS 66062
Phone: (913) 791-3380
Fax: (913) 791-3481
E-mail: admissions@mnu.edu

Pittsburg State University
Pittsburg, KS 66762
Phone: (620) 235-4251
Fax: (620) 235-6003
E-mail: psuadmit@pittstate.edu
http://www.pittstate.edu

KENTUCKY

Eastern Kentucky University
521 Lancaster Avenue
Richmond, KY 40475
Phone: (859) 622-2106
Fax: (859) 622-8024
E-mail: admissions@eku.edu

Northern Kentucky University
Highland Heights, KY 41099
Phone: (859) 572-5220
E-mail: admitnku@nku.edu
http://www.nku.edu

Murray State University
PO Box 9
Murray, KY 42071
Phone: (270) 762-3035
Fax: (270) 762-3050
E-mail: admissions@murraystate.edu
http://www.murraystate.edu

Western Kentucky University
One Big Red Way
Bowling Green, KY 42101
Phone: (270) 745-2551
Fax: (270) 745-6133
E-mail: admission@wku.edu
http://www.wku.edu

LOUISIANA

University of Louisiana at Lafayette
PO Box 44652
Lafayette, LA 70504
Phone: (337) 482-6473
E-mail: admissionsl@louisiana.edu
http://www.louisiana.edu

MAINE

New England School of Communications
1 College Circle
Bangor, ME 04401
Phone: (207) 941-7176
Fax: (207) 947-3987
E-mail: info@nescom.edu
http://www.nescom.edu

MARYLAND

Bowie State University
Bowie, MD 20715
Phone: (301) 860-3415
Fax: (301) 860-3518
E-mail: undergraduateadmissions@ bowiestate.edu
http://www.bowiestate.edu

MASSACHUSETTS

Boston University
121 Bay State Road
Boston, MA 02215
Phone: (617) 353-2000
E-mail: admissions@bu.edu
http://www.bu.edu

Curry College
Milton, MA 02186
Phone: (617) 333-2210
Fax: (617) 333-2114
E-mail: curryadm@curry.edu
http://www.curry.edu

Emerson College
120 Boylston Street
Boston, MA 02116
Phone: (617) 824-8500
E-mail: admission@emerson.edu
http://www.emerson.edu

Salem State College
352 Lafayette Street
Salem, MA 01970
Phone: (978) 542-6200

Simmons College
300 The Fenway
Boston, MA 02115
Phone: (800) 345-8468
Fax: (617) 521-3190
http://www.simmons.edu

Suffolk University
8 Ashburton Place
Boston, MA 02108
Phone: (800) 6-SUFFOLK
Fax: (617) 742-4291
E-mail: admission@suffolk.edu
http://www.suffolk.edu

MICHIGAN

Andrews University
Berrien Springs, MI 49104
Phone: (800) 253-2874
Fax: (269) 471-3228
E-mail: enroll@andrews.edu
http://www.andrews.edu

Central Michigan University
Mt. Pleasant, MI 48859
Phone: (989) 774-3076
Fax: (989) 774-7267
E-mail: cmuadmit@cmich.edu
http://www.cmich.edu

Eastern Michigan University
Ypsilanti, Michigan 48197
Phone: (734) 487-3060
Fax: (734) 487-6559
E-mail: admissions@emich.edu
http://www.emich.edu

Ferris State University
901 State Street
Big Rapids, MI 49307
Phone: (231) 591-2000
E-mail: admissions@ferris.edu
http://www.ferris.edu

Grand Valley State University
One Campus Drive
Allendale, MI 49401
Phone: (616) 895-6611
E-mail: go2gvsu@gvsu.edu
http://www.gvsu.edu

Madonna University
36600 Schoolcraft Road
Livonia, MI 48150
Phone: (734) 432-5317
Fax: (734) 432-5393
E-mail: muinfo@madonna.edu
http://www.madonna.edu

Northern Michigan University
1401 Presque Isle Avenue
Marquette, MI 49855
Phone: (906) 227-2650
Fax: 906-227-1747
E-mail: admiss@nmu.edu
http://www.nmu.edu

Spring Arbor University
106 East Main Street
Spring Arbor, MI 49283
Phone: (517) 750-1200
Fax: (517) 750-6620
E-mail: admissions@arbor.edu
http://www.arbor.edu

Wayne State University
Detroit, MI 48202
Phone: (313) 577-3581
Fax: (313) 577-7536
E-mail: admissions@wayne.edu
http://www.wayne.edu

MINNESOTA

Concordia College-Moorhead
901 S. Eighth Street
Moorhead, MN 56562
Phone: (218) 299-4000
E-mail: admissions@cord.edu
http://www.cord.edu

Minnesota State University Mankato,
Mankato, MN 56001
Phone: (507) 389-6670
Fax: (507) 389-1511
E-mail: admissions@mnsu.edu
http://www.mnsu.edu

Minnesota State University Moorhead
Owens Hall
Moorhead, MN 56563
Phone: (218) 477-2161
Fax: (218) 477-4374
E-mail: dragon@mnstate.edu
http://www.mnstate.edu

Northwestern College
3003 Snelling Avenue North
St. Paul, MN 55113
Phone: (651) 631-5209
Fax: (651) 631-5680
E-mail: admissions@nwc.edu
http://www.nwc.edu

St. Cloud State University
720 4th Avenue South
St. Cloud, MN 56301

Phone: (320) 308-2244
Fax: (320) 308-2243
http://www.stcloudstate.edu/

Saint Mary's University of Minnesota
700 Terrace Heights #2
Winona, MI 55987
Phone: (507) 457-1700
Fax: (507) 457-1722
E-mail: admissions@smumn.edu
http://www.smumn.edu

Winona State University
PO Box 5838
Winona, MN 55987
Phone: (507) 457-5100
E-mail: admissions@winona.edu
http://www.winona.edu

MISSOURI

Lindenwood University
209 South Kings Highway
St. Charles, MO 63301
Phone: (636) 949-4949
Fax: (636) 949-4989
http://www.lindenwood.edu

Northwest Missouri State University
800 University Drive
Maryville, MO 64468
Phone: (660) 562-1146
Fax: (660) 562-1121
E-mail: admissions@nwmissouri.edu
http://www.nwmissouri.edu

Stephens College
Columbia, MO 65215
Phone: (573) 876-7207
Fax: (573) 876-7237
E-mail: apply@stephens.edu
http://www.stephens.edu

University of Central Missouri
1400 Ward Edwards
Warrensburg, MO 64093
Phone: (660) 543-4170
Fax: (660) 543-8517
E-mail: admit@ucmo.edu
http://www.ucmo.edu

Webster University
470 E. Lockwood Avenue
St. Louis, MO 63119
Phone: (314) 961-2660
Fax: (314) 968-7115
E-mail: admit@webster.edu
http://www.webster.edu

William Woods University
1 University Avenue
Fulton, MO 65251
Phone: : (573) 592-4221
E-mail: admissions@williamwoods.
edu
http://www.williamwoods.edu

MONTANA

Carroll College
1601 North Benton Avenue
Helena, MT 59625
Phone: (406) 447-4384
E-mail: admit@carroll.edu
http://www.carroll.edu

**Montana State University–
Billings**
1500 University Drive
Billings, MT 59101
Phone: (406) 657-2158
Fax: (406) 657-2302
E-mail: admissions@msubillings.edu
http://www.msubillings.edu

MISSISSIPPI

Mississippi College
PO Box 4026
200 South Capitol Street
Clinton, MS 39058
Phone: (601) 925-3800
Fax: (601) 925-3804
E-mail: enrollment-services@
mc.edu
http://www.mc.edu

NEBRASKA

Union College
3800 South 48th Street
Lincoln, NE 68506
Phone: (402) 486-2504

Fax: (402)486-2566
E-mail: ucenroll@ucollege.edu

Hastings College
710 North Turner Avenue
Hastings, NE 68901
Phone: (402)461-7320
Fax: (402) 461-7490
E-mail: mmolliconi@hastings.edu
http://www.hastings.edu

NEVADA

University of Nevada, Reno
Reno, NV 89557
Phone: (775) 784-4700
E-mail: asknevada@unr.edu
http://www.unr.edu

NEW HAMPSHIRE

New England College
26 Bridge Street
Henniker, NH 03242
Phone: (800) 521-7642
Fax: (603) 428-3155
E-mail: admission@nec.edu
http://www.nec.edu

**Southern New Hampshire
University**
2500 North River Road
Manchester, NH 03106
Phone: (603) 645-9611
Fax: (603) 645-9693
http://www.snhu.edu

NEW JERSEY

Rider University
2083 Lawrenceville Road
Lawrenceville, NJ 08648
Phone: (609) 896-5000
E-mail: admissions@rider.edu
http://www.rider.edu

NEW YORK

Buffalo State College
1300 Elmwood Avenue
Buffalo, NY 14222
Phone: (716) 878-4017
Fax: (716) 878-6100

E-mail: admissions@buffalostate.
edu
http://www.buffalostate.edu

Hofstra University
100 Hofstra University
Hempstead, NY 11549
Phone: (516) 463-6700
Fax: (516) 463-5100
http://www.hofstra.edu

Iona College
715 North Avenue
New Rochelle, NY 10801
Phone: (914) 633-2502
Fax: (914) 637-2778
E-mail: admissions@iona.edu
http://www.iona.edu

Ithaca College
Ithaca, NY 14850
Phone: (607) 274-3124
E-mail: admission@ithaca.edu
http://www.ithaca.edu

**Long Island University, C.W.
Post Campus**
720 Northern Boulevard
Brookville, NY 11548
Phone: (516) 299-2900
Fax: (516) 299-2137
E-mail: enroll@cwpost.liu.edu
http://www.liu.edu

Marist College
3399 North Road
Poughkeepsie, NY 12601
Phone: (845) 575-3226
E-mail: admissions@marist.edu
http://www.marist.edu

Mount Saint Mary College
330 Powell Avenue
Newburgh, NY 12550
Phone: (845) 569-3248
E-mail: mtstmary@msmc.edu
http://www.msmc.edu

**Rochester Institute of
Technology**
Director of Undergraduate
Admissions
60 Lomb Memorial Drive

Rochester, NY 14623
Phone: (585) 475-6631
Fax: (585) 475-7424
E-mail: admissions@rit.edu
http://www.rit.edu

State University of New York College at Brockport

350 New Campus Drive
Brockport, NY 14420
Phone: (585) 395-2751
Fax: (585) 395-5452
E-mail: admit@brockport.edu

State University of New York at Oswego

229 Sheldon Hall
Oswego, NY 13126
Phone: (315) 312-2250
Fax: (315) 312-3260
E-mail: admiss@oswego.edu
http://www.oswego.edu

St. John's University

8000 Utopia Parkway
Queens, NY 11439
Phone: (718) 990-2000
Fax: (718) 990-2160
E-mail: admhelp@stjohns.edu
http://www.stjohns.edu

Utica College

1600 Burrstone Road
Utica, NY 13502
Phone: (315) 792-3006
E-mail: admiss@ucsu.edu
http://www.utica.edu

NORTH CAROLINA

Appalachian State University

Boone, NC 28608
Phone: (828) 262-2000
E-mail: admissions@appstate.edu
http://www.appstate.edu

Campbell University

P.O. Box 546
Buies Creek, NC 27506
Phone: (910) 893-1320
E-mail: adm@mailcenter.campbell.
   edu
http://www.campbell.edu

North Carolina State University

Box 7103
112 Peele Hall
Raleigh, NC 27695
Phone: (919) 515-2434
Fax: (919) 515-5039
E-mail: undergrad_admissions@
   ncsu.edu
http://www.ncsu.edu

NORTH DAKOTA

University of Mary

7500 University Drive
Bismarck, ND 58504
Phone: (701) 355-8191
Fax: (701) 255-7687
E-mail: marauder@umary.edu
http://www.umary.edu

OHIO

Bowling Green State University

110 McFall Center
Bowling Green, OH 43403
Phone: (419) 372-BGSU
Fax: (419) 372-6955
E-mail: choosebgsu@bgnet.bgsu.edu
http://www.bgsu.edu

Baldwin-Wallace College

275 Eastland Road
Berea, OH 44017
Phone: (440) 826-2222
Fax: (440) 826-3830
E-mail: info@bw.edu
http://www.bw.edu

Capital University

1 College and Main
Columbus, Ohio 43209
Phone: (614) 236-6101
Fax: (614) 236-6926
E-mail: admissions@capital.edu
http://www.capital.edu

Cleveland State University

1806 East 22nd Street
Cleveland, OH 44114
Phone: (216) 687-2100
Fax: (216) 687-9210
E-mail: admissions@csuohio.edu
http://csuohio.edu

Heidelberg College

310 East Market Street
Tiffin, OH 44883
Phone: (419) 448-2330
Fax: (419) 448-2334
E-mail: adminfo@heidelberg.edu
http://www.heidelberg.edu

Kent State University

PO Box 5190
Kent, OH 44242
Phone: (330) 672-2121
E-mail: kentadm@kent.edu
http://www.kent.edu

Marietta College

Marietta, OH 45750
Phone: (800) 331-7896
E-mail: admit@marietta.edu
http://www.marietta.edu

Otterbein College

One Otterbein College
Westerville, OH 43081
Phone: (614) 823-1500
E-mail: uotterb@otterbein.edu
http://uotterb@otterbein.edu

Ohio Northern University

Ada, OH 45810
Phone: (888) 408-4668
Fax: (419) 772-2313
E-mail: admissions-ug@onu.edu
http://www.onu.edu

Ohio University

Athens, OH 45701
Phone: (740) 593-4100
E-mail: admissions.freshmen@
   ohiou.edu
http://www.ohiou.edu

University of Dayton

300 College Park
Dayton, OH 45469
Phone: (937) 229-4411
E-mail: admission@udayton.edu
http://www.dayton.edu

University of Findlay

1000 North Main Street
Findlay, OH 45840
Phone: (419) 434-4732

E-mail: admissions@findlay.edu
http://www.findlay.edu

University of Rio Grande
PO Box 500
Rio Grande, OH 45674
Phone: (740) 245-7208
Fax: (740) 245-7260
E-mail: admissions@rio.edu
http://www.rio.edu

Ursuline College
2550 Lander Road
Pepper Pike, OH 44124
Phone: (440) 449-4203
Fax: (440) 684-6138
E-mail: admission@ursuline.edu
http://www.ursuline.edu

Xavier University
3800 Victory Parkway
Cincinnati, OH 45207
Phone: (513) 745-3301
E-mail: xuadmit@xavier.edu
http://www.xavier.edu

OKLAHOMA

East Central University
1100 East 14th Street
Ada, OK 74820
Phone: (580) 310-5233
E-mail: pdenny@ecok.edu
http://www.ecok.edu

Northeastern State University
601 North Grand
Tahlequah, OK 74464
Phone: (918) 444-2211
Fax: (918) 458-2342
E-mail: cain@nsuok.edu
http://www.nsuok.edu

Oklahoma City University
2501 North Blackwelder
Oklahoma City, OK 73106
Phone: (405) 521-5050
E-mail: mlockhart@okcu.edu
http://www.okcu.edu

University of Central Oklahoma
100 North University Drive
Edmond, OK 73034
Phone: (405) 974-2338

Fax: (405) 341-4964
E-mail: admituco@ucok.edu
http://ucok.edu

University of Oklahoma
1000 Asp Avenue
Norman, OK 73019
Phone: (405) 325-2151
Fax: (405) 325-7124
E-mail: admrec@ou.edu
http://www.ou.edu

OREGON

George Fox University
Newberg, OR 97132
Phone: (800) 765-4369
E-mail: admissions@georgefox.edu
http://www.georgefox.edu

University of Oregon
1217 University of Oregon
Eugene, OR 97403
Phone: (541) 346-3201
http://www.uoregon.edu

PENNSYLVANIA

La Salle University
1900 West Olney Avenue
Philadelphia, PA 19141
Phone: (215) 951-1500
Fax: (215) 951-1656
E-mail: admiss@lasalle.edu
http://www.lasalle.edu

Keystone College
One College Green
La Plume, PA 18440
Phone: (570) 945-8111
E-mail: admissions@keystone.edu
http://www.keystone.edu

Marywood University
2300 Adams Avenue
Scranton, PA 18509
Phone: (570) 348-6211
E-mail: ugadm@ac.marywood.edu
http://www.marywood.edu

Mansfield University of Pennsylvania
Mansfield, PA 16933

Phone: (570) 662-4813
Fax: (570) 662-4121
E-mail: admissions@mansfield.edu
http://www.mansfield.edu

Mercyhurst College Admissions
501 East 38th Street
Erie, PA 16546
Phone: (814) 824-2202
E-mail: admissions@mercyhurst.edu
http://www.mercyhurst.edu

Susquehanna University
514 University Avenue
Selinsgrove, PA 17870
Phone: (570) 372-4260
Fax: (570) 372-2722
E-mail: suadmiss@susqu.edu
http://www.susqu.edu

Temple University
Philadelphia, PA 19122
Phone: (215) 204-7200
E-mail: tuadm@temple.edu
http://www.temple.edu

University of Pittsburgh at Bradford
300 Campus Drive
Bradford, PA 16701
Phone: (814) 362-7555
http://www.upb.pitt.edu

Westminster College
319 South Market Street
New Wilmington, PA 6172
Phone: (724) 946-7100
E-mail: admis@westminster.edu
http://www.westminster.edu

York College of Pennsylvania
York, PA 17405
Phone: (717) 849-1600
Fax: (717) 849-1607
E-mail: admissions@ycp.edu
http://www.ycp.edu

RHODE ISLAND

Johnson & Wales University
8 Abbott Park Place
Providence, RI 02903

Phone: (401) 598-1000
Fax: (401) 598-4901
E-mail: petersons@jwu.edu
http://www.jwu.edu

SOUTH CAROLINA

Columbia College
1301 Columbia College Drive
Columbia, SC 29203
Phone: (803) 786-3765
Fax: (803) 786-3674
E-mail: admissions@colacoll.edu
http://www.colacoll.edu

University of South Carolina-Columbia
Columbia, SC 29208
Phone: (803) 777-7000
E-mail: admissions-ugrad@sc.edu
http://www.sc.edu

TENNESSEE

Belmont University
1900 Belmont Boulevard
Nashville, TN 37212
Phone: (615) 460-6785
Fax: (615) 460-5434
E-mail: buadmission@mail.
   belmont.edu
http://www.belmont.edu

Freed-Hardeman University
158 East Main Street
Henderson, TN 38340
Phone: (731) 989-6651
Fax: (731) 989-6047
E-mail: admissions@fhu.edu
http://www.fhu.edu

Lambuth University
705 Lambuth Boulevard
Jackson, TN 38301
Phone: (731) 425-3223
E-mail: admit@lambuth.edu
http://www.lambuth.edu

Lipscomb University
3901 Granny White Pike
Nashville, TN 37204
Phone: (615) 269-1000
Fax: (615) 269-1804

E-mail: admissions@lipscomb.edu
http://www.lipscomb.edu

Middle Tennessee State University
1301 East Main Street
Murfreesboro, TN 37132
Phone: (615) 898-2111
Fax: (615) 898-5478
E-mail: admissions@mtsu.edu
http://www.ntsu.edu

Union University
1050 Union University Drive
Jackson, TN 38305
Phone: (731) 661-5100
E-mail: info@uu.edu
http://www.uu.edu

TEXAS

Hardin-Simmons University
Box 16050
Abilene, TX 79698
Phone: (325) 670-5890
Fax: (325) 671-2115
E-mail: breynolds@hsutx.edu
http://www.hsutx.edu

Howard Payne University
1000 Fisk Avenue
Brownwood, TX 76801
Phone: (325) 649-8027
Fax: (325) 649-8901
E-mail: enroll@hputx.edu
http://www.hputx.edu

Sam Houston State University
PO Box 2418
Huntsville, TX 77341
Phone: (936) 294-1111
E-mail: admissions@shsu.edu
http://www.shsu.edu

Southern Methodist University
PO Box 750181
Dallas, TX 75275
Phone: (214) 768-2000
E-mail: ugadmission@smu.edu
http://www.smu.edu

Texas A&M University
217 John J. Koldus Building

College Station, TX 77843-1265
Phone: (979) 845-3741
Fax: (979) 845-8737
E-mail: admissions@tamu.ed
http://www.tamu.edu

Texas State University-San Marcos
San Marcos, TX 78666
Phone: (512) 245-2364
Fax: (512) 245-8044
E-mail: admissions@txstate.edu
http://www.txstate.edu

Texas Tech University
Box 45005
Lubbock, TX 7940
Phone: (806) 742-2011
E-mail: admissions@ttu.edu
http://www.ttu.edu

University of Houston
122 E. Cullen Building
Houston, TX 77204
Phone: (713) 743-1010
E-mail: admissions@uh.edu
http://www.uh.edu

University of Texas at Arlington
PO Box 19111
701 South Nedderman Drive
Arlington, TX 76019
Phone: (817) 272-6287
Fax: (817) 272-3435
E-mail: admissions@uta.edu
http://www.uta.edu

University of Texas-Austin
Main Building, Room 7
Austin, TX 78712
Phone: (512) 471-3434
E-mail: frmn@uts.cc.utexas.edu
http://www.utexas.edu

UTAH

Brigham Young University
A-153 Abraham Smoot Building
Provo, UT 84602
Phone: (801) 422-2507
Fax: (801) 422-0005
E-mail: admissions@byu.edu
http://www.byu.edu

University of Utah
201 South
Salt Lake City, UT 84112
Phone: (801) 581-8761
Fax: (801) 585-7864
E-mail: admissions@sa.utah.edu

Weber State University
1137 University Circle
3750 Harrison Boulevard
Ogden, UT 84408-1137
Phone: (801) 626-6050
Fax: (801) 626-6744
E-mail: admissions@weber.edu
http://www.weber.edu

VERMONT

Castleton State College
Castleton, VT 05735
Phone: (802) 468-1213
Fax: (802) 468-1476
E-mail: info@castleton.edu
http://www.castleton.edu

Champlain College
163 South Willard Street
P.O. Box 670
Burlington, VT 05402
Phone: (802) 860-2727
Fax: (802) 860-2767
E-mail: admission@champlain.
    edu
http://www.champlain.edu

University of Vermont
194 South Prospect Street
Burlington, VT 05401
Phone: (802) 656-3370
Fax: (802) 656-8611
E-mail: admissions@uvm.edu
http://www.uvm.edu

VIRGINIA

Hampton University
Tyler Street
Hampton, VA 23668
Phone: (757) 727-5070
E-mail: admissions@hamptonu.
    edu
http://www.hamptonu.edu

Virginia State University
Petersburg, VA 23806
Phone: (804) 524-5902
Fax: (804) 524-5055
E-mail: ilogan@vsu.edu
http://www.vsu.edu

WASHINGTON

Central Washington University
400 East University Way
Ellensburg, WA 98926
Phone: (509) 963-1211
Fax: (509) 963-3022
E-mail: cwuadmis@cwu.edu
http://www.cwu.edu

Gonzaga University
Spokane, WA 99258
Phone: (800) 322-2584
E-mail: mcculloh@gu.gonzaga.edu
http://www.gonzaga.edu

Seattle University
900 Broadway
Seattle, WA 98122
Phone: (206) 296-2000
E-mail: admissions@seattleu.edu
http://www.seattleu.edu

Walla Walla College
204 South College Avenue
College Place, WA 99324
Phone: (509) 527-2327
Fax: (509) 527-2397
E-mail: info@wwc.edu
http://www.wwc.edu

WEST VIRGINIA

**West Virginia Wesleyan
    College**
59 College Avenue
Buckhannon, WV 26201
Phone: (304) 473-8510
E-mail: admission@wvwc.edu
http://www.wvwc.edu

WISCONSIN

Cardinal Stritch University
6801 North Yates Road

Milwaukee, WI 53217
Phone: (414) 410-4040
E-mail: admityou@stritch.edu
http://www.stritch.edu

Carroll College
100 North East Avenue
Waukesha, WI 53186
Phone: (262) 524-7220
E-mail: ccinfo@cc.edu
http://www.cc.edu

Mount Mary College
2900 North Menomonee River
    Parkway
Milwaukee, WI 53222
Phone: (414) 256-1219
Fax: (414) 256-0180
E-mail: admiss@mtmary.edu
http://www.mtmary.edu

Marquette University
PO Box 1881
Milwaukee, WI 53201
Phone: (414) 288-7250
E-mail: admissions@marquette.
    edu
http://www.marquette.edu

**University of Wisconsin–
    Madison**
716 Langdon Street
Madison, WI 53706
Phone: (608) 262-3961
Fax: (608) 262-7706
E-mail: on.wisconsin@admissions.
    wisc.edu
http://www.wisc.edu

**University of Wisconsin–River
    Falls**
410 South Third Street
River Falls, WI 54022
Phone: (715) 425-3500
Fax: (715) 425-0676
E-mail: admit@uwrf.edu
http://www.urf.edu

D. FOUR-YEAR COLLEGES AND UNIVERSITIES OFFERING MAJORS IN ADVERTISING

A degree or background in advertising is helpful in many jobs in the retail and wholesale industries. A college background may give an applicant an edge in marketability and advancement prospects, as well as providing experience not otherwise available.

The following is a listing of selected four-year schools offering majors in advertising. They are grouped by state. School names, addresses, phone numbers, Web addresses, and e-mail addresses are included when available.

The author does not endorse any one school over another. Use this list as a beginning. Check the reference section of libraries or guidance counseling centers for additional schools offering majors in this field.

ALABAMA

University of Alabama
Box 870132
Tuscaloosa, AL 35487
Phone: (205) 348-5666
Fax: (205) 348-9046
E-mail: admissions@ua.edu
http://www.ua.edu

ARIZONA

Art Institute of Phoenix
2233 West Dunlap Avenue
Phoenix, AZ 85021
Phone: (602) 331-7500
Fax: (602) 331-5300
http://www.artinstitutes.edu/
    phoenix

Northern Arizona University
PO Box 4084
Flagstaff, AZ 86011
Phone: (928) 523-5511
E-mail: undergraduate.
    admissions@nau.edu
http://www.nau.edu

ARKANSAS

Harding University
Box 12255
Searcy, AR 72149
Phone: (501) 279-4407
Fax: (501) 279-4129
E-mail: admissions@harding.edu
http://www.harding.edu

University of Arkansas at Little Rock
2801 South University Avenue
Little Rock, AR 72204
Phone: (501) 569-3127
Fax: (501) 569-8956
E-mail: twharrison@ualn.edu
http://www.ualn.edu

CALIFORNIA

Academy of Art University
79 New Montgomery Street
San Francisco, CA 94105
Phone: (415) 274-2222
Fax: (415) 618-6287
http://www.academyart.edu

Art Center College of Design
1700 Lida Street
Pasadena, CA 91103
Phone: (626) 396-2200
E-mail: admissions@artcenter.edu
http://www.artcenter.edu

The Art Institute of California-San Francisco
1170 Market Street
San Francisco, CA 94102
Phone: (415) 865-0198
Fax: (415) 863-6344
http://www.artinsitutes.edu/
    sanfrancisco

California State University, Fullerton
PO Box 6900
800 North State College Boulevard
Fullerton, CA 92834
Phone: (714) 278-2370
E-mail: admissions@fullerton.edu
http://www.fullerton.edu

California State University, Hayward
25800 Carlos Bee Boulevard
Hayward, CA 94542
Phone: (510) 885-3248
Fax: (510) 885-3816
E-mail: adminfo@csuhayward.edu
http://www.csuhayward.edu

Pepperdine University
24255 Pacific Coast Highway
Malibu, CA 90263
Phone: (310) 506-4392
Fax: (310) 506-4861
E-mail: admission-seaver@
    pepperdine.edu
http://www.pepperdine.edu

San Diego State University
5500 Campanile Drive
San Diego, CA 92182
Phone: (619) 594-6886
Fax: (619) 594-1250
E-mail: admissions@sdsu.edu
http://www.sdsu.edu

COLORADO

University of Colorado at Boulder
552 UCB
Boulder, CO 80309
Phone: (303) 492-6301
http://www.colorado.edu

CONNECTICUT

Quinnipiac University
Hamden, Connecticut 06518
Phone: (203) 582-8600
Fax: (203) 582-8906
E-mail: admissions@quinnipiac.
    edu
http://www.quinnipiac.edu

DISTRICT OF COLUMBIA

University of the District of Columbia
4200 Connecticut Avenue NW
Washington, DC 20008
Phone: (202) 274-6110
Fax: (202) 274-5553
http://www.udc.edu

FLORIDA

Barry University
11300 N.E. Second Avenue
Miami Shores, FL 33161
Phone: (305) 899-3000
E-mail: admissions@mail.barry.edu
http://www.barry.edu

Florida Southern College
111 Lake Hollingsworth Drive
Lakeland, FL 33801
Phone: (800) 274-4131
E-mail: fscadm@flsouthern.edu
http://www.flsouthern.edu

Florida State University
Tallahassee, FL 32306
Phone: (850) 644-2525
E-mail: admissions@admin.fsu.edu
http://www.fsu.edu

Johnson & Wales University
1701 Northeast 127th Street
North Miami, FL 33181
Phone: (305) 892-7002
Fax: (305) 892-7020
E-mail: admissions.mia@jwu.edu
http://wwwjwu.edu

University of Florida
PO Box 114000
Gainesville, FL 32611
Phone: (352) 392-3261
E-mail: freshman@ufl.edu
http://www.ufl.edu

University of Miami
PO Box 248025
Coral Gables, FL 33124
Phone: (305) 284-2211
E-mail: admission@miami.edu
http://www.miami.edu

Northwood University, Florida Campus
2600 North Military Trail
West Palm Beach, FL 33409
Phone: (561) 478-5500
E-mail: fladmit@northwood.edu
http://www.northwood.edu

University of Central Florida
P.O. Box 160111
Orlando, FL 32816
Phone: (407) 823-3000
E-mail: admission@mail.ucf.edu
http://www.ucf.edu

GEORGIA

Art Institute of Atlanta
6600 Peachtree Dunwoody Road, N.E.
100 Embassy Row
Atlanta, GA 30328
Phone: (770) 394-8300
Fax: (770) 394-0008
http://www.artinstitutes.edu/atlanta

University of Georgia
212 Terrell Hall
Athens, GA 30602
Phone: (706) 542-3000
E-mail: undergrad@admissions.
uga.edu
http://www.uga.edu

Wesleyan College
4760 Forsyth Road
Macon, GA 31210
Phone: (478) 757-5206
E-mail: admission@wesleyancollege.
edu
http://www.wesleyancollege.edu

HAWAII

Hawaii Pacific University
1164 Bishop Street
Honolulu, HI 96813
Phone: (808) 544-0200
E-mail: admissions@hpu.edu
http://www.hpu.edu

IDAHO

Boise State University
1910 University Drive

Boise, ID 83725
Phone: (208) 426-1177
E-mail: bsuinfo@boisestate.edu
http://www.boisestate.edu

University of Idaho
PO Box 444264
Moscow, ID 83844
Phone: (208) 885-6326
Fax: (208) 885-9119
E-mail: carolynl@uidaho.edu
http://www.uidaho.edu

ILLINOIS

American Academy of Art
332 South Michigan Avenue
Chicago, IL 60604
Phone: (312) 461-0600
E-mail: stuartrnet@comcast.net
http://www.aart.edu

Bradley University
1501 W. Bradley Avenue
Peoria, IL 61625
Phone: (309) 676-7611
E-mail: admissions@bradley.edu
http://www.bradley.edu

Columbia College Chicago
600 South Michigan Avenue
Chicago, IL 60605
Phone: (312) 344-7130
Fax: (312) 344-8024
http://www.colum.edu

Illinois Institute of Art—Schaumburg
1000 North Plaza Drive
Schaumburg, IL 60173
Phone: (847) 619-3450
Fax: (847) 619-3064
http://www.artinstitutes.edu/
schaumburg

Loyola University Chicago
820 North Michigan Avenue
Chicago, IL 60611
Phone: (312) 915-6500
E-mail: admission@luc.edu
http://www.luc.edu

University of Illinois at Urbana–Champaign
901 West Illinois
Urbana, IL 61801
Phone: (217) 333-0302
Fax: (217) 244-4614
E-mail: ugradadmissions@uiuc.edu
http://www.uinc.edu

INDIANA

Ball State University
2000 University Avenue
Muncie, IN 47306
Phone: (765) 285-8300
E-mail: askus@bsu.edu
http://www.bsu.edu

Purdue University
475 Stadium Mall Drive
Schleman Mall
West Lafayette, IN 47907
Phone: (765) 494-1776
Fax: (765) 494-0544
E-mail: admissions@purdue.edu
http://www.purdue.edu

University of Southern Indiana
8600 University Boulevard
Evansville, IN 47712
Phone: (812) 464-8600
E-mail: enroll@usi.edu
http://www.usi.edu

IOWA

Clarke College
1550 Clarke Drive
Dubuque, IA 52001
Phone: (563) 588-6300
E-mail: admissions@clarke.edu
http://www.clarke.edu

Drake University
2507 University Avenue
Des Moines, IA 50311
Phone: (515) 271-2011
E-mail: admitinfo@acad.drake.edu
http://www.drake.edu

St. Ambrose University
518 West Locust Street
Davenport, IA 52803

Phone: (563) 333-6300
E-mail: admit@sau.edu
http://www.sau.edu

Simpson College
701 North C Street
Indianola, IA 50125
Phone: (515) 961-1624
E-mail: admiss@simpson.edu
http://www.simpson.edu

Iowa State University of Science and Technology
100 Alumni Hall
Ames, IA 50011
Phone: (515) 294-5836
Fax: (515) 294-2592
E-mail: admissions@iastate.edu
http://www.iastate.edu

KENTUCKY

University of Kentucky
100 W. D. Funkhouser Building
Lexington, KY 40506
Phone: (859) 257-2000
E-mail: admissio@uky.edu
http://www.uky.edu

Western Kentucky University
One Big Red Way
Bowling Green, KY 42101
Phone: (270) 745-2551
Fax: (270) 745-6133
E-mail: admission@wku.edu
http://www.wku.edu

LOUISIANA

Louisiana College
1140 College Drive
Pineville, LA 71359
Phone: (318) 487-7439
Fax: (318) 487-7550
E-mail: admissions@lacollege.edu
http://www.lacollege.edu

MAINE

New England School of Communications
1 College Circle
Bangor, ME 04401

Phone: (207) 941-7176
Fax: (207) 947-3987
E-mail: info@nescom.edu
http://www.nescom.edu

Saint Joseph's College of Maine
278 Whites Bridge Road
Standish, ME 04084
Phone: (207) 893-7746
Fax: (207) 893-7862
E-mail: admission@sjcme.edu
http://www.sjcme.edu

MASSACHUSETTS

Eastern Nazarene College
23 East Elm Avenue
Quincy, MA 02170
Phone: (800) 883-6288
Fax: (617) 745-3992
E-mail: admissions@enc.edu
http://www.enc.edu

Emerson College
120 Boylston Street
Boston, MA 02116
Phone: (617) 824-8500
E-mail: admission@emerson.edu
http://www.emerson.edu

Simmons College
300 The Fenway
Boston, MA 02115
Phone: (800) 345-8468
Fax: (617) 521-3190
http://www.simmons.edu

Western New England College
1215 Wilbraham Road
Springfield, MA 01119
Phone: (413) 782-1321
Fax: (413) 782-1777
E-mail: ugradmis@wnec.edu
http://www.wnec.edu

MICHIGAN

Central Michigan University
Mt. Pleasant, MI 48859
Phone: (989) 774-3076
Fax: (989) 774-7267
E-mail: cmuadmit@cmich.edu
http://www.cmich.edu

Ferris State University
901 State Street
Big Rapids, MI 49307
Phone: (231) 591-2000
E-mail: admissions@ferris.edu
http://www.ferris.edu

Grand Valley State University
One Campus Drive
Allendale, MI 49401
Phone: (616) 895-6611
E-mail: go2gvsu@gvsu.edu
http://www.gvsu.edu

Michigan State University
250 Administration Building
East Lansing, MI 48824
Phone: (517) 355-8332
Fax: (517) 353-1647
E-mail: admis@msu.edu
http://www.msu.edu

Western Michigan University
1903 West Michigan Avenue
Kalamazoo, MI 49008
Phone: (269) 387-2000
http://www.wmich.edu

MINNESOTA

Art Institutes International Minnesota
15 South 9th Street
Minneapolis, MN 55402
Phone: (612) 332-3361
Fax: (612) 332-3934
http://www.artinsitutes.edu/minneapolis

Concordia College-Moorhead
901 S. Eighth Street
Moorhead, MN 56562
Phone: (218) 299-4000
E-mail: admissions@cord.edu
http://www.cord.edu

Metropolitan State University
700 East 7th Street
St. Paul, MN 55106
Phone: (651) 793-1303
Fax: (651) 793-1310
E-mail: monir.johnson@metrostate.edu
http://www.metrostate.edu

Minnesota State University Moorhead
Owens Hall
Moorhead, MN 56563
Phone: (218) 477-2161
Fax: (218) 477-4374
E-mail: dragon@mnstate.edu
http://www.mnstate.edu

Minneapolis College of Art and Design
2501 Stevens Avenue South
Minneapolis, MN 55404
Phone: (612) 874-3762
E-mail: admissions@mn.mcad.edu
http://www.mcad.edu

St. Cloud State University
720 4th Avenue South
St. Cloud, MN 56301
Phone: (320) 308-2244
Fax: (320) 308-2243
http://www.stcloudstate.edu

Winona State University
PO Box 5838
Winona, MN 55987
Phone: (507) 457-5100
E-mail: admissions@winona.edu
http://www.winona.edu

MISSOURI

Drury University
900 North Benton
Springfield, MO 65802
Phone: (417) 873-7205
Fax: (417) 866-3873
E-mail: druryad@drury.edu
http://www.drury.edu

Fontbonne University
6800 Wydown Boulevard
St. Louis, MO 63105
Phone: (314) 889-1400
Fax: (314) 889-1451
E-mail: pmusen@fontbonne.edu
http://www.fontbonne.edu

Northwest Missouri State University
800 University Drive
Maryville, MO 64468

Phone: (660) 562-1146
Fax: (660) 562-1121
E-mail: admissions@nwmissouri.edu
http://www.nwmissouri.edu

Stephens College
Columbia, MO 65215
Phone: (573) 876-7207
Fax: (573) 876-7237
E-mail: apply@stephens.edu
http://www.stephens.edu

University of Missouri–Columbia
230 Jesse Hall
Columbia, MO 65211
Phone: (573) 882-7786
Fax: (573) 882-7887
E-mail: mu4u@missouri.edu
http://www.missouri.edu

Washington University in St. Louis
Campus Box 1089
One Brookings Drive
St. Louis, MO 63130
Phone: (314) 935-6000
Fax: (314) 935-4290
E-mail: admissions@wustl.edu
http://www.wusl.edu

Webster University
470 E. Lockwood Avenue
St. Louis, MO 63119
Phone: (314) 961-2660
Fax: (314) 968-7115
E-mail: admit@webster.edu
http://www.webster.edu

William Woods University
1 University Avenue
Fulton, MO 65251
Phone: (573) 592-4221
E-mail: admissions@williamwoods.edu
http://www.williamwoods.edu

MISSISSIPPI

University of Mississippi
145 Martindale Student Services Center
University, MS 38677

Phone: (662) 915-7226
Fax: (662) 915-5869
E-mail: admissions@olemiss.edu
http://www.olemiss.edu

NEBRASKA

Hastings College
710 North Turner Avenue
Hastings, NE 68901
Phone: (402)461-7320
Fax: (402) 461-7490
E-mail: mmolliconi@hastings.edu
http://www.hastings.edu

University of Nebraska—Lincoln
1410 Q Street
Lincoln, NE 68588
Phone: (402) 472-2023
Fax: (402) 472-0670
E-mail: admissions@unl.edu
http://www.unl.edu

NEVADA

University of Nevada, Reno
Reno, NV 89557
Phone: (775) 784-4700
E-mail: asknevada@unr.edu
http://www.unr.edu

NEW HAMPSHIRE

Franklin Pierce University
40 University Drive
Rindge, NH 03461
Phone: (603) 899-4050
Fax: (603) 899-4394
E-mail: admissions@franklinpierce.
edu
http://www.franklinpierce.edu

New England College
26 Bridge Street
Henniker, NH 03242
Phone: : (800) 521-7642
Fax: (603) 428-3155
E-mail: admission@nec.edu
http://www.nec.edu

Southern New Hampshire University
2500 North River Road

Manchester, NH 03106
Phone: (603) 645-9611
Fax: (603) 645-9693
http://www.snhu.edu

NEW JERSEY

Rider University
2083 Lawrenceville Road
Lawrenceville, NJ 08648
Phone: (609) 896-5000
E-mail: admissions@rider.edu
http://www.rider.edu

NEW YORK

Baruch College of the City University of New York
One Bernard Baruch Way
Box H-0720
New York, NY 10010
Phone: (646) 312-1400
Fax: (646) 312-1363
E-mail: admissions@baruch.cuny.
edu
http://www.baruch.cuny.edu

Fashion Institute of Technology
Seventh Avenue at 27th Street
New York, NY 10001
Phone: (212) 217-3760
E-mail: fitinfo@fitnyc.edu
http://www.fitnyc.edu

Iona College
715 North Avenue
New Rochelle, NY 10801
Phone: (914) 633-2502
Fax: (914) 637-2778
E-mail: admissions@iona.edu
http://www.iona.edu

Marist College
3399 North Road
Poughkeepsie, NY 12601
Phone: (845) 575-3226
E-mail: admissions@marist.edu
http://www.marist.edu

Pace University
1 Pace Plaza
New York, NY 10038
Phone: (800) 874-7223

E-mail: infoctr@pace.edu
http://www.pace.edu

Rochester Institute of Technology
60 Lomb Memorial Drive
Rochester, NY 14623
Phone: (585) 475-6631
Fax: (585) 475-7424
E-mail: admissions@rit.edu
http://www.rit.edu

St. John's University
8000 Utopia Parkway
Queens, NY 11439
Phone: (718) 990-2000
Fax: (718) 990-2160
E-mail: admhelp@stjohns.edu
http://www.stjohns.edu

Syracuse University
900 South Crouse Avenue
Syracuse, NY 13244
Phone: (315) 443-3611
http://www.syr.edu

NORTH CAROLINA

Appalachian State University
Boone, NC 28608
Phone: (828) 262-2000
E-mail: admissions@appstate.edu
http://www.appstate.edu

Campbell University
P.O. Box 546
Buies Creek, NC 27506
Phone: (910) 893-1320
E-mail: adm@mailcenter.campbell.
edu
http://www.campbell.edu

OHIO

Kent State University
PO Box 5190
Kent, OH 44242
Phone: (330) 672-2121
E-mail: kentadm@kent.edu
http://www.kent.edu

Ohio University
Athens, OH 45701

Phone: (740) 593-4100
E-mail: admissions.freshmen@
ohiou.edu
http://www.ohiou.edu

Xavier University
3800 Victory Parkway
Cincinnati, OH 45207
Phone: (513) 745-3301
E-mail: xuadmit@xavier.edu
http://www.xavier.edu

Youngstown State University
One University Plaza
Youngstown, OH 44555
Phone: (330) 941-2000
Fax: (330) 941-3674
E-mail: enroll@ysu.edu
http://www.ysu.edu

OKLAHOMA

East Central University
1100 East 14th Street
Ada, OK 74820
Phone: (580) 310-5233
E-mail: pdenny@ecok.edu
http://www.ecok.edu

Northeastern State University
601 North Grand
Tahlequah, OK 74464
Phone: (918) 444-2211
Fax: (918) 458-2342
E-mail: cain@nsuok.edu
http://www.nsuok.edu

Oklahoma City University
2501 North Blackwelder
Oklahoma City, OK 73106
Phone: (405) 521-5050
E-mail: mlockhart@okcu.edu
http://www.okcu.edu

Oklahoma Christian
University
Box 11000
Oklahoma City, OK 73136
Phone: (405) 425-5050
Fax: (405) 425-5208
E-mail: info@oc.edu
http://www.oc.edu

University of Central
Oklahoma
100 North University Drive
Edmond, OK 73034
Phone: (405) 974-2338
Fax: (405)341-4964
E-mail: admituco@ucok.edu
http://ucok.edu

University of Oklahoma
1000 Asp Avenue
Norman, OK 73019
Phone: (405) 325-2151
Fax: (405) 325-7124
E-mail: admrec@ou.edu
http://www.ou.edu

OREGON

Art Institute of Portland
1122 N.W. Davis Street
Portland, OR 97209
Phone: (503) 228-6528
Fax: (503) 227-1945
http://www.artinstitutes.edu/
portland

Portland State University
PO Box 751
Portland, OR 97207
Phone: (503) 725-3511
Fax: (503) 725-5525
E-mail: admissions@pdx.edu
http://www.pdx.edu

University of Oregon
1217 University of Oregon
Eugene, OR 97403
Phone: (541) 346-3201
http://www.uoregon.edu

PENNSYLVANIA

Art Institute of Pittsburgh
420 Boulevard of the Allies
Pittsburgh, PA 15219
Phone: (412) 263-6600
Fax: (412) 263-6667
http://www.artinsittues.edu/
pittsburgh

Gannon University
109 University Square
Erie, PA 16541

Phone: (814) 871-7240
Fax: (814) 871-5803
E-mail: admissions@gannon.edu
http://www.gannon.edu

Penn State Erie, The Behrend
College
5091 Station Road
Erie, PA 16563
Phone: (814) 898-6100
E-mail: behrend.admissions@psu.
edu
http://www.behrend.psu.edu

Penn State Abington
201 Shields Building, Box 3000
University Park, PA 16804
Phone: (814) 865-4700
Fax: (814) 863-7590
E-mail: admissions@psu.edu
http://www.psu.edu

Penn State Altoona
200 Shields
University Park, PA 16804
Phone: (814) 865-4700
http://www.aa.psu.edu

Penn State Beaver
100 University Drive
Monaca, PA 15061
Phone: (814) 865-5471
E-mail: admissions@psu.edu
http://www.psu.edu

Penn State Berks
201 Shields Building, Box 3000
University Park, PA 16804
Phone: (814) 865-4700
Fax: (814) 863-7590
E-mail: admissions@psu.edu
http://www.bk.psu.edu

Penn State Brandywine
25 Yearsley Mill Road
Media, PA 19063
Phone: (814) 865-5471
E-mail: admissions@psu.edu
http://www.de.psu.edu

Penn State DuBois
College Place
DuBois, PA 15801
Phone: (814) 865-5471

E-mail: admissions@psu.edu
http://www.ds.psu.edu

Penn State Fayette
1 University Drive
PO Box 519
Uniontown, PA 15401
Phone: (814) 865-5471
E-mail: admissions@psu.edu
http://www.fe.psu.edu

Penn State Greater Allegheny
4000 University Drive
McKeesport, PA 15132
Phone: (814) 865-5471
E-mail: admissions@psu.edu
http://www.mk.psu.edu

Penn State Hazleton
Hazleton, PA 18202
Phone: (814) 865-5471
E-mail: admissions@psu.ed
http://www.hn.psu.edu

Penn State Mont Alto
Campus Drive
Mont Alto, PA 17237
Phone: (814) 865-5471
E-mail: admissions@psu.edu
http://www.ma.psu.edu

Penn State New Kensington
3550 7th Street Road
New Kensington, PA 15068
Phone: (814) 865-5471
E-mail: admissions@psu.edu
http://www.nk.psu.edu

Penn State Schuylkill
200 University Drive
Schuylkill Haven, PA 17972
Phone: (814) 865-5471
E-mail: admissions@psu.edu
http://www.sl.psu.edu

Penn State Shenango
147 Shenango Avenue
Sharon, PA 16146
Phone: (814) 865-5471
E-mail: admissions@psu.edu
http://www.shenango.psu.edu

Point Park University
201 Wood Street
Pittsburgh, PA 15222
Phone: (412) 392-3430
Fax: (412) 392-3902
E-mail: enroll@pointpark.edu
http://www.pointpark.edu

Temple University
Philadelphia, PA 19122
Phone: (215) 204-7200
E-mail: tuadm@temple.edu
http://www.temple.edu

Waynesburg University
51 West College Street
Waynesburg, PA 15370
Phone: (724) 852-3333
Fax: (724) 627-8124
E-mail: admissions@waynesburg.
    edu
http://www.waynesburg.edu

Westminster College
319 South Market Street
New Wilmington, PA 6172
Phone: (724) 946-7100
E-mail: admis@westminster.edu
http://www.westminster.edu

Widener University
One University Place
Chester, PA 19013
Phone: (610) 499-4126
E-mail: admissions.office@widener.
    edu
http://www.widener.edu

York College of Pennsylvania
York, PA 17405
Phone: (717) 849-1600
Fax: (717) 849-1607
E-mail: admissions@ycp.edu

RHODE ISLAND

Johnson & Wales University
8 Abbott Park Place
Providence, RI 02903
Phone: (401) 598-1000
Fax: (401) 598-4901
E-mail: petersons@jwu.edu
http://www.jwu.edu

SOUTH CAROLINA

University of South Carolina-Columbia
Columbia, SC 29208
Phone: (803) 777-7000
E-mail: admissions-ugrad@sc.edu
http://www.sc.edu

TENNESSEE

Belmont University
1900 Belmont Boulevard
Nashville, TN 37212,
Phone: (615) 460-6785
Fax: (615) 460-5434
E-mail: buadmission@mail.
    belmont.edu

Memphis College of Art
1930 Poplar Avenue
Memphis, TN 38104
Phone: (901) 272-5151
Fax: (901) 272-5158
E-mail: info@mca.edu
http://www.mca.edu

Union University
1050 Union University Drive
Jackson, TN 38305
Phone: (731) 661-5100
E-mail: info@uu.edu
http://www.uu.edu

University of Tennessee
Knoxville, TN 37996
Phone: (865) 974-2184
Fax: (865) 974-6341
E-mail: admissions@tennessee.
    edu
http://www.tennessee.edu

TEXAS

Sam Houston State University
PO Box 2418
Huntsville, TX 77341
(936) 294-1111
E-mail: admissions@shsu.edu
http://www.shsu.edu

Southern Methodist University
PO Box 750181
Dallas, TX 75275

Phone: (214) 768-2000
E-mail: ugadmission@smu.edu
http://www.smu.edu

Texas State University-San Marcos
San Marcos, TX 78666
Phone: (512) 245-2364
Fax: (512) 245-8044
E-mail: admissions@txstate.edu
http://www.txstate.edu

Texas Tech University
Box 45005
Lubbock, TX 7940
Phone: (806) 742-2011
E-mail: admissions@ttu.edu
http://www.ttu.edu

University of Texas at Arlington
PO Box 19111
701 South Nedderman Drive
Arlington, TX 76019
Phone: (817) 272-6287
Fax: (817) 272-3435
E-mail: admissions@uta.edu
http://www.uta.edu

University of Texas-Austin
Main Building, Room 7

Austin, TX 78712
Phone: (512) 471-3434
E-mail: frmn@uts.cc.utexas.edu
http://www.utexas.edu

West Texas A&M University
PO Box 60999
Canyon, TX 79016
Phone: (806) 651-2000
E-mail: apifer@mail.wtamu.edu
http://www.wtamu.edu

UTAH

Brigham Young University
A-153 Abraham Smoot Building
Provo, UT 84602
Phone: (801) 422-2507
Fax: (801) 422-0005
E-mail: admissions@byu.edu
http://www.byu.edu

VIRGINIA

Hampton University
Tyler Street
Hampton, VA 23668
Phone: (757) 727-5070
E-mail: admissions@hamptonu.edu
http://www.hamptonu.edu

WEST VIRGINIA

West Virginia State College
PO Box 1000
Institute, WV 25112
Phone: (304) 766-3032
Fax: (304) 766-4158
E-mail: meeksjd@wvsc.edu

West Virginia University
Box 6009
Morgantown, WV 26506
Phone: (304) 293-2124
Fax: (304) 293-3080
E-mail: go2wvu@mail.wvu.edu

WISCONSIN

Marquette University
PO Box 1881
Milwaukee, WI 53201
Phone: (414) 288-7250
E-mail: admissions@marquette.edu
http://www.marquette.edu

University of Wisconsin–Madison
716 Langdon Street
Madison, WI 53706
Phone: (608) 262-3961
Fax: (608) 262-7706
E-mail: on.wisconsin@admissions.wisc.edu
http://www.wisc.edu

E. TWO-YEAR COLLEGES OFFERING MAJORS IN RETAILING

The following is a listing of selected two-year schools offering majors in retailing. They are grouped by state. School names, addresses, phone numbers, Web addresses, and e-mail addresses are included when available.

The author does not endorse any one school over another. Use this list as a beginning. Check the reference section of libraries or guidance counseling centers for additional schools offering degrees in this field.

CALIFORNIA

American River College
4700 College Oak Drive
Sacramento, CA 95841
Phone: (916) 484-8171
http://www.arc.losrios.edu

Orange Coast College
2701 Fairview Road
Costa Mesa, CA 92926

Phone: (714)432-5788
Fax: (714) 432-5072
E-mail: kclark@occ.cccd.edu
http://www.orangecoastcollege.com

Orange Coast College
2701 Fairview Road
Costa Mesa, CA 92926
Phone: (714) 432-5788

Fax: (714) 432-5072
E-mail: kclark@occ.cccd.edu
http://www.cccd.edu

Pasadena City College
1570 East Colorado Boulevard
Pasadena, CA 91106
Phone: (626) 585-7614
Fax: (626) 585-7915
http://www.pasadena.edu

FLORIDA

Florida Community College at Jacksonville
501 West State Street
Jacksonville, FL 32202
Phone: (904) 632-3131
Fax: (904) 632-5105
E-mail: admissions@fccj.edu
http://www.fccj.edu

ILLINOIS

Black Hawk College
6600 34th Avenue
Moline, IL 61265
Phone: (309) 796-5342
Fax: (309) 792-5976
http://www.bhc.edu

College of DuPage
SRC 2048, 45 Fawell Boulevard
Glen Ellyn, IL 60137
Phone: (630) 942-2442
Fax: (630) 790-2686
E-mail: hauenstein@cod.edu
http://www.cod.edu

Elgin Community College
1700 Spartan Drive
Elgin, IL 60123
Phone: (847) 214-7414
E-mail: admissions@elgin.edu
http://www.elgin.edu

Moraine Valley Community College
9000 West College Parkway
Palos Hills, IL 60465
Phone: (708) 974-5357
Fax: (708) 974-0681
E-mail: roselli@morainevalley.edu
http://www.morainevalley.edu

Waubonsee Community College
Route 47 at Waubonsee Drive
Sugar Grove, IL 60554
Phone: (630)466-7900
Fax: (630) 466-4964
E-mail: recruitment@waubonsee.
edu
http://www.waubonsee.edu

IOWA

Ellsworth Community College
1100 College Avenue
Iowa Falls, IA 50126
Phone: (641)648-4611

Iowa Lakes Community College
19 South 7th Street
Estherville, IA 51334
Phone: (712) 852-5254
Fax: (712) 362-3639
E-mail: info@iowalakes.edu
http://www.iowalakes.edu

KANSAS

Garden City Community College
801 Campus Drive
Garden City, KS 67846
Phone: (620) 276-9531
E-mail: nikki.geier@gcccks.edu
http://www.gcccks.edu

Hutchinson Community College and Area Vocational School
1300 North Plum
Hutchinson, KS 67501
Phone: (620) 665-3536
Fax: (620) 665-3301
E-mail: strobelc@hutchcc.edu
http://www.hutchcc.edu

Johnson County Community College
12345 College Park Boulevard
Overland Park, KS 66210
Phone: (913) 469-8500 Ext. 3806
http://www.johnco.cc.ks.us

MASSACHUSETTS

Holyoke Community College
Holyoke, MA 01040
Phone: (413) 552-2000
Fax: (413) 552-2045
E-mail: admissions@hcc.mass.
edu
http://www.hcc.mass.edu

MINNESOTA

Minnesota State College–Southeast Technical
PO Box 409
Winona, MN 55987
Phone: (507) 453-2700
http://www.southeastmn.edu

NEBRASKA

Northeast Community College
801 East Benjamin Avenue
PO Box 469
Norfolk, NE 68702
Phone: (402) 844-7258
Fax: (402) 844-7400
E-mail: admission@northeast.edu
http://www.northeast.edu

NEW HAMPSHIRE

Southern New Hampshire University
2500 North River Road
Manchester, NH 03106
Phone: (603) 645-9611
Fax: (603) 645-9693
http://www.snhu.edu

NEW JERSEY

Burlington County College
Route 530
Pemberton, NJ 08068
Phone: (609) 894-9311
http://www.bcc.edu

NORTH CAROLINA

Pitt Community College
PO Drawer 7007
1986 Pitt Tech Road
Greenville, NC 27835
Phone: (252) 321-4217
Fax: (252)321-4612
http://www.pittcc.edu

Wayne Community College
PO Box 8002
Goldsboro, NC 27533
Phone: (919) 735-5151
Fax: (919) 736-3204
http://www.waynecc.edu

PENNSYLVANIA

**Community College of
 Allegheny County**
800 Allegheny Avenue
Pittsburgh, PA 15233
Phone: (412) 237-4581
http://www.ccac.edu

RHODE ISLAND

Johnson & Wales University
8 Abbott Park Place
Providence, RI 02903
Phone: (977) 598-3368
Fax: (303) 256-9333
E-mail: den.admissions@jwu.edu
http://www.jwu.edu

TENNESSEE

Draughons Junior College
1860 Wilma Rudolph Boulevard
Clarksville, TN 37040
Fax: (931) 552-3624
http://www.draughons.edu

TEXAS

Border Institute of Technology
9611 Acer Avenue
El Paso, TX 79925
Phone: (915) 593-7328
http://bitelp.edu

North Central Texas College
1525 West California Street
Gainesville, TX 76240
Phone: (940) 668-7731
Fax: (940) 668-6049
E-mail: nctcgainesville@nctc.edu
http://www.nctc.edu

WASHINGTON

Bates Technical College
1101 South Yakima Avenue
Tacoma, WA 98405
Phone: (253) 680-7000
http://www.bates.ctc.edu/

Centralia College
600 West Locust
Centralia, WA 98531
Phone: (360) 736-9391
Fax: (360) 330-7503
E-mail: admissions@centralia.ctc.
 edu
http://www.centralia.edu

Clark College
1800 East McLoughlin Boulevard
Vancouver, WA 98663
Phone: (360) 992-2308
Fax: (360) 992-2867
E-mail: sanderson@clark.edu
http://www.clark.edu

WISCONSIN

Western Technical College
PO Box 908
La Crosse, WI 54602
Phone: (608) 785-9158
Fax: (608) 785-9094
E-mail: mildes@wwtc.edu
http://www.wwtc.edu

**Waukesha County Technical
 College**
800 Main Street
Pewaukee, WI 53072
Phone: (262) 691-5464
http://www.wctc.edu

**Wisconsin Indianhead
 Technical College**
505 Pine Ridge Drive
Shell Lake, WI 54871
Phone: (715) 468-2815
Fax: (715) 468-2819
E-mail: mcrandal@witc.edu
http://www.witc.edu

WYOMING

Casper College
125 College Drive
Casper, WY 82601
Phone: (307) 268-2111
Fax: (307) 268-2611
E-mail: kfoltz@caspercollege.edu
http://www.caspercollege.edu

APPENDIX II
TRADE ASSOCIATIONS, UNIONS, AND OTHER ORGANIZATION

The following is a listing of trade associations, unions, and organizations discussed in this book. There are also a number of other associations listed that might be useful to you.

The names, addresses, phone numbers, fax numbers, Web addresses, and e-mail addresses are included (when available) to help you easily get in touch with any of the organizations.

Many of the associations have branch offices located throughout the country. Organization headquarters can get you the phone number and address of your local branch.

Advertising Research Foundation
432 Park Avenue South
New York, NY 10016
Phone: (212) 751-5656
Fax: (212) 319-5265
E-mail: info@thearf.org
http://www.thearf.org

Advertising and Marketing International Network (AMIN)
c/o B. Vaughn Sink, Executive Director
12323 Nantucket
Wichita, KS 67235
Phone: (316) 531-2342
Fax: (316) 722-8353
E-mail: vaughn.sink@shscom.com
http://www.aminworldwide.com

Advertising Club of New York (ACNY)
235 Park Avenue South
New York, NY 10003
Phone: (212) 533-8080
Fax: (212) 533-1929
E-mail: gina@theadvertisingclub.org
http://www.theadvertisingclub.org

Advertising Women of New York (AWNY)
25 W. 45th Street
New York, NY 10036

Phone: (212) 221-7969
Fax: (212) 221-8296
E-mail: awny@awny.org
http://www.awny.org

American Advertising Federation (AAF)
1101 Vermont Avenue NW
Washington, DC 20005
Phone: (202) 898-0089
Fax: (202) 898-0159
E-mail: aaf@aaf.org
http://www.aaf.org

American Artists Professional League (AAPL)
47 5th Avenue
New York, NY 10003
Phone: (212) 645-1345
Fax: (212) 645-1345
E-mail: aaplinc@aol.com
http://www.americanartists professionalleague.org

American Assembly of Collegiate Schools of Business (AACSB)
AACSB International
777 South Harbour Island Boulevard
Tampa, FL 33602
Phone: (813)769-6500
Fax: (813)769-6559
http://www.aacsb.edu

American Association of Advertising Agencies (AAAA)
405 Lexington Avenue
New York, NY 10174
Phone: (212) 682-2500
Fax: (212) 682-8391
E-mail: barbara@aaaa.org
http://www.aaaa.org

American Association of Retired Persons (AARP)
1100 N. Market Street
Wilmington, DE 19801
Phone: (302) 571-8791
Fax: (302) 571-1984
E-mail: destate@aarp.org
http://www.aarp.org/de

American Automotive Leasing Association (AALA)
675 N. Washington Street
Alexandria, VA 22314
Phone: (703) 548-0777
Fax: (703) 548-1925
E-mail: peters@aalafleet.com
http://www.aalafleet.com

American Booksellers Association
200 White Plains Road
Tarrytown, NY 10591
Phone: (914) 591-2665
Fax: (914) 591-2720

E-mail: info@bookweb.org
http://www.bookweb.org

American Wholesale Booksellers Association (AWBA)
c/o Patty Walsh, Executive Secretary
702 S. Michigan
South Bend, IN 46601
Phone: (574) 288-4141
Fax: (303) 265-9292
E-mail: info@awba.com
http://www.awba.com

American Collegiate Retailing Association (ACRA)
c/o Robert Robicheaux,
     Membership Chairman
219 Business-Engineering Complex
1150 10th Avenue South
Birmingham, AL 35294
Phone: (205) 934-4648
Fax: (205) 934-0058
E-mail: bobr@uab.edu
http://www.acraretail.org

American Institute of Certified Public Accountants
1211 Avenue of the Americas
New York, NY 10036
Phone: (212)596-6200
Fax: (212)596-6213
E-mail: center@aicpa.org
http://www.aicpa.org

American Institute of Graphic Arts (AIGA)
164 5th Avenue
New York, NY 10010
Phone: (212)807-1990
Fax: (212)807-1799
E-mail: comments@aiga.org
http://www.aiga.org

American Management Association (AMA)
1601 Broadway
New York, NY 10019
Phone: (212) 586-8100
Fax: (212) 903-8168
E-mail: customerservice@amanet.
     org
http://www.amanet.org

American Marketing Association (AMA)
311 S. Wacker Drive
Chicago, IL 60606
Phone: (312)542-9000
Fax: (312)542-9001
http://www.marketingpower.com

American Purchasing Society (APS)
8 East Galena Boulevard
Aurora, IL 60506
Phone: (630) 859-0250
Fax: (630) 859-0270
E-mail: support@american-
     purchasing.com
http://www.american-purchasing.
     com

American Society for Training & Development
1640 King Street
PO Box 1443
Alexandria, VA 22313
Phone: (703) 683-8100
Fax: (703) 683-8103
E-mail: publications@astd.org
http://www.astd.org

American Society of Artists
PO Box 1326
Palatine, IL 60078
Phone: (312) 751-2500
E-mail: asoa@webtv.net
http://www.americansocietyof
     artists.org

American Specialty Toy Retailing Association (ASTRA)
116 W. Illinois Street
Chicago, IL 60610
Phone: (312) 222-0984
Fax: (312) 222-0986
E-mail: info@astratoy.org
http://www.astratoy.org

American Truck Stop Owners Association (ATSOA)
PO Box 4949
Winston-Salem, NC 27115
Phone: (336) 744-5555
Fax: (336) 744-1184
E-mail: salem1@alltel.net

American Wholesale Marketers Association (AWMA)
2750 Prosperity Avenue
Fairfax, VA 22031
Phone: (703) 208-3358
Fax: (703) 573-5738
E-mail: info@awmanet.org
http://www.awmanet.org

Apparel Guild
2655 Park Circle
East Meadow, NY 11554
Phone: (516) 735-1595

Art Directors Club (ADC)
106 W. 29th Street
New York, NY 10001
Phone: (212) 643-1440
Fax: (212) 643-4266
E-mail: info@adcglobal.org
http://www.adcglobal.org

Association for Business Communication (ABC)
Baruch College
Communication Studies
One Bernard Baruch Way
Box B8-240
New York, NY 10010
Phone: (646) 312-3726
     (646) 312-3723
Fax: (646) 349-5297
E-mail: myers@business
     communication.org
http://www.businesscommunication.
     org

Association for Retail Technology Standards (ARTS)
325 7th Street NW
Washington, DC 20004
Phone: (202) 626-8140
Fax: (202) 626-8145
E-mail: arts@nrf.com
http://www.nrf-arts.org

Association of Coupon Professionals (ACP)
200 E. Howard Street
Des Plaines, IL 60018
Phone: (847) 297-7773
Fax: (847) 297-8428

E-mail: acphq@aol.com
http://www.couponpros.org

Association of Retail Marketing Services Inc.
10 Drs James Parker Boulevard
Red Bank, NJ 07701
Phone: (732) 842-5070
Fax: (732) 219-1938
E-mail: info@goarms.com
http://www.goarms.com

Association of Sales Administration Managers (ASAM)
c/o Bill Martin, Sec.-Treas.
Box 1356
Laurence Harbor, NJ 08879
Phone: (732) 264-7722
E-mail: asamnet@aol.com

Association for Women in Communications (AWC)
3337 Duke Street
Alexandria, VA 22314
Phone: (703) 370-7436
Fax: (703) 370-7437
E-mail: info@womcom.org
http://www.womcom.org

Building Owners & Managers Association International
1201 New York Avenue NW
Washington, DC 20005
Phone: (202)408-2662
Fax: (202)326-6377
E-mail: info@boma.org
http://www.boma.org

California Retailers Association (CRA)
c/o Bill Dombrowski, Pres./CEO
980 9th Street
Sacramento, CA 95814
Phone: (916) 443-1975
Fax: (916) 441-4218
E-mail: cra@calretailers.com
http://www.calretailers.com

Canadian Booksellers Association (CBA)
789 Don Mills Road
Toronto, ON, Canada M3C 1T5

Phone: (416) 467-7883
Fax: (416) 467-7886
Toll-Free: (866) 788-0790
E-mail: sdayus@cbabook.org
http://www.cbabook.org

Canadian Federation of Independent Grocers (CFIG)
Federation Canadienne des Epiciers Independants
2235 Sheppard Avenue East
Willowdale, ON, Canada M2J 5B5
Phone: (416) 492-2311
Fax: (416) 492-2347
Toll-Free: (800) 661-2344
E-mail: info@cfig.ca
http://www.cfig.ca

Catalog and Multichannel Marketing Council
1120 Avenue of the Americas
New York, NY 10036-6700
Phone: (212) 768-7277
Fax: (212) 302-6714
E-mail: councils@the-dma.org
http://www.the-dma.org

Christian Booksellers Association (CBA)
PO Box 62000
Colorado Springs, CO 80962
Phone: (719) 265-9895
Fax: (719) 272-3510
E-mail: info@cbaonline.org
http://www.cbaonline.org

Clothing Manufacturers Association of the U.S.A.
730 Broadway
New York, NY 10003
Phone: (212) 529-0823
Fax: (212) 529-1739
E-mail: kaplancma730@hotmail.com

Direct Marketing Association (DMA)
1120 Avenue of the Americas
New York, NY 10036
Phone: (212) 768-7277
Fax: (212) 302-6714
E-mail: president@the-dma.org
http://www.the-dma.org

Direct Marketing Club of New York
224 7th Street
Garden City, NY 11530
Phone: (516)746-6700
Fax: (516)294-8141
E-mail: info@dmcny.org
http://www.dmcny.org

Direct Marketing Educational Foundation (DMEF)
1120 Avenue of the Americas
New York, NY 10036
Phone: (212) 768-7277
Fax: (212) 790-1561
E-mail: dmef@the-dma.org
http://www.the-dma.org/dmef

Direct Marketing Insurance and Financial Services Council (IFSC)
c/o Direct Marketing Association
1120 Avenue of the Americas
New York, NY 10036
Phone: (212) 768-7277
Fax: (212) 302-6714
E-mail: hr@the-dma.org
http://www.the-dma.org

Distribution Research and Education Foundation (DREF)
c/o Ron Schreibman, Executive Director
1725 K Street NW
Washington, DC 20006
Phone: (202) 872-0885
Fax: (202) 785-0586
E-mail: rschreibman@nawd.org

Electronic Funds Transfer Association (EFTA)
11350 Random Hills Road
Fairfax, VA 22030
Phone: (703) 934-6052
Fax: (703) 934-6058
E-mail: eftassoc@efta.org
http://www.efta.org

Electronic Retailing Association
2000 North 14th Street
Arlington, VA 22201
Phone: (703) 841-1751
Fax: (703) 841-1860

E-mail: contact@retailing.org
http://www.retailing.org

Food Industry Association Executives (FIAE)

PO Box 2510
Flemington, NJ 08822
Phone: (908) 782-7833
Fax: (908) 782-6907
E-mail: bmcconnell@fiae.net
http://www.fiae.net

Food Marketing Institute (FMI)

655 15th Street NW
Washington, DC 20005
Phone: (202) 452-8444
Fax: (202) 429-4519
E-mail: fmi@fmi.org
http://www.fmi.org

General Merchandise Distributors Council (GMDC)

1275 Lake Plaza Drive
Colorado Springs, CO 80906
Phone: (719) 576-4260
Fax: (719) 576-2661
E-mail: info@gmdc.org
http://gmdc.com

Graphic Artists Guild

90 John Street, Suite 403
New York, NY 10038
Phone: (212)791-3400
Fax: (212)791-0333
E-mail: admin@gag.org
http://www.gag.org

Grocery Manufacturers of America (GMA)

2401 Pennsylvania Avenue NW
Washington, DC 20037
Phone: (202) 337-9400
Fax: (202) 337-4508
E-mail: info@gmabrands.com
http://www.gmabrands.com

Independent Insurance Agents and Brokers of America (IIABA)

127 S. Peyton Street
Alexandria, VA 22314
Fax: (703) 683-7556

E-mail: info@iiaba.org
http://www.independentagent.com

Institute of Internal Auditors Inc.

247 Maitland Avenue
Altamonte Springs, FL 32701
Phone: (407)937-1100
Fax: (407)937-1101
E-mail: iia@theiia.org
http://www.theiia.org

Institute of Real Estate Management (IREM)

430 N. Michigan Avenue
Chicago, IL 60611
Phone: (312)329-6000
Fax: (800)-338-4736
E-mail: custserv@irem.org
http://www.irem.org

Indiana Retail Council (IRC)

c/o Grant Monahan, Pres.
One N. Capitol
Indianapolis, IN 46204
Phone: (317) 632-7391
Fax: (317) 632-7399
E-mail: inretail@indy.net
http://www.indianaretailers.com

Institute of Store Planners (ISP)

25 North Broadway
Tarrytown, NY 10591
Phone: (914) 332-0040
Fax: (914) 332-1541
E-mail: info@ispo.org
http://ww3.ispo.org

International Association of Administrative Professionals (IAAP)

10502 NW Ambassador Drive
PO Box 20404
Kansas City, MO 64195
Phone: (816) 891-6600
Fax: (816) 891-9118
E-mail: rstroud@iaap-hq.org
http://www.iaap-hq.org

International Association of Airport Duty Free Stores (IAADFS)

2025 M Street, NW

Washington, DC 20036
Phone: (202) 367-1184
Fax: (202) 429-5154
E-mail: iaadfs@iaadfs.org
http://www.iaadfs.org

International Association of Business Communicators

1 Hallidie Plaza
San Francisco, CA 94102
Phone: (415)544-4700
Fax: (415)544-4747
E-mail: service_centre@iabc.com
http://www.iabc.com

International Association of Ice Cream Vendors (IAICV)

100 N. 20th Street
Philadelphia, PA 19103
Phone: (215) 564-3484
Fax: (215) 564-2175
E-mail: iaicv@fernley.com
http://www.iaicv.org

International Council of Shopping Centers

1221 Avenue of the Americas
New York, NY 10022
Phone: (646)728-3800
Fax: (732)694-1755
E-mail: icsc@icsc.org
http://www.icsc.org

International Foundation of Employee Benefit Plans

18700 W. Bluemound Road
PO Box 69
Brookfield, WI 53008
Phone: (262)786-6710
Fax: (262)786-8670
Toll-Free: (888) 334-3327
E-mail: ebinfo@ifebp.org,
    research@ifebp.org
http://www.ifebp.org

International Mass Retail Association

1700 N. Moore
Arlington, VA 22209
Phone: (703)841-2300
Fax: (703)841-1184
E-mail: erin.dimuzio@retail-
    leaders.org
http://www.retail-leaders.org

Joint Labor Management Committee of the Retail Food Industry (JLMC)
c/o Robert F. Harbrant, Chairman
3720 Farragut Avenue
Kensington, MD 20895
Phone: (301) 942-5400
Fax: (301) 942-5409
E-mail: harbrant@thejlmc.com
http://www.thejlmc.com

Kentucky Retail Federation (KRF)
512 Capitol Avenue
Frankfort, KY 40601
Phone: (502) 875-1444
Fax: (502) 875-1595
E-mail: info@kyretail.com
http://www.kyretail.com

Louisiana Retailers Association (LRA)
PO Box 44034
Baton Rouge, LA 70804
Phone: (225) 344-9481
Fax: (225) 383-4145
E-mail: lra@laretail.org
http://www.laretail.org

Mail & Fulfillment Service Association
1421 Prince Street
Alexandria, VA 22314
Phone: (703) 836-9200
Fax: (703) 548-8204
Toll-Free: (800) 333-6272
E-mail: mfsa-mail@mfsanet.org
http://www.mfsanet.org

Manufacturers' Agents National Association
1 Spectrum Pointe
Lake Forest, CA 92630
Phone: (949) 859-4040
Fax: (949) 855-2973
E-mail: mana@manaonline.org
http://www.manaonline.org

Manufacturers Representatives Educational Research Foundation (MRERF)
8329 Cole Street
Arvada, CO 80005

Phone: (303) 463-1801
Fax: (303) 463-3198
E-mail: info@mrerf.org
http://www.mrerf.org

Marketing Agencies Association Worldwide (MAA)
460 Summer Street
Stamford, CT 06901
Phone: (203) 978-1590
Fax: (203) 969-1499
E-mail: keith.mccracken@maaw.org
http://www.maaw.org

Marketing Research Association (MRA)
110 National Drive
Glastonbury, CT 06033
Phone: (860)682-1000
Fax: (860)682-1010
E-mail: E-mail@mra-net.org
http://www.mra-net.org

Maryland Retailers Association (MRA)
171 Conduit Street
Annapolis, MD 21401
Phone: (410) 269-1440
Fax: (410) 269-0325
E-mail: tsaquella@mdra.org
http://www.mdra.org

Michigan Association of College Stores (MACS)
c/o Michael Kuzak
Northern Michigan University Bookstore
1401 Presque Isle
Marquette, MI 49855-5389
Phone: (906) 227-1126
Fax: (906) 227-1344
E-mail: mkuzak@nmu.edu
http://www.michigancollegestores.org

Michigan Association of Convenience Stores
c/o Mark A. Griffin, President
7521 Wetshire Drive
Lansing, MI 48917
Phone: (517) 622-3530
Fax: (517) 622-3420
E-mail: mpamacs@mpamacs.org
http://mpamacs.org

Michigan Retailers Association (MRA)
c/o Larry L. Meyer
603 South Washington Avenue
Lansing, MI 48933
Phone: (517) 372-5656
Fax: (517) 372-1303
E-mail: mra@retailers.com
http://www.retailers.com

Missouri Retailers Association (MRA)
c/o Mr. Samuel Overfelt, President
PO Box 1336
Jefferson City, MO 65102
Phone: (573) 636-5128
Fax: (573) 636-6846
E-mail: moretailer@aol.com

Montana Food Distributors Association (MFDA)
PO Box 5775
Helena, MT 59604
Phone: (406) 449-6394
Fax: (406) 449-0647
E-mail: bigskypower@msn.com

Museum Store Association (MSA)
c/o Nora Weiser, Assistant Director
4100 E. Missisippi Avenue
Denver, CO 80246
Phone: (303) 504-9223
Fax: (303) 504-9585
E-mail: nweiser@msaweb.org
http://www.museumdistrict.com

National Association of College Stores
500 E. Lorain Street
Oberlin, OH 44074
Phone: (440)775-7777
Fax: (440)775-4769
E-mail: info@nacs.org
http://www.nacs.org

National Association of Convenience Stores (NACS)
1600 Duke Street
Alexandria, VA 22314
Phone: (703) 684-3600
Fax: (703) 836-4564
E-mail: nacs@nacsonline.com
http://www.nacsonline.com

National Association of Professional Insurance Agents (NAPIA)
400 N. Washington Street
Alexandria, VA 22314
Phone: (703) 836-9340
Fax: (703) 836-1279
E-mail: piainfo@pianet.org
http://www.pianet.com

National Association of Realtors (NAR)
430 North Michigan Avenue
Chicago, IL 60611
Phone: (800) 874-6500
Fax: (312) 329-5962
http://www.realtor.org

National Association of Resale and Thrift Shops (NARTS)
PO Box 80707
St. Clair Shores, MI 48080
Phone: (586) 294-6700
Fax: (586) 294-6776
E-mail: info@narts.org
http://www.narts.org

National Association of Retail Collection Attorneys (NARCA)
1620 I Street NW
Washington, DC 20006
Phone: (202) 861-0706
Fax: (202) 463-8498
E-mail: narca@narca.org
http://www.narca.org

National Association of Schools of Art and Design
11250 Roger Bacon Drive
Reston, VA 20190
Phone: (703)437-0700
Fax: (703)437-6312
E-mail: info@arts-accredit.org
http://nasad.arts-accredit.org

National Association of Wholesaler-Distributors (NAW)
1725 K Stret, NW
Washington, DC 20006
Phone: (202) 872-0885
Fax: (202) 785-0586

E-mail: naw@nawd.org
http://www.nawd.org

National Automobile Dealers Association
8400 Westpark Drive
Mc Lean, VA 22102
Phone: (703)821-7000
Fax: (703)821-7234
Toll-Free: 800-252-6232
E-mail: nadainfo@nada.org
http://www.nada.org

National Catalog Managers Association (NCMA)
c/o Automotive Aftermarket Industry Association
7101 Wisconsin Avenue
Bethesda, MD 20814
Phone: (301) 654-6664
Fax: (301) 654-3299
E-mail: ncma@aftermarket.org
http://www.ncmacat.org

National Confectionery Sales Association (NCSA)
c/o Teresa M. Tarantino, Co-Executive Director
10225 Berea Road
Cleveland, OH 44102
Phone: (216) 631-8200
Fax: (216) 631-8210
E-mail: ttarantino@mail.propressinc.com
http://www.candyhalloffame.com

National Convenience Store Advisory Group (NCSAG)
PO Box 624
Brookfield, IL 60513
Fax: (708) 344-4444
Toll-Free: (877) 466-2724
http://www.ncsag.org

National Grocers Association (NGA)
1005 N Glebe Road
Arlington, VA 22201
Phone: (703)516-0700
Fax: (703)516-0115
E-mail: info@NationalGrocers.org
http://www.nationalgrocers.org

National Independent Automobile Dealers Association (NIADA)
2521 Brown Boulevard
Arlington, TX 76006
Phone: (817) 640-3838
Fax: (817) 649-5866
E-mail: mike@niada.com
http://www.niada.com

National Independent Flag Dealers Association (NIFDA)
214 North Hale Street
Wheaton, IL 60187
Fax: (630) 510-4501
E-mail: nifda@flaginfo.com
http://www.flaginfo.com

National Nutritional Foods Association (NNFA)
3931 MacArthur Boulevard
Newport Beach, CA 92660
Phone: (949)622-6272
Fax: (949)622-6266
E-mail: nnfa@nnfa.org
http://www.nnfa.org

National Piggly Wiggly Operators Association (NPWOA)
Piggly Wiggly, LLC
2605 Sagebrush Drive
Flower Mound, TX 75028
Phone: (972) 906-7191
E-mail: mrpig@pigglywiggly.com
http://www.pigglywiggly.com

National Retail Federation (NRF)
325 7th Street, NW
Washington, DC 20004
Phone: (202) 783-7971
Fax: (202) 737-2849
E-mail: mullint@nrf.com
http://www.nrf.com

National Safety Council (NSC)
1121 Spring Lake Drive
Itasca, IL 60143
Phone: (630) 285-1121
Fax: (630) 285-1315
E-mail: info@nsc.org
http://www.nsc.org

National Society of Accountants (NSA)

1010 N. Fairfax Street
Alexandria, VA 22314
Phone: (703) 549-6400
Fax: (703) 549-2984
E-mail: members@nsacct.org
http://www.nsacct.org

NATSO (Representing the Travel Plaza and Truckstop Industry)

1737 King Street
Alexandria, VA 22314
Phone: (703) 549-2100
Fax: (703) 684-4525
E-mail: headquarters@natso.com
http://www.natso.com

New England Booksellers Association (NEBA)

c/o Wayne A. Drugan, Jr., Executive Director
1770 Massachusetts Avenue
Cambridge, MA 02140
Phone: (617) 576-3070
Fax: (617) 576-3091
E-mail: rusty@neba.org
http://www.newenglandbooks.org

New Jersey Retail Merchants Association (NJRMA)

332 W. State Street
Trenton, NJ 08618
Phone: (609) 393-8006
Fax: (609) 393-8463
E-mail: rsantoro@njrma.org
http://www.njrma.org

North American Retail Dealers Association (NARDA)

10 E. 22nd Street
Lombard, IL 60148
Phone: (630) 953-8950
Fax: (630) 953-8957
E-mail: nardasvc@narda.com
http://www.narda.com

Ohio Council of Retail Merchants (OCRM)

c/o John C. Mahaney, Jr., President
50 W. Broad Street
Columbus, OH 43215
Phone: (614) 221-7833
Fax: (614) 221-7020
http://www.ocrm.net

Oklahoma Retail Merchants Association

c/o Mr. Joel Scott Mitchell, Exec. Vice President
2519 NW 23rd Street
Oklahoma City, OK 73107
Phone: (405) 947-5503
Fax: (405) 946-9203

Oregon Retail Council

c/o Ms. Julie Brandis, Director
PO Box 12519
Salem, OR 97309-0519
Phone: (503) 588-0050
Fax: (503) 588-0052
E-mail: jbrandis@aoi.com

Pacific Northwest Hardware and Implement Association (PNWA)

PO Box 17819
Salem, OR 97305
Phone: (503) 375-9024
Fax: (503) 375-7980
http://www.pnwassoc.com

Petroleum Marketers Association of America (PMAA)

1901 N. Ft. Myer Drive
Arlington, VA 22209
Phone: (703) 351-8000
Fax: (703) 351-9160
E-mail: info@pmaa.org
http://www.pmaa.org

Promotion Marketing Association (PMA)

257 Park Avenue South
New York, NY 10010
Phone: (212) 420-1100
Fax: (212) 533-7622
E-mail: pma@pmalink.org
http://www.pmalink.org

Public Relations Society of America (PRSA)

33 Maiden Lane
New York, NY 10038
Phone: (212) 460-1400
Fax: (212) 995-0757
E-mail: exec@prsa.org
http://www.prsa.org

Radio Advertising Bureau Inc. (RAB)

22 Cortlandt Street
New York, NY 10007
Phone: (212)681-7200
Fax: (212)681-7223
E-mail: renee@rab.com
http://www.rab.com

Sales and Marketing Executives International (SMEI)

PO Box 1390
Sumas, WA 98295
Phone: (312) 893-0751
Fax: (604) 855-0165
http://www.smei.org

Society for Human Resource Management

1800 Duke Street
Alexandria, VA 22314
Phone: (800) 283-7476
http://www.shrm.org

Society for Technical Communication (STC)

901 N. Stuart Street
Arlington, VA 22203
Phone: (703) 522-4114
Fax: (703) 522-2075
E-mail: stc@stc.org
http://www.stc.org

Society of American Florists (SAF)

1601 Duke Street
Alexandria, VA 22314
Phone: (703) 836-8700
Fax: (703) 836-8705
E-mail: info@safnow.org
http://www.safnow.org

Society of Illustrators

128 E. 63rd Street
New York, NY 10021
Phone: (212)838-2560
Fax: (212)838-2561
E-mail: info@societyillustrators.org
http://www.societyillustrators.org

The One Club for Art & Copy
21 East 26th Street
New York, NY, 10010
Phone: (212) 979-1900
Fax: (212) 979-5006
http://www.oneclub.org

United Food and Commercial Workers International Union (UFCW)
1775 K Street, NW
Washington, DC 20006
Phone: (202) 223-3111
Fax: (202) 466-1562
E-mail: press@ufcw.org
http://www.ufcw.

U.S. Department of Labor
Frances Perkins Building
200 Constitution Avenue NW
Washington, DC 20210
Phone: (202)693-4650
http://www.dol.gov

U.S. Small Business Administration
409 3rd Street, SW
Washington, DC 20416
Phone: (202)205-6740
Fax: (202)205-6913
http://www.sba.gov

US Office of Personnel Management
Division for Strategic Human Resources Policy
Center for Pay and Performance Policy
1900 E. Street NW
Washington, DC 20415
Phone: (202)606-2880
Fax: (202)606-4264
http://www.opm.gov/

Women in Direct Marketing International (WDMI)
c/o Wunderman
285 Madison Avenue
New York, NY 10017
Phone: (732) 469-5900
E-mail: bladden@directmaildepot.com
http://www.wdmi.org

World Organization of Webmasters (WOW)
9580 Oak Avenue Parkway
Folsom, CA 95630
Phone: (916) 989-2933
Fax: (916) 987-3022
E-mail: info@joinwow.org
http://www.joinwow.org

Writers Guild of America, East (WGAE)
555 W. 57th Street
New York, NY 10019
Phone: (212) 767-7800
Fax: (212) 582-1909
E-mail: info@wgaeast.org
http://www.wgaeast.org

Writers Guild of America, West (WGA)
7000 W. Third Street
Los Angeles, CA 90048
Phone: (323) 951-4000
Fax: (323) 782-4800
E-mail: website@wga.org
http://www.wga.org

APPENDIX III
DIRECTORY OF CHAIN STORES

The following is a directory of the corporate offices of selected chain stores. The classification of some chain stores may overlap with those in the department store, grocery/supermarket listing or other appendixes. Be sure to check all the appendixes when looking for specific stores or companies.

Names, addresses, phone numbers, fax numbers, and websites are included when available. Stores are listed alphabetically by name.

Use this list to get started in locating internships, training programs, summer employment or to send your resume when you are ready to go job hunting.

This list is provided as a starting point. There are many more manufacturers and other companies located throughout the country. Inclusion or exclusion does not constitute endorsement or the lack of it by the author.

7-Eleven, Inc.
1722 Routh Street
Dallas, TX 75202
Phone: (972) 828-7011
Fax: (972) 828-7848
http://www.7-eleven.com

Ace Hardware
2200 Kensington Court
Oak Brook, IL 60523
Phone: (630) 990-6600
Fax: (630) 990-6838
http://www.acehardware

A.C. Moore Arts and Crafts
130 A.C. Moore Drive
Berlin, NJ 08009
Phone: (856) 768-4930
Fax: (856)753-4723
http://www.acmoore.com

Advance Autoparts
5008 Airport Road
Roanoke, VA 24012
Phone: (540) 362-4911
Fax: (540) 561-1448
http://www.advanceautoparts.com

A.J. Wright
770 Cochituate Road.
Framingham, MA 01701
Phone: (508) 390-1000
http://www.ajwright.com

Altmeyer Home Stores
PO Box 710
New Kensington, PA 15068
Phone: (724) 468-3434
Fax: (724) 468-3233
http://www.altmeyers.com

Ann Taylor
7 Times Square
New York, NY 10036
Phone: (212) 541-3300
Fax: (212) 541-3379
http://www.anntaylor.com

Athletes Foot
1412 Oakbrook Drive
Norcross, GA 30093
Phone: (770) 514-4500
Fax: (770) 514-4903
http://www.theathletesfoot.com

AutoZone
123 S. Front Street
Memphis, TN 38103
Phone: (901) 495-6500
Fax: (901) 495-8300
http://www.autozone.com

Banana Republic
2 Folsom Street
San Francisco, CA 94105
Phone: (650) 952-4400
Fax: (415) 427-2553
http://www.bananarepublic.com

Barnes and Noble
122 5th Avenue
New York, NY 10011
Phone: (212) 633-3300
Fax: (212) 675-0413
http://www.barnesandnobleinc

Bartell Drug Company
4727 Denver Avenue South
Seattle, WA 98134
Phone: (206) 763-2626
Fax: (206) 763-2062
http://www.bartelldrugs.com

Bath and Body Works
7 Limited Parkway
Reynoldsburg, OH 43068
Phone: (614) 856-6000
Fax: (614) 856-6013
http://www.bathandbodyworks.com

B.C. Moore and Sons, Inc.
PO Drawer 72
Wadesboro, NC 28170
Phone: (704) 694-2171
Fax: (704)694-6748

Bed, Bath & Beyond
650 Liberty Avenue
Union, NJ 07083
Phone: (908) 688-0888
Fax: (908) 688-6483
http://www.bedbathandbeyond.com

Best Buy
7601 Penn Avenue, South
Richfield, MN 55423
Phone: (612) 291-1000
Fax: (612) 292-4001
http://www.bestbuyinc.com

Big Lots
300 Phillipi Road
Columbus, OH 43228
Phone: (614) 278-6800
Fax: (614) 278-6676
http://www.biglots.com

BJs Wholesale Club
1 Mercer Road
Natick, MA 01760
Phone: (508) 651-7400
Fax: (508) 651-6114
http://www.bjswholesale.com

Blockbuster
1201 Elm Street
Dallas, TX 75270
Phone: (214) 854-3000
Fax: (214) 854-3677
http://www.blockbuster.com

Bob's Stores
160 Corporate Court
Meriden, CT 06450
Phone: (203) 235-5775
Fax: (203) 634-0129
http://www.bobstores.com

The Body Shop
5036 One World Way
Wake Forest, NC 27587
Phone: (919) 554-4900
Fax: (919) 554-4361
http://www.thebodyshop.com

Books-A-Million
02 Industrial Lane
Birmingham, AL 35211
Phone: (205) 942-3737
Fax: (205) 942-6601
http://www.bamm.com

Bon Ton
2801 E. Market Street
York, PA 17402
Phone: (717) 757-7660

Fax: (717)751-3108
http://www.bonton.com

Borders
100 Phoenix Drive
Ann Arbor, MI 48108
Phone: (734) 477-1100
Fax: (734) 477-1285
http://www.bordersgroupinc.com

Brookstone, Inc.
1 Innovation Way
Merrimack, NH 03054
Phone: (603) 880-9500
Fax: (603) 577-8005
http://www.brookstone.com

Burlington Coat Factory
1830 Route 130
Burlington, NJ 08016
Phone: (609) 387-7800
Fax: (609) 387-7071
http://www.burlingtoncoatfactory.com

Caché
1440 Broadway
New York, NY 10018
Phone: (212) 575-3200
Fax: (212) 944-2842
http://www.cache.com

Casual Male
555 Turnpike Street
Canton, MA 02021
Phone: (781) 828-9300
Fax: (781) 821-6094
http://www.casualmalexl.com

Children's Place
915 Secaucus Rd.
Secaucus, NJ 07094
Phone: (201) 558-2400
Fax: (201) 558-2630
http://www.childrensplace.com

CompUSA
7795 W. Flagler Street
Miami, FL 33144
Phone: (305) 415-2199
http://www.compusa.com

Costco
999 Lake Drive
Issaquah, WA 98027

Phone: (425) 313-8100
http://www.costco.com

Crate and Barrel
1250 Techny Road
Northbrook, IL 60062
Phone: (847) 272-2888
Fax: (847)272-5366
http://www.crateandbarrel.com

CSK Auto Parts
645 E. Missouri Avenue
Phoenix, AZ 85012
Phone: (602) 265-9200
Fax: (602) 631-7321
http://www.cskauto.com

CVS
1 CVS Drive
Woonsocket, RI 02895
Phone: (401) 765-1500
Fax: (401) 762-9227
http://www.cvs.com

Dick's Sporting Goods
300 Industry Drive
RIDC Park West
Pittsburgh, PA 15275
Phone: (724) 273-3400
Fax: (724) 227-1904
http://www.dickssportinggoods.
  com

Discount Drug Mart
211 Commerce Drive
Medina, OH 44256
Phone: (330) 725-2340
Fax: (330) 722-2990
http://www.discount-drugmart.com

Dollar General
100 Mission Ridge
Goodlettsville, TN 37072
Phone: (615) 855-4000
Fax: (615) 855-5252
http://www.dollargeneral.com

Dollar Tree
500 Volvo Parkway
Chesapeake, VA 23320
Phone: (757) 321-5000
Fax: (757) 321-5111
http://www.dollartree.com

Dress Barn
30 Dunnigan Drive
Suffern, NY 10901
Phone: (845) 369-4500
Fax: (845) 369-4829
http://www.dressbarn.com

Eddie Bauer
10401 NE 8th Street
Bellevue, WA 98004
Phone: (425) 755-6544
Fax: (425) 755-7696
http://www.eddiebauer.com

Ethan Allen Interiors
Ethan Allen Drive
Danbury, CT 06811
Phone: (203) 743-8000
Fax: (203) 743-8298
http://www.ethanallen.com

Fashion Bug
450 Winks Lane
Bensalem, PA 19020
Phone: (215) 245-9100
Fax: (215) 633-4640
http://www.fashionbug.com

Filene's Basement
25 Corporate Drive
Burlington, MA 01803
Phone: (617) 348-7000
Fax: (617) 348-7128
http://www.filenesbasement.com

Fortunoff
70 Charles Lindbergh Boulevard
Uniondale, NY 11553
Phone: (516) 832-9000
Fax: (516) 237-1703
http://www.fortunoff.com

Footlocker
112 W. 34th Street
New York, NY 10120
Phone: (212)720-3700
Fax: (212) 720-4397
http://www.footlocker-inc.com

The Gap
2 Folsom Street
San Francisco, CA 94105
Phone: (650) 952-4400

Fax: (415) 427-2553
http://www.gap.com

Hallmark
2501 McGee Street
Kansas City, MO 64108
Phone: (816) 274-5111
Fax: (816) 274-5061
http://www.hallmark.com

Home Depot
2455 Paces Ferry Road
Atlanta, GA 30339
Phone: (770) 433-8211
Fax: (770) 384-2356
http://www.homedepot.com

IKEA
Plymouth Commons
Plymouth Meeting, PA 19462
Phone: (610) 834-0872
Fax: (610) 834-0872
http://www.ikea.com

JC Penney
6501 Legacy Drive
Plano, TX 75024
Phone: (972) 431-1000
Fax: (972) 431-1362
http://www.jcpenney.net

KB Toys
100 West Street
Pittsfield, MA 01201
Phone: (413) 496-3000
Fax: (413) 496-3616
http://www.kbtoys.com

Kmart
3333 Beverly Road
Hoffman Estates, IL 60179
Phone: (847) 286-2500
Fax: (847) 286-5500
http://www.kmartcorp.com

Medicine Shoppe
1 Rider Trail Plaza Drive
Earth City, MO 63045
Phone: (314)993-6000
Fax: (314) 872-5500
http://www.medicineshoppe.com

Michaels
PO Box 619566
Dallas, Texas 75261
Phone: (972) 409-1300
Fax: (972) 409-1556
http://www.michaels.com

Office Depot
2200 Old Germantown Road
Delray Beach, FL 33445
Phone: (561) 438-4800
Fax: (561) 438-4001
http://www.officedepot.com

Office Max
263 Shuman Boulevard
Naperville, IL 60563
Phone: (630) 438-7800
http://www.officemax.com

Old Navy
2 Folsom Street
San Francisco, CA 94105
Phone: (650) 952-4400
http://www.oldnavy.com

PetSmart
19601 N. 27th Avenue
Phoenix, Arizona 85027
Phone: (623) 580-6100
Fax: (623)580-6183
http://www.petsmart.com

Pier 1 Imports
100 Pier 1 Place
Fort Worth, TX 76102
Phone: (817) 252-8000
Fax: (817) 252-8174
http://www.pier1.com

Rite Aid
PO Box 3165
Harrisburg, PA 17105
Phone: (717) 761-2633
Fax: (717)975-5871
http://www.riteaid.com

Ritz Camera Centers
6711 Ritz Way
Beltsville, MD 20705
Phone: (301) 419-0000
Fax: (301-419-2995
http://www.ritzcamera.com

Saks Fifth Avenue
12 E. 49th Street
New York, NY 10017
Phone: (212) 940-5305
Fax: (212) 940-4299
http://www.saksfifthavenue.com

Sally's Beauty
3001 Colorado Boulevard
Denton, TX 76210
Phone: (940) 898-7500
Fax: (940) 898-7927
http://www.sallybeauty.com

Sam's Club
608 SW 8th Street
Bentonville, AR 72712
Phone: (479) 277-7000
http://www.samsclub.com

Sears
3333 Beverly Road
Hoffman Estates, IL 60179
Phone: (847) 286-2500
Fax: (800)326-0485
http://www.sears.com

Sports Authority
1050 W. Hampden Avenue
Englewood, CO 80110
Phone: (303)789-5266
Fax: (303) 863-2240
http://www.sportsauthority.com

Staples
500 Staples Drive
Framingham, MA 01702

Phone: (508)253-5000
Fax: (508)253-8989
http://www.staples.com

Striderite
191 Spring Street
Lexington, MA 02420
Phone: (617)824-6000
Fax: (617) 824-6549
http://www.strideritecorp.com

TJ Maxx
770 Cochituate Road
Framingham, MA 01701
Phone: (508) 390-1000
http://www.tjmaxx.com

Target
1000 Nicollet Mall
Minneapolis, MN 55403
Phone: (612) 304-6073
Fax: (612) 696-5400
http://www.target.com

Toys R Us
1 Geoffrey Way
Wayne, NJ 07470
Phone: (973) 617-3500
Fax: (973) 617-4006
http://www.toysrus.com

US Vision
1 Harmon Drive
Glen Oaks Industrial Park
Glendora, NJ 08029
Phone: (856)228-1000
Fax: (856) 228-3339
http://www.usvision.com

Victoria's Secret
4 Limited Parkway, East
Reynoldsburg, OH 43068
Phone: (614) 577-7000
Fax: (614) 577-7844
http://www.victoriassecret.com

Waldenbooks
100 Phoenix Drive
Ann Arbor, MI 48108
Phone: (734)477-1100
Fax: (734)477-1435
http://www.waldenbooks.com

Walgreens
200 Wilmot Road
Deerfield, IL 60015
Phone: (847) 914-2500
Fax: (847) 914-2804
http://www.walgreens.com

Wal-Mart
702 SW 8th Street
Bentonville, AR 72716
Phone: (479) 273-4000
Fax: (479) 277-1830
http://www.walmartstores.com

Zales
901 West Walnut Hill Lane
Irving, TX 75038
Phone: (972) 580-4000
Fax: (972) 580-5523
http://www.zalecorp.com

APPENDIX IV
DIRECTORY OF DEPARTMENT STORES

The following is a directory of the corporate offices of selected department stores. The classifications of some department stores may overlap with those in the chain store listing. Be sure to check all of the appendixes when looking for specific stores.

Names, addresses, phone number, fax numbers, Web sites, and e-mail addresses are included when available. Stores are listed alphabetically by name.

Use this list to get started in locating internships, training programs, summer employment or to send your résumé when you are ready to go job hunting.

This list is provided as a starting point. There are many more department stores located throughout the country. Inclusion or exclusion does not constitute endorsement or the lack of it by the author.

B.C. Moore and Sons Inc.
101 South Greene Street
Wadesboro, NC 28170
Phone: (704) 694-2171
Fax: (704) 694-6748
http://www.mooresonline.com

Beall's Inc.
1806 38th Avenue East
Bradenton, FL 34208
Phone: (941) 747-2355
Fax: (941) 746-1171
http://www.beallsinc.com/

Belk Brothers Co.
2801 W. Tyvola Road
Charlotte, NC 28230
Phone: (704) 423-9600
Fax: (704)342-4320
E-mail: contact@belk.com
http://www.belk.com

Bergdorf Goodman Inc.
754 5th Avenue
New York, NY 10019
Phone: (212) 753-7300
Fax: (212)872-8677
http://www.bergdorfgoodman.com

Bloomingdale's Inc.
1000 3rd Avenue
New York, NY 10022
Phone: (212) 705-2000
Fax: (212)705-2502
http://www.bloomingdales.com

Bon Inc.
1601 3rd Avenue
Seattle, Washington 98101
Phone: (206) 344-2121
Fax: (206)506-7722
http://www.federated-fds.com

Bon-Ton Department Stores Inc.
PO Box 2821
York, PA 17405
Phone: (717) 757-7660
Fax: (717)751-3198
E-mail: contactus@bonton.com
http://www.bonton.com

Boscov's Department Stores Inc.
4500 Perkiomen Avenue
Reading, PA 19606
Phone: (610) 779-2000
Fax: (610)370-3495
E-mail: ifabrizio@boxcovs.com
http://www.boscovs.com

Century 21 Department Stores
22 Cortlandt Street
New York, NY 10007
Phone: (212) 227-9092
E-mail: customerservice@c21stores.com
http://www.c21stores.com
http://www.century21deptstores.com

Dillards
1600 Cantrell Road
Little Rock, AR 72201
Phone: (501) 376-5200
E-mail: questions@dillards.com
http://www.dillards.com

Dunlaps Co.
200 Bailey Avenue
Fort Worth, TX 76107
Phone: (817) 336-4985
Fax: (817) 877-1302
E-mail: info@dunlaps.com
http://www.dunlaps.com

Filene's Basement Corp.
25 Corporate Avenue
Burlington, MA 01803
Phone: (617) 348-7000
Fax: (617)348-7128
http://www.filenesbasement.com

Filene's
426 Washington Street
Boston, MA 02108
Phone: (617) 357-2100
Fax: (617)357-2996
http://www.filenes.com

Famous-Barr
601 Olive Street
St. Louis, MO 63101
Phone: (314) 444-3111
http://www.famousbarr.com

J.C. Penney Company
6501 Legacy Drive
Plano, TX 75024
Phone: (972) 431-1000
Fax: (972) 431-9140
E-mail: jcpis@jcpenney.net
http://www.jcpenney.net

Kmart Corp.
3100 West Big Beaver Road
Troy, MI 48084
Phone: (248) 643-1000
Fax: (248) 463-5636
http://www.kmartcorp.com

Kohl's Corp.
N56 West 17000 Ridgewood Drive
Menomonee Falls, WI 53051
Phone: (262) 703-7000
Fax: (262)703-7115
http://www.kohls.com

Lord and Taylor
424 5th Avenue
New York, NY 10018
Phone: (212) 391-3344
http://www.lordandtaylor.com

Macy's
Macy's Inc.
151 W. 34th Street

New York, NY 10001
Phone: (212) 695-4400
http://www.federated-fds.com
http://www.macys.com

Macy's
7 W. Seventh Street
Cincinnati, OH 45202
Phone: (212) 494-1602
http://www.federated-fds.com

Montgomery Ward
1 Montgomery Ward Plaza
Chicago, IL 60671
Phone: (800) 227-7598
http://www.mward.com

Neiman-Marcus
1618 Main Street
Dallas, TX 75201
Phone: (214) 741-6911
Fax: (214) 742-4904
http://www.neimanmarcus.com

Nordstrom Inc.
1617 6th Avenue
Seattle, WA 98101
Phone: (206) 628-2111
Fax: (206) 628-1795
http://www.nordstrom.com

Saks Fifth Avenue
12 East 49th Street
New York, NY 10017
Phone: (212) 940-5305
http://www.saksfifthavenue.com

Sears
3333 Beverly Roads
Hoffman Estates, IL 60179
Phone: (847) 286-2500
http://www.sears.com

Sterling Department Stores
221 W. Capitol Avenue
Little Rock, AR
Phone: (501) 375-8181

Target
1000 Nicollet Mall
Minneapolis, MN 55403
Phone: (612) 304-6073
Fax: (612)304-0730
http://www.target.com

Wal-Mart
702 SW 8th Street
Bentonville, AR 72716
Phone: (501) 273-4000
Fax: (501) 273-4053
E-mail: cserve@wal-mart.com
http://www.wal-mart.com

APPENDIX V
DIRECTORY OF SUPERMARKETS/GROCERIES

The following is a directory of the corporate offices of some of the larger supermarket and grocery parent companies as well as the stores which they include. The classifications of some supermarkets and grocery stores may overlap with those in the chain store listing. Be sure to check all of the appendixes when looking for specific stores.

Names, addresses, phone number, fax numbers, and Web sites are included when available. Companies are listed alphabetically by name.

Use this list to get started in locating internships, training programs, summer employment or to send your resume when you are ready to go job hunting.

This list is provided as a starting point. There are many more supermarkets and groceries located throughout the country. Inclusion or exclusion does not constitute endorsement or the lack of it by the author.

Ahold USA, Inc.
1385 Hancock Street
Quincy Center Plaza
Quincy, MA 02169
Phone: (781) 380-8000
Fax: (617) 770-8190
http://www.aholdusa.com
(Includes Stop & Shop, Giant-
    Landover, and Giant-Carlisle)

Albertson's LLC
PO Box 20
Boise, ID 83726
Phone: (208) 395-6200
Fax: (208)395-6349
http://www.albertsons.com
(Includes Albertsons, Super Saver
    Store and Grocery Warehouse)

Aldi, Inc.
1200 North Kirk Road
Batavia, IL 60510
Phone: (630) 879-8100
http://www.aldi.us
(includes Aldi)

Alex Lee, Inc.
120 4th Street SW
Hickory, NC 28602
Phone: (828) 725-4424

Fax: (828) 725-4435
http://www.alexlee.com
(Includes Lowe's Food Store and
    IGA)

Bashas' Inc.
22402 S. Basha Road
Chandler, AZ 85248
Phone: (480) 895-9350
Fax: (480) 895-5394
http://www.bashas.com
(Includes Bashas', Food City Bashas'
    and AJ's)

Big Y Foods, Inc.
2145 Roosevelt Avenue
Springfield, MA 01102
Phone: (413) 784-0600
http://www.bigy.com
(Includes Big Y)

Brookshire Grocery Co.
1600 West South West Loop 323
Tyler, TX 75701
Phone: (903) 534-3000
Fax: (903) 534-2206
http://www.brookshires.com
(Includes Brookshire, Super 1
    Foods SW and ALPS Market)

Central Grocers Co-Op, Inc.
11100 Belmont Avenue
Franklin Park, IL 60131
Phone: (847) 451-0660
Fax: (847) 288-8710
http://www.central-grocers.com
(includes Ultra Foods, Strack & Van
    Til)

Delhaize America, Inc.
2110 Executive Drive
Salisbury, NC 28145
Phone: (704) 633-8250
Fax: (704) 636-5024
http://www.delhaizegroup.com
(Includes Food Lion, Hannaford,
    Sweetbay Supermarket)

**DeMoulas/Supermarket/
    Market Basket**
875 East Street
Tewksbury, MA 01876
Phone: (978) 851-8000
Fax: (978) 640-8390
(Includes DeMoulas Market Basket)

Foodarama Supermarkets, Inc.
922 Highway 33
Building 6
Freehold, NJ 07728

Phone: (732) 462-4700
Fax: (732) 294-2322
(Includes Shoprite)

Giant Eagle, Inc.
101 Kappa Drive
Pittsburgh, PA 15238
Phone: (412) 963-6200
Fax: (412) 968-1617
http://www.gianteagle.com
(Includes Giant Eagle)

Great Atlantic & Pacific Tea Company
2 Paragon Drive
Montvale, NJ 07645
Phone: (201) 573-9700
Fax: (201) 505-3054
http://www.aptea.com
(Includes Pathmark, Super Fresh and Waldbaum's)

Grocers Supply Co., Inc.
3131 E. Holcombe Boulevard
Houston, TX 77221
Phone: (713) 747-5000
Fax: (713) 746-5611
http://www.grocerssupply.com
(Includes Fiesta Mart)

H.E. Butt Grocery Company
646 South Main Avenue
San Antonio, TX 78204
Phone: (210) 938-8000
Fax: (210) 938-8169
http://www.heb.com
(Includes HEB, HEB Plus and HEB Central Market)

Houchens Industries, Inc.
700 Church Street
Bowling Green, KY 42102
Phone: (270) 843-3252
Fax: (270) 780-2877
(Includes Save-A-Lot, Piggly Wiggly AL and Sureway Supermarkets)

Hy-Vee Food Stores, Inc.
5820 Westown Parkway
West Des Moines, IA 50266
Phone: (515) 267-2800
Fax: (515) 267-2817

http://www.hy-vee.com
(Includes Hy-Vee)

Ingles Markets, Inc.
2913 US Highway, 70 West
Black Mountain, NC 28711
Phone: (828) 669-2941
Fax: (828) 669-2941
http://www.ingles-markets.com
(Includes Ingles, Sav-Mo Foods)

King Kullen Grocery Company, Inc.
185 Central Avenue
Bethpage, NY 11714
Phone: (516) 33-7100
Fax: (516) 827-6325
http://www.kingkullen.com
(Includes King Kullen)

Kroger Company
1014 Vine Street
Cincinnati, OH 45202
Phone: (513) 762-4000
Fax: (513) 762-1160
http://www.kroger.com
(Includes Kruger, Ralphs, Smith's Food & Drug)

K-VA-T Food Stores, Inc.
201 Trigg Street
Abingdon, VA 24211
Phone: (276) 628-5503
Fax: (276) 623-5440
http://www.foodcity.com
(Includes Food City K-VA-T and Super Dollar Market)

Lone Star Funds
2711 North Haskell Avenue
Dallas, TX 75204
Phone: (214) 754-8300
http://www.bi-lo.com
(Includes Bi-Lo, Food World and Bruno's)

Marsh Supermarkets, Inc.
9800 Crosspoint Boulevard
Indianapolis, IN 46256
Phone: (317) 594-2100
Fax: (317) 594-2704
http://www.marsh.net

(Includes Marsh The Marketplace, Marsh Hometown Market and O'Malia's)

Meijer, Inc.
2929 Walker Avenue, NW
Grand Rapids, MI 49544
Phone: (616) 453-6711
Fax: (616) 791-2572
http://www.meijer.com
(Includes Meijer)

Penn Traffic Company
1200 State Fair Boulevard
Syracuse, NY 13221
Phone: (315) 453-7284
Fax: (315) 461-2645
http://www.penntraffic.com
(Includes P&C, Quality Market and BiLo Market)

Price Chopper/Golub Corporation
01 Duanesburg Road
Schenectady, NY 12306
Phone: (518) 355-5000
Fax: (518) 379-3536
http://www.pricechopper.com
(Includes Price Chopper)

Publix Super Markets, Inc.
300 Publix Corporate Parkway
Lakeland, FL 33811
Phone: (863) 688-1188
Fax: (863) 284-5532
http://www.publix.com
(Includes Publix and Publix GreenWise)

Raley's Supermkts
500 W. Capitol Avenue
West Sacramento, CA 95605
Phone: (916) 373-3333
Fax: (916) 371-1323
http://www.raleys.com
(Includes Raley's, Nob Hill, and Food Source)

Roundy's Supermarkets, Inc.
875 East Wisconsin Avenue
Milwaukee, WI 53202
Phone: (414) 231-5000

Fax: (414) 231-7939
http://www.roundys.com
(Includes Pick 'n Save Store, Rainbow Food Store and Metro Market)

Ruddick Corp.
301 S. Tryon Street
Charlotte, NC 28202
Phone: (704) 372-5404
Fax: (704) 372-6409
http://www.ruddickcorp.com
(Includes Harris Teeter)

Safeway, Inc.
5918 Stoneridge Mall Road
Pleasanton, CA 94588
Phone: (925) 467-3000
Fax: (925) 467-3321
http://www.safeway.com
(Includes Safeway, Vons, Tom Thumb)

Save Mart Supermarkets, Inc.
800 Standiford Avenue
Modesto, CA 95350
Phone: (209) 577-1600
Fax: (209) 577-3857
http://www.savemart.com
(Includes Save Mart, Lucky Store/ Save Mart, S Mart)

Schnuck Markets, Inc.
11420 Lackland Road
St. Louis, MO 63146
Phone: (314) 994-9900
Fax: (314) 994-4465
http://www.schnucks.com
(Includes Schnuck and Logli Supermarket)

Smart & Final, Inc.
PO Box 512377
Los Angeles, CA 90051
Phone: (323) 869-7606
Fax: (323) 869-7868
http://www.smartandfinal.com
(Includes Smart & Final, Henry's and Sun Harvest)

Spartan Stores, Inc.
850 76th Street SW
Grand Rapids, MI 49315

Phone: (616) 878-2000
Fax: (616) 878-8802
http://www.spartanstores.com
(Includes Glen's Market, Felpausch and Save-A-Lot)

Stater Bros Markets
301 S. Tippecanoe Avenue
San Bernardino, CA 92408
Phone: (909) 733-5000
Fax: (909) 733- 3930
http://www.staterbros.com
(Includes Stater Brothers)

Supervalu, Inc.
11840 Valley View Road
Eden Prairie, MN 55344
Phone: (952) 828-4000
Fax: (952) 828-899
http://www.supervalu.com
(Iincludes Albertsons, Store/ Supervalu, Save-A-Lot, Shaw's)

Target Corporation
1000 Nicollet Mall
Minneapolis, MN 55403
Phone: (612) 304-6073
Fax: (612) 696-5400
http://www.target.com
(Includes Super Target Center)

Tops Markets, Inc.
6363 Main Street
Williamsville, NY 14221
Phone: (716) 635-5000
http://www.topsmarkets.com
(Includes Tops and Martin's Super Food Stores)

Trader Joe's Company
800 S. Shamrock Avenue
Monrovia, CA 91016
Phone: (626) 599-3700
Fax: (626) 301-4431
http://www.traderjoes.com
(Includes Trader Joe's)

United Supermarkets, Inc.
7830 Orlando Avenue
Lubbock, TX 79423
Phone: (806) 791-7457

Fax: (806) 791-7476
http://www.unitedtexas.co
(Includes United, Market Street and Amigos United)

Village Super Market, Inc.
733 Mountain Avenue
Springfield, NJ 07081
Phone: (973) 467-2200
Fax: (973) 467-6582
http://www.shoprite.com
(Includes ShopRite)

Wakefern Food Corp.
600 York Street
Elizabeth, NJ 07207
Phone: (908) 527-3300
Fax: (908) 527-3397
http://www.shoprite.com
(Includes ShopRite and Price Rite)

Wal-mart
702 SW 8th Street
Bentonville, AR 72716
Phone: (479) 273-4000
Fax: (479) 273-4000
http://www.wal-mart.com
(Includes Wal-mart Supercenters)

Wegmans Food Markets, Inc.
1500 Brooks Avenue
Rochester, NY 14603
Phone: (585) 328-2550
Fax: (585) 328-2550
http://www.wegmans.com
(Includes Wegmans)

Weis Markets, Inc.
1000 S. 2nd Street
Sunbury, PA 17801
Phone: (570) 286-4571
Fax: (570) 286-3286
http://www.weis.com
(Includes Weis, Scot's Lo-Cost and Save-A-Lot)

Whole Foods Market
550 Bowie Street
Austin, TX 78703
Phone: (512) 477-4455
Fax: (512) 482-7000

http://www.wholefoods.com
(Includes Whole Foods and Wild
   Oats)

WinCo Foods, Inc.
650 North Armstrong Place
Boise, ID 83704

Phone: (208) 377-0110
Fax: (208) 377- 0474
http://www.wincofoods.com
(Includes Winco)

Winn-Dixie Stores, Inc.
050 Edgewood Court

Jacksonville, FL 32254
Phone: (904) 783-5000
Fax: (904) 370-7224
http://www.winn-dixie.com
(Includes Winn-Dixie and
   SaveRite)

APPENDIX VI
DIRECTORY OF CATALOG COMPANIES

The following is a directory of the corporate offices of selected catalog companies. The classifications of some catalog companies may overlap with those in the chain or department store listing. Be sure to check all of the appendixes when looking for specific catalog companies.

Names, addresses, phone number, fax numbers, and Web sites are included when available. Catalogs are listed alphabetically by name.

Use this list to get started in locating internships, training programs, summer employment or to send your résumé when you are ready to go job hunting.

This list is provided as a starting point. There are many more catalogs located throughout the country. Inclusion or exclusion does not constitute endorsement or the lack of it by the author.

1-800-Flowers.com
1 Old Country Road
Carle Place, NY 11514
Phone: (800) 356-7478
Fax: (516) 237-6060
http://www.1800flowers.com

All American Rider
2811 Mcgaw A
Irvine, CA 92714
Phone: (800) 932-2103
Fax: (800) 932-8701
http://www.allamericanrider.com

Allen-Edmonds Shoe Corporation
201 E. Seven Hills Road
Port Washington, WI 53074
Phone: (262) 235-6000
Fax: (262) 268-7427
http://www.allenedmonds.com

American Girl
8400 Fairway Place
Middleton, WI 53562
Phone: (608) 836-4848
Toll Free: (800)360-1861
Fax: (608) 836-1999
http://www.americangirl.com

Athleta
1450 Technology Lane
Petaluma, CA 94954
Phone: (707) 559-2200
Toll Free: (888) 322-5515

Fax: (707)769-2610
http://www.athleta.com

Avon
1345 Avenue of the Americas
New York, NY 10105
Phone: (212) 282-5000
Fax: (212) 282-6049
http://www.avoncompany.com

Blair Corporation
220 Hickory Street
Warren, PA 16366
Phone: (814) 723-3600
Toll Free: (800) 458-6057
Fax: (814) 726-6376
http://www.blair.com

Bloomingdales, Inc.
1000 3rd Avenue
New York, NY 10022
Phone: (212) 705-2000
http://www.bloomingdales.com

Boker, USA
1550 Balsam Street
Lakewood, CO 80214
Phone: (303) 462-0662
Fax: (303) 462-0668
https://www.bokerusa.com

Boston Proper
6500 Park of Commerce Boulevard
Boca Raton, FL 33487
Phone: (561)241-1700

Fax: (561) 241-1055
http://www.bostonproper.com

Brooks Brothers
346 Madison Avenue
New York, NY 10017
Phone: (212) 682-8800
Fax: (212) 309-7273
http://www.brooksbrothers.com

Brookstone Inc.
1 Innovation Way
Merrimack, NH 03054
Phone: (603) 880-9500
Fax: (603) 577-8005
http://www.brookstone.com

Bath & Body Works
7 Limited Parkway
Reynoldsburg, OH 43068
Phone: (614) 856-6000
Toll Free: (800) 395-1001
Fax: (614) 856-6013
http://www.bathandbodyworks.com

Cabela's
1 Cabela Drive
Sidney, NE 69160
Phone: (308) 254-5505
Fax: (308) 254-4800
http://www.cabelas.com

CaHall's Brown Duck Catalog
P.O. Box 450
Mount Orab, OH 45154

Phone: (800) 445-9675
Fax: (937) 444-6813
http://www.cahallsworkwear.com

Calyx Flowers
Phone: (800) 877-0998
http://www.calyxflowers.com

Campmor, Inc.
400 Corporate Drive
Mahwah, NJ 07430
Phone: (201)825-8300
Fax: (201) 236-3601
http://www.campmor.com

Carvin
12340 World Trade Drive
San Diego, CA 92128
Phone: (858) 487-1600
Toll Free: (800) 854-2235
Fax: (858) 487-7620
http://www.carvin.com

CDW Computer Corporation
200 N. Milwaukee Avenue
Vernon Hills, IL 60061
Phone: (847) 465-6000
http://www.cdw.com

Chadwick's of Boston
35 United Drive
West Bridgewater, MA 02379
Phone: (508) 583-8110
Toll Free: (800) 677-0340
Fax: (508) 588-7994
http://www.chadwicks.com

Charles Keath Ltd.
1265 Oakbrook Drive
Norcross, GA 30093
Phone: (770) 449-3100
Fax: (561) 241-6621
Toll free (800) 388-6565
http://www.charleskeath.com

Chico's
11215 Metro Parkway
Fort Myers, FL 33966
Phone: (239) 277-6200
Fax: (239) 274-4018
http://www.chicos.com

Coldwater Creek
1 Coldwater Creek Drive
Sandpoint, ID 83864
Phone: (208) 263-2266
Fax: (208) 263-1582
http://www.coldwater-creek

Container Store
500 Freeport Parkway
Coppell, TX 75019
Phone: (972) 538-6000
Toll Free: (888) 266-8246
Fax: (972) 538-7623
http://www.containerstore

Crate and Barrel
1250 Techny Road
Northbrook, IL 60062
Phone: (847) 272-2888
Fax: (847) 272-5366
http://www.crateandbarrel.com

Crosstown Traders
3740 E. 34th Street
Tucson, AZ 85713
Phone: (520) 745-4500
Fax: (520) 747-1068
http://www.oldpueblotraders.com

Current USA
1025 E. Woodmen Road
Colorado Springs, CO 80920
Phone: (719) 594-4100
Fax: (719) 531-2283
http://www.currentinc.com

Dean & Duluca
560 Broadway
New York, NY 10012
Phone: (212) 226-6800
Fax: (800) 781-4050
http://www.deandeluca.com

Eddie Bauer
10401 NE 8th Street
Bellevue, WA 98004
Phone: (425) 755-6544
Fax: (425) 755-7696
http://www.eddiebauer

Donna Salyers Fabulous Furs Inc.
25 W Robbins Street
Covington, KY 41011

Phone: (859) 291-3300
Fax: (800) 292-4331
http://www.fabulousfurs.com

Figi's Fruit and Nuts
3200 South Maple Avenue
Marshfield, WI 54449
Phone: (715) 387-1771
Fax. (715) 384-1129
http://www.figis.com

Fingerhut
7777 Golden Triangle Drive
Eden Prairie, MN 55344
Phone: (952) 656-3700
Fax: (952) 656-4112
http://www.fingerhut.com

Frederick's of Hollywood
6255 W. Sunset Boulevard
Hollywood, CA 90028
Phone: (323) 466-5151
Fax: (323) 464-5149
http://www.fredericks.com

Gateway
7565 Irvine Center Drive
Irvine, CA 92618
Phone: (949) 471-7000
Fax: (949) 471-7041
http://www.gateway.com

Green Mountain Coffee
33 Coffee Lane
Waterbury, VT 05676
Phone: (802) 244-5621
Fax: (802) 244-5436
http://www.GreenMountainCoffee.
com

Hammacher Schlemmer
9307 N. Milwaukee Avenue
Niles, IL 60714
Phone: (847) 581-8600
Fax: (847) 581-8616
http://www.hammacher.com

Harry and David
2500 S. Pacific Highway
Medford, OR 97501
Phone: (541) 864-2362
Fax: (541) 864-2194
http://www.harryanddavid.com

HCI Direct, Inc
Tillman Drive
Bensalem, PA 19020
Phone: (215) 244-9600
Fax: (215) 244-0328
http://www.hcidirect.com

Hello Direct
75 Northeastern Boulevard
Nashua, NH 03062
Phone: (603) 598-1100
Fax: (800) 456-2566
http://www.hello-direct

Home Depot
2455 Paces Ferry Road, NW
Atlanta, GA 30339
Phone: (770) 433-8211
Fax: (770) 384-2356
http://www.homedepot.com

Horchaw
1618 Main Street
Dallas, TX 75201
Phone: (214) 743-7600
Fax: (214) 573-5320
http://www.horchow.com

Hy Cite Locations
333 Holtzman Road
Madison, WI 53713
Phone: (608) 273-3373
Fax: (608) 273-0936
http://www.hycite.com

Indiana Botanic Gardens
3401 W. 37th Avenue
Hobart, IN 46342
Phone: (219) 947-4040
Fax: (219) 947-4148
http://www.botanicchoice.com

Insight Enterprises
1305 W. Auto Drive
Tempe, AZ 85284
Phone: (480) 902-1001
Fax: (480) 902-1157
http://www.insight.com

IKEA
Olof Palmestraat 1
NL-2616 LN Delft, Sweden
Phone: +46-42-267-100
http://www.ikea

Intimate Brands
3 Limited Parkway
Columbus, OH 43230
Phone: (614) 415-8000
Fax: (614) 415-7278
http://www.intimatebrands.com

J. Crew Group
770 Broadway
New York, NY 10003
Phone: (212) 209-2500
Fax: (212) 209-2666
http://www.jcrew.com

J.C. Penney
6501 Legacy Drive
Plano, TX 75024
Phone: (972) 431-1000
Fax: (972) 431-1362
http://www.jcpenney.net

J. Jill Group
4 Batterymarch Park
Quincy, MA 02169
Phone: (617) 376-4300
Fax: (617) 769-0177
http://www.jjill.com

Just My Size
1000 E. Hanes Mill Road
Winston-Salem, NC 27105
Phone: (336) 519-4400
http://www.jms.com

King Arthur Flour
135 Route 5 South
Norwich, VT 05055
Phone: (802) 649-3881
Fax: (802) 649-3365
http://www.kingarthurflour.com

Lamps Plus
20250 Plummer Street
Chatsworth, CA 91311
Phone: (818) 886-5267
Fax: (818) 886-1011
http://www.lampsplus.com

LL Bean, Inc.
3 Campus Drive
Freeport, ME 04033
Phone: (800) 441-5713
Fax: (207) 552-3080
http://www.llbean.com

Lands' End
1 Lands' End Lane
Dodgeville, WI 53595
Phone: (800) 963-4816
Fax: (608) 935-4831
http://www.landsend.com

Levenger
420 S. Congress Avenue
Delray Beach, FL 33445
Phone: (888) 592-7461
Fax: (561) 266-2181
http://www.levenger.com

Lillian Vernon Corporation
2600 International Parkway
Virginia Beach, VA 23452
Phone: (757) 427-7700
Fax: (757) 427-7819
http://www.lillianvernon.com

Miles Kimball
250 City Center
Oshkosh, WI 54906

Neiman Marcus
1618 Main Street
Dallas, TX 75201
Phone: (888) 888-4757
Fax: (214) 573-5320
http://www.neimanmarcus.com

Newport News
711 3rd Avenue
New York, NY 10017
Phone: (212) 986-2585
Fax: (212) 916-8281
http://www.newport-news.com

New York & Company
450 W. 33rd Street
New York, NY 10001
Phone: (212) 884-2000
Fax: (212) 884-2396
http://www.nyandcompany.com

OfficeMax Inc.
263 Shuman Boulevard
Naperville, IL 60563
Phone: (630) 438-7800
http://www.officemax.com

Patagonia
259 W. Santa Clara Street
Ventura, CA 93001
Phone: (800) 638-6464
Fax: (800) 543-5522
http://www.patagonia.com

Plow and Hearth
1107 Emmet Street, North
Charlottesville, VA 22903
Phone: (800) 494-7544
http://www.plowhearth.com

Ross-Simons
9 Ross-Simons Drive
Cranston, RI 02920
Phone: (800) 835-0919
Fax: (401) 463-8599
http://www.ross-simons.com

Santa's Smokehouse
2400 Davis Road
Fairbanks, AK 99701
Phone: (907) 456-3885
Fax: (907) 456-3889
http://www.santassmokehouse.com

Sears, Roebuck and Company
3333 Beverly Road
Hoffman Estates, IL 60179
Phone: (847) 286-2500
Fax: (800) 326-0485
http://www.sears.com

SkyMall
1520 E. Pima Street
Phoenix, AZ 85034
Phone: (800) 759-6255

Fax: (602) 254-6075
http://www.skymall.com

Spiegel
711 3rd Avenue
New York, NY 10017
Phone: (212) 986-2585
Fax: (212) 916-8281
http://www.spiegel.com

Swiss Colony
1112 7th Avenue
Monroe, WI 53566
Phone: (608)328-8400
Fax: (608)328-8457
http://www.swisscolony.com

Talbots
1 Talbots Drive
Hingham, MA 02043
Phone: (800) 825-2687
Fax: (781) 741-4369
http://www.talbots.com

The Popcorn Factory
13970 W. Laurel Drive
Lake Forest, IL 60045
Phone: (847) 362-00278
Fax: (847) 362-9680
http://www.thepopcornfactory.
  com

Urban Outfitters
5000 S. Broad Street
Philadelphia, PA 19112
Phone: (215) 454-5500
Fax: (215) 454-5163
http://www.urbanoutfittersinc

Vermont Country Store
5650 Main Street
Manchester Center, VT 05255
Phone: (802) 362-8460
Fax: (802) 362-8288
http://www.vermontcountrystore.
  com

Victoria's Secret
8655 E. Broad Street
Reynoldsburg, OH 43068
Phone: (800) 888-1500
Fax: (614) 337-5075
http://www.victoriassecret.com

Williams Sonoma, Inc.
3250 Van Ness Avenue
San Francisco, CA 94109
Phone: (415) 421-7900
Fax: (415) 616-8359
http://www.williams-sonomainc.com

Woodcraft Supply
1177 Rosemar Road
Parkersburg, WV 26102
Phone: (800) 225-1153
Fax: (304) 428-8271
http://www.woodcraft.com

Young Pecan Company
1200 Pecan Street
Florence, SC 29501
Phone: (800) 829-6864
Fax: (843) 664-2344
http://www.youngpecan.com

APPENDIX VII
DIRECTORY OF TELEVISION SHOPPING CHANNELS

The following is a directory of the corporate offices of selected television shopping channels. Names, addresses, phone numbers, fax numbers, and Web addresses are included when available.

Use this list to get started locating internships, training programs, summer employment or to send your résumé when you are ready to go job hunting.

This list is provided as a beginning. Inclusion or exclusion does not constitute endorsement or the lack of it by the author.

Access Television
2600 Michelson Drive
Irvine, CA 92612
Phone: (949) 263-9900
Fax: (949) 622-6295
http://www.AccessTV.com

HSN (Home Shopping Network)
1 HSN Drive
St. Petersburg, FL 33729
Phone: (727) 872-1000
http://www.hsn.com

JTV (Jewelry Television)
10001 Kingston Pike
Knocksvill, TN 37822
Phone: (800) 619-3000
http://www.jewelrytelevision.com

QVC
1200 Wilson Drive
West Chester, PA 19380
Phone: (484)701-1000
Fax: (484) 701-8170
http://www.qvc.com

Shop At Home, Inc.
14101 Southcross Drive West
Burnsville, MN 55337
Phone: (888-) 870-6342
http://www.sathsite.com

Shop NBC
6740 Shady Oak Road
Eden Prairie, MN 55344
Phone: (952) 943-6000
Fax: (952) 943-6711
http://www.shopnbc.com

ValueVision Media
6740 Shady Oak Road
Eden Prairie, MN 55344
Phone: (952)943-6000
Fax: (952) 943-6711
http://www.valuevisionmedia.com

APPENDIX VIII
DIRECTORY OF MANUFACTURERS AND OTHER COMPANIES

The following is a directory of the corporate offices of selected U.S. companies and manufacturers. The classification may overlap with those in other appendixes. This listing may be valuable to those seeking careers in the wholesale as well as retail trade.

Names, addresses, phone numbers, toll-free numbers, fax numbers, Web sites, and e-mail addresses are included when available. Companies are listed alphabetically by name.

Use this list to get started in locating internships, training programs, summer employment or to send your resume when you are ready to go job hunting.

This list is provided as a starting point. There are many more manufacturers and other companies located throughout the country. Inclusion or exclusion does not constitute endorsement or the lack of it by the author.

A&W Restaurants, Inc.
1900 Colonel Sanders Lane
Louisville, KY 40213
Phone: (866) 456-2929
http://www.awrestaurants.com

A.J. Wright
770 Cochituate Road
Framingham, MA 01701
Phone: (877) 746-7259
http://www.aj-wright.com

AAMCO Transmissions, Inc.
201 Gibraltar Road
Horsham, PA 19044
Phone: (610) 668-2900 or (800) 292-8500
Fax: (610) 664-5897
E-mail: awright@AAMCO.com
http://www.aamco.com

Abbott Laboratories
100 Abbott Park Road
Abbott Park, IL 60064
Phone: (800) 255-5162
http://www.abbott.com

Abbott Nutrition Products Division
625 Cleveland Ave.
Columbus, OH 43215
Phone: (800) 227-5767

Fax: (614) 624-7616
http://www.abbottnutrition.com

ABC, Inc.
500 S. Buena Vista Street
Burbank, CA 91521
Phone: (818) 460-7477
http://www.abc.com

Accor North America
4001 International Parkway
Carrollton, TX 75007
Phone: (972) 360-9000
http://www.accor-na.com

ACE USA Companies
PO Box 1000
436 Walnut Street
Philadelphia, PA 19106
Phone: (215) 640-4555
Fax: (215) 640-2489
http://www.ace-ina.com

Activision Blizzard
6060 Center Drive
Los Angeles, CA 90045
Phone: (800) 757-7707
http://www.activisionblizzaRoadcom

Adidas America
5055 North Greeley Avenue
Portland, OR 97217
Phone: (800) 448-1796

Fax: (971) 234-4515
E-mail: consumer.relations@adidas.com
http://www.adidas.com

Adobe Systems Inc.
345 Park Avenue
San Jose, CA 95110
Phone: (800) 833-6687
Fax: (408) 537-6000
http://www.adobe.com

Aerus Electrolux Corporation
300 East Valley Drive
Bristol, VA 24201
Phone: (800) 243-9078
Fax: (276) 645-2863
E-mail: customerservice@aerusonline.com
http://www.aerusonline.com

AETNA, Inc.
151 Farmington Avenue
Hartford, CT 06156
Phone: (800) US-AETNA
http://www.aetna.com

Alamo Rent A Car
8421 Saint John Industrial Drive
Saint Louis, MO 63114
Phone: (800) 445-5664
E-mail: crelations@alamo.com
http://www.alamo.com

Alberto Culver Co.
2525 Armitage Avenue
Melrose Park, IL 60160
Phone: (800) 333-0005
Fax: (708) 450-2299
http://www.alberto.com

Albertsons Inc.
250 Parkcenter Boulevard
Boise, ID 83706
Phone: (877) 932-7948
http://www.albertsons.com

Alcon Laboratories, Inc.
6201 South Freeway
Fort Worth, TX 76134
Phone: (800) 757-9780
Fax: (817) 551-3092
E-mail: consumeraffairs.ft.worth@
alconlabs.com
http://www.alconlabs.com

Allied Van Lines, Inc.
PO Box 4403
Chicago, IL 60680
Phone: (800) 510-7469
Fax: (630) 717-3123
E-mail: custsvc@alliedvan.com
http://www.allied.com

Allstate Insurance Co.
2775 Sanders Road
Northbrook, IL 60062
Phone: (800) 255-7828
Fax: (847) 418-5966
http://www.allstate.com

Alltel Corporation
2001 NW Sammamish Road
Issaquah, WA 98027
Phone: (425) 313-5200
http://www.alltel.com

Alltel Corporation
One Allied Drive
Little Rock, AR 72202
Phone: (800) 255-8351
http://www.alltel.com

Amana Appliances
553 Benson Road
Benton Harbor, MI 549022
Phone: (800) 628-5782
http://www.amana.com

Amazon.com, Inc.
PO Box 81226
Seattle, WA 98108
Phone: (800) 201-7575
Fax: (206) 266-2335
http://www.amazon.com

AMD
One AMD Place
PO Box 3453
Sunnyvale, CA 94088
Phone: (800) 538-8450
http://www.amd.com

America Online, Inc.
22000 AOL Way
Dulles, VA 20166
Phone: (800) 827-6364
Fax: (703) 918-1400
http://www.aol.com

American Airlines, Inc.
PO Box 619612
MD 2400
Dallas/Fort Worth Airport, TX
75261
Phone: (817) 967-2000
Fax: (817) 967-4162
http://www.aa.com

**American Automobile
Association**
1000 AAA Drive
Heathrow, FL 32746
Phone: (407) 444-8391
Fax: (407) 444-8416
http://www.aaa.com

American Express Co.
777 American Express Way
Ft. Lauderdale, FL 33337
Phone: (212) 640-2000
http://www.americanexpress.com

American Greetings Corp.
One American Road
Cleveland, OH 44144
Phone: (800) 777-4891
E-mail: consumer.relations@
amgreetings.com
http://www.corporate.american
greetings.com

American Standard, Inc.
PO Box 6820
1 Centennial Plaza
Piscataway, NJ 08855

Phone: (800) 442-1902
Fax: (732) 980-6170
http://www.americanstandard-us.com

American Tourister
575 West Street
Mansfield, MA 02048
Phone: (800) 262-8282
http://www.americantourister.com

**America's Favorite Chicken Co.
(AFC Enterprises)**
5555 Glenridge Connector, NE
Atlanta, GA 30342
Phone: (800) 222-5857
http://www.afce.com

Amgen, Inc.
One Amgen Center Drive
Thousand Oaks, CA 91320
Phone: (800) 28-AMGEN
Fax: (805) 447-1010
http://www.amgen.com

Amway Corporation
7575 Fulton Street East
Ada, MI 49355
Phone: (800) 253-6500
Fax: (616) 682-4000
E-mail: order.support@quixtar.com
http://www.amway.com

Andersen Windows, Inc.
100 Fourth Avenue North
Bayport, MN 55003
Phone: (888) 888-7020
Fax: (651) 264-5827
http://www.andersenwindows.com

Anheuser-Busch, Inc.
One Busch Place
St. Louis, MO 63118
Phone: (800) 342-5283
http://www.budweiser.com

Apple Computer, Inc.
1 Infinite Loop
Cupertino, CA 95014
Phone: (800) 676-2775
http://www.apple.com

Applebee's
11201 Renner Boulevard
Lenexa, KS 66219
Phone: (913) 890-0100
http://www.applebees.com

Appleseed's
PO Box 176
Jessup, PA 18434
Phone: (888) 430-5711
Fax: (800) 755-7557
E-mail: CustomerService@Apple
seeds.com
http://www.appleseeds.com

Arby's Restaurant Group, Inc.
1155 Perimeter Center West
Atlanta, GA 30338
Phone: (678) 514-4100
Fax: (678) 514-5347
http://www.arbys.com

Arizona Mail Order
PO Box 27800
Tucson, AZ 85713
Phone: (800) 362-8410
Fax: (800) 964-1975
E-mail: CustomerService@
OldPuebloTraders.com
http://www.oldpueblotraders.com

Armstrong World Industries, Inc.
PO Box 3001
2500 Columbia Avenue
Lancaster, PA 17604
Phone: (800) 233-3823
Fax: (717) 396-4270
http://www.armstrong.com

A.T. Cross Company
One Albion Road
Lincoln, RI 02865
Phone: (800) 282-7677
Fax: (401) 334-4351
E-mail: consumerre@cross.com
http://www.cross.com

AT&T
Glenridge Highlands Two
5565 Glenridge Connector
Atlanta, GA 30342
Phone: (800) 331-0500
Fax: (888) 938-4715
http://www.att.com

AT&T
675 West Peachtree Street, NE
Atlanta, GA 30375

Phone: (800) 346-9000
Fax: (404) 584-6545
E-mail: Headquarters.Appeals@
att.com
http://www.att.com

AT&T Wireless Services, Inc.
http://www.attwireless.com

AT&T, Inc.
175 E. Houston Street
San Antonio, TX 78205
Phone: (800) 464-7928
Fax: (210) 351-2071
http://www.att.sbc.com

Ateeco, Inc.
PO Box 606
600 East Center Street
Shenandoah, PA 17976
Phone: (800) 233-3170
Fax: (570) 462-1392
http://www.pierogies.com

Atlas World Group, Inc
1212 St. George Road
Evansville, IN 47711
Phone: (800) 638-9797
Fax: (812) 421-7129
http://www.atlasworldgroup.com

Avis Rent-A-Car System
4500 South 129th East Avenue
PO Box 699000
Tulsa, OK 74169-9000
Phone: (800) 352-7900
Fax: (918) 621-4819
E-mail: custserv@avis.com
http://www.avis.com

Avon Products, Inc.
1251 Avenue of the Americas
New York, NY 10020
Phone: (800) 367-2866
http://www.avon.com

AXA Financial, Inc.
1290 Avenue of the Americas
New York, NY 10104
Phone: (212) 554-1234
http://www.equitable.com

B&H Photo Video
420 9th Avenue
New York, NY 10001
Phone: (800) 336-7408
Fax: (212) 239-7759
http://www.bhphotovideo.com

Bacardi U.S.A., Inc.
Consumer Services
2100 Biscayne Boulevard
Miami, FL 33137
Phone: (800) BACARDI
http://www.bacardi.com

Bali Company
PO Box 450
Winston-Salem, NC 27102
Phone: (800) 225-4872
http://www.balicompany.com

Bally Total Fitness Corporation
PO Box 1090
Norwalk, CA 90651
Phone: (800) 515-2582
Fax: (773) 693-2982
http://www.ballyfitness.com

Bank of America Corporation
100 North Tryon Street
Mail Code NC1-007-58-16
Charlotte, NC 28255
Phone: (800) 432-1000
http://www.bankofamerica.com

BankUnited
7815 NW 148th Street
Miami Lakes, FL 33016
Phone: (877) 779-2265
http://www.bankunited.com

Baskin Robbins
130 Royall Street
Canton, MA 02021
Phone: (781) 737-3000
Fax: (781) 737-4000
http://www.baskinrobbins.com

Bass Pro Shops, Inc.
2500 East Kearney
Springfield, MO 65898
Phone: (800) 227-7776

Fax: (417) 873-5060
http://www.basspro.com

Bath & Body Works
Seven Limited Parkway East
Reynoldsburg, OH 43068
Phone: (800) 756-5005
http://www.bathandbodyworks.com

Bayer HealthCare Consumer Care
36 Columbia Road
PO Box 1910
Morristown, NJ 07962
Phone: (800) 331-4536
Fax: (973) 408-8000
http://www.consumercare.bayer.com

BD (Becton, Dickinson and Company)
1 Becton Drive MC376
Franklin Lakes, NJ 07417
Phone: (201) 847-6800
http://www.bd.com

Bear Creek Corp.
2500 South Pacific Highway
PO Box 299
Medford, OR 97501
Phone: (800) 345-5655 (Harry and David)
Fax: (541) 776-2194
http://www.harryanddavid.com

Beech-Nut Nutrition Corporation
13023 Tesson Ferry Road
St Louis, MO 63128
Phone: (800) 233-2468
Fax: (314) 436-7679
http://www.beechnut.com

Beiersdorf Inc
Wilton Corporate Center
187 Danbury Road
Wilton, CT 06897
Phone: (800) 227-4703
Fax: (203) 563-5890
http://www.beiersdorf.com

Bellisio
PO Box 16630
Duluth, MN 55816

Phone: (218) 723-5555
Fax: (218) 723-5580
http://www.bellisiofoods.com

Benihana Inc.
8685 Northwest 53rd Terrace
Miami, FL 33166
Phone: (800) 327-3369
Fax: (305) 592-6371
E-mail: customerrelations@benihana.com
http://www.benihana.com

Best Buy Company, Inc.
7601 Penn Avenue South
Richfield, MN 55423
Phone: (888) 237-8289
http://www.bestbuy.com

Best Foods
2816 S. Kilbourn Aveue
Chicago, IL 60623
Phone: (773) 247-5800
Fax: (773) 247-6146
http://www.bestfoods.com

Best Western International, Inc.
PO Box 42007
Phoenix, AZ 85080
Phone: (800) 528-1238
Fax: (623) 780-6199
http://www.bestwestern.com

BIC Corp
One Bick Way
Shelton, CT 06484
Phone: (203) 783-2000
http://www.bicworld.com

Big Lot Stores, Inc.
300 Phillipi Road
Columbus, OH 43228
Phone: (800) 877-1253
http://www.biglots.com

Birds Eye Foods, Inc.
P.O. Box 20670
Rochester, NY 14602
Phone: (800) 563-1786
http://www.birdseyefoods.com

Bissell Homecare, Inc.
2345 Walker Avenue, NW

Grand Rapids, MI 49544
Phone: (800) 237-7691
http://www.bissell.com

Black and Decker (US) Inc.
101 Schilling Road
Hunt Valley, MD 21031
Phone: (800) 544-6986
http://www.blackanddecker.com

Blockbuster Entertainment Corp.
1201 Elm Street
Dallas, TX 75270
Phone: (866) 692-2789
E-mail: online.comsumerrelations@blockbuster.com
http://www.blockbuster.com

Bloomingdale's, Inc.
1000 Third Avenue
New York, NY 10022
Phone: (212) 705-2000
http://www.bloomingdales.com

Bob Evans Farms, Inc.
3776 South High Street
Columbus, OH 43207
Phone: (800) 272-7675
Fax: (614) 497-4330
E-mail: tammy.myers@bobevans.com
http://www.bobevans.com

BP Corporation
PO Box 3011
Naperville, IL 60563
Phone: (800) 333-3991
Fax: (630) 300-5254
E-mail: bpconsum@bp.com
http://www.bp.com

Braun
Proctor & Gamble
1 Gillette Park
Boston, MA 02127
Phone: (800) 272-8611
http://www.braun.com

Breathe Right Company
CNS, Inc.
20 Troy Road
Whippany, NJ 07981

Phone: (800) 858-6673
E-mail: cnsinfo@consumerfirst.com
http://www.breatheright.com

Bridgestone Firestone LLC
PO Box 7988
Chicago, IL 60680
Phone: (800) 367-3872
Fax: (204) 987-1359
http://www.firestonecompleteauto
  care.com

Bristol-Myers Squibb Company
PO Box 4000
Princeton, NJ 08543
Phone: (800) 332-2056
Fax: (609) 897-6016
http://www.bms.com

**Brother International
  Corporation**
100 Somerset Corporation
  Boulevard
Bridgewater, NJ 08807
Phone: (877) 276-8437
Fax: (877) 268-9575
http://www.brother-usa.com

Brown Shoe Company, Inc.
8300 Maryland Avenue
St. Louis, MO 63105
Phone: (800) 766-6465
Fax: (314)854-4274
E-mail: info@brownshoe.com
http://www.brownshoe.com

**Brown-Forman Beverages
  Worldwide**
PO Box 1080
Louisville, KY 40201
Phone: (800) 753-4567
http://www.brown-forman.com

Brunswick Corporation
1 North Field Court
Lake Forest, IL 60045
Phone: (847) 735-4700
Fax: (847) 735-4765
E-mail: services@brunswick.com
http://www.brunswick.com

Buca di Beppo
Buca, Inc.

1300 Nicollet Mall
Minneapolis, MN 55403
Phone: (866) 328-2822
Fax: (612) 827-6446
E-mail: famiglia@bucainc.com

Budget Rent A Car System, Inc.
4500 S. 129th East Avenue
PO Box 69084
Tulsa, OK 74169
Phone: (800) 214-6094
http://www.budget.com

Bulova Corporation
One Bulova Avenue
Woodside, NY 11377
Phone: (718) 204-4603
Fax: (718) 204-3546
http://www.bulova.com

**Burlington Coat Factory Direct
  Corporation**
1830 Route 130 North
Burlington, NJ 08016
Phone: (888) 223-2628
Fax: (609) 387-7071
http://www.burlingtoncoatfactory.
  com

Bush Brothers & Company
PO Box 52330
Knoxville, TN 37950
Phone: (865) 558-5445
E-mail: letters@bushbros.com
http://www.bushbeans.com

Cabela's Government Outfitter
Government Sales
One Cabela Drive
Sidney, NE 69160
Phone: (800) 242-1596
Fax: (888) 248-8311
E-mail: government@cabelas.com
http://www.cabelas.com

Cablevision Systems, Inc.
1111 Stewart Avenue
Bethpage, NY 11714
Phone: (800) 244-2328
http://www.cablevision.com

Calvin Klein
1001 Frontier Road

Bridgewater, NJ 08807
Phone: (212) 719-2600
Fax: (212) 221-4541
http://www.calvinklein.com

Campbell Soup Co.
One Campbell Place
Camden, NJ 08103
Phone: (800) 257-8443
http://www.campbellsoup.com

Candelis
18821 Bardeen Avenue
Irvine, CA 92612
Phone: (800) 800-8600
Fax: (949) 752-7317
E-mail: info@candelis.com
http://www.candelis.com

Canon USA, Inc
One Canon Plaza
Lake Success, NY 11042
Phone: (800) 828-4040
http://www.usa.canon.com

Captain D's Seafood
1717 Elm Hill Pike
Nashville, TN 37210
Phone: (800) 314-4819 opt. 1
Fax: (615) 231-2309
http://www.captainds.com

Carrier Air Conditioning Co.
PO Box 4808
Syracuse, NY 13221
Phone: (800) 227-7437
Fax: (315) 432-6620
http://www.global.carrier.com

Casio, Inc.
570 Mt. Pleasant Avenue
Dover, NJ 07801
Phone: (800) 962-2746
Fax: (973) 537-8926
http://www.casio.com

Casual Male Retail Group
555 Turnpike Street
Canton, MA 02021
Phone: (800) 767-0319
Fax: (800) 225-6072
http://www.cmrginc.com

Chanel, Inc.
9 West 57th Street
New York, NY 10019
Phone: (800) 550-0005
http://www.chanel.com

Chevron Corporation
6001 Bollinger Canyon Road
San Ramon, CA 94583
Phone: (800) 962-1223
http://www.chevron.com

Chicken of the Sea International
9330 Scranton Road
PO Box 85568
San Diego, CA 92121
Phone: (800) 456-1511
Fax: (858) 597-4248
http://www.chickenofthesea.com

Church & Dwight Company, Inc.
469 North Harrison Street
Princeton, NJ 08543-5297
Phone: (800) 524-1328
http://www.churchdwight.com

CIBA Vision
11460 Johns Creek Parkway
Duluth, GA 30097
Phone: (800) 227-1524
http://www.cibavision.com

Cingular Wireless
175 E Houston Street
San Antonio, TX 78205
Phone: (800) 331-0500
Fax: (210) 351-2071
http://www.wireless.att.com

Circuit City Stores, Inc.
9954 Mayland Drive
Richmond, VA 23233
Phone: (800) 843-2489
http://www.circuitcity.com

Citizen Watch Company of America, Inc.
1000 W. 190 Street
Torrance, CA 90502
Fax: (310) 532-8171

E-mail: customerservice_us@citizenwatch.com
http://www.citizenwatch.com

Clopay Building Products Co. (a subsidiary of Griffon Company)
8585 Duke Boulevard
Mason, OH 45040
Phone: (800) 225-6729
http://www.clopaydoor.com

Clorox Company
1221 Broadway
Oakland, CA 94612
Phone: (800) 292-2200
http://www.thecloroxcompany.com

Coats & Clark Inc
PO Box 12229
Greenville, SC 29612
Phone: (800) 648-1479
http://www.coatsandclark.com

The Coca-Cola Co.
PO Box 1734
Atlanta, GA 30301
Phone: (800) 438-2653
Fax: (404) 676-4903
E-mail: crreview@na.ko.com
http://www.thecocacolacompany.com

Coldwell Banker Real Estate Corporation
One Campus Drive
Parsippany, NJ 07054
Phone: (877) 373-3829
http://www.coldwellbanker.com

Colgate-Palmolive Company
300 Park Avenue
New York, NY 10022
Phone: (800) 468-6502
Fax: (212) 310-3243
http://www.colgate.com

Colonial Penn Life Insurance
399 Market Street
Philadelphia, PA 19181
Phone: (877) 877-8052.
http://www.colonialpenn.com

The Columbia House Company
PO Box 91602
Indianapolis, IN 46291
Phone: (800) 562-4046
Fax: (800) 590-6656
http://www.columbiahouse.com

Combe Incorporated
1101 Westchester Avenue
White Plains, NY 10604
Phone: (914) 694-5454
Fax: (914) 696-6233
http://www.combe.com

ConAgra Foods
P.O. Box 3768
Omaha, NE 68103
Phone: (800) 722-1344
Fax: (402) 595-7880
http://www.conagrafoods.com

Conair Cuisinart Corporation
150 Milford Road
East Windsor, NJ 08520
Phone: (800) 366-5391
Fax: (609) 426-9475
http://www.conair.com

Congoleum Corporation
3700 Quakerbridge Road
PO Box 3127
Mercerville, NJ 08619
Phone: (800) 274-3266
http://www.congoleum.com

ConocoPhillips
600 N. Dairy Ashford Road
Houston, TX 77079
Phone: (281) 293-1000
http://www.conocophillips.com

Continental Tire North America, Inc.
1800 Continental Boulevard
Charlotte, NC 28273
Phone: (800) 847-3349
Fax (888) 847-3329
http://www.continentaltire.com

Contour Beds
3550 Tillman Drive
Bensalem, PA 19020
Phone: (800) 828-1033
Fax: (215) 639-4891

E-mail: consumeraf@aol.com
http://www.contour.com

Converse, Inc.
One High Street
North Andover, MA 01845
Phone: (800) 547-2667
E-mail: ewtore@converce.com
http://www.converse.com

Conwood Company, L.P.
813 Ridge Lake Boulevard
Memphis, TN 38120
Phone: (800) 238-5990
http://www.cwdlp.com

Coors Brewing Co.
311 10th Street
Golden, CO 80401
Phone: (800) 642-6116
Fax: (303) 277-5415
http://www.coors.com

Corel Corporation
46430 Fremont Boulevard
Fremont, CA 94538
Phone: (613) 728-8200
http://www.corel.com

Coty Inc.
406 American Road
Morris Plains, NJ 07950
Phone: (800) 715-4023
Fax: (973) 290-8913
http://www.coty.com

Creative Labs
1523 Cimarron Plaza
Stillwater, OK 74075
Phone: (405) 742-6622
http://www.creativehelp.com

Cuisinart
One Cumming Point
Stanford, CT 06902
Phone: (800) 726-0190
Fax: (203) 975-4660
E-mail: cuisinart@conair.com
http://www.cuisinart.com

Cumberland Packing Corporation
Sweet 'N Low Division

Two Cumberland Street
Brooklyn, NY 11205
Phone: (718) 858-4200
Fax: (718) 260-9017
http://www.sweetnlow.com

Current, Inc.
1005 East Woodmen Road
Colorado Springs, CO 80920
Phone: (719) 594-4100
http://www.currentinc.com

Dairy Queen Corporation
7505 Metro Boulevard
Minneapolis, MN 55439
Phone: (952) 830-0200
http://www.dairyqueen.com

The Dannon Co., Inc.
PO Box 90296
Allentown, PA 18109
Phone: (877) 326-6668
http://www.dannon.com

Danskin
4075 E Market Street
York, PA 17402
Phone: (800) 288-6749
E-mail: edanskin@danskin.com
http://www.danskin.com

DAP Products, Inc
2400 Boston Street
Baltimore, MD 21224
Phone: (800) 543-3840
Fax: (410) 534-2650
http://www.dap.com

Deere & Company
One John Deere Place
Moline, IL 61265
Phone: (309) 765-8000
http://www.deere.com

Del Laboratories, Inc.
Consumer Relations
PO Box 9357
Uniondale, NY 11553
Phone: (516) 844-2020
Fax: (516) 349-0904
E-mail: dell@dellabs.com
http://www.dellabs.com

Del Monte Foods Company
PO Box 80
Pittsburgh, PA 15230
Phone: (800) 543-3090
http://www.delmonte.com

Dell Inc.
1 Dell Way
Round Rock, TX 78682
Phone: (800) 624-9897
http://www.dell.com

Delta Faucets Company
55 East 111th Street
PO Box 40980
Indianapolis, IN 46280
Phone: (800) 345-3358
http://www.deltafaucet.com

Deneba Software
8550 NW 33rd Street
Miami, FL 33122
Phone: (800) 733-6322
Fax: (305) 406-9802
http://www.acdsystems.com

The Dial Corporation
15101 North Scottsdale Road
Scottsdale, AZ 85254
Phone: (480) 754-3425
http://www.dialcorp.com

Diners Club International
7958 S. Chester
Englewood, CO 80112
Phone: (800) 234-6377
Fax: (303) 649-2891
http://www.dinersclub.com

DIRECTV Enterprises, Inc.
2230 E. Imperial Highway
El Segundo, CA 90245
Phone: (800) 494-4388
http://www.directtv.com

Discover Financial Services, Inc.
2500 Lake Cook Road
Riverwoods, IL 60015
Phone: (800) 347-2683
Fax: (224)405-4993
http://www.discoverfinancial.com

D-Link Systems, Incorporated
17595 Mt. Hermann Street
Fountain Valley, CA 92708
Phone: (800) 326-1688
Fax: (866) 743-4684
E-mail: customerservice@dlink.com
http://www.dlink.com

Dole Food Company, Inc.
One Dole Drive
Westlake Village, CA 91362
Phone: (800) 232-8888
Fax: (818) 874-4997
http://www.dole.com

Dollar Rent A Car Systems, Inc.
CIMS 7082
5330 East 31st St.
PO Box 33167
Tulsa, OK 74153
Phone: (800) 800-5252
Fax: (918) 669-8596
http://www.dollar.com

Domino's Pizza, Inc.
30 Frank Lloyd Wright Drive
PO Box 997
Ann Arbor, MI 48106
Phone: (734) 930-3030
http://www.dominos.com

Dot Hill Systems Corporation
2200 Faraday Avenue
Carlsbad, CA 92008
Phone: (760) 931-5500
Fax: (760) 931-5527
E-mail: mark.odell@dothill.com
http://www.dothill.com

Dr Pepper/Seven Up, Inc.
PO Box 869077
Plano, TX 75086
Phone: (800) 527-7096
http://www.dpsu.com

Dreyer's Grand Ice Cream
5929 College Avenue
Oakland, CA 94618
Phone: (877) 437-3937 (Dreyer's)
Phone: (888) 590-3397 (Edy's)
Phone: (800) 767-0120 (Häagen-Dazs)

Phone: (800) 441-2525 (Nestlé Ice Cream)
Phone: (888) 442-3722 (The Skinny Cow)
http://www.icecream.com

DS Waters of America
4170 Tanners Creek Drive
Flowery Branch, Georgia 30542
Phone: (800) 492-8377
E-mail: customerservice@water.com
http://www.water.com

Dunkin Donuts
130 Royall Street
Canton, MA 02021
Phone: (800) 859-5339
http://www.dunkindonuts.com

Dunlop Tire Corp.
P.O. Box 1109
Buffalo, NY 14240
Phone: (716) 639-5439
http://www.dunloptire.com

DuPont Co.
Chestnut Run Plaza - 705/GS38
Wilmington, DE 19880
Phone: (800) 441-7515
E-mail: info@dupont.com
http://www.dupont.com

Duracell North America
Berkshire Corporate Park
Bethel, CT 06801
Phone: (800) 551-2355
Fax: (800) 796-4565
http://www.duracell.com

DWS Scudder
PO Box 219669
210 W 10th Street
Kansas City, MO 64105
E-mail: service@dws.com
http://www.dws-scudder.com

Eagle Family Foods
735 Taylor Road
Suite 200
Gahanna, OH 43230
Phone: (877) 645-6681

Fax: (614) 501-4295
http://www.eaglefamilyfoods.com

EarthLink, Inc.
1375 Peachtree Street, NE
Atlanta, GA 30309
Phone: (800) 719-4660
E-mail: support@earthlink.net
http://www.earthlink.net

Eastman Kodak Company
343 State Street
Rochester, NY 14650
Phone: (800) 242-2424
http://www.kodak.com

e-Bay, Inc.
2145 Hamilton Avenue
San Jose, CA 95125
Phone: (800) 322-9266
http://www.eBay.com

Eddie Bauer, Inc.
PO Box 7001
Groveport, OH 43125
Phone: (800) 625-7935
http://www.eddiebauer.com

Edmund Scientific Co.
60 Pearce Avenue
Tonawanda, NY 14150
Phone: (800) 728-6999
Fax: (800) 828-3299
http://www.scientificsonline.com

Eizo Nanao Technologies
5710 Warland Drive
Cypress, CA 90630
Phone: (562) 431-5011
Fax: (562) 431-4811
http://www.eizo.com

The Electrolux Group
PO Box 212378
Augusta, GA 30917
Phone: (800) 724-7519
http://www.electrolux.com

Eli Lilly & Co.
Lilly Corporate Center
Indianapolis, IN 46285
Phone: (800) 545-5979
http://www.lilly.com

Elizabeth Arden, Inc.
309 South Street
New Providence, NJ 07974
Phone: (800) 326-7337
E-mail: consumer@elizabetharden.
  com
http://www.elizabetharden.com

E-Machines
7565 Irvine Center Drive
Irvine, CA 92618
Phone: (408) 273-0888
http://www.e4me.com

Encyclopedia Britannica, Inc.
331 La Salle Boulevard
Chicago, IL 60610
Phone: (800) 323-1229
Fax: (312) 294-2104
http://www.britannica.com

Epson America, Inc.
3840 Kilroy Airport Way
Long Beach, CA 90806
Phone: (800) 463-7766
http://www.epson.com

Equifax
PO Box 105851
Atlanta, GA 30348
Phone: (800) 685-1111
http://www.equifax.com

Ernest & Julio Gallo Winery
600 Yosemite Boulevard
Modesto, CA 95354
Phone: (209) 341-6600
E-mail: consumerrelations@ejgallo.
  com
http://www.gallo.com

The Estee Lauder Companies,
  Inc.
767 Fifth Avenue
New York, NY 10153
Phone: (888) 378-3359
http://www.elcompanies.com

Ethan Allen, Inc.
PO Box 1966
Danbury, CT 06813
Phone: (888) 324-3571
Fax: (203) 743-8298

E-mail: orders@ethanallen.com
http://www.ethanallen.com

The Eureka Co.
PO Box 3900
Peoria, IL 61612
Phone: (800) 282-2886
http://www.eureka.com

Expedia, Inc.
13810 SE Eastgate Way
Bellevue, WA 98005
Phone: (800) 397-3342
E-mail: travel@customercare.expedia.
  com
http://www.expedia.com

Experian
PO Box 2104
Allen, TX 75013
Phone: (888) 397-3742
http://www.experian.com

Exxon Mobil
PO Box 1049
Buffalo, NY 14240
Phone: (800) 243-9966
http://www.exxonmobil.com

Faultless Starch/Bon Ami Co.
1025 W. 8th Street
Kansas City, MO 64101
Phone: (816) 842-1230
E-mail: info@faultless.com
http://www.bonami.com
http://www.faultless.com

Federated Department Stores,
  Inc
7 West 7th Street
Cincinnati, OH 45202
Phone: (800) 264-0069
http://www.fds.com

FedEx Corp.
3875 Airways
Module H3 Department 4634
Memphis, TN 38116
Phone: (800) 463-3339
http://www.fedex.com

FedExKinko's
PO Box 1935

Provo, UT 84603
Phone: (800) 254-6567
Fax: (801) 342-9263
E-mail: customerrelations@
  fedexkinkos.com
http://www.FedExKinkos.com

Fingerhut Direct Marketing,
  Inc.
6250 Ridgewood Road
Street Cloud, MN 56396
Phone: (800) 208-2500
http://www.fingerhut.com

Fisher-Price
636 Girard Avenue
East Aurora, NY 14052
Phone: (800) 432-5437
Fax: (716) 687-3494
http://www.fisher-price.com

Florsheim, Inc.
333 W. Estabrook Boulevard
Glendale, WI 53212
Phone: (866) 454-0449
E-mail: us.consumers@florsheim.
  com
http://www.florsheim.com

Flowers Foods, Inc.
1919 Flowers Circle
Thomasville, GA 31757
Phone: (229) 226-9110
http://www.flowersfoods.com

Food Lion, Inc.
PO Box 1330
Salisbury, NC 28145
Phone: (800) 210-9569
http://www.FoodLion.com

Fortune Brands
520 Lake Cook Road
Deerfield, IL 60015
Phone: (847) 484-4400
E-mail: mail@fortunebrands.com
http://www.fortunebrands.com

The Franklin Mint
801 Springdale Drive
Exton, PA 19341
Phone: (800) 523-7622
http://www.franklinmint.com

Frigidaire Home Products
P.O. Box 21378
Augusta, GA 30917
Phone: (706) 860-4110
http://www.frigidaire.com

Frito-Lay
7701 Legacy Drive
Plano, TX 75024
Phone: (800) 352-4477
Fax: (972) 334-5071
http://www.fritolay.com

Fruit of the Loom, Inc.
One Fruit of the Loom Drive
Bowling Green, KY 42103
Phone: (270) 781-6400
Fax: (270) 781-6400
E-mail: consumer.srv@fruit.com
http://www.fruit.com

FTD Inc.
3113 Woodcreek Drive
Downers Grove, IL 60515
Phone: (800) 736-3383
http://www.ftd.com

Fuji Photo Film U.S.A., Inc.
1100 King George Post
Edison, NJ 08837
Phone: (800) 800-3854
Fax: (732) 857-3487
http://www.fujifilm.com

Fuller Brush Company
PO Box 1247
One Fuller Way
Great Bend, KS 67530
Phone: (800) 522-0499
Fax: (620) 792-1906
http://www.fuller.com

Gateway, Inc.
610 Gateway Drive
North Sioux City, SD 57049
Phone: (800) 846-2000
Fax: (605) 232-2450
http://www.gateway.com

General Electric Company
3135 Easton Turnpike
Fairfield, CT 06828
Phone: (203) 373-2211

Fax: (203) 373-3131
http://www.ge.com

General Mills, Inc.
PO Box 9452
Minneapolis, MN 55440
Phone: (800) 249-0562
Fax: (763) 764-8330
http://www.generalmills.com

General Motors Acceptance Corp. (GMAC)
PO Box 217062
Auburn Hills, MI 48321
Phone: (800) 200-4622
Fax: (316) 652-6349
http://www.gmacfs.com

The Generra Company
499 Seventh Avenue South
New York, NY 10018
Phone: (212) 594-5801
Fax: (212) 594-5802
http://www.generra.com

Georgia-Pacific Corp.
PO Box 105605
Atlanta, GA 30348
Phone: (800) 283-5547
http://www.gp.com

Gerber Products Company
445 State Street
Fremont, MI 49413-0001
Phone: (800) 4-GERBER
Fax: (231) 928-2423
http://www.gerber.com

Giant Food, Inc.
8301 Professional Place
Landover, MD 20785
Phone: (301) 341-4322
Fax: (301) 618-4968
http://www.giantfood.com

Gillette Company
PO Box 61
Boston, MA 02199
Phone: (800) GILLETTE
Fax: (617) 463-3410
http://www.gillette.com

GlaxoSmithKline Consumer Healthcare
PO Box 1467
Pittsburgh, PA 15205
Phone: (800) 245-1040
Fax: (412) 928-5864
http://www.GSK.com

Glidden Paints
15885 Prague Rd.
Strongsville, OH 44136
Phone: (800) 454-3336
http://www.glidden.com

The Golden Grain Co.
PO Box 049003
Chicago, IL 60604
Phone: (800) 421-2444
http://www.ricearoni.com

Gold's Gym International
125 East John Carpenter.
Suite 1300
Irving, TX 75062
Phone: (866) 465-3775
Fax: (214) 296-5097
http://www.goldsgym.com

Goodrich Corporation
PO Box 19001
Greenville, SC 29602
Phone: (877) 788-8899
http://www.bfgoodrichtires.com

The Goodyear Tire & Rubber Co.
Department 728
1144 East Market Street
Akron, OH 44316
Phone: (800) 321-2136
Fax: (330) 796-2222
http://www.goodyear.com

Greyhound Lines, Inc.
PO Box 660362
MS 490
Dallas, TX 75266
Phone: (800) 231-2222
http://www.greyhound.com

Guess? Inc.
1444 South Alameda Street
Los Angeles, CA 90021

Phone: (877) 444-8377
Fax: (213) 744-0855
http://www.guess.com

Guinness
801 Main Avenue
Norwalk, CT 06851
Phone: (800) 521-1591
Fax: (203) 229-8901
E-mail: guinness@consumer-care.
net
http://www.guiness.com

H&R Block, Inc.
One HR Block Way
Kansas City, MO 64105
Phone: (800) 829-7733
http://www.hrblock.com

Hain Celestial Group, Inc.
4600 Sleepytime Drive
Boulder, CA 80301
Phone: (800) 434-4246
http://www.hain-celestial.com

Hallmark Cards, Inc.
PO Box 419034
MD #216
Kansas City, MO 64141
Phone: (800) 425-5627
http://www.hallmark.com

Hanes and Hanes Her Way Underwear
PO Box 6088
Bethania, NC 27105
Phone: (800) 832-0594
http://www.hanes.com

Hanes Hosiery
PO Box 450
1000 E. Hanes Mill Road
Winston-Salem, NC 27105
Phone: (800) 342-7070
Fax: (336) 519-2154
http://www.haneshosiery.com

Hartz Mountain Corp.
400 Plaza Drive
Secaucus, NJ 07094
Phone: (800) 275-1414
http://www.hartz.com

Hasbro, Inc.
PO Box 200
Pawtucket, RI 02862
Phone: (800) 255-5516
Fax: (401) 431-8082
http://www.hasbro.com

Hearth & Home Technologies Inc
20802 Kensington Boulevard
Lakeville, MN 55044
Phone: (888) 427-3973
E-mail: info@hearthnhome.com
http://www.fireplaces.com

Heinz North America
Heinz 57 Center
357 6th Avenue
Pittsburgh, PA 15222
Phone: (800) 255-5750
Fax: (412) 237-5291
http://www.heinz.com

Hershey Food Corporation
100 Crystal A Drive
Hershey, PA 17033
Phone: (800) 468-1714
http://www.hersheys.com

Hertz Corp.
225 Brae Boulevard
Park Ridge, NJ 07656
Phone: (201) 307-2000
Toll Free: (888) 777-6095
http://www.hertz.com

Hewlett-Packard Co.
3000 Hanover Street
Building 6A, Mail Stop 1247
Palo Alto, CA 94304
Phone: (800) 752-0900
Fax: (650) 857-5518
http://www.hp.com

Highfalls Brewing Company, Inc.
445 Street Paul Street
Rochester, NY 14605
Phone: (800) 729-4366
http://www.highfalls.com

Hilton Hospitality Inc.
755 Crossover Lane

Building A2
Memphis, TN 38117
Phone: (800) 445-8667
http://www.hilton.com

Home Depot, Inc.
2455 Paces Ferry Road
Atlanta, GA 30339
Phone: (800) 553-3199
Fax: (877) 496-9470
http://www.homedepot.com

Home Goods
Phone: (800) 614-4663
http://www.homegoods.com

Home Shopping Network (HSN)
One HSN Drive
Street Petersburg, FL 33729
Phone: (727) 872-1000
http://www.hsn.com

Honeywell International Inc
101 Columbia Road
Morristown, NJ 07962
Phone: (800) 601-3099
Fax: (973) 455-4807
http://www.honeywell.com

Hoover Company
240 Edwards Street
Cleveland, TN 37311
Phone: (800) 944-9200
http://www.hoover.com

Hormel Foods Co.
One Hormel Place
Austin, MN 55912
Phone: (800) 523-4635
Fax: (507) 437-9852
E-mail: media@hormel.com
http://www.hormel.com

Houston's Restaurant
Hillstone Restaurant Group
147 South Beverly Drive
Beverly Hills, CA 90212
Phone: (800) 230-9787
Fax: (310) 385-7119
http://www.hillstone.com

Howard Johnson, Inc.
PO Box 4090
1910 8th Aveue, NE
Aberdeen, SD 57402
Phone: (800) 544-9881
http://www.hojo.com

Huffy Corporation
6551 Centerville Business Parkway
Centerville, OH 45459
Phone: (800) 872-2453
Fax: (937) 865-5470
E-mail: customer.service@
    huffybikes.com
http://www.huffybikes.com

Humana Inc.
500 West Main Street
Louisville, KY 40202
Phone: (800) 4-HUMANA
http://www.humana.com

Hyatt Hotels & Resorts
71 South Wacker Drive
Chicago, IL 60606
Phone: (800) 228-3336
Fax: (402) 593-5151
http://www.hyatt.com

IBM Corporation
One New Orchard Road
Armonk, NY 10504
Phone: (800) 426-4968
Fax: (866) 722-9226
http://www.ibm.com

ICI Paints in North America
15885 West Sprague Road
Strongsville, OH 44136
Phone: (800) 984-5444
Fax: (216) 344-8900
http://www.ici.com

In-N-Out Burger
4199 Campus Drive
Irvine, CA 92612
Phone: (800) 786-1000
http://www.in-n-out.com

Intel
1900 Prairie City Road
Folsom, CA 95630
Phone: (916) 356-8080
http://www.intel.com

InterContinental Hotels Group
3 Ravinia Drive
Atlanta, GA 30346
Phone: (770) 604-2000
http://www.ihgplc.com

Iomega
500 West 500 North Lindon
Roy, UT 84067
Toll Free: (888) 516-8467
E-mail: customersupport_super@
    cs.iomega.com
http://www.iomega.com

Jack In The Box
9330 Balboa Avenue
San Diego, CA 92123
Phone: (800) 955-5225
http://www.jackinthebox.com

**Jackson & Perkins Nursery
    Stock**
2 Floral Avenue
Hodges, SC 29653
Phone: (800) 872-7673
Fax: (800) 242-0329
http://www.jacksonandperkinsservice.
    com

Jameson Inns, Inc.
4770 S. Atlanta Road
Smyrna, GA 30080
Phone: (770) 901-9020
E-mail: comments@jamesoninns.
    com
http://www.jamesoninns.com

JanSport, Inc.
PO Box 1817
Appleton, WI 54912
Phone: (800) 558-3600
E-mail: consumer_relations@vfc.
    com
http://www.jansport.com

**Jarden Consumer Solutions,
    Inc.**
2381 Executive Center Drive
Boca Raton, FL 34331
Phone: (800) 458-8407
Fax: (800) 478-6737
http://www.sunbeam.com

JCPenney Co., Inc.
PO Box 10001
Dallas, TX 75301
Phone: (972) 431-1000
http://www.jcpenney.com

Jenn-Air
553 Benson Road
Benton Harbor, MI 49022
Phone: (800) 688-1100
http://www.jennair.com

Jenny Craig, Inc.
5770 Fleet Street
Carlsbad, CA 92008
Phone: (800) 597-Jenny
E-mail: jennycraig@tpli.com
http://www.jennycraig.com

JetBlue Airways Corporation
PO Box 17435
Salt Lake City, UT 84117
Phone: (800) 538-2583
Fax: (801) 365-2440
http://www.jetblue.com

Jiffy Lube International, Inc.
PO Box 4427
Houston, TX 77210
Phone: (800) 344-6933
http://www.jiffylube.com

Jockey International, Inc.
2300 60th Street
PO Box 1417
Kenosha, WI 53141
Phone: (800) 562-5391
http://www.jockey.com

**John Hancock Financial
    Services, Inc.**
PO Box 111
Boston, MA 02117
Phone: (800) 732-5543
Fax: (617) 572-8707
http://www.johnhancock.com

Johns-Manville Corporation
PO Box 5108
Denver, CO 80217
Phone: (800) 654-3103
http://www.jm.com

Johnson & Johnson Consumer Products, Inc.
199 Grandview Road
Skillman, NJ 08558
Phone: (800) 526-3967
http://www.jnj.com

Johnson Publishing Co., Inc.
820 South Michigan Avenue
Chicago, IL 60605
Phone: (312) 322-9200
http://www.johnsonpublishing.
com

Jordache Enterprises, Inc.
1400 Broadway
New York, NY 10018
Phone: (212) 944-1330
E-mail: contact@jordachevintage.
com
http://www.jordache.com

Jostens, Inc.
3601 Minnesota Drive
Minneapolis, MN 55435
Phone: (800) 413-3857
http://www.jostens.com

Just Born, Inc
1300 Stefko Boulevard
Bethlehem, PA 18017
Phone: (800) 445-5787
Fax: (800) 543-4981
http://www.justborn.com

Just My Size Clothing Co.
P.O. Box 748
Rural Hall, NC 27098
Phone: (800) 261-6098
Fax: (800) 848-1237
http://www.jms.com

Just My Size Panties
475 Corporate Square Drive
Winston-Salem, NC 27105
Phone: (800) 994-4348
Fax: (336) 519-4226
http://www.jms.com

JVC Company of America
1700 Valley Road
Wayne, NJ 07494
Phone: (800) 252-5722

Fax: (973) 315-5042
E-mail: customerrelation@jvc
america.com
http://www.jvcservice.com

Kawasaki Motor Corporation, USA
PO Box 25252
Santa Ana, CA 92799
Phone: (800) 661-7433
http://www.kawasaki.com

KB Toys Inc.
100 West Street
Pittsfield, MA 01201
Phone: (877) 452-5437
Fax: (413) 496-3616
http://www.kbtoys.com

Kellogg Company
PO Box CAMB
Battle Creek, MI 49016
Phone: (800) 962-1413
http://www.kelloggcompany.com

Kemper Insurance Companies
1 Kemper Drive
Long Grove, IL 60049
Phone: (800) 833-0355
http://www.kemperinsurance.com

KFC (Kentucky Fried Chicken)
P.O. Box 725489
Atlanta, GA 31139
Phone: (800) 225-5532
http://www.kfc.com

Kimberly-Clark Corporation
401 North Lake
Neenah, WI 54956
Phone: (800) 553-3639
Fax: (920) 721-4766
http://www.kimberly-clark.com

Kinetico
10845 Kinsman Road
PO Box 193
Newbury, OH 44065
Phone: (800) 944-9283
Fax: (440) 564-9541
E-mail: custserv@kinetico.com
http://www.kinetico.com

The Kirby Company
1920 West 114th Street
Cleveland, OH 44102
Phone: (800) 494-8586
Fax: (216)529-6146
E-mail: consumer@kirbywhq.com
http://www.kirby.com

KitchenAid
553 Benson Road
Benton Harbor, MI 49022
Phone: (800) 541-6390
http://www.kitchenaid.com

Kmart Corp.
3333 Beverly Road
Hoffman Estates, IL 60179
Phone: (866) 562-7848
E-mail: help@customerservice.
kmart.com
http://www.kmart.com

Kohler Co.
444 Highland Drive
Mail Stop 10
Kohler, WI 53044
Phone: (800) 456-4537
http://www.kohler.com

Kohl's Corporation
17000 Ridgewood Drive
Menomonee Falls, WI 53051
Phone: (800) 694-2647
Fax: (262) 703-6363
E-mail: customerservice@kohls.
com
http://www.kohls.com

Kona Grill, Inc.
7150 E. Camelback Road
Scottsdale, AZ 85251
Phone: (866) 328-5662
Fax: (480) 991-6811
E-mail: information@konagrill.com
http://www.konagrill.com

Kraft Foods, Inc.
One Kraft Court
Glenview, IL 60025
Phone: (800) 323-0768
Fax: (570) 301-5275
http://www.kraftfoods.com

Kroger Co.
1014 Vine Street.
Cincinnati, OH 45202
Phone: (800) 632-6900
http://www.kroger.com

Kyocera Optics
Panurgy
701 Ford Road
Rockaway, NJ 07866
Phone: (800) 421-5735
Fax: (973) 625-9489
E-mail: info@panurgyoem.com
http://www.panurgyoem.com

LA Gear
844 Moraga Drive
Los Angeles, CA 90049
Phone: Phone: (800) 252-4327
Fax: (310) 889-3500
http://www.lagear.com

Land O'Lakes, Inc.
PO Box 64101
Mail Station 1070
Parkway Paul, MN 55164
Phone: (800) 328-4155
Fax: (651) 481-2128
http://www.landolakes.com

Lands' End, Inc.
1 Lands' End Lane
Dodgeville, WI 53595
Phone: (800) 963-4816
Fax: (800) 332-0103
http://www.landsend.com

Lane Furniture
PO Box 1627
Highway 145 South
Tupelo, MS 38802
Phone: (662) 566-7211
http://www.lanefurniture.com

La-Z-Boy, Inc.
1284 North Telegraph Road
Monroe, MI 48162
Phone: (734) 242-1444
E-mail: cservice@la-z-boy.com
http://www.la-z-boy.com

Leap Wireless International
10307 Pacific Center Center

San Diego, CA 92121
Phone: (877) 977-5327
Fax: (858) 882-6010
http://www.leapwireless.com

Lee Jeans
9001 West 67th Street
Merriam, KS 66202
Phone: (800) 453-3348
E-mail: leE-mail@vfc.com
http://www.lee.com

L'eggs Products
1000 E. Hanes Mill Road
Winston-Salem, NC 27105
Phone: (800) 925-3447
Fax: (336) 519-2154
http://www.leggs.com

LEGO Systems Inc
555 Taylor Road
PO Box 1138
Enfield, CT 06083
Phone: (800) 422-5346
Fax: (888) 329-5346
http://www.lego.com

Lennox Industries, Inc.
PO Box 799900
Dallas, TX 75379
Phone: (800) 953-6669
Fax: (972) 497-5331
http://www.davelennox.com

Levi Strauss & Company
1155 Battery Street
San Francisco, CA 94111
Phone: (800) 872-5384
http://www.levi.com

Levolor/Kirsch Window Fashion
4110 Premier Drive
High Point, NC 27265
Phone: (800) 538-6567
Fax: (336) 881-5873
E-mail: info@levolor.com
http://www.levolor.com

Lexmark International, Inc.
740 W. New Circle Road
Lexington, KY 40550
Phone: (800) 539-6275

E-mail: custrep@lexmark.com
(general inquiries)
http://www.lexmark.com

LG Electronics Inc.
PO Box 240007
201 James Record Road
Huntsville, AL 35824
Phone: (800) 243-0000
Fax: (800) 448-4026
http://www.us.lgservice.com

Liberty Mutual Insurance Group
175 Berkeley Street
MS 10B
Boston, MA 02116
Phone: (800) 344-0197
Fax: (617) 574-6688
E-mail: : PresidentialSvcTeam@
LibertyMutual.com
http://www.libertymutual.com

Lillian Vernon Corporation
2600 International Parkway
Virginia Beach, VA 23452
Phone: (800) 901-9291
http://www.lillianvernon.com

Limited Brands, Inc.
Three Limited Parkway
Columbus, OH 43230
Phone: (800) 945-5088
http://www.limitedbrands.com

Lincoln Electric Co.
22801 Parkway Claire Avenue
Cleveland, OH 44117
Phone: (800) 833-9353
Fax: (216) 486-1751
http://www.lincolnelectric.com

L.L. Bean, Inc.
15 Casco Parkway
Freeport, ME 04033
Phone: (800) 441-5713
Fax: (207) 552-3080
http://www.llbean.com

Long John Silver's Restaurants, Inc.
1900 Colonel Snaders Lane
Louisville, KY 40213

Phone: (888) 806-3474
http://www.ljsilvers.com

The Longaberger Company
One Market Square
1500 East Main Parkway
Newark, OH 43055
Phone: (740) 322-7800
Fax: (740) 322-7807
E-mail: info@longaberger.com
http://www.longaberger.com

Longhorn Steakhouse
Parden Restaurants
PO Box 593330
Orlando, FL 32859
Phone: (407) 245-4000
http://www.longhornsteakhouse.
com

L'Oreal USA
575 Fifth Avenue
New York, NY 10017
Phone: (212) 818-1500
http://www.lorealusa.com

Los Angeles Times
202 W. First Parkway
Los Angeles, CA 90012
Phone: (800) 252-9141
Fax: (213) 237-7679
http://www.latimes.com

Lowe's
PO Box 1111
North Wilkesboro, NC 28659
Phone: (800) 445-6937
http://www.lowes.com

MAACO Enterprises, Inc.
381 Brooks Road
King of Prussia, PA 19406
Phone: (800) 523-1180
http://www.maaco.com

Macy's
151 West 34th Street
New York, NY 10001
Phone: (212) 695-4400 (East)
Phone: (206) 344-2121 (Northwest)
Phone: (305) 835-5000 (Florida)
Phone: (612) 375-2200 (North)
Phone: (314) 342-6300 (Midwest)

Phone: (770) 913-4000 (South)
http://www.macys.com

Magic Chef
553 Benson Road
Benton Harbor, MI 49022
Phone: (800) 688-1120
http://www.magicchef.com

Marshalls Inc.
Phone: (888) 627-7425
http://www.marshallsonline.com

Massachusetts Mutual Insurance Co.
1295 State Street
Springfield, MA 01111
Phone: (800) 487-7844
Fax: (888) 599-0010
http://www.massmutual.com

Masterfoods USA
800 High Parkway
Hackettstown, NJ 07840
Phone: (800) 222-0293
E-mail: askus@masterfoodsusa.com
http://www.masterfoods.com

Mattel, Inc.
333 Continental Boulevard
El Segundo, CA 90245
Phone: (800) 524-8697
Fax: (310) 252-4190
E-mail: http://www.service.mattel.
com
http://www.mattel.com

Maybelline, Inc.
PO Box 1010
Clark, NJ 07066
Phone: (800) 944-0730
http://www.maybelline.com

Mayflower Transit, LLC.
One Premier Drive
Fenton, MO 63026
Phone: (800) 428-1234
http://www.mayflower.com

Maytag
553 Benson Road
Benton Harbor, MI 49022
Phone: (800) 688-9900
http://www.maytag.com

McCormick & Co., Inc.
211 Schilling Circle
Hunt Valley, MD 21031
Phone: (800) 632-5847
Fax: (410) 527-6005
http://www.mccormick.com

McCormick and Schmick's Seafood Restaurants
720 SW Washington Parkway
Portland, OR 97205
Phone: (503) 226-3440
Fax: (503) 228-5074
http://www.mccormickand
schmicks.com

McDonald's Corp.
2111 McDonald's Drive
Oak Brook, IL 60523
Phone: (800) 244-6227
http://www.mcdonalds.com

McGraw-Hill Companies, Inc.
PO Box 182604
Columbus, OH 43272
Phone: (877) 833-5524
Fax: (614) 759-3749
E-mail: customer.service@mcgraw-
hill.com
http://www.mcgraw-hill.com

McKee Foods Corp.
PO Box 750
Collegedale, TN 37315
Phone: (800) 522-4499
http://www.mckeefoods.com

Medco Health Solutions Inc.
100 Parsons Pond Drive
Franklin Lakes, NJ 07417
Phone: (800) 631-7780
http://www.medco.com

Meineke Car Care Centers, Inc.
PO Box 32401
128 S Tryon Street
Charlotte, NC 28232
Phone: (800) 447-3070
http://www.meineke.com

Melitta USA, Inc.
13925 58th Parkway North
Clearwater, FL 33760

Phone: (888) 635-4882
http://www.melitta.com

Mellon Financial Corp.
One Mellon Center
Pittsburgh, PA 15258
Phone: (412) 234-5000
http://www.mellon.com

The Mentholatum Co., Inc.
707 Sterling Drive
Orchard Park, NY 14127
Phone: (800) 688-7660
Fax: (716) 674-3696
http://www.mentholatum.com

Mercury Marine
   (Brunswick Corporation)
W6250 W. Pioneer Road
PO Box 1939
Fond Du Lac, WI 54936
Phone: (920) 929-5040
Fax: (920) 929-5893
http://www.mercurymarine.com

Merillat Industries
5353 West U.S. 223
Adrian, MI 49221
Phone: (866) 850-8557
http://www.merillat.com

Merisant Worldwide, Inc.
33 North Deerborn
Chicago, IL 60602
Phone: (800) 323-5316
http://www.merisant.com

Merrill Lynch & Co., Inc.
250 Vesey Street
New York, NY 10080
Phone: (212) 449-1000
http://www.merrilllynch.com

Mervyn's
22301 Foothill Boulevard
Mailstop 2115
Hayward, CA 94541
Phone: (800) 637-8967
E-mail: Parkwayrelations@
   mervyns.com
http://www.mervyns.com

MetLife, Inc.
500 Schoolhouse Road
Johnstown, PA 15904
Phone: (800) METLIFE
http://www.metlife.com

Michelin North America, Inc.
PO Box 19001
Greenville, SC 29602
Phone: (800) 847-3435
http://www.michelin-us.com

Michelina's
525 S. Lake Avenue
Duluth, MN 55082
Phone: (218) 723-5555
http://www.michelinas.com

Michigan Bulb Co.
PO Box 4180
Lawrenceburg, IN 47025
Phone: (513) 354-1497
E-mail: service@michiganbulb.com
http://www.michiganbulb.com

Microsoft Corporation
1 Microsoft Way
Redmond, WA 98052
Phone: (800) 642-7676
Fax: (425) 936-7329
http://www.microsoft.com

Midas Inc.
1300 Arlington Heights Road
Itasca, IL 60143
Phone: (800) 621-0144
http://www.midas.com

Midas Mutual Funds
PO Box 6110
Indianapolis, IN 46209
Phone: (800) 400-6432
Fax: (212) 363-1101
E-mail: info@mutualfunds.net
http://www.mutualfunds.net

Miles Kimball Co.
250 City Center
Oshkosh, WI 54906
Phone: (800) 255-4590
Fax: (920) 231-6942
http://www.mileskimball.com

Miller Coors
3939 W. Highland Boulevard
Milwaukee, WI 53208
Phone: (414) 931-2000
Fax: (414) 931-3735
http://www.millercoors.com

Minwax
10 Mountain View Road
Upper Saddle River, NJ 07458
Phone: (800) 523-9299
E-mail: askminwax@sherwin.com
http://www.minwax.com

Mitsubishi Digital Electronics
   America, Inc.
9351 Jeronimo Road
Irvine, CA 92618
Phone: (800) 332-2119
Fax: (949) 465-6147
http://www.mitsubishi-tv.com

Morgan Stanley
1585 Broadway
New York, NY 10036
Phone: (800) 733-2307
http://www.morganstanley.com

Morton International, Inc.
123 North Wacker Drive
Chicago, IL 60606
Phone: (800) 725-8847
Fax: (312) 807-2769
http://www.mortonsalt.com

Motorola, Inc.
1303 East Algonquin Road
Schaumburg, IL 60196
Phone: (800) 331-6456
http://www.motorola.com

Motts, Inc.
5301 Legacy Drive
PO Box 869077
Plano, TX 75024
Phone: (800) 426-4891
http://www.motts.com

Movado Group, Inc.
650 From Road
Paramus, NJ 07652
Phone: (201) 267-8000
http://www.movadogroupinc.com

MSN Internet Services
MSN Consumer Advocate
One Microsoft Way
Redmond, WA 98052
Phone: (800) 386-5550
http://www.msn.com

Mutual of Omaha Insurance Co.
Mutual of Omaha Plaza
Omaha, NE 68175
Phone: (402) 342-7600
Fax: (402) 351-3768
E-mail: individualclaims@
    mutualofomaha.com
http://www.mutualofomaha.com

Nabisco Foods Group
100 DeForest Avenue
East Hanover, NJ 07936
Phone: (800) NABISCO
http://www.nabiscoworld.com

National Amusements, Inc.
200 Elm Parkway
PO Box 9126
Dedham, MA 02027
Phone: (781) 461-1600
E-mail: customer_service@
    national-amusements.com
http://www.national-amusements.
    com

National Car Rental System, Inc.
208 Parkway James Avenue
Goose Creek, SC 29445
Phone: (800) 468-3334
http://www.nationalcar.com

National Fuel Gas Company
6363 Main Street
Williamsville, NY 14221
Phone: (800) 453-3513 (NY); (800) 352-1900 (PA)
Fax: (716) 857-7061
http://www.nationalfuelgas.com

National Presto Industries, Inc.
3925 North Hastings Way
Eau Claire, WI 54703
Phone: (715) 839-2121
Fax: (715) 839-2122
http://www.gopresto.com

Nationwide Financial Network
300 Continental Drive
Newark, DE 19713
Phone: (800) 523-4681
Fax: (302) 452-7634
http://www.nationwideprovident.
    com

NaturaLawn of America
1 E. Church Parkway
Fredrick, MD 21701
Phone: (301) 694-5440
Fax: (301) 846-0320
E-mail: natural@nl-amer.com
http://www.nl-amer.com

Nautica Enterprises, Inc.
40 West 57th Street
New York, NY 10019
Phone: (877) NAUTICA
Fax: (212) 887-8136
http://www.nautica.com

NBC Universal, Inc.
30 Rockefeller Plaza
New York, NY 10112
Phone: (212) 664-2333
http://www.nbc.com

Near East Food Products
PO Box 049003
Chicago, IL 60604
Phone: (800) 822-7423
http://www.neareaParkwaycom

The Neiman-Marcus Group, Inc.
111 Customer Way
Irving, TX 75039
Phone: (800) 685-6695
Fax: (214) 761-2650
http://www.neimanmarcus.com

Nestlé Purina PetCare Company
Checkerboard Square
Parkway Louis, MO 63164
Phone: (800) 778-7462
Fax: (314) 982-4580
http://www.purina.com

Nestlé USA
800 North Brand Boulevard
Glendale, CA 91203

Phone: (800) 225-2270
http://www.nestle.com

Nestlé Waters North America Inc.
777 West Putnam Avenue
Greenwich, CT 06830
Phone: (203) 531-4100
http://www.nestle-watersna.com

Neutrogena Corp.
5760 West 96th Street
Los Angeles, CA 90045
Phone: (800) 582-4048
Fax: (310) 337-5564
E-mail: ntgweb@neuus.jnj.com
http://www.neutrogena.com

New England Financial
700 Quacker Lane
Warwick, RI 02886
Phone: (800) 388-4000
http://www.nefn.com

New York Life Insurance Company
One Rockwood Road
Sleepy Hollow, NY 10591
Phone: (914) 846-3876
Fax: (914) 846-5497
http://www.newyorklife.com

New York Magazine Holdings LLC
75 Varick Street
New York, NY 10013
Phone: (800) 678-0900
http://www.newyorkmag.com

New York Times Co.
620 Eighth Avenue
New York, NY 10018
Phone: (212) 556-1234
http://www.nytco.com

Newport News
5100 City Line Road
Hampton, VA 23630
Phone: (800) 759-3950
Fax: (757) 825-4103
E-mail: customercare@newport-
    news.com
http://www.newport-news.com

Newsweek, Inc.
PO Box 5711
Harlan, IA 51593
Phone: (800) 631-1040
Fax: (888) 385-1428
http://www.newsweek.com

Nexxus Products Co.
2525 Armitage Avenue
Melrose Park, IL 60160
Phone: (800) 444-6399
http://www.nexxusproducts.com

Niagara Mohawk
300 Erie Boulevard West
Syracuse, NY 13202
Phone: (800) 642-4272
http://www.nationalgridus.com/
    niagaramohawk

Nike, Inc.
PO Box 4027
One Bowerman Drive
Beaverton, OR 97076
Phone: (800) 344-6453
http://www.nike.com

Nikon Inc.
1300 Walt Whitman Road
Melville, NY 11747
Phone: (631) 547-4200
Fax: (631) 547-4025
http://www.nikonusa.com

Nine West Group Inc.
9 West Plaza
1129 Westchester Avenue
White Plains, NY 10604
Phone: (800) 999-1877
http://www.ninewest.com

Nokia USA
4630 Woodland Corporate
    Boulevard
Tampa, FL 33614
Phone: (888) 665-4228
Fax: (813) 243-1256
E-mail: : customercare@nokia.com
http://www.nokiausa.com

Norelco Consumer Products Co.
1251 Avenue of the Americas
New York, NY 10020

Phone: (800) 243-3050
http://www.philips.com/Norelco

The North Face, Inc.
2013 Farallon Drive
San Leandro, CA 94577
Phone: (800) 447-2333
Fax: (510) 618-3541
E-mail: tnf_consumerservices@
    vfc.com
http://www.thenorthface.com

Northwest Airlines
C6590
5101 Northwest Drive
Parkway Paul, MN 55121
Phone: (800) 692-6955
http://www.nwa.com

**Northwestern Mutual Life
    Insurance Co.**
720 East Wisconsin Avenue
Milwaukee, WI 53202
Phone: (414) 271-1444
http://www.northwesternmutual.
    com

Norwegian Cruise Line
7665 Corporate Center Drive
Miami, FL 33126
Phone: (305) 436-4000
http://www.ncl.com

**Novartis Pharmaceuticals
    Corporation**
One Health Plaza
East Hanover, NJ 07936
Phone: (800) 742-2422
Fax: (973) 781-8265
http://www.pharma.us.novartis.
    com

Novell, Inc.
404 Wyman Street
Waltham, MA 02451
Phone: (800) 529-3400
E-mail: customer_service@novell.
    com
http://www.novell.com

Nu Tone, Inc.
9825 Kenwood Road
Cincinnati, OH 45227

Phone: (888) 336-3948
E-mail: ask@nutone.com
http://www.nutone.com

The NutraSweet Company
1762 Lovers Lane
Augusta, GA 30901
Phone: (800) 323-5321
http://www.nutrasweet.com

NutriSystem, Inc.
300 Welsh Road
Horsham, PA 19044
Phone: (800) 585-5483
Fax: (215) 706-5388
http://www.nutrisystem.com

Ocean Spray Cranberries Inc.
One Ocean Spray Drive
Lakeville-Middleboro, MA 02349
Phone: (800) 662-3263
Fax: (508) 923-0036
http://www.oceanspray.com

Office Depot, Inc.
2200 Old Germantown Road
Delray Beach, FL 33445
Phone: (800) 463-3768
Fax: (561) 438-4760
http://www.officedepot.com

OfficeMax, Inc.
263 Shuman Boulevard
Naperville, IL 60563
Phone: (877) 633-4236
Fax: (800) 995-9644
E-mail: customerresolution@
    officemax.com
http://www.officemax.com

Okidata
2000 Bishops Gate Boulevard
Mt Laurel, NJ 08054
Phone: (800) 654-3282
http://www.okidata.com

Olan Mills, Inc.
4325 Amnicola Highway
PO Box 23456
Chattanooga, TN 37422
Phone: (800) 251-6320
Fax: (423) 499-3864
http://www.olanmills.com

Olive Garden
Darden Restaurants
PO Box 593330
Orlando, FL 32859
Phone: (407) 245-4000
http://www.olivegarden.com

Olympus America
3500 Corporate Parkway
PO Box 610
Center Valley, PA 18034
Phone: (888) 553-4448
http://www.olympusamerica.com

Oneida, Ltd.
PO Box 1
Oneida, NY 13421
Phone: (888) 263-7195
http://www.oneida.com

Orbitz, Inc.
500 W. Madison
Chicago, IL 60661
Phone: (888) 656-4546
Fax: (312) 894-5001
http://www.orbitz.com

Orkin
2170 Piedmont Road
Atlanta, GA 30324
Phone: (800) 346-7546
Fax: (404) 633-2315
http://www.orkin.com

Oster Professional Products
150 Cadillac Lane
McMinnville, TN 37110
Phone: (800) 830-3678
Fax: (913) 668-1647
http://www.osterpro.com

Outback Steakhouse
2202 N. West Shore Boulevard
Tampa, FL 33607
Phone: (813) 282-1225
http://www.outback.com

Owens Corning
One Owens Corning Parkway
Toledo, OH 43659
Phone: (800) GET-PINK
http://www.owenscorning.com

Palm, Inc.
950 West Maude Avenue
Sunnyvale, CA 94085
Phone: (800) 881-7256
Fax: (408) 617-0100
http://www.palm.com

Panasonic Company
One Panasonic Way
Secaucus, NJ 07094
Phone: (800) 211-7262
http://www.panasonic.com

Panera Bread
6710 Clayton Road
Richmond Heights, MO 63117
Phone: (800) 301-5566
Fax: (314) 633-7200
http://www.panerabread.com

Papa John's International, Inc.
PO Box 99900
Louiseville, KY 40269
Phone: (502) 261-4987
http://www.papajohns.com

Parker Brothers
PO Box 200
Pawtucket, RI 02862
Phone: (888) 836-7025
http://www.hasbro.com

Pathmark Stores, Inc.
2 Paragon Drive
Montvale, NJ 07645
Phone: (866) 443-7374
E-mail: customers@pathmark.com
http://www.pathmark.com

Pella Corporation
102 Main Parkway
Pella, IA 50219
Phone: (641) 628-1000
http://www.pella.com

Pennzoil
Pennzoil Place
PO Box 2967
Houston, TX 77252
Phone: (800) 237-8045
http://www.pennzoil.com

Pentair Pool Products, Inc.
1620 Hawkins Avenue

Sanford, NC 27330
Phone: (800) 831-7133
Fax: (800) 284-4151
http://www.pentairpool.com

Pep Boys Auto
311 West Allegheny Avenue
Philadelphia, PA 19132
Phone: (800) 737-2697
Fax: (205) 430-4622
E-mail: custserv@pepboys.com
http://www.pepboys.com

Pepperidge Farm, Inc.
595 Westport Avenue
Norwalk, CT 06851
Phone: (888) 737-7374
http://www.pepperidgefarm.com

Pepsi-Cola Co.
700 Anderson Hill Road
Purchase, NY 10577
Phone: (800) 433-2652
Fax: (914) 767-6177
http://www.pepsico.com

Perdue Farms Incorporated
PO Box 1656
Horsham, PA 19044
Phone: (800) 473-7383
http://www.perdue.com

P.F. Chang's China Bistro, Inc.
7676 E. Pinnacle Peak Road
Scottsdale, AZ 85265
Phone: (480) 888-3000
http://www.pfchangs.com

Pfizer Inc.
235 East 42nd Parkway
New York, NY 10017
Phone: (800) 879-3477
http://www.pfizer.com

Pharmavite Corporation
PO Box 9606
Mission Hills, CA 91346
Phone: (818) 221-6200
http://www.pharmavite.com

Philip Morris USA
PO Box 26603
Richmond, VA 23261

Phone: (800) 343-0975
http://www.philipmorris.com

Philips Consumer Electronics North America
64 Perimeter Center East
PO Box 467300
Atlanta, GA 31146
Phone: (888) 744-5477
http://www.philipsusa.com

Phillips-Van Heusen Corporation
1001 Frontier Road
Bridgewater, NJ 08807
Phone: (800) 388-9122
http://www.pvh.com

Pioneer Electronics Service, Inc.
PO Box 1760
Long Beach, CA 90810
Phone: (800) 421-1404
Fax: (310) 952-2821
http://www.pioneerelectronics.com

Pirelli Tire Corporation
100 Pirelli Drive
Rome, GA 30161
Phone: (800) 747-3554
Fax: (706) 368-5832
E-mail: : consumer.affairs@
us.pirelli.com
http://www.us.pirelli.com

Pizza Hut
14841 Dallas Parkway
Dallas, TX 75254
Phone: (800) 948-8488
http://www.pizzahut.com

Playskool
PO Box 200
Pawtucket, RI 02862
Phone: (800) 752-9755
E-mail: customersupport@hasbro.
com
http://www.hasbro.com/playskool

Playtex Products Inc.
75 Commerce Drive
PO Box 701
Allendale, NJ 07401

Phone: (888) 310-4290
Fax: (201) 785-8202
http://www.playtexproductsinc.
com

Plextor America
830 Hillview Court
Milpitas, CA 95035
Phone: (866) 204-0332
Fax: (408) 719-3030
http://www.plextor.com

Polaroid Corp.
300 Baker Avenue
Concord, MA 01742
Phone: (800) 343-5000
Fax: (781) 386-5605
http://www.polaroid.com

Polo/Ralph Lauren Corp.
4100 Beachwood Drive
Greensboro, NC 27410
Phone: (888) 475-7674
Fax: (336) 632-9097
E-mail: customerassitance@
ralphlauren.com
http://www.polo.com

Price Chopper Supermarkets
PO Box 1074
Schenectady, NY 12306
Phone: (518) 355-5000
http://www.pricechopper.com

The Procter & Gamble Co.
PO Box 599
Cincinnati, OH 45202
Phone: (513) 983-1100
http://www.pg.com

Prudential Financial, Inc.
PO Box 1136
Minneapolis, MN 55440
Phone: (800) 201-6690
http://www.prudential.com

Public Clothing Company
1407 Broadway
New York, NY 10018
Phone: (212) 768-8440
http://www.publicclothing.com

Publishers Clearing House
382 Channel Drive
Port Washington, NY 11050
Phone: (800) 337-4724
Fax: (516) 883-5769
E-mail: cirving@pch.com
http://www.pch.com

Qdoba Mexican Grill
4865 Ward Road
Wheat Ridge, CO 80033
Phone: (303) 629-5000
Fax: (303) 629-2396
E-mail: info@qdoba.com
http://www.qdoba.com

The Quaker Oats Co.
PO Box 049003
Chicago, IL 60604
Phone: (312) 821-1000
http://www.quakeroats.com

Quantum Corp.
1650 Technology Drive
San Jose, CA 95110
Phone: (800) 677-6268
http://www.quantum.com

Quark, Inc.
PO Box 12027
Cheyenne, WY 82003
Phone: (800) 676-4575
Fax: (307) 772-7122
E-mail: : cservice@quark.com
http://www.quark.com

QuikTrip Corporation
PO Box 3475
Tulsa, OK 74101
Phone: (918) 615-7700
http://www.quiktrip.com

Quizno's
1475 Lawrence Street
Denver, CO 80202
Phone: (866) 486-2783
http://www.quiznos.com

QVC Inc.
1200 Wilson Drive at Studio Park
West Chester, PA 19380
Phone: (800) 367-9444
http://www.qvc.com

Qwest Communications International, Inc.
4600 South Syracuse Street
Denver, CO 80237
Phone: (800) 899-7780
Fax: (303) 256-6271

Radio Shack Corporation
300 Radio Shack Circle
Fort Worth, TX 76102
Phone: (800) 843-7422
http://www.radioshack.com

Rayovac Corporation
PO Box 44960
Madison, WI 53744
Phone: (800) 237-7000
Fax: (888) 677-4770
E-mail: consumers@rayovac.com
http://www.rayovac.com

Readers Digest Association, Inc.
Readers Digest Road
Pleasantville, NY 10570
Phone: (800) 635-5006
Fax: (914) 238-4559
http://www.readersdigest.com

Reckitt Benckiser, Inc.
Morris Corporate Center IV
399 Interpace Parkway
PO Box 225
Parsippany, NJ 07054
Phone: (800) 333-3899
E-mail: corpcomms@
reckittbenckiser.com
http://www.reckittbenckiser.com

Regal Ware Inc.
1675 Reigle Drive
Kewaskum, WI 53040
Phone: (262) 626-2121
http://www.regalware.com

Remington Arms Company, Inc.
870 Remington Drive
PO Box 700
Madison, NC 27025
Phone: (800) 243-9700

Fax: (336) 548-7801
http://www.remington.com

Remington Products Co.
PO Box 44960
Madison, WI 53744
Phone: (800) 736-4648
http://www.remington-products.com

Rich Products
PO Box 20670
127 Airport Road
St. Simons Island, GA 31522
Phone: (888) 732-7251
Fax: (912) 634-3105
http://www.rich.com

Ricoh Corporation
5 Dedrick Place
West Caldwell, NJ 07006
Phone: (800) 327-8349
E-mail: tech@ricohdms.com
http://www.ricoh-usa.com

Rite Aid Corporation
PO Box 3165
Harrisburg, PA 17105
Phone: (800) 748-3243
http://www.riteaid.com

Rodale, Inc.
33 E. Minor Street
Emmaus, PA 18098
Phone: (800) 848-4735
Fax: (610) 967-8963
E-mail: customer_service@rodale.com
http://www.rodale.com

Rolex Watch U.S.A. Inc.
665 Fifth Avenue
New York, NY 10022
Phone: (212) 758-7700
Fax: (212) 980-2166
http://www.rolex.com

Roto-Rooter Corp.
300 Ashworth Road
West Des Moines, IA 50265
Phone: (515) 223-1343
http://www.roto-rooter.com

Royal Caribbean International
1050 Caribbean Way
Miami, FL 33132
Phone: (800) 398-9819
http://www.royalcarribean.com

Rubbermaid
3320 West Market Street
Fairlawn, OH 44333
Phone: (888) 895-2110
http://www.rubbermaid.com

Ruth's Chris Steakhouse
Ruth's Hospitality Group, Inc.
500 International Parkway
Heathrow, FL 32746
Phone: (407) 333-7440
http://www.ruthschris.com

Safeway, Inc.
MS 10501
PO Box 29093
Phoenix, AZ 85038
Phone: (877) 723-3929
Fax: (623) 869-4397
http://www.safeway.com

Saks Fifth Avenue
12 East 49th Street
New York, NY 10017
Phone: (800) 238-3089
Fax: (212) 940-5031
http://www.saks.com

Sam's Club
608 Southwest Eighth Street
Bentonville, AR 72712
Phone: (888) 746-7726
http://www.samsclub.com

Samsonite Corporation
575 W Street
Mansfiled, MA 02048
Phone: (800) 262-8282
Fax: (610) 871-3343
http://www.samsonite.com

Samsung Electronics America
400 Valley Road
Mount Arlington, NJ 07856
Phone: (800) 726-7864
Fax: (973) 601-6001
http://www.samsung.com

Sanofi-Aventis
55 Corporate Drive
Bridgewater, NJ 08807
Phone: (800) 981-2491
http://www.sanofi-aventis.us

Sara Lee Foods
PO Box 756
Neenah, WI 54957
Phone: (800) 328-2426
Fax: (888) 514-5970
http://www.saraleefoods.com

Sargento Foods Inc.
One Persnickety Place
Plymouth, WI 53073
Phone: (800) 243-3737
Fax: (920) 893-8399
http://www.sargento.com

SC Johnson and Son, Inc.
1525 Howe Street
Racine, WI 53403
Phone: (800) 494-4855
Fax: (262) 260-4805
http://www.scjohnsonwax.com

Schering-Plough HealthCare Products, Inc.
3030 Jackson Avenue
Memphis, TN 38151
Phone: (800) 842-4090
Fax: (901) 320-2292
http://www.sphcp.com

The Scotts Company
14111 Scottslawn Road
Marysville, OH 43041
Phone: (800) 543-8873
http://www.scotts.com

Seagate Technology, Inc.
920 Disc Drive
Scotts Valley, CA 95066
Phone: (831) 438-6550
http://www.seagate.com

Sealy Corporation
One Office Parkway at Sealy Drive
Trinity, NC 27370
Phone: (336) 861-3500
http://www.sealy.com

Sears, Roebuck and Co.
3333 Beverly Road
Hoffman Estates, IL 60179
Phone: (800) 549-4505
Fax: (800) 427-3049
http://www.sears.com

Seiko Instruments USA, Inc.
12301 Technology Boulevard
Austin, TX 78727
Phone: (800) 757-1011
Fax: (512) 349-3000
E-mail: customerservice@siu-austin.com
http://www.seikoinstruments.com

Sempra Energy
101 Ash Street
San Diego, CA 92101
Phone: (619) 696-2000
http://www.sempra.com

Seneca Foods Corporation
3736 South Main Street
Marian, NY 14505
Phone: (800) 872-1110
Fax: (315) 926-8300
E-mail: consumer_affairs@senecafoods.com
http://www.senecafoods.com

Serta, Inc.
3 Golf Center #392
Hoffman Estates, IL 60169
Phone: (800) 426-0371
Fax: (847) 645-0205
E-mail: customer.service@serta.com
http://www.serta.com

7-Eleven, Inc
1722 Routh Street
Dallas, TX 75201
Phone: (800) 255-0711
E-mail: http://www.7-Eleven.com
http://www.7-Eleven.com

Sharp Electronics Corp.
1300 Naperville Drive
Romeoville, IL 60441
Phone: (800) 237-4277
http://www.sharpusa.com

Shell Oil Co.
PO Box 2463
Houston, TX 77252
Phone: (888) 467-4355
http://www.localshell.com
http://www.shellus.com

Sherwin-Williams Company
Midland Building
101 Prospect Aveue, NW
PO Box 647
Cleveland, OH 44115
Phone: (216) 566-2000
Toll Free: (800) 474-3794
http://www.sherwin-williams.com

Shoney's Inc.
1717 Elm Hill Pike
Nashville, TN 37210
Phone: (877) 474-6639
Fax: (615) 231-2621
http://www.shoneys.com

Simmons Bedding Company
1900 Beaver Ridge Circle
Norcross, GA 30071
Phone: (877) 399-9397
Fax: (770) 613-8575
E-mail: customerassistance@simmons.com
http://www.simmons.com

Simon and Schuster
1230 Avenue of the Americas
New York, NY 10020
Phone: (800) 223-2336
Fax: (800) 943-9831
http://www.simonsays.com

Simple Tech, Inc.
1830 E. Warner Avenue
Santa Ana, CA 92705
Phone: (949) 477-7700
Fax: (949) 476-1209
http://www.fabrik.com

Singer Sewing Company
1224 Heil Quaker Boulevard
PO Box 7017
LaVergne, TN 37086
Fax: (615) 213-0994
E-mail: talktous@singerco.com
http://www.singerco.com

Slim-Fast Foods Co.
PO Box 6065
Englewood, NJ 07631
Phone: (877) 375-4632
E-mail: support@slimfast.com
http://www.slimfast.com

Snapper
535 Macon Road
McDonough, GA 30253
Phone: (888) 477-8650
Fax: (770) 957-7981
http://www.snapper.com

Snapple Beverage Corporation
5301 Legacy Drive
PO Box 869077
Plano , TX 75024
Phone: (800) 426-4891
http://www.snapple.com

Sonesta International Hotels Corp.
116 Huntington Avenue
Boston, MA 02116
Phone: (617) 421-5400
Fax: (617) 421-5402
E-mail: info@sonesta.com
http://www.sonesta.com

Sony Corp. of America
12451 Gateway Boulevard
Fort Myers, FL 33913
Phone: (800) 222-7669
http://www.sony.com

Southwest Airlines
PO Box 36647-1CR
Dallas, TX 75235
Phone: (214) 792-4223
Fax: (214) 792-5099
http://www.southwest.com

Spencer's
6826 Black Horse Pike
Egg Harbor Township, NJ 08234
Phone: (800) 527-7977
http://www.spencersonline.com

Spiegel Brands, Inc
One Spiegel Avenue
Hampton, VA 23630
Phone: (800) 474-5555

E-mail: clientservices@spiegel.com
http://www.spiegel.com

Spiegel Catalog
5100 City Line Road
Hampton, VA 23630
Phone: (800) 222-5680
http://www.spiegel.com

Springs Global U.S., Inc.
PO Box 70
Fort Mill, SC 29716
Phone: (888) 926-7888
http://www.springs.com

Sprint Nextel
6391 Sprint Parkway
Overland Park, KS 66151
Phone: (888) 211-4727
http://www.sprint.com/
consumerinfo

Stanley Hardware
480 Myrtle Stree
New Britain, CT 06053
Phone: (800) 622-4393
http://www.stanleyhardware.com

Staples, Inc.
500 Staples Drive
Framingham, MA 01702
Phone: (800) 378-2753
http://www.staples.com

Starbucks
PO Box 3717
Seattle, WA 98124
Phone: (800) 334-5553
http://www.starbucks.com

State Fair Foods, Inc.
PO Box 756
Neenah, WI 54957
Phone: (800) 328-2426
Fax: (888) 514-5970
http://www.statefairbrand.com

State Farm Mutual Automobile Insurance Co.
One State Farm Plaza
Bloomington, IL 61710
Phone: (309) 766-6393
http://www.statefarm.com

Stop & Shop Supermarket Co., Inc.
PO Box 55888
Boston, MA 02205
Phone: (800) 767-7772
Fax: (617) 770-6033
http://www.stopandshop.com

Subway
325 Bic Drive
Milford, CT 06461
Phone: (203) 877-4281
Toll Free: (800) 888-4848
http://www.subway.com

Swatch Watch USA
55 Metro Way
Secaucus, NJ 07094
Phone: (800) 879-2824
E-mail: swatch.cservice.estore@
swatch.com
http://www.swatch.com

The Swiss Colony, Inc
1112 Seventh Avenue
Monroe, WI 53566
Phone: (800) 544-9036
Fax: (608) 242-1001
E-mail: swisscolony@sccompanies.
com
http://www.swisscolony.com

Symantec Corporation
20330 Stephens Creek Boulevard
Cupertino, CA 95014
Phone: (408) 517-8000
Fax: (408) 517-8186
http://www.symantec.com

Syngenta
410 Swing Road
Greensboro, NC 27409
Phone: (800) 334-9481
Fax: (336) 632-7353
http://www.syngenta-us.com

Taco Bell
17901 Von Karman
Irvine, CA 92614
Phone: (800) TacoBell
http://www.tacobell.com

Talbots
One Talbots Drive

Hingham, MA 02043
Phone: (800) 992-9010
Fax: (781) 741-4136
http://www.talbots.com

Target Stores
PO Box 9350
Minneapolis, MN 55440
Phone: (800) 440-0680
Fax: (612) 307-8870
http://www.target.com

TEAC America, Inc.
7733 Telegraph Road
Montebello, CA 90640
Phone: (323) 726-0303
Fax: (323) 727-7656
http://www.teac.com

Techville Computer Center
11343 N. Central Expressway
Dallas, TX 75243
Phone: (214) 739-7033
Fax: (214) 739-7042
http://www.techville.com

Teleflora
11444 West Olympic Boulevard
Los Angeles, CA 90064
Phone: (800) 421-4051
Fax: (310) 966-3666
http://www.teleflora.com

Tenneco, Inc.
500 North Field Drive
Lake Forest, IL 60045
Phone: (847) 482-5000
Fax: (847) 482-5940
http://www.tenneco.com

Tetley USA Inc.
PO Box 856
100 Commerce Drive
Shelton, CT 06484
Phone: (800) 728-0084
Fax: (203) 929-9263
http://www.tetleyusa.com

Texas Instruments, Inc.
PO Box 660199
Dallas, TX 75266
Phone: (800) 842-2737
Fax: (972) 917-0747
http://www.ti.com

T.G.I. Friday's
Carlson Restaurants Worldwide
4201 Marsh Lane
Carrollton, TX 75007
Phone: (800) 800-FRIDAYS
http://www.tgifridays.com

3COM Corporation
350 Campus Drive
Marlborough, MA 01752
Phone: (800) 876-3266
Fax:(508) 323-1111
http://www.3com.com

3M
3M Center
St. Paul, MN 55144
Phone: (800) 364-3577
Fax: (800) 713-6329
http://www.3m.com

Thrifty Rent A Car System, Inc.
5310 East 31st Street
Tulsa, OK 74135
Phone: (800) 334-1705
Fax: (918) 669-2060
E-mail: customercare@thrifty.com
http://www.thrifty.com

Time Warner Inc.
One Time Warner Center
New York, NY 10019
Phone: (212) 484-8000
http://www.timewarner.com

Time, Inc.
3000 University Center Drive
Tampa, FL 33612
Phone: (800) 541-1000
Fax: (813) 979-6615
http://www.time.com

Timex Corp.
1302 Pike Avenue
North Little Rock, AR 72114
Phone: (800) 448-4639
Fax: (501) 370-5747
E-mail: custserv@timex.com
http://www.timex.com

TJ Maxx
770 Cochituate Road.

Framingham, MA 01701
Phone: (800) 926-6299
http://www.tjmaxx.com

TJX Companies, Inc.
770 Cochituate Road.
Framingham, MA 01701
Phone: (877) 746-7259 (A. J. Wright)
Phone: (800) 926-6299 (TJ Maxx)
Phone: (800) 888-0776 (Home Goods)
Phone: (800) (888) 627-7425 (Marshalls)
Fax: (508) 390-2091
http://www.tjx.com

T-Mobile Wireless
PO Box 37380
Albuquerque, NM 87176
Phone: (800) T-MOBILE
Fax: (505) 998-3775
http://www.tmobile.com

Tone Brothers, Inc.
2301 S.E. Tone's Drive
Ankeny, IA 50021
Phone: (800) 247-5251
http://www.spiceadvice.com

Top-Flite Professional Golf Company
425 Meadow Street
Chicopee, MA 01013
Phone: (413) 536-1200
Toll Free: (866) 834-6532
http://www.topflite.com

The Toro Co.
8111 Lyndale Avenue South
Bloomington, MN 55420
Phone: (800) 348-9939
E-mail: consumer.service@toro.com
http://www.toro.com

Toshiba America
82 Totowa Road
Wayne, NJ 07470
Phone: (800) 631-3811
E-mail: customersupport@tacp.com
http://www.tacp.toshiba.com

Totes/Isotoner
9655 International Boulevard
Cincinnati, OH 45246
Phone: (800) 762-8712
Fax: (513) 682-8606
E-mail: consumeraffairs@totes.
   com
http://www.totes.com

Tourneau, Inc.
3 East 54th Street
New York, NY 10022
Phone: (800) 348-3332
http://www.tourneau.com

Toys
1 Geoffrey Way
Wayne, NJ 07470
Phone: (800) 869-7787
http://www.toysrus.com

Trane
PO Box 9010
Tyler, TX 75707
Phone: (903) 581-3200 (Residential)
Phone: (931) 645-6471 (Commercial)
http://www.trane.com

TransUnion, LLC
PO Box 1000
Chester, PA 19022
Phone: (800) 888-4213
Fax: (610) 546-4605
http://www.transunion.com

Travelers Companies, Inc.
One Tower Square 5MS
Hartford, CT 06183
Phone: (800) 328-2189
http://www.travelers.com

Travelocity.com L.P.
11603 Crosswinds Way
San Antonio, TX 78233
Phone: (800) 709-5983
http://www.travelocity.com

Tripp Lite
1111 W 35th Street
Chicago, IL 60609
Phone: (773) 869-1111
Fax: (773) 869-1329
http://www.tripplite.com

True Value Company
8600 West Bryn Mawr
Chicago, IL 60631
Phone: (773) 695-5000
http://www.truevalue.com

Tupperware Corporation
PO Box 2353
Orlando, FL 32802
Phone: (800) 366-3800
http://www.tupperware.com

Turtle Wax, Inc.
Consumer Affairs
PO Box 247
Willowbrook, IL 60559
Phone: (800) 805-7695
Fax: (708) 563-4302
http://www.turtlewax.com

TV Guide
PO Box 37360
Boone, IA 50037
Phone: (800) 866-1400
Fax: (515) 433-5001
http://www.tvguide.com

TXU Energy
TXU Electric and Gas Company
1601 Bryan Street
Dallas, TX 75201
Phone: (800) 242-9113
Fax: (800) 232-9448
E-mail: txuenergy@txu.com
http://www.txu.com

Tyson Foods
PO Box 2020
Springdale, AR 72765
Phone: (800) 233-6332
Fax: (479) 290-7930
E-mail: willie.barber@tyson.com
http://www.tyson.com

UBS Financial Services Inc.
PO Box 766
Union City, NJ 07087
Phone: (800) 354-9103
E-mail: onlineservices@ubs.com
http://www.financialservicesinc.
   ubs.com

U-Haul International
PO Box 21502
Phoenix, AZ 85036
Phone: (800) 528-0463
http://www.uhaul.com

Uniden America Corporation
4700 Amon Carter Boulevard
Fort Worth, TX 76155
Phone: (800) 297-1023
Fax: (800) 323-2641
E-mail: cservice@uniden.com
http://www.uniden.com

Unilever
800 Sylvan Avenue
Englewood Cliffs, NJ 07632
Phone: (800) 621-2013
http://www.unilever.com

Uniroyal Tires
PO Box 19001
Greenville, SC 29602
Phone: (877) 458-5878
http://www.uniroyal.com

United Airlines
77 West Wacker Drive
Chicago, IL 60601
Phone: (877) 228-1327
Fax: (877) 406-1059
http://www.ual.com

United Online Inc.
LNR Warner Center
21301 Burbank Boulevard
Woodland Hills, CA 91367
Phone: (805) 418-2000
Fax: (818) 287-2001
http://www.unitedonline.com

United Van Lines, Inc.
One United Drive
Fenton, MO 63026
Phone: (800) 948-4885
http://www.unitedvanlines.com

Uno Chicago Grill
100 Charles Park Road
Boston, MA 02132
Phone: (866) 600-8667
E-mail: mail@unos.com
http://www.unos.com

UPS (United Parcel Service of America, Inc.)
55 Glenlake Parkway, NE
Atlanta, GA 30328
Phone: (800) 742-5877
Fax: (404) 828-6204
http://www.ups.com

US Airways
PO Box 1501
Winston-Salem, NC 27102
Phone: (866) 523-5333
Fax: (336) 661-8187
http://www.usairways.com

US Bancorp
U S Bancorp Center
800 Nicollet Mall
Minneapolis, MN 55402
Phone: (800) 872-2657
http://www.usbank.com

The Valvoline Company
PO Box 14000
Lexington, KY 40512
Phone: (800) TEAM-VAL
http://www.valvoline.com

Verizon Communications Inc.
140 West Street
New York, NY 10007
Phone: (800) 621-9900
http://www.verizon.com

Viacom, Inc.
1515 BRoadway
New York, NY 10036
Phone: (212) 258-6000
http://www.viacom.com

Victoria's Secret Stores
North American Office
PO Box 16589
Columbus, OH 43216
Phone: (800) 411-5116
E-mail: service@victoriassecret.com
http://www.victoriassecret.com

Wachovia Corporation
1525 West W.T. Harris Boulevard
Charlotte, NC 28212
Phone: (800) 922-4684
http://www.wachovia.com

Wachovia Securities, LLC
901 East Byrd Street
Richmond, VA 23219
http://www.wachoviasec.com

Wagner Spray Tech Corp.
1770 Fernbrook Lane
Plymouth, MN 55447
Phone: (800) 328-8251
Fax: (763) 519-3563
E-mail: custserv@wagnerspraytech.
   com
http://www.wagnerspraytech.com

Walgreen Co.
200 Wilmot Road
Deerfield, IL 60015
Phone: (800) 289-2273
Fax: (847) 914-3105
http://www.walgreens.com

Wal-Mart Stores, Inc.
702 SW Eighth Street
Bentonville, AR 72716
Phone: (800) WAL-MART
Fax: (479) 204-9798
E-mail: letters@wal-mart.com
http://www.wal-mart.com

Walter Drake, Inc.
4630 Forge Road
Colorado Springs, CO 80907
Phone: (800) 525-9291
Fax: (888) 252-8462
http://www.wdrake.com

Waste Management, Inc.
1001 Fannin Street
Houston, TX 77002
Phone: (713) 512-6200
http://www.wastemanagement.com

Water Pik Inc.
1730 East Prospect Road
Fort Collins, CO 80553
Phone: (800) 525-2774
Fax: (970) 221-8715
http://www.waterpik.com

Weider Publications
21100 Erwin Street
Woodland Hills, CA 91367
Phone: (800) 423-5590
http://www.weider.com

Weight Watchers Gourmet Food Company
11 Madison Avenue
New York, NY 10010
Phone: (800) 651-6000
E-mail: customerservice@
   weightwatchers.com
http://www.weightwatchers.com

Wells Fargo & Company
420 Montgomery Street
San Francisco, CA 94104
Phone: (800) 869-3557
http://www.wellsfargo.com

Wendy's International, Inc.
One Dave Thomas Blvd
Dublin, OH 43017
Phone: (800) 443-7266
Fax: (614) 764-6707
http://www.wendys.com

West Bend Cookware
1100 Schmidt Road
West Bend, WI 53090
Phone: (262) 626-8623
Fax: (262) 626-8532
E-mail: info@westbendcookware.
   com
http://www.westbendcookware.
   com

West Point Home Inc
PO Box 71
West Point, GA 31833
Phone: (800) 533-8229
E-mail: consumer.affairs@wpstv.
   com
http://www.martex.com

Western Digital
20511 Lake Forest Drive
Lake Forest, CA 92630
Phone: (800) 275-4932
http://www.wdc.com

Wet Seal, Inc.
26972 Burbank
Foothill Ranch, CA 92610
Phone: (866) 745-7938
E-mail: customerservice@wetseal.
   com
http://www.wetseal.com

Whirlpool Corporation
2000 North M-63
Benton Harbor, MI 49022
Phone: (866) 698-2538
Fax: (269) 923-5443
http://www.whirlpool.com

Whirlpool Corporation
2000 N. M-63
Benton Harbor, MI 49022
Phone: (800) 253-1301
E-mail: whirlpool_customer
    experience@whirlpool.com
http://www.whirlpoolcorp.com

The White Rain Company
410 Ware Boulevard
Brandon, FL 33510
Phone: (800) 575-7960
Fax: (800) 789-0828
E-mail: comments@whiterain.com
http://www.whiterain.com

Wilke/Thornton, Inc.
545 Metro Place South
Dublin, OH 43017
Phone: (614) 792-6900
Fax: (614) 792-6901
E-mail: info@wilke-thornton.com
http://www.wilke-thornton.com

Williams-Sonoma, Inc.
10000 Covington Cross Drive
Las Vegas, NV 89144
Phone: (800) 541-1262
Fax: (702) 363-2541
http://www.williams-sonoma.com

Winn Dixie Stores, Inc.
PO Box B
Jacksonville, FL 32203
Phone: (866) 946-6349
Fax: (904) 370-7789
http://www.winn-dixie.com

Winnebago Industries
605 West Crystal Lake Road
PO Box 152
Forest City, IA 50436
Phone: (800) 537-1885
Fax: (641) 585-6966
E-mail: or@winnabagoind.com
http://www.winnebagoind.com

Woodworker's Supply, Inc.
1108 North Glenn Road
Casper, WY 82601
Phone: (800) 231-2748
Fax: (800) 853-9663
http://www.woodworker.com

Wrangler
400 N. Elm Street
Greensboro, NC 27401
Phone: (888) 784-8571
E-mail: wranglerweb@vfc.com
http://www.wrangler.com

Wm. Wrigley Jr. Co.
410 North Michigan Avenue
Chicago, IL 60611
Phone: (800) 824-9681
http://www.wrigley.com

Wyeth Consumer Health Care
PO Box 26609
Richmond, VA 23261
Phone: (800) 934-5556
http://www.wyeth.com

Wyse Technology
3471 North First Street
San Jose, CA 95134
Phone: (800) 438-9973
http://www.wyse.com

Xerox Corporation
PO Box 4505
45 Glover Avenue
Norwalk, CT 06856

Phone: (800) 275-9376
E-mail: webmaster@xerox.com
http://www.xerox.com

Yahoo! Online
701 First Avenue
Sunnyvale, CA 94089
Phone: (866) 562-7219
Fax: (408) 349-3301
http://www.yahoo.com

Yamaha Motor Corporation
6555 Katella Avenue
Cypress, CA 90630
Phone: (800) 962-7926
Fax: (714) 761-7303
http://www.yamaha-motor.com

YUM! Brands, Inc.
1441 Gardiner Lane
Louisville, KY 40213
Phone: (800) 544-5774
http://www.yum.com

Zale Corporation
901 W. Walnut Hill Lane
MS 6A-6
Irving, TX 75038
Phone: (800) 311-5393
Fax: (972) 580-5219
E-mail: CustomerService@zales.com
http://www.zalecorp.com

Zenith Electronics Corp.
2000 Millbrook Drive
Lincolnshire, IL 60069
Phone: (800) 243-0000
http://www.zenithservice.com

Zoom Technologies, Inc.
207 South Street
Boston, MA 02111
Phone: (617) 423-1072
http://www.zoom.com

GLOSSARY

The following is a list of abbreviations, acronyms, and terms that should prove helpful to individuals interested in working in the retail and wholesale industries.

accounts receivable Monies due for merchandise which has been sold

add-on merchandise Additional merchandise which may be sold to a customer

addressable advertising A type of advertising that gives television programmers and advertisers the ability to deliver targeted television commercials to individual households based on specific criteria

advertised item Products featured in ads, flyers, or commercials

advertising Promoting a product through paid ads, commercials, or other media

all sales final No refunds, credits, or exchanges after the sale of a product or merchandise

approval code A special code given by a credit card company when a transaction for a sale is approved and authorized

authorization code A series of numbers or letters given by a credit card company when a transaction is authorized

automated A process that is completed by a computer or other machine

B2B Business to Business; a wholesaler is generally a business-to-business retailer

B2C Business to consumer; a retailer generally is a business-to-consumer company

back order Merchandise that is not currently in stock, but is on order and will be available at a later date

banner ad A graphic advertising unit used on websites

bar code A set of encoded lines and spaces that can be scanned to identify merchandise

benchmark Achievement standards in the industry

bins Boxes, containers, or enclosed shelving used to display store merchandise

Black Friday A retail term referring to the day after Thanksgiving in the United States. It is the start of the Christmas holiday shopping season, and for many retailers, the biggest shopping day of the year.

blog Short for *web log*; a Web site or Web page with regular entries, much like a Web journal where people share comments, thoughts, opinions, stories, etc.; may include text, images, videos, and links

blogger A person who blogs

brackets The fixtures that hold up the displays on a store's wall

building a display Arranging merchandise samples in a visually pleasing manner in the store

C.O.D. Cash On Delivery; see below

cash discount The retail price of a product less a percentage if a customer pays cash

Cash On Delivery Customer pays on delivery of merchandise

cash refund Monies received for returned merchandise

cash register tape Paper tape in the cash register on which transactions are recorded

cash register The machine that records transactions

comparison shopping Shopping at competing retailers to compare their merchandise, prices, and service

competition Similar retailers targeting the same customers

computerized inventory system A computer program which tracks a retailer's or wholesaler's inventory

consumer Customer

cost The price of merchandise

CRM Customer relationship management; focuses on customer relationships instead of transactions

customer satisfaction How pleased and satisfied customers are with a company; providing good service in a pleasant manner and meeting the customer's expectations

customer service The art of providing good service that meets or exceeds customers' expectations

daily sales audit A review of daily sales journals against the receipt of funds

date of invoice The date a credit period begins

demographics The breakdown of an area into statistical categories; demographics are often used to determine placement of stores

distressed goods Merchandise that has been damaged or soiled

distributor Individual or company that moves merchandise from a manufacturer to retail outlets

DOI Date of invoice

DRTV Direct Response TV

EAS Electronic article surveillance; electronic device utilized to help control shoplifting

E-Commerce Buying and selling merchandise through the Internet

electronic scanner a machine or computer that reads bar codes

expenses The cost of operating a business

forecasting Predicting future sales or trends in sales

freestanding store A retail store which is not in a mall or shopping center

gross margin The profit a business has before it deducts the expenses of operations

hypermart/hypermarket A retail outlet with a warehouse appearance such as Sam's or BJ's

impulse purchase A purchase made without prior planning by a customer

infomercial Short or regular-length television programs which combine information with a suggestion or sales pitch to purchase a particular product or service

initial markup The first or original price markup on merchandise

inventory A method of checking the value and amount of merchandise on hand by taking a physical count of stock

journal roll The cash register tape on which transactions are recorded. These are kept by the store for records.

kiosk A leased booth, car, or area inside of a store or mall

long form Television commercials which are longer than two minutes; also called infomercial

loss leader Merchandise sold at an extremely low or attractive price to entice customers to come into the store or make a purchase from a retailer

mail order retailing Sale of merchandise through the mail from items such as catalogs or direct mail

manufacturer Producer of products

markdown A reduction of the selling price

markup Used in retail; the difference between the selling price of merchandise and the cost of that merchandise

merchandising The buying and selling of merchandise

percentage-of-salesmethod Method of developing the advertising budget based on a percentage of past or anticipated sales

One-Stop Wholesale distributor of specialty merchandise

podcast An audio or video multimedia broadcast hosted on a website and can be downloaded to computers as well as portable devices such as iPods

promotional advertising Advertising by a retailer used to attract customers

rack jobber A wholesaler allowed by a store to stock and replenish merchandise on display racks; many department stores have rack jobbers handle their CD or book stock

receipt Paper from the cash register or credit card machine given to a customer

referral premium Gift or cash reimbursement awarded to current customers who refer potential new customers; car salespeople and dealers often utilize referral premiums

register Machine that records customer transactions

retail price The price a consumer pays for merchandise

retailer Company that sells merchandise to a consumer

retailing Selling goods and services to customers

ROG Receipt of goods

sales per square foot Refers to the net sales of a retailer divided by the square feet of selling space of the store

search the net Going on-line to visit various sites on the Internet

short form Direct response television commercials which are less than two minutes in length

shrinkage The loss of merchandise as a result of shoplifting, internal theft, and damage

SKU See Stock Keeping Unit

standards The brackets used to hold up wall displays

stock A store's supply of goods and merchandise

stock Keeping Unit The identification number given to each item by the retailer

stuffers A promotional piece or advertisement accompanying a billing or credit card statement or placed in customers' shopping bags

tearsheet Copy of an advertisement from the newspaper or magazine; most companies will not pay for ads without a tearsheet

trades Newspapers and magazines that are geared to a specific industry

turnover Determines how quickly merchandise is sold; may also refer to employee retention rates

unit-of-sales method Means by which an advertising budget is established based on the number or projected number of sales of an item, instead of the dollar amount

union card A card that is used to identify members of a specific union

universal Product Code A set of encoded lines and spaces which can be scanned to identify a product

UPC See Universal Product Code

visual merchandising The arrangement of items in a pleasing manner for display

Web The World Wide Web

Web site A place on the World Wide Web

WWW World Wide Web

BIBLIOGRAPHY

A. BOOKS

There are thousands of books written on all aspects of the retail and wholesale industries. The books listed below are separated into general categories. The subject matter in many of the books overlaps into other categories.

These books can be found in bookstores and libraries. If your local library does not have the books you want, you might ask your librarian to order them for you through the interlibrary loan system.

The list is meant as a beginning. For other books that might interest you, look in the career section of the bookstores and libraries. You can also check *Books in Print* (found in the reference section or online in libraries) for other books on the subject.

ADVERTISING

Arens, William F. *Essentials of Contemporary Advertising*. Burr Ridge, Ill.: McGraw-Hill Higher Education, 2008.

Aspatore Staff. *Advertising as a Branding Tool: Industry Leaders on Catching the Consumer's Attention, Creating Economic and Emotional Value, and Developing Resonating Messages (Inside the Minds)*. Boston: Aspatore Books, Incorporated, 2008.

Claxton, Lena. *How to Say It - Marketing with New Media: A Guide to Promoting Your Small Business Using Websites, E-Zines, Blogs, and Podcasts*. Paramus, N.J.: Prentice Hall, 2008.

Marshall, Stephen W. *Television Advertising That Works: An Analysis of Commercials from Effective Campaigns*. Youngstown, Ohio: Cambria Press, 2008.

Minsky, Laurence. *How To Succeed In Advertising When All You Have Is Talent*. Chicago: The Copy Workshop, 2007.

Sokotch, Mel. *Shortcuts to the Obvious: How to Get More Effective Advertising More Efficiently*. New York: Aspetuck River Publishing, 2006.

ADVERTISING CAREERS

Field, Shelly. *Career Opportunities in Advertising and Public Relations*. New York: Facts On File, 2005.

AUTOMOBILE SALES

Hensley, Douglas. *Automobile Sales Training and Tips from the Pros*. Morrisville, N.C.: Lulu.com, 2006.

Lawson, Helene M. *Ladies on the Lot: Women, Car Sales, and the Pursuit of the American Dream*. Lanham, Md.: Rowman & Littlefield Publishers, Incorporated, 2000.

BRANDING

Adamson, Allen P. *BrandDigital: Simple Ways Top Brands Succeed in the Digital World*. New York: Palgrave Macmillan, 2008.

Baskin, Jonathan Salem. *Branding Only Works on Cattle: The New Way to Get Known (And Drive Your Competitors Crazy)*. New York: Grand Central Marketing, 2008.

BUYING AND PURCHASING

Cash, Patrick, R. *Management of Retail Buying*. Hoboken, N.J.: John Wiley and Sons, 2005.

Clodfelter, Richard. *Retail Buying: From Basics To Fashion*. New York: Fairchild Books, 2008.

Diamond, Jay and Pintel, Gerald. *Retail Buying*. East Rutherford, N.J.: Prentice Hall, 2007.

Jacobsen, Marie-Louise. *The Art of Retail Buying: An Introduction to Best Practices from the Industry*. Hoboken, N.J.: John Wiley and Sons, 2008.

Moe, Daniel J. *Retail: The Fundamentals of Retail Buying*. Philadelphia: Xlibris Corporation, 2008.

Van den Broek, Michel. *The Naked Buyer: Part 1 What Sales People Must Know About Purchasing*. Morrisville, N.C.: Lulu, 2008.

Rosemary Varley. *Retail Product Management and Merchandising*. New York: Routledge, 2006.

Tepper, Bette K. *Mathematics For Retail Buying*. New York: Fairchild Books, 2008.

BUSINESS AND ECONOMICS OF RETAILING

Bianco, Anthony. *The Bully of Bentonville: The High Cost of Wal-Mart's Everyday Low Prices*. New York: Doubleday Publishing, 2006.

Jacobson, Ira. *A Quest for Excellence: The Incredible Story of the Most Beautiful Store in the World*. Deal, N.J.: R & J Press, 2008.

Lowrey, Tina M. *Brick and Mortar Shopping In The 21st Century*. New York: Lawrence Erlbaum Associates, Incorporated, 2007.

Ratner, Gerald. *The Rise and Fall . . . and Rise Again*. Hoboken, N.J.: John Wiley and Sons, 2008.

Mayhew, Anne. *Narrating the Rise of Big Business in the USA: How Economists Explain Standard Oil and Wal-Mart*. New York: Routledge, 2008.

Smit, Barbara. *Sneaker Wars: The Enemy Brothers Who Founded Adidas and Puma and the Family Feud That Forever Changed the Business of Sport*. New York: Harper Collins, 2008.

The Power of Marketing At-Retail: 3rd Edition. Alexandria, Va.: Point-Of-Purchase Advertising International, 2008.

Togyer, Jason. *For the Love of Murphy's: The Behind-The-Counter Story of a Great American Retailer*. University Park, Pa.: Pennsylvania State University Press, 2008.

CONVENIENCE STORES

Renn, Leslie D. *How to Start and Manage a Convenience Food Store Business: Step by Step Guide to Starting Your Own Business*. Mesa, Ariz.: Lewis & Renn Associates, 2007.

Scott, Robert Garrett. *The Mystery of the Convenience Store Robberies*. Bloomington, Ind.: Authorhouse, 2008.

COPYWRITING

Bayan, Richard. *Words That Sell: More Than 6,000 Entries to Help You Promote Your Products, Services, and Ideas*. New York: McGraw-Hill Companies, 2006.

Oliver, Vicky. *Power Sales Words: How to Write It, Say It and Sell It with Sizzle*. Naperville, Ill.: Sourcebooks, Incorporated, 2006.

Shaw, Mark. *Copywriting: Successful Writing for Design, Advertising and Marketing*. London, U.K.: Laurence King Publishing, 2008.

Gunelius, Susan. *Kick Ass Copywriting In 10 Easy Steps: Build the Buzz and Sell the Sizzle*. Irvine, Calif.: Entrepreneur Press, 2008.

CUSTOMER SERVICE

Barlow, Janelle. *A Complaint Is a Gift: Recovering Customer Loyalty When Things Go Wrong*. San Francisco: Berrett-Koehler Publishers, Incorporated: 2008.

Beemer, C Britt. *The Customer Rules: The 14 Indespensible, Irrefutable, and Indisputable Qualities of the Greatest Service Companies in the World*. New York: McGraw-Hill Companies, 2008.

Brandon, P S. *Clients Driving Innovation*. Hoboken, N.J.: John Wiley and Sons, 2008.

Gallagher, Richard S. *What to Say to a Porcupine: 20 Humorous Tales That Get to the Heart of Great Customer Service*. New York: Amacom, 2008.

Kennedy, Dan S. *No B. S. Marketing to the Affluent: The No Holds Barred, Kick Butt, Take No Prisoners Guide to Getting Really Rich*. Irvine, California: Entrepreneur Press, 2008.

Livingston, Bob. *How You Do... What You Do: Create Service Excellence That Wins Clients for Life*. New York: McGraw-Hill Companies, 2008.

Martinez, Mario. *Building a Customer Service Culture: The Seven Service Elements of Customer Success*. Greenwich, Conn.: Information Age Publishing, Incorporated, 2008.

Michelli, Joseph. *The New Gold Standard: 5 Leadership Principles for Creating a Legendary Customer Experience Courtesy of the Ritz-Carlton Hotel Company*. New York: McGraw-Hill Companies, 2008.

O'Boyle, Kathleen. *Eight to Great: Eight Steps to Delivering an Exception Customer Experience*. North Charleston, S.C.: BookSurge, 2008.

Rauch, Marc, J. *Marceting: Unique Advice and Proven Techniques from a Hands-on Advertising Expert That Make Your Cash Register Ring: the Book on Effective Advertising and Promotion on a Shoestring Budget*. Frederick, Md.: PublishAmerica, Incorporated, 2006.

DIRECT MARKETING

Imbriale, Robert. *Direct Mail Marketing Secrets: The Ultimate Crash-Course in Marketing by Mail*. Fallbrook, Calif.: Ultimate Wealth, Inc, 2008.

Jones, Susan K. *Creative Strategy in Direct and Interactive Marketing*. Chicago: Racom Communications, 2008.

Patten, Dave. *How to Market Your Business: A Practical Guide to Advertising, PR, Selling, and Direct and Online Marketing*. London, U.K.: Kogan Page, Limited, 2008.

Vanella, Mari Anne. *42 Rules of Cold Calling Executives: A Practical Guide for Telesales, Telemarketing, Direct Marketing and Lead Generation*. Cupertino, Calif.: Happy About, 2008.

ELECTRONIC RETAILING

Blacharski, Dan W. *EBay's Secrets Revealed: The Insiders Guide to Advertising, Marketing, and Promoting*

Your eBay Store with Little or No Money. Ocala, Fla.: Atlantic Publishing Company, 2007.

Beener, Stephanie. *How to Open and Operate a Financially Successful Florist and Floral Business Both Online and Off.* Ocala, Fla.: Atlantic Publishing Company, 2008.

Campanelli, Melissa. *Design and Launch an Online Boutique in a Week.* Irvine, Calif.: Entrepreneur Press, 2008.

Ennico, Cliff. *The eBay Business Answer Book: The 500 Most Frequently Asked Questions about Making Big Money on eBay.* New York: Amacom, 2008.

Miller, Michael. *Absolute Beginner's Guide to EBay.* Indianapolis: Que, 2008.

Smith, Sandi. *Start Your Own Online Store: Guide to Shopping Carts and Online Merchant Accounts.* Dallas: Panna Press, 2005.

Sweeney, Susan. *101 Internet Businesses You Can Start from Home: How to Choose and Build Your Own Successful E-Business.* Gulf Breeze, Fla.: Maximum Press, 2008.

Turban, Efraim. *Introduction to Electronic Commerce.* Boston: Prentice Hall Higher Education, 2008.

FRANCHISING

Bennett, Julie. *Franchise Times Guide to Selecting, Buying and Owning a Franchise.* New York: Sterling, 2008.

Dummies Technical Press Staff. *Franchising For Dummies.* Edison, N.J.: John Wiley and Sons, 2007.

Franchising Your Business: An Owner's Guide to Franchising as a Growth Option. Olympia Fields, Ill.: Francorp, Incorporated, 2008.

Judd, Richard J. *Franchising: An Entrepreneur's Guide.* Mason, Ohio: CENGAGE Learning Custom Publishing, 2007.

Massetti, Ralph Jr. *Is Your Business Right for Franchising?* Morrisville, N.C.: Lulu, 2007.

Palmer, Andrew P. *The Seven Pillars of Franchising Success.* Philadelphia: Xlibris Corporation, 2007.

GRAPHIC DESIGN

Cyr, Lisa L. *Graphic Workshop, Innovative Promotions That Work: A Quick Guide to the Essentials of Effective Design.* Minneapolis: Quayside, 2006.

HUMAN RESOURCES

Goodwin, Clifford R. *Supervisor's Survival Kit.* Boston: Prentice Hall Higher Education, 2008.

Leonard, Barry. *High End Department Stores, Their Access to and Use of Diverse Labor Markets: Technical Report.* Indianapolis: DIANE Publishing Company, 2005.

LEASING

Continuing Education of the Bar. *Retail Leasing: August 2008* Update. Oakland, Calif.: Continuing Education of the Bar-California, 2008.

Continuing Education of the Bar. *Retail Leasing: Drafting and Negotiating the Lease.* Oakland, Calif.: Continuing Education of the Bar-California, 2007.

LOSS PREVENTION

Hayes, Read. *Retail Security and Loss Prevention.* New York: Palgrave Macmillan, 2007.

Monson, Thomas N. *Loss Prevention Threats and Strategies: How People Steal from Your Business and What You Can Do to Stop It.* Medford, Ore.: Advantage Source, Incorporated, 2004.

Purpura, Philip. *Security and Loss Prevention: An Introduction.* Burlington, Mass.: Elsevier Science & Technology Books, 2007.

Sennewald, Charles A. *Retail Crime, Security, and Loss Prevention: An Encyclopedic Reference.* Burlington, Mass.: Elsevier Science & Technology Books, 2008.

MANAGEMENT

Stern, Neil Z. *Greentailing and Other Revolutions in Retail: Hot Ideas That Are Grabbing Customers' Attention and Raising Profits.* Hoboken, N.J.: John Wiley & Sons, 2008.

Segel, Rick. *Retail Business.* Hoboken, N.J.: John Wiley & Sons, 2008.

MARKETING

Brown, Bruce, C. *The Secret Power of Blogging: How to Promote and Market Your Business, Organization, or Cause with Free Blogs.* Ocala, Fla.: Atlantic Publishing Company, 2008.

Guertin, Bill. *Reality Sells: How to Bring Customers Back Again and Again by Marketing Your Genuine Story.* Elmonte, Calif.: New Win Publishing: 2007.

Phillips, Michael. *Marketing Without Advertising: Inspire Customers to Rave about Your Business and Create Lasting Success.* Berkeley, Calif.: NOLO, 2008.

The Power of Marketing At-Retail: 3rd Edition. Alexandria, Va.: Point-Of-Purchase Advertising International, 2008.

MERCHANDISING

Harvard Business School Press Staff. *Harvard Business Review on Retailing and Merchandising.* Boston: Harvard Business School Press, 2008.

Morgan, Tony. *Visual Merchandising: Windows and In-Store Displays for Retail.* London, U.K.: Laurence King Publishing. 2008.

Pie Books Staff. *Fashion Brand Graphics.* New York: Rizzoli International Publications, Incorporated, 2008.

Tungate, Mark. *Fashion Brands: Branding Style from Armani to Zara.* London, U.K.: Kogan Page, Limited, 2008.

Institute of Store Planners. *Institute of Store Planners.* Cincinnati: ST Media Group International, Incorporated, 2008.

NETWORK MARKETING

Brooke, Richard B. *Mailbox Money: The Promise of Network Marketing.* Spokane, Wash.: High Performance People, LLC, 2008.

Blakeman, Robyn. *The Bare Bones Introduction to Integrated Marketing Communication.* Lanham, Md.: Rowman & Littlefield Publishers, Incorporated, 2008.

Christensen, Mary. *Be a Recruiting Superstar: The Fast Track to Network Marketing Millions.* New York: Amacom, 2008.

POINT OF PURCHASE

Zukin, Sharon. *Point of Purchase: How Shopping Changed American Culture.* New York: Routledge, 2005.

PUBLICITY

Hartunian, Paul. *Power Publicity for Retailers.* Upper Montclair, N.J.: Clifford Publishing, 2006.

Hartunian, Paul. *Power Publicity for Florists.* Upper Montclair, N.J.: Clifford Publishing, 2006.

Hartunian, Paul. *Power Publicity for Book Stores.* Upper Montclair, N.J.: Clifford Publishing, 2006.

McIntyre, Catherine. *Writing Effective News Releases, 2nd Edition: How to Get Free Publicity for Yourself, Your Business or Your Organization.* Colorado Springs, Colo.: Piccadilly Books, Limited, 2008.

Seaman, David. *Dirty Little Secrets of Buzz: How to Attract Massive Attention for Your Business, Your Product or Yourself.* Naperville, Ill.: Sourcebooks, Incorporated, 2008.

Yudkin, Marcia. *6 Steps to Free Publicity.* Franklin Lakes, N.J.:Career Press, Incorporated, 2008.

RETAILING

Ander, Willard N. Jr. *Winning At Retail: Developing a Sustained Model for Retail Success.* Hoboken, N.J.: John Wiley & Sons, Incorporated, 2004.

Barreneche, Raul A. *New Retail.* London, U.K.: Phaidon Press, 2008.

Bond, Ronald L. *Retail In Detail.* Irvine, Calif.: Entrepreneur Press, 2008.

Diamond, Ellen. *Fashion Retailing: A Multi-Channel Approach.* East Rutherford, N.J.: Prentice Hall PTR, 2005.

Dunne, Patrick M. *Retailing.* Mason, Ohio: Cengage South-Western, 2007.

Easterling, Cynthia R. *Merchandising Mathematics for Retailing.* East Rutherford, N.J.: Prentice Hall PTR, 2007.

Kraft, Manfred. *Retailing in the 21st Century: Current and Future Trends.* New York: Springer, 2008.

Levy, Michael. *Retailing Management.* Burr Ridge, Ill.: McGraw-Hill/Irwin, 2008.

Levinson, Jay Conrad. *Guerrilla Retailing: Unconventional Ways to Make Big Profits from Your Retail Business.* Golden Colo.: Guerrilla Group, Incorporated, 2004.

Point of Purchase Advertising, Int. Ed. *The Power of Marketing At-Retail: 3rd Edition.* Alexandria, Va.: Point-Of-Purchase Advertising International, 2008.

Pierce, Julie. *The Walmart Way. Not Sam's Way: An Associate View from Inside the Stores.* Philadelphia: Xlibris, 2006.

Schroeder, Carol, L. *Specialty Shop Retailing: Everything You Need to Know to Run Your Own Store.* Hoboken, N.J.: John Wiley and Sons, 2007.

RETAIL MARKETING AND PROMOTION

Ranchhod, Ashok. *Strategic Marketing in Practice.* Burlington, Mass.: Elsevier Science & Technology Books, 2008.

Daly, Donald. *Select Selling: Strategies to Win Customers by Defining the Ultimate Target Profile and Discovering What They Really Want.* Taylorville, Ill.: Oak Tree Publishing, 2004.

Falk, Edgar A. *One Thousand Ideas To Create Retail Excitement.* Paramus, N.J.: Prentice Hall Press, *2003.*

Fragasso, Phil. *Marketing for Rainmakers: 52 Rules of Engagement to Attract and Retain Customers for Life.* Hoboken, N.J.: John Wiley & Sons, Incorporated, 2008.

Kaplan, Steve. *Bag the Elephant: How to Win and Keep Big Customers.* New York: Workman Publishing Company, Incorporated, 2008.

Lincoln, Keith. *Private Label: Turning the Retail Brand Threat into Your Biggest Opportunity.* London, U.K.: Kogan Page, Limited, 2008.

————. *How To Succeed In Retail*. London, U.K.: Kogan Page, Limited, 2007.

Moran, Mike. *Search Engine Marketing, Inc: Driving Search Traffic to Your Company's Web Site*. Upper Saddle River, N.J.: Pearson Education, 2008.

Patten, Dave. *How to Market Your Business: A Practical Guide to Advertising, PR, Selling, and Direct and Online Marketing*. London, U.K.: Kogan Page, Limited, 2008.

Schmidt, Les. *So, You're in the People Business: Everything You Need to Know to Win and Keep Customers*. Parker, Colo.: Outskirts Press, Inc, 2007.

Sullivan, Malcolm. *Retail Marketing*. Boston: International Thomson Business Press, 2002.

RETAIL STORE DESIGN

Institute of Store Planners. *Stores and Retail Spaces 7*. Cincinnati: ST Media Group International, Incorporated, 2007.

teNeues. *Ultimate Shop Design*. New York: teNeues Publishing Company, 2006.

Manuelli, Sara. *Design for Shopping: New Retail Interiors*. New York: Abbeville Press, Incorporated, 2006.

Vernet, David. *Boutiques and Other Retail Spaces: The Architecture of Seduction*. New York: Routledge, 2007.

RETAIL STORE OPERATION

Dion, James. *The Complete Idiots Guide to Starting and Running a Retail Store*. New York: Penguin Group, 2008.

Ramsey, Dan and Ramsey, Judy. *The Everything Guide To Starting and Running a Retail Store: All you need to get started and succeed in your own retail adventure*. Cincinnati: Adams Media Corporation, 2009.

SALES

Kennon, Terry. *How to Avoid Just Looking: And Other Ways to Increase Your Retail Sales*. Bloomington, Ind.: AuthorHouse, 2006.

Phibbs, Bob. *Sales RX: The Five Parts to a Successful Sale Workbook*. Long Beach, Calif.: Retail Doc Publications, 2005.

Veedell, Herman. *Birth of a Salesman: From Stitches to Sticks and Bricks*. North Charleston, S.C.: BookSurge, LLC, 2007.

SALES JOBS

Carson, Mitch. *The Silent Salesmen: Guaranteed Strategies for Increasing Sales and Profits Using Promotional Products*. Hoboken, N.J.: John Wiley and Sons, 2008.

Friedman, Walter. *Birth of a Salesman: The Transformation of Selling in America*. Cambridge, Mass.: Harvard University Press, 2005.

Melfa, Frank A. *Pharmaceutical Landing: How to Land the Pharmaceutical Sales Job You Want and Succeed in It!* North Bergen, N.J.: Power Writings, 2005.

SPECIAL EVENTS

Goldblatt, Joe. *The Roots and Wings of Celebration*. Hoboken, N.J.: John Wiley & Sons, 2008.

SHOPPING CENTERS

International Council of Shopping Centers. *Shopping Center Specialty Leasing*. New York: International Council of Shopping Centers, 2004.

Malhotra, Naresh, K. *Marketing Research: An Applied Approach*. Paramus, N.J.: Financial Times/Prentice Hall, 2007.

Muhlebach, Richard F. *Shopping Center Management and Leasing*. Chicago: Institute of Real Estate Management, 2004.

SPECIALTY STORES

Finell, Dorothy. *The Specialty Shop: How to Create Your Own Unique and Profitable Retail Business*. New York: Amacom, 2007.

Schroeder, Carol L. *Specialty Shop Retailing: Everything You Need to Know to Run Your Own Store*. Hoboken, N.J.: John Wiley & Sons, 2007.

TELEVISION SHOPPING

Daugard, Craig. *How to Make Big Money on TV: Accessing the Home Shopping Explosion Behind the Screens*. Darby, Pa.: DIANE Publishing Company, 2004.

Romer, Nick. *Make Millions Selling on QVC: Insider Secrets to Launching Your Product on Television and Transforming Your Business (and Life) Forever*. Hoboken, N.J.: John Wiley and Sons, 2008.

Sugarman, Joseph. *Television Secrets for Marketing Success: How to Sell Your Product on Infomercials, Home Shopping Channels and Spot TV Commercials from the Entrepreneur Who Gave You BluBlocker(R) Sunglasses*. Las Vegas: DelStar Books, 1998.

WHOLESALING

Ambrose, James. *5 Fundamentals for the Wholesale Distribution Sales Manager*. Washington, D.C.: National Association of Wholesaler Distributors, 2007.

American Wholesalers and Distributors Directory: A Comprehensive Guide Offering Industry Details on Approximately 29,000 Wholesalers and Distributors in the United States. Farmington Hills, Mich.: Gale, 2008.

Levering, Susan. *Smart Investments: Developing Top Performers in Wholesale Distribution.* Washington, D.C.: National Association of Wholesaler Distributors, 2006.

McCrea, Bridget. *Start Your Own Wholesale Distribution Business.* Irvine, Calif.: Entrepreneur Press, 2006.

B. PERIODICALS

Magazines, newspapers, membership bulletins, and newsletters may be helpful in finding information about a specific job category, finding information about a specific job category, finding a job in a specific field, or giving you insight into what certain jobs entail.

As with the books in the previous section, this list should serve as a beginning. There are many periodicals that are not listed because of space limitations. Periodicals also tend to come and go. Look in your local library or in a newspaper or magazine shop for other periodicals that might interest you.

ADVERTISING—GENERAL INTEREST

AAF Communicator
American Advertising Federation
1101 Vermont Avenue, N W
Washington, DC 20005
http://www.aaf.org

Ad Agency Insider
InfoCom Group
5900 Hollis Street
Emeryville, CA 94608
Phone: (510) 596-9300
Fax: (510) 596-9331
http://www.infocomgroup.com/aai.html

Ad Ideas
National System, Inc.
56 Worthington Access Drive
Maryland Heights, MO 64043
Phone: (800) 231-8179
Fax: (314) 205-1996

Advertising and Marketing Review
622 Gardenia Court
Golden, CO 80401
Phone: (303) 277-9840
Fax: (303) 278-9909
E-mail: kencuster@aol.com
http://www.ad-mkt-review.com

Advertising Age
Crain Communications, Inc
711 Third Avenue
New York, NY 10017
Phone: (212) 210-0281
Fax: (212) 210- 0200
E-mail: info@crain.com
http://www.adage.com

AdWeek
Nielsen Business Publications
770 Broadway
New York, NY 10003
Phone: (646) 654-5000
Fax: (646) 654-5365
E-mail: info@adweek.com
http://www.adweek.com

Brandweek
Nielsen Business Publications
PO Box 17018
North Hollywood, CA 91615
Phone: (800) 562-2706
Fax: (646) 654-5518
E-mail: info@brandweek.com
http://www.brandweek.com

ADVERTISING RESEARCH

Journal of Advertising Research
Advertising Research Foundation
641 Lexington Avenue
New York, NY 10022
Phone: (212) 751-5656
Fax: (212) 319-5265
E-mail: jareditor@warc.com
http://www.jar.warc.com

CHAIN STORES

Chain Store Age
Lebhar-Friedman, Inc.
425 Park Avenue
New York, NY 10022
Phone: (212) 756-5000
Fax: (212) 756-5215
E-mail: info@lf.com
http://www.chainstoreage.com

CUSTOMER SERVICE

Customer Service Advantage
370 Technology Drive
Malvern, PA 19355
Phone: (610) 695-8600
Fax: (610) 695-8089
http://www.pbp.com/CSA.asp

The Customer Communicator
712 Main Street
Boonton, NJ 07005
Phone: (973) 265-2300
Fax: (973) 402-6056
E-mail: info@customerservicegroups.com
http://www.customerservicegroup.com

COLLEGE STORES

Campus Marketplace
National Association of College Stores
500 E. Lorain Street
Oberlin, OH 44074
Phone: (440) 775-7777
Fax: (440) 775-4769
E-mail: thecollegestore@nacs.org
http://www.nacs.org

College Store Executive
825 Old Country Road
Westbury, NY 11590
Phone: (516) 334-3030
Fax: (516) 334-8958
E-mail: ebm-mail@ebmpubs.com
http://www.ebmpubs.com

The College Store
National Association of College Stores
500 E. Lorain Street
Oberlin, OH 44074
Phone: (440) 775-7777
Fax: (440) 775-4769

E-mail: thecollegestore@nacs.org
http://www.nacs.org

CREATIVE (ARTISTS, ART DIRECTORS, ETC.)

Trace
American Institute of Graphic Arts
164 Fifth Avenue
New York, NY 10010
Phone: (212) 807-1990
Fax: (212) 807-1799
http://www.aiga.org

Creative
42 W. 38th Street
New York, NY 10018
Phone: (212) 840-0160
Fax: (212) 819-0945
E-mail: creativemag@comvision.com
http://www.creativemag.com

DEPARTMENT STORES

Department Store Workers' Union, Local 1-S
140 W. 31st Street
New York, NY 10001
Phone: (212) 594-6910
Fax: (212) 594-6917
http://www.local1srwdsu.org

Directory of Department Stores
3922 Coconut Palm Drive
Tampa, FL 33619
Phone: (813) 664-6800
Fax: (813) 664-6882

DIRECT MARKETING

Direct Marketing
Direct Marketing Association
1120 Ave of the Americas
New York, NY 10036
Phone: (212) 768-7277
Fax: (212) 768-4547

Direct Marketing News
114 West 26th Street
New York, NY 10001
Phone: (646) 638-6000
Fax: (646) 638-6117
E-mail: edtor@dmnews.com
http://www.dmnews.com

Direct Response
2360 Plaza Del Amo
Torrance, CA 90501
Phone: (310) 212-5727
Fax: (310) 212-5773

Direct Selling News
200 Swisher Road
Lake Dallas, TX 75065
Phone: (800) 279-5249
Fax: (940) 497-9987
http://www.directsellingnews.com

DISCOUNT & CHAIN STORES

Chain Store Guide
3922 Coconut Palm Drive
Tampa, FL 33619
Phone: (800) 778-9794
Fax: (813) 627-6883
E-mail: info@csgis.com
http://www.csgis.com

Discount Store News
Lebhar-Friedman, Inc.
425 Park Avenue
New York, NY 10022
Phone: (212) 756-5000
Fax: (212) 756-5395
E-mail: info@lf.com
http://www.lf.com

Nationwide Major Mass Market Merchandisers
Douglas Publications, Inc.
2807 N. Parham Road
Richmond, VA 23294
Phone: (804) 762-4455
Fax: (804) 935-0271
http://www.douglaspublications.com

Off Price Retail Directory
International Council of Shopping Centers
29399 US Highway 19 North
Clearwater, FL 33761
Phone: (727) 781-7557
Fax: (727) 781-9717

Retail Merchandiser
Nielsen Business Publications
PO Box 2016
Skokie, IL 60076
E-mail: debbie@retail-merchandiser.com
http://www.retail-merchandiser.com

Sullivan's Retail Performance Monitor
7519 Hurstbourne Green Drive
Charlotte, NC 28277
Phone: (516) 265-3900
Fax: (516) 265-3281

E-COMMERCE

E-marketing and Commerce
1500 Spring Garden Street
Philadelphia, PA 19130
Phone: (215) 238-5300
Fax: (215) 238-5457
http://www.emarketingandcommerce.com

FRANCHISES

Business Franchise Guide
C C H Inc.
2700 Lake Cook Road
Riverwoods, IL 60015
Phone: (847) 267-7000
E-mail: custserv@cch.com
http://www.cch.com

The Franchise Handbook
Enterprise Magazines, Inc.
1020 N. Broadway
Milwaukee, WI 53202
Phone: (800) 272-0246
E-mail: infor@franchise1.com
http://www.franchise1.com

GROCERY/SUPERMARKETS

Progressive Grocer
Nielsen Business Publications
770 Broadway
New York, NY 10003
Phone: (646) 654-7604
E-mail: tweir@progressivegrocer.com
http://www.progressivegrocer.com

LEASING

Square Foot Magazine
2741 W. Palm Lane
Phoenix, AZ 85009
E-mail: lross@squarefootmag.com
http://www.commercialleasingupdate.com

LOSS PREVENTION

Loss Prevention Letter for Supermarket Executives
Food Marketing Institute

655 15th Street NW
Washington, DC 20005
Phone: (202) 452-8444
Fax: (202) 429-4519
E-mail: fmi@fmi.org
http://www.fmi.org

MARKETING

Journal of Food Products Marketing
Haworth Press, Inc.
325 Chestnut Street
Philadelphia, PA 19106
Phone: (215) 625-8900
Fax: (215) 625-2940
E-mail: getinfo@haworthpress.com
http://www.haworthpress.com/web/JFPM

Journal of Marketing
American Marketing Association
311 S. Wacker Drive
Chicago, IL 60606
Phone: (312) 542-9000
Fax: (312) 542-9001
E-mail: info@ama.org
http://www.marketingpower.com

Journal of Research in Marketing & Entrepreneurship
Eastern Washington University
College of Business and Public Administration
668 N. Riverpoint Boulevard
Spokane, WA 99202
Phone: (509) 358-2254
Fax: (509) 358-2267
E-mail: rschwartz@mail.ewu.edu
http://www.ewu.edu/x20494.xml

Retailers Forum Magaizne
383 E. Main Street
Centerport, NY 11721
Phone: (631) 754-5000

Retailer and Marketing News
3111 Cole Avenue
Dallas, TX 75204
Phone: (214) 871-2930
Fax: (214) 871-2931

MERCHANDISING

Accessory Merchandising
400 Knightsbridge Parkway

Lincolnshire, IL 60069
Phone: (847) 634-2600
Fax: (847) 634-7885
http://www.accessorymerchandising.net

Apparel Merchandising
425 Park Avenue
New York, NY 10022
Phone: (212) 756-5269

OUTLETS

Value Retail Directory
International Council of Shopping Centers
29399 US Highway 19 North
Clearwater, FL 33761
Phone: (727) 781-7557
Fax: (727) 781-9717
http://www.valueretailnews.com/directories

Value Retail News
International Council of Shopping Centers
29399 US Highway 19 North
Clearwater, FL 33761
Phone: (727) 781-7557
Fax: (727) 781-9717
E-mail: lhumphers@icsc.com
http://www.valueretail.news

PUBLIC RELATIONS, PUBLICTY, COMMUNITY RELATIONS

Community Relations Report
Joe Williams Communications, Inc.
PO Box 924
Bartlesville, OK 74005
Phone: (918) 336-2267

PR Week
114 W. 26th Street
New York, NY 10001
Phone: (646) 638-6000
Fax: (646) 638-6117
E-mail: subscriptions@prweek.com
http://www.prweek.com

RETAIL AND WHOLESALE

Billboard Record Retailing Directory
Billboard Directories
770 Broadway
New York, NY 10003
Phone: (732) 363-4156

Fax: (732) 363-0338
http://www.billboard.com

Bureau News
Bureau of Wholesale Sales Representatives
1100 Spring Street, N W
Atlanta, GA 30309
Phone: (404) 351-7355
Fax: (404) 352-5298

Car Dealer Insider
United Communications Group
11300 Rockville Pike
Rockville, MD 20852

Confection & Snack Retailing
B N P Media
155 Pfingsten Road
Deerfield, IL 60015
Phone: (847) 405-4000
Fax: (847) 405-4100
http://www.confectioner.com

Cost of Doing Business for Retail Sporting Goods Stores
National Sporting Goods Association
1601 Feehanville Drive 60056
Mt. Prospect, IL
Phone: (847) 296-6742
Fax: (847) 391-9827
http://www.nsga.org

Deal Maker
K O Real Estate Advisory Group
PO Box 2630
Mercerville, NJ 08690
Phone: (609) 587-6200
Fax: (609) 587-6200
E-mail: dealmaker@dealmaker.net
http://www.dealmaker.net

Electronic Retailing
G P G Publishing, Inc.
9200 Sunset Boulevard
Los Angeles, CA 90068
Phone: (818) 782-7328
Fax: (818) 782-7450
E-mail: webmaster@elrond.worldshop.com
http://www.eretail.com

Food Retailing Industry Speaks
Food Marketing Institute
2345 Crystal Drive

Arlington, VA 22202
Phone: (202) 452-8444
Fax: (202) 429-4519
E-mail: fmi@fmi.org
http://www.fmi.org

The Magazine Retail Sales Experience
Harrington Associates
12 Main Street
Norwalk, CT 06851
203-838-1701
203-838-1861
jharrington@nscopy.com
http://www.nscopy.com/mrse.htm

Manufacturing & Distribution U S A
27500 Drake Road
Farmington Hills, MI 4833
Phone: (248) 699-4253
E-mail: gale.customerservice@cengage.com
http://gale.cengage.com

Marketing at Retail
NewBay Media, LLC
810 Seventh Avenue
New York, NY 10019
Phone: (212) 378-0400
Fax: (212) 378-2160
E-mail: scneditor@aol.com
http://www.marketingatretail.com

N A R D A Independent Retailer
North American Retail Dealers Association
4700 West Lake Avenue
Glenview, IL 60025
Phone: (847) 375-4713
Fax: (866) 879-7505
E-mail: nardahdq@narda.com
http://www.narda.com

Retail In$ights
6421 W. Weaver Drive
Littleton, CO 80123
Phone: (800) 837-3662
http://www.retailinsghts.com

Retail Kiosk & Self-Service Summary
NetWorld Alliance
13100 Eastpoint Park Boulevard
Louisville, KY 40223
Phone: (502) 241-7545
Fax: (502) 241-1385
http://www.networldalliance.com

Retail Observer
1442 Sierra Creek Way
San Jose, CA 95132
Phone: (408) 272-8974
Fax: (408) 272-3344
E-mail: retailobs@aol.com

Retailing Today
425 Park Avenue
New York, NY 10022
Phone: (212) 756-5000
Fax: (212) 756-5395
http://www.retailingtoday.com

Weekly Insiders Retail
PO Box 389
Toms River, NJ 08754
Phone: (732) 240-5330
Fax: (732) 341-0891

Wholesale Source Magazine
Show Communications
423 Lenni Road
Lenni, PA 19052
Phone: (610) 361-0117
E-mail: showcomm@aol.com

INDEX

Entries in **boldface** indicate major treatment of a topic.

A

AAF (American Advertising Federation) 20, 21, 115, 136, 139, 172, 174

AALA (American Automobile Leasing Association) 159

ACA (American Compensation Association) 67, 69

accountant 37

accounting clerk, department or specialty store 123, 125

accounting clerk, shopping center or mall office 36, 37

account representative, wholesale 212

ACRA (American Collegiate Retailing Association) 56, 58, 61, 91, 94, 98, 110, 112, 115, 146, 148, 150, 152

ad assistant, shopping center/mall 18, 21, 22, 141

ADC (Art Directors Club, Inc.) 136, 139

ad manager 113

administrative assistant 28, 30, 34, 35, 73

administrative assistant, shopping center or mall office **32–33**

advancement prospects, explanation of xviii

advertising agency art director 136

advertising art director, retail 135, 135

advertising assistant 113

advertising assistant, shopping center/mall 15, 18, **21–22**

advertising director, retail store **113–115**

advertising director, shopping center/mall **18–20**

advertising manager, retail store 113

advertising manager, shopping center/mall 18, 20

Advertising Research Foundation (ARF) 107

advertising trainee, shopping center/mall 21

AFTRA (American Federation of Television and Radio Artists) 181

AICA (Association of Image Consultants International) 187

AIGA (American Institute of Graphic Arts) 136, 139

AIPA (American Institute of Public Accountants) 37

alteration tailor 121

alternate titles, explanation of xvii

AMA (American Management Association) 200, 214

AMA (American Marketing Association) 14, 16, 107, 115, 148, 150, 172, 174, 190

American Advertising Federation (AAF) 20, 21, 115, 136, 139, 172, 174

American Automobile Leasing Association (AALA) 159

American Chopper (television show) xv

American Collegiate Retailing Association (ACRA) 56, 58, 61, 91, 94, 98, 110, 112, 115, 141, 146, 148, 150, 152

American Compensation Association (ACA) 67, 69

American Federation of Television and Radio Artists (AFTRA) 181

American Heart Association 9

American Institute of Graphic Arts (AIGA) 136, 139

American Institute of Public Accountants (AIPA) 37

American Management Association (AMA) 200, 211, 214

American Marketing Association (AMA) 14, 16, 107, 115, 148, 150, 172, 174, 190

American Purchasing Society (APS) 110, 112, 225

American Society for Training and Development (ASTD) 75, 132, 214

American Wholesale Marketers Association (AWMA) 176, 200, 203, 211, 214, 220, 222, 227

antique shows 49

APS (American Purchasing Society) 110, 112, 225

area manager, department store 54, 55

area manager, grocery/supermarket 151, 152

area manager, specialty or chain store 97

area manager, wholesale manufacturer or distributor 226

ARF (Advertising Research Foundation) 107

art director, retail **135–137,** 138, 139

Art Directors Club, Inc. (ADC) 136, 139

artist 166

artist, retail 138, 139

ASC (Association of Stylists and Coordinators) 187

assistant advertising director, retail store 113

assistant advertising manager, shopping center/mall 18, 21, 22

assistant brand manager 106

assistant buyer **111–112,** 149, 150, 182

assistant customer service manager 86

assistant director of human resources 67, 70, 75

assistant director of leasing 33

assistant director of public relations, shopping center/mall 33

assistant janitorial supervisor 38

assistant leasing director 46

assistant loss prevention manager 78

assistant maintenance supervisor 40

assistant mall manager 5, 23, 32, 33

assistant mall marketing director 15, 16

ABOUT THE AUTHOR

Shelly Field is a nationally recognized motivational speaker, career expert, stress management specialist, personal career and life coach, and author of over 35 best selling books in the business and career fields.

Her books help people find careers in a wide variety of areas including the hospitality, music, sports and communications industries, casinos and casino hotels, advertising and public relations, theater, the performing arts, and entertainment animal rights, heath care, writing, and art. She is a frequent guest on local, regional and national radio, cable, and television talk, information and news shows; and has also been the subject of numerous print interviews for articles and news stories.

Field is a featured speaker at conferences, conventions, expos, corporate functions, spouse programs, employee training and development sessions, career fairs, casinos, and events nationwide. A former comedienne, she adds a humorous spin whether speaking on empowerment, motivation, stress management, staying positive, the power of laughter, careers, attracting, retaining and motivating employees or customer service. Her popular presentations, "STRESS BUSTERS: Beating the Stress in Your Work and Your Life" and "The De-Stress Express" are favorites around the country.

A career consultant to businesses, educational institutions, employment agencies, women's groups and individuals, Field is sought out by executives, celebrities, and sports figures for personal life and career coaching and stress management.

In her role as a corporate consultant to businesses throughout the country she provides assistance with human resources issues such as attracting, retaining and motivating employees, customer service training, and stress management in the workplace

President and CEO of the Shelly Field Organization, a public relations, marketing and management firm handling national clients, she has represented celebrities in the sports, music, and entertainment industries as well as authors, businesses, and corporations.

For media inquiries, information about personal appearances, seminars or workshops or personal coaching please contact the Shelly Field Organization at P.O. Box 711, Monticello, NY 12701 or visit Shelly on the web at www.shellyfield.com.